Library of
Davidson College

Representing
the Professions

Representing the Professions

Administration, Law, and Theater in Early Modern England

Edward Gieskes

Newark: University of Delaware Press

©2006 by Rosemont Publishing & Printing Corp.

All rights reserved. Authorization to photocopy items for internal or personal use, or the internal or personal use of specific clients, is granted by the copyright owner, provided that a base fee of $10.00, plus eight cents per page, per copy is paid directly to the Copyright Clearance Center, 222 Rosewood Drive, Danvers, Massachusetts 01923. [0-87413-929-5/06 $10.00 + 8¢ pp, pc.]

Other than as indicated in the foregoing, this book may not be reproduced, in whole or in part, in any form (except as permitted by Sections 107 and 108 of the U.S. Copyright Law, and except for brief quotes appearing in reviews in the public press).

Associated University Presses
2010 Eastpark Boulevard
Cranbury, NJ 08512

The paper used in this publication meets the requirements of the American National Standard for Permanence of Paper for Printed Library Materials Z39.48-1984.

Library of Congress Cataloging-in-Publication Data

Gieskes, Edward, 1968-
   Representing the professions : administration, law, and theater in early modern England / Edward Gieskes
     p. cm.
   Includes bibliographical references (p.) and index.
   ISBN 0-87413-929-5 (alk. paper)
   1. English drama—Early modern and Elizabethan, 1500-1600—History and Criticism. 2. English drama—17th century—History and criticism. 3. Professions in literature. 4. Literature—History and criticism—Theory, etc. 5. Professions—England—History—16th century. 6. Professions—England—History—17th century. 7. Lawyers in literature. I. Title.
   PR658.P375G54 2006
   822'.309921—dc22
                                           2005016236

PRINTED IN THE UNITED STATES OF AMERICA

For Lisa

Contents

Acknowledgments   9

Introduction   13

1. "To sound the depths of what thou wilt profess":
The Professions in Early Modern England   38

2. "I mean to learn":
Status and Service in the History Plays   68

3. "This! Why it outfrowns ink!":
Social Conflict and the Legal Profession   114

4. "The Art of Revels Hath a Settled Place in the City":
The Revels, Civic Drama, and
the Theater Professions   162

5. "Honesty and Vulgar Praise":
The Poet's War and the Literary Field   215

6. Conclusions   249

Notes   277
Bibliography   345
Index   359

Acknowledgments

IN THE COURSE OF A PROJECT THAT HAS TAKEN MANY YEARS TO complete, I have incurred many debts to many people and I have likely left people out—omissions I apologize for in advance.

In Boston, my teachers and friends James Siemon, Jon Klancher, and William Carroll offered commentary on the work in its earliest stages, providing patient encouragement that has continued since my leaving graduate school. Diana Henderson wrote extensive and detailed notes on my dissertation and those notes became a vital part of the revision process.

Thanks are due to my fellow students in the English Department at Boston University who commiserated as the work progressed—especially to Kirk Melnikoff who read drafts of several chapters and has been a much-valued collaborator and friend these many years. The Boston Playwrights' Theatre provided me a most accommodating and supportive work environment and coworkers—Tom McClellan, Kate Snodgrass, and Marc Olivere—who tolerated my endless typing. I owe a debt to Professor David Seipp of the Boston University Law School for invaluable references and a look at an early draft of a manuscript on legal education. The acting company Willing Suspension Productions allowed me (and many others) an opportunity to learn firsthand about early modern plays in production.

At the University of South Carolina, my colleagues and friends have been more than supportive. At various times, Nina Levine, Larry Rhu, Andy Shifflett, and Greg Wilsbacher have read and helped me improve elements of this book, and their clear-eyed commentary and their friendship has been enormously important. The English Department, the College of Liberal Arts, and the University have been forthcoming with generous research support. The English Department's summer support, the College's CLASS grant program, and the University's Research and Productive Scholarship program have underwritten much of the research for this book.

The Folger Shakespeare Library has fostered my scholarship through its collections and through the Folger Institute's seminar program, which has given me invaluable opportunities to learn, to test ideas, and to study. Linda Charnes, Lynne Magnusson, and Coppélia Kahn led seminars that have had a profound effect on my work. Susan Cerasano offered me some good advice and a host of references in the library stacks one afternoon. The Folger staff has been unfailingly supportive of my work, as of so many others.

Many of the chapters in this book had their origins as contributions to the Shakespeare Association of America's Annual Meetings and the responses from fellow seminarians at meetings of the SAA have helped me hone my argument as well as revealed areas of research I had to consider.

Thanks also to the editors of *ELH*, *Medieval and Renaissance Drama in England*, and the Oxford Middleton for permission to use revised versions of essays first published in their respective publications.

Thanks for various things are owed (in no particular order) to Barbara Hodgdon, Shankar Raman, Steve Lynn, Bill Rivers, Pete Smith, Andrew Hartley, Gary Taylor, Lauren Kehoe, Sarah Lyons, Joris and Barbara Gieskes, Anita Sulewski, Jonathan Mulrooney, Margo Hendricks, Joan Pong-Linton, Ted Leinwand, Mike Walker, and others whom I am likely forgetting.

I would like to thank the anonymous readers at the Press for their comments and encouraging words about the manuscript.

Finally, in the place of honor, I must thank my wife, Lisa Gieskes, for her tolerance, support, editorial skills, and kindness over the many years this project has taken to complete. Without that support, this work would have been impossible. This book is for her.

Representing the Professions

Introduction

> The autonomization of intellectual and artistic production is correlative with the constitution of a socially distinguishable category of professional artists or intellectuals who are less inclined to recognize rules other than the specifically intellectual or artistic traditions handed down by their predecessors, which serve as a point of departure or rupture.
> —Pierre Bourdieu, *The Field of Cultural Production*

MODERN PROFESSIONAL ARTISTS AND INTELLECTUALS TAKE THE autonomy that Bourdieu describes for granted, often acting as if that autonomy were without a history.[1] Autonomy means precisely the ability of professional artists and intellectuals to recognize only rules that derive from the practice of their predecessors, not rules imposed from outside their field by kings, states, or markets. This autonomy is, in fact, the product of historical struggles within each of these fields. For example, the constitution of a "socially distinguishable category" of professional writers has a history and that history is one of the subjects of this book. In what follows, I describe the emergence of four related professions (administration, law, theater, and playwriting) in the context of the slow breakdown of the late medieval polity. This breakdown led to the erosion of traditional principles of social order, particularly those related to the role of birth in the construction of social identity. These principles were subsequently replaced by an array of relatively autonomous fields—such as the occupations later called professions—that disembedded subjects from the premodern order and eventually reembedded them in a recognizably modern one.[2] The redefinition of "profession" in the sixteenth and seventeenth centuries responds to this shift. Occupations grew into principles of social order that could compete with the established categories of birth and estate in defining the identity of the individual as society itself came to be understood in terms of the professional market, or, better (as I will demonstrate) the professional field.[3] This book is therefore a literary history of the professions in sixteenth-century England and in pursuing this project reads plays by Shakespeare, Jonson, Middleton, Dekker, Beaumont, and Marston, among others in conjunction with noncanonical texts such as legal manuals, pamphlets, pageants, theatrical records, and handbooks for administrators.[4]

Professions offer means of self-fashioning not directly linked to traditional hierarchies of rank or of birth. Each chapter that follows develops an analysis of the ways in which the individual professions under discussion provide increasingly coherent alternatives to traditional hierarchies. In the first part of the book, I examine early modern changes in the ideas of profession and vocation. In the period the sacred and secular senses of these terms became increasingly intermingled as various occupations claimed status as professions in order to dignify their practice. I turn from this general discussion to show how administration and law move from a clerical or guild model of training and practice toward more systematic and "professional" methods of education and advancement. In the law and in administration, the titles and forms of nobility remain metaphors for achievement and goals for the ambitious, but these images of authority depend in the first instance on talent with birth serving as a helpful additional qualification. The second part of the book focuses more specifically on the theater and playwriting. Tudor and Stuart theater has long been described as professional and my intention in the two chapters that deal with the theater professions and playwriting respectively is to characterize the effects that that professional status has on both stage practices and playwriting. All of these professional groups are relatively autonomous—operating in distinct social arenas—but are related by their interest in producing representations of the social world. The literary production of early modern writers and thinkers contributed to a developing discourse about society and that discourse is profoundly influenced by its professional context.

I

Much recent literary criticism concerned with the sixteenth and seventeenth centuries has focused on the transition from a feudal to a capitalist social order—emphasizing "self-fashioning" in the case of Stephen Greenblatt's *Renaissance Self-Fashioning*, the market and theater in Jean-Christophe Agnew's *Worlds Apart*, and the "laureate system" in Richard Helgerson's *Self-Crowned Laureates*. What these works (and many others, including Catherine Belsey's *Subject of Tragedy* and Joel Fineman's *Shakespeare's Perjured Eye*) share is a concentration on the individual agent in a changing culture.[5] Stephen Greenblatt argues that the works of writers such as Sir Thomas More and Tyndale document a "radical and momentous social crisis: the disintegration of the stable world order, the desacramentalization of church and state, the subversive perception of the role of the mind, and specifically the imagination, in the creation of oppressive institutions."[6] This social crisis, Greenblatt suggests, led to the creation of "new models, precisely as a way of containing and channeling the energies which had been released."[7] These "new models" of man and the state turn out to depend on a phenom-enon Greenblatt terms "self-fashioning," the active formation of "selves" in society. Greenblatt acknowledges the role of "institutions" in developing these new models but focuses most of his attention on individual agents engaged in the narrative improvisation of selfhood.[8] This focus downplays the role of the social space within which such improvisation takes place.

Richard Helgerson's *Self-Crowned Laureates* takes as its subject "the literary system" and discusses how writers such as Spenser, Jonson, and Milton strove to place themselves within it. His study has more of an institutional focus than Greenblatt's, yet it still centers on the efforts of each writer to differentiate himself from a rabble of others in a version of self-fashioning focused on establishing himself as a laureate, not a common versifier.[9] Though this distinguishing operation occurs within an acknowledged system (as with Greenblatt), Helgerson pays more attention to the efforts of the three poets to mark themselves as distinct than he does to the "system" in which these distinguishing efforts take place.[10] I plan to outline that system—an emerging literary field with internal pressures and conflicts that generate, for example, the constructed opposition (and hierarchy) of "poetaster" and "laureate."

Jean-Christophe Agnew's history of the market and the theater links developments in the cultural and economic orders. He argues that as markets become free of traditional constraints of place, time, and ritual and shift from a barter to a money economy in the later middle ages, social life comes to be "imbued" with a "pervasive and ongoing sense of risk, a recurrent anticipation of profit and loss that lends to all social intercourse a pointed, transactional quality."[11] This "transactional quality" calls forth new strategies to cope with anxieties about self and the society within which that self exists. Agnew grounds cultural changes in the early modern development of what he calls a "placeless market" and a kind of exchange that stripped social representations from goods, people, and resources.[12] Much as Greenblatt does, Agnew focuses on strategies of self-representation, drawing on a variety of literary sources. He writes, "the new liquidity of mercantile relations, like the growing fluidity of social relations in general, made itself most vividly felt in those literary genres devoted to social description and moral instruction."[13] These genres (initially character books and conduct manuals) strove to establish controls over the "fluidity" of social relations and identities by providing models of self-formation and interaction.[14] Agnew devotes his attention to drama, as the best representation of experiments with alternate self-formations, modes of interaction, and imagined dislocations of traditional structures of being and acting. He writes, "By deliberately effacing the line between the self's iconic representation in art and ritual and its instrumental presentation in ordinary life, Renaissance theater formally reproduced the same symbolic confusion that a boundless market had already introduced into the visual codes and exchange relations of a waning feudal order."[15] A historically developing drama makes manifest the dynamic of increasingly fluid social relations and helps to provide, Agnew argues, interpretive structures for a problematic social world. However, his insistence on the importance of economic change tends to elide other important factors such as residual cultural traditions, the influence of other changes in the social order, and, particularly, the role played by the notion of profession. While Agnew might suggest that all these phenomena are related to the changes he documents in market relations (and ideas about market relations), this study treats them as coeval factors, mutually influencing and influenced, not necessarily developing out of some common root.[16] Agnew's argument makes the transition to modernity a function of a changing relation to the ideas of the market and of exchange; however these are only two among many interacting factors which produced the social formation we call modernity.

More recently, scholars have moved away from the large theoretical and historical claims of the early New Historicism engaging less with questions about "the" self, or "the" theater, or other large categories whether philosophical or historical, and have turned toward more narrowly defined issues that in turn illuminate aspects of early modern culture. One example is in theater history where scholars have been doing fruitful work on individual acting companies, on particular theaters, and on commerce.[17] Historicist scholarship seems to have been defining its object ever more narrowly—striving to avoid the dangers of narrative history pointed out by the poststructuralist suspicion of metanarratives—in order to produce more accurate or more detailed microhistorical accounts of early modern society and culture that can in turn provide insights into the totality of that culture.[18] Unlike some versions of the New Historicism, which reads anecdote or individual events as synecdoches for the culture, microhistory aims to provide an exhaustive account of a figure, a place, a short span of time. This account then serves as an allegory for the broader culture.[19] This book moves between these two prevailing approaches to describe how institutional and individual histories construct early modern versions of professionalization. For example, in chapter 4 I discuss changes in royal administration in relation to changes in Shakespeare's dramaturgy using theater texts and historical documents to illuminate both the development of an administrative profession and cultural responses to this development. *Representing the Professions* thus advances a structural history of the early modern professions by producing a literary history of representations of professionals.

I focus on governmental (particularly royal) administration, law, theater, and playwriting because these disciplines are closely linked in the period. Lawyers were often administrators, Inns of Court men wrote plays (Marston being only one example), and a large portion of the audience for theater was composed of lawyers and other legal workers. Secular law, especially common law, was rapidly becoming the dominant legal code; the theatrical profession held an increasingly visible and legitimate place in London; playwriting was becoming a grudgingly accepted career even for gentlefolk; and political administration was moving out of the hands of the clergy and into the hands of a secular bureaucracy trained for public service.[20] Furthermore, each of these activities intersects with the others, overlapping, competing, and sharing interests. Tudor education trained lawyers and administrators who could and often did read and write poetry; literary production contributed to a developing discourse about society; and plays expressed concerns about changes in that society.[21] As Agnew argues, representations of a changing social order helped to shape those changes as well as conditioned responses to it.[22]

Moreover, writing was the occupation to which many educated men turned when frustrated in a search for a position. As Richard Helgerson writes, "The extraordinary recourse of gentlemen's sons to the seats of learning had, however, an unforeseen result. It quickly saturated the offices of the state with men trained in good letters, leaving few openings for those who came behind. So in order to support themselves in as gentlemanly a fashion as possible and to catch the attention of potential benefactors, they turned to writing."[23] Educated commoners also met with this lack of openings, and, as Helgerson notes, their frustration found voice in the work of the satirists of the 1590s. Thus, lawyers, administrators, and writers were all shaped by and contended with the legacy of humanist education. This shared frame of values and practices makes these fields a logical constellation for this study.[24]

The category of "profession" is, like that of "artist," a recent invention; a product of both sixteenth-century history and twentieth-century sociology. Bourdieu's cautions about the dangers of anachronism and the need to construct objects of research carefully serve as a reminder and a warning not to confuse earlier and later phenomena with one another. In light of these cautions, this study will examine both early modern occupations and the modern system of "professions" in an effort to avoid these pitfalls. While I do not propose a thoroughgoing study of the system of "professions" in modern culture, an examination of the modern definition of profession and professionalism will clarify which elements of the early modern "professions" carry over into modernity at the same time as it guards against the importation of contemporary professional attitudes into an object that predates them.

II

> Divinity, adieu!
> These necromantic books are heavenly,
> Lines, circles, scenes, letters and characters:
> Ay, these are those that Faustus most desires.
> Oh what a world of profit and delight,
> Of power, of honour, of omnipotence,
> Is promised to the studious artisan!
> All things that move between the quiet poles
> Shall be at my command. Emperors and kings
> Are but obeyed in their several provinces . . .
> But his dominion that exceeds in this
> Stretcheth as far as the mind of man.
> —Christopher Marlowe, *Doctor Faustus* (1588)

As one example of an early modern text that deals with "professional" issues, Marlowe's *Doctor Faustus* concerns itself in part with the consequences of what is basically a professional choice: magic over humanist academic disciplines. Faustus himself can be seen as a "modern" agent and his career as an allegory of what Anthony Giddens terms the "dark side" of modernity: he is a well-educated, ambitious professional who is fascinated by the magic of abstraction.[25] Faustus is, significantly, a professional—an academic, a divine, a physician, and a lawyer.[26] His opening meditation enumerates many of the learned disciplines available to an educated man of the later sixteenth century. Faustus examines them, finds them all wanting, and therefore turns to necromancy for the fulfillment of his aspirations, referring to the rewards necromancy promises to the "studious artisan"—to the craftsman of magic. Occupations such as law were held to confer gentle status on their professors, a status legally denied to artisans and craftsmen.[27] However, Faustus's speech never makes a distinction between the statuses of various occupations—all seem equal in his list of options—and, more importantly, he refers to magic, his newfound profession, as a craft. In this he conflates occupations defined by their relation to book learning—to theoretical knowledge—and those defined as crafts—the work of hands—in ways excluded by the norms of his society. In other words, the status traditionally attached to an occupation is, at least on the surface, indifferent to him. This attitude toward occupational hierarchies points to the development of a new, more modern, disposition toward work that places more emphasis on the conduct of one's work than on its nature. Granting a fundamental difference in their attitudes toward the *ends* of vocation, this position approximates that to be found in the theology of William Perkins, who argues that diligence in one's calling dignifies the work regardless of the calling's status. Such a disposition is one of the ideological bases of modern professionalism.[28]

Faustus's stated interest, like that of many modern professionals, is more in the power, delight, and knowledge that occupations can offer him, than in the status they might confer.[29] Faustus's search, like that of the subject that will typify the Enlightenment, is for knowledge that will afford both personal satisfaction and power over the world.[30] Faustus breaks with tradition because of these aspirations. The quest for personal fulfillment represented in this speech by his listing and dismissing a variety of professional disciplines is one sign of this break. However, Marlowe's play not only concerns itself with the question of what Faustus's break with tradition implies for the individual agent, but it also examines the culture that makes such a break possible. In 1588, Faustus's modernity lies in his willingness to break with tradition, while the play's modernity lies in its questioning of that same break.[31]

Debate over the value and constitution of modernity has become a common feature of recent work in social theory, literary criticism, and philosophy. Thinkers as diverse as Jürgen Habermas and Anthony Giddens have offered book-length investigations of "modernity" that argue for the continuing power and authority of "modern" cultural forms.[32] On the other side of the debate, Fredric Jameson argues that contemporary culture, if not properly "postmodern," is at least "late modern," suggesting that it is in a process of transition to something different and new.[33] Jean François Lyotard makes a case for contemporary culture as postmodern in *The Postmodern Condition*. He argues that where modern culture understood itself in terms of "master narratives" that included Enlightenment rationalism, teleological visions of a progressive history, and various economic theories (Marxism, laissez-faire capitalism, etc.), the postmodern condition is typified by multiple competing micronarratives that cannot be subsumed under one (or even more than one) "metanarrative." Peter Sloterdijk's *Critique of Cynical Reason* debates the future of Enlightenment ideals in what he describes as an age of pervading cynicism about those ideals.[34] Sloterdijk asserts that "cynicism is *enlightened false consciousness*. It is that modernized, unhappy consciousness, on which enlightenment has labored both successfully and in vain."[35] This "enlightened false consciousness" is both a product of and a problem for modern philosophy rooted in the Enlightenment. His solution is to imagine a kind of post-Enlightenment philosophy that resolves some of the modern philosophical project's contradictions, and he argues that such a philosophy is urgently needed in a changing contemporary society.[36] He does not, however, imagine that this change will result in a postmodern social order that is radically different from that of modernity.[37] In his analysis of what he calls the "modern constitution," Bruno Latour argues that not only are we not postmodern, but that we are not even modern.[38] All these theorists are deeply involved with the idea of modernity—questioning it, debating it, and redefining it—pointing to the contemporary importance of the question of what constitutes modernity.

Thus, it is understandable that Renaissance English society and culture have recently been redescribed as "early modern" in an effort better to historicize study of the period. The newer term reflects the idea that what was formerly called the Renaissance represents an early stage in England's (and, more generally, Europe's) transition from the "Middle Ages" to modernity.[39] This intentionally vague designation calls attention to the fact that the period, roughly 1500–1700, was marked by a transition that took place in fits and starts, progressing in different areas of society at different rates. Early modern is the most useful and accurate label for this epoch of transition because it emphasizes that uneven and often sluggish transition. While it is impossible to designate when "early modern" literature or society begins, by the sixteenth and seventeenth centuries the evidence of transition becomes historically undeniable. Yet, despite its wide acceptance, use of the term remains problematic. As Heather

Dubrow writes, "*Early modern* has the salutary effect of emphasizing economic continuities between periods that are rigidly separated by the designation *Renaissance*. Yet the shift from *Renaissance* to *early modern* has created a number of problems, including some of the very difficulties that the newer term was designed to avoid."[40] Dubrow argues that current usage still designates the Middle Ages as "Other" and, more importantly, "risks imposing an unjustly teleological perspective on" the sixteenth and seventeenth centuries.[41] David Aers's 1992 essay "A Whisper in the Ear of Early Modernists; or, Reflections on Literary Critics Writing the 'History of the Subject,'" serves as another reminder that the sixteenth and seventeenth centuries do not have a corner on the emergence of "modern" subjectivity.[42] In addition to these problems there is the question of what exactly is modern about the sixteenth century. In other words, if we call sixteenth-century England "early modern," we need to be specific about what we mean by "modern" and how the term applies to a culture still pervaded by institutions and practices dating from the Middle Ages.[43] This is one of the questions this book intends to address.

Recently, "modern" has tended to be defined in two ways. First, as a term describing an historical period beginning sometime in late eighteenth century and (arguably) ending sometime in the decades following the Second World War. This is consistent with the word's use to describe things "of or relating to the present and recent times, as opposed to the remote past; of, relating to, or originating in the current age or period."[44] Used in this way, "modern" is a descriptive term devoid of specific content and does little to characterize a period beyond marking it as recent. The second sense relates more specifically to the socioeconomic and cultural conditions of the West (and later much of the world due to a combination of Western colonialism and imperialism as well as indigenous adoption of "modern" techniques and technologies) since the latter part of the sixteenth century.[45] It relates to economic, intellectual, and social changes that have been characterized as distinct from what has been defined as the premodern world of the Middle Ages. This sense is related to the *OED*'s definition of "modernity": "An intellectual tendency or social perspective characterized by departure from or repudiation of traditional ideas, doctrines, and cultural values in favour of contemporary or radical values and beliefs (chiefly those of scientific rationalism and liberalism)."[46] This definition is likewise broad but has the virtue of referring to specific changes—away from "tradition" and toward "contemporary or radical values" related to intellectual and political change. Clearly, the sixteenth and seventeenth centuries are implicated in these changes even though "scientific rationalism and liberalism" as the definition uses the term were only in their infancy. This book defines "modern" and "modernity" somewhere between the open definition of "modern" cited above and a more specific definition of "modernity." The breadth I allow modernity is both intentional and polemical because the term is often defined too narrowly as referring only to the late nineteenth and twentieth centuries. I follow scholars like Alan MacFarlane, who maintains that the signal characteristics of modernity appear much earlier than the nineteenth century: "The majority of ordinary people in England from at least the thirteenth century were rampant individualists, highly mobile both geographically and socially, economically 'rational,' market-oriented and acquisitive, ego-centred in kinship and social life."[47] MacFarlane may overstate the case, but a number of scholars have recently argued that the basic constituent elements of modernity are evident in the early modern period (and even earlier) and continue to develop along lines already apparent in the sixteenth and seventeenth centuries.[48]

Modernity has often been understood to refer to the period following the Industrial Revolution and to be descriptive of the social and cultural changes concomitant with the transition from an agricultural economy to an industrial one.[49] "Modern" often refers to social developments such as the dominance of wage labor, a shift in the relations of work to life and workers to work, a radical population shift from rural to urban settings, and the replacement of status categories based on birth by categories based on wealth. More broadly, Anthony Giddens writes of a specifically modern "dynamism": "The dynamism of modernity derives from the *separation of time and space* and their recombination in forms which permit the precise time-space "zoning" of social life; the *disembedding* of social systems (a phenomenon which connects closely with the factors involved in time-space separation); and the *reflexive ordering and reordering* of social relations in light of continual inputs of knowledge affecting the actions of individuals and groups."[50] Giddens argues that "modern" society is premised on the dissolution of older social bonds—

those of the kin group, of the religious group, and of the feudal estates. These formerly structuring principles have been replaced by social schemata that situate subjects in systems that are understood to operate according to abstract laws—laws, that is, that can be rationally derived. As one example, the medieval idea of the three estates (those who fight, those who pray, and those who toil) that defined an individual's place in the social order primarily by function and birth—with the principle of identity descending from God—is transformed through a rationalizing process into the modern notion of self-determined identity formed by autonomous subjects who choose places in the modern social order.[51] Giddens stresses the formative role of relatively autonomous "abstract systems" in modern social structure. His primary examples of "abstract systems" are the professions that began to gain autonomy in the early modern period. Under pressure from the increasing importance of institutions such as professional associations and school-based education, the medieval estates eroded as a formative principle of identity in the course of the sixteenth and seventeenth centuries. In the changing social system of early modern England, the idea of divine election eventually came to be replaced by secular merit as an ordering principle.[52] In early modern England, institutions and professions began the lengthy process of developing into what Pierre Bourdieu calls autonomous fields with their own internal structuring principles and legitimacy independent of divine or temporal authority—hence their disruptive effects on traditional order. The development of increasingly autonomous fields fragmented the more inclusive and static premodern order in the transition to modernity.

The above general and schematic description of modernity—including a shift from particularized domestic production to "rationalized" production, a move from small farming to big farms run for a landlord's profit, a population shift from the country to the city, and a fragmentation and reorganization of social bonds and structures—provides a generally accurate description of social and economic developments evident in sixteenth- and seventeenth-century England.[53] Among the institutions that underwent significant change are the formally structured occupations we have come to know as "professions." Before the later fifteenth century, none of the four occupations discussed below existed in a form that modern sociology would recognize as professional. Administration was dominated by the clergy before the advent of the lay administrators who staffed the Tudor government;[54] the law remained essentially a guild until the sixteenth-century boom in litigation; professional theater with permanent playing spaces had not appeared; and professional writers did not exist as such before the mid-sixteenth century brought an enlarged demand for the production of books and plays. All four occupations developed in the context of and under pressure from a rapidly changing society that created new needs at the same time as it eroded old certainties.

III

> By forcing one to discover externality at the heart of internality, banality in the illusion of rarity, the common in the pursuit of the unique, sociology does more than denounce all the impostures of egoistic narcissism, it offers perhaps the only means of contributing, if only through awareness of determinations, to the construction, otherwise abandoned to the forces of the world, of something like a subject.
> —Pierre Bourdieu, *The Logic of Practice*

Pierre Bourdieu's social analysis offers means to understand how social phenomena such as the professions take shape, change, and remain the same.[55] For Bourdieu, the modern professions as commonly conceived are a product of "impostures of egoistic narcissism" that hide historical and social determinations under the mask of professional autonomy.[56] Despite the negative overtones of such a depiction of the professions, the factor of professional misrecognition appears to Bourdieu as useful to both its practitioners and their society. Bourdieu is particularly helpful in pointing out the utility of such determinations: such misrecognitions are socially necessary. Misrecognition allows agents to forget or ignore the determinations that structure their actions, even the actions that seem most free.[57] An examination of the origins of the professions in early modern England will contribute to an awareness of how the misrecognized contingencies of professional practice have structured and continue to structure the trajectories of human agents.[58] The protoprofessions I examine below offered their practitioners ways to define and organize new "careers" in a society where traditional models of social interaction were fading in importance in the face of a growing population, changing forms of government, and, not least important, the economic changes attendant on these and other related demographic and political changes.

As John Guillory notes, Bourdieu's work has had a mixed reception in the American academy as a whole and specifically in the field of literary studies.[59] Guillory argues that American readers of Bourdieu reject "his apparent reduction of social action to self-interest, in the form of the accumulation of 'capital,' and further, his implicit foreclosure of any action that transcends individual interest or has progressive social change as its end."[60] Guillory's analysis of what he calls "Bourdieu's refusal" by the American academy demonstrates that this refusal is based on a fundamental but nevertheless logical misreading of the work. Guillory suggests that the American academy's deep investment in an ideology of voluntarism directed toward and capable of producing social change leads to this kind of misreading of Bourdieu's work. Far from being a kind of deterministic economism, Bourdieu's analysis is intended to produce knowledge of the limitations of human agency in order to produce at least the potential for greater freedom.[61] As he writes in the preface to *The Logic of Practice* cited above, sociology "offers perhaps the only means of contributing, if only through awareness of determinations, to the construction, otherwise abandoned to the forces of the world, of something like a subject."[62] Rather than arguing that all interaction can be reduced to economistic self-interest, Bourdieu explicitly analyzes choices in which agents reject, qualify, or transform the economies in which they exist and, more importantly, construct versions of subjectivity.

Bourdieu's social theory is intimately concerned with interactions—between agents, between fields of activity, between classes—and provides a way to ground the more abstract elements of the transition to modernity discussed above in concrete social and historical developments.[63] Bourdieu sees society as constituted by an array of fields (contemporary examples studied in his work include academia, politics, and cultural production among others) that interact with each other in complex ways as relatively autonomous spheres of activity—each governed by internal rules and dominated by internal competitions for success in terms defined by the field:[64]

The field as a field of possible forces, presents itself to each agent as a *space of possibles* which is defined in the relationship between the structure of average chances of access to the different positions (measured by the "difficulty" of attaining them and, more precisely, by the relationship between the number of positions and the number of competitors) and the dispositions of each agent, the subjective and objective basis of the perception and appreciation of the objective chances.[65]

These "spaces of possibles" operate to define for agents the available positions and the steps necessary to achieve them. One of Bourdieu's favorite examples is the literary field (specifically that of nineteenth-century France). Success in this iteration of the literary field is defined in terms that reverse the terms of success in the economic field—in other words, limited sales and the lack of monetary reward signal artistic success.[66] Agents engaged in the field define their activities in relation to this reversed economy—either seeking popular success or avant-garde recognition.[67] Agents succeed or fail based on the objective availability of positions as well as on their individual capacity to judge the "objective chances" of attaining a given position in the field. These capacities or dispositions enable an agent to recognize, understand, and exploit his or her own social capital.[68] This social capital is the product of both the individual agent's background and the operations of the field. Writing of twentieth-century France, Bourdieu argues:

> The members of the professions (esp. doctors and lawyers), relatively well endowed with both forms of capital, but too little integrated into economic life to use their capital in it actively, invest in their children's education but also and especially in cultural practices which symbolize possession of the material and cultural means of maintaining a bourgeois lifestyle and which provide a social capital, a capital of social connections, honourability and respectability that is often essential in winning and keeping the confidence of high society, and with it a clientele, and may be drawn on, for example, in making a political career.[69]

In this example, members of groups like doctors or lawyers who are "well endowed with both forms of capital" (economic and cultural) but are marginal to "economic life" read as commerce or industry make use of both species of capital in ways that work to ensure the conservation of that capital and the reproduction of their positions in social space. Early modern lawyers (and other professionals) often strove to ensure that their offspring would at least not lose the social position they achieved. As one example, John Marston's father was a reader of the Middle Temple, a prominent barrister, and he placed his son in the Temple in hopes that he would become a lawyer. Marston did not practice law but did make use of the cultural and economic capital handed down to him to become a successful playwright and then a divine. A particular agent's set of dispositions, or habitus, is structured by the demands of the field, that agent's background, and the history of his or her engagement with the field (or fields) he or she encounters.[70]

The organized set of dispositions that Bourdieu calls the habitus is a structuring structure that is itself structured. This compressed and abstract formulation serves as a kind of shorthand for a theory of social activity. For Bourdieu, the activity of particular agents owes much, but not everything, to a series of social determinations, expressed through the habitus. Habitus represents Bourdieu's effort to "escape from under the philosophy of the subject, as well as from under the philosophy of the structure but without forgetting to take into account the effect [the structure] wields upon and through the agent."[71] In other words, habitus represents a theoretical effort to escape from the false alternatives of a totally uncontextualized subjectivity and one that is totally determined by society. Habitus preserves both individual agency and the sense that that agency is conditioned and limited by society. It is the internalization of social and economic structures—"society written into the body"—as dispositions that encourage agents to act in objectively regular ways that are related to their position in social space. As a structuring structure, it shapes the possibilities for action available to an agent in a particular situation. For example, the dispositions of the dominant and dominated classes toward art are structurally related to their respective positions in society.[72] As a structured structure, habitus is shaped by the fields that it encounters and that shaping in turn changes the possibilities available to a particular agent. Education, for example, exerts a structuring effect on habitus, altering an agent's class habitus into something resembling, but never becoming identical, to that of another.[73] Habitus is the central term in Bourdieu's sociology: it enacts the logic of the fields, it structures the misrecognitions that allow society to function, and it registers the value of the various species of social capital:[74]

> The habitus, as society written into the body, into the biological individual, enables the infinite number of acts of the game—written into the game as possibilities and objective demands—to be produced; the constraints and demands of the game, although they are not restricted to a code of rules, *impose themselves* on those people—and those people alone—who, because they have a feel for the game, a feel, that is, for the immanent necessity of the game, are prepared to perceive them and carry them out.[75]

This "society written into the body" produces dispositions in agents that render them able to recognize and reproduce the practices particular to a given field. Agents with a particular habitus have a "feel for the game" of the field that ensures the reproduction of the rules of that game.[76]

Habitus, however deterministic it may sound, is not a monolithic structure that precludes individual variation or agency. When Bourdieu writes of a "class habitus" he refers to dispositions that members of a particular group or social class have in common that make their collective practices objectively regular, though not identical. In *Distinction*, he shows how agents from various classes tend to share the tastes, habits, and the social destinies of their peers.[77] Bourdieu asserts that "each individual system of dispositions is a structural variant of the others, expressing the singularity of position within the class and its trajectory."[78] Every agent possesses a variant of a class habitus that derives from the collective history and social trajectory of his or her class. This is why individual agents from a given class tend to behave similarly (but not identically) in similar situations. Habitus *is* individual, however, because the givens of each agent's class habitus are changed by that particular agent's history of encounters with society. Thus, habitus "expresses the singularity of position within the class and its trajectory." In other words, each agent is in possession of (and is possessed by) an individual system of dispositions that is a structural variant of those possessed by other members of his or her "class." These individual variations derive from a particular agent's trajectory through the diversity of fields that constitute social space.[79]

These relatively autonomous fields operate within the larger system of fields that constitutes society as a whole. Bourdieu argues that all fields are positioned within the all embracing fields of power (political or social or economic) and class relations.[80] A particular field has no simple, direct relation to the larger field of power; in other words, there is no *immediate* correspondence between a struggle within a field and the social and economic conditions of its historical moment.[81] For example, Bourdieu harshly criticizes the reduction of cultural production to a mere reflection of the social or economic order, arguing that one must first understand the relations within a field before attempting to relate developments in that field to anything external to it. Additionally, there are always layers of mediation—interactions with related fields, conflicts over legitimacy, etc.—between a field and the larger field of power.[82] The series of mediations Bourdieu describes explains why his work never succumbs to the language of reflection in his work on literature—artistic works are never passive reflections of any aspect of a society but instead refract myriad determinations and engagements not least among them the artist's personal ambition. No simple base-superstructure relation prevails with the political or economic situation determining cultural phenomena. Bourdieu replaces this simplifying model with an explication of the complex series of relations that complicate any linkage analytically connecting a given cultural practice with the larger field of power in which it exists.

Despite these layers of mediation, Bourdieu asserts that there are analyzable structural relationships between fields in the form of homologies:

> We can observe a whole range of structural and functional homologies between the field of philosophy, the political field, the literary field, etc., and the structure of the social space (or class structure): each has its dominant and dominated, its struggles for usurpation and exclusion, its mechanisms of reproduction, and so on. But every one of these characteristics takes a specific and irreducible form in each field (a homology may be defined as a resemblance within a difference). Thus, being contained within the field of power, the struggles that go on within the philosophical field, for instance, are always overdetermined and tend to function in a double logic. They have political effects and perform political functions by virtue of the homology of position that obtains between such and such a philosophical contender and such and such a political or social group in the totality of the social field.[83]

The professions discussed in detail below share numerous "structural and functional homologies" despite the fundamental differences between their goals, social roles, and respectability. To pick an example, the struggles for distinction characteristic of all four fields—though quite different in content, in the forms of contestation, and in the definition of success—are homologous in that they all show attempts to define both the individual agent's position and his profession as legitimate. In order to chart the specific nature of such homologies, fields have to be researched and understood on their own terms. In the case of early modern England this analysis demands detailed and rigorous historical and cultural study that considers any field in the context of related fields and of the "totality of the social field." Bourdieu demands close attention to both the microlevel of the individual field defined as narrowly and specifically as possible and the macrolevel at which fields and agents interact with other fields and agents.

Toril Moi's postscript to the special issue of *MLQ* titled *Pierre Bourdieu and Literary History*, in which Guillory's essay on Bourdieu's American reception appears makes the important and too often forgotten point that a properly Bourdieuian approach to literary criticism requires use of the full array of Bourdieu's ideas because his categories are mutually dependent. She writes: "If we remove Bourdieu's concepts from every specific context of significant use, we will never be able to do anything interesting, or even remotely relevant, with them."[84] The context she refers to is, at least in part, the broad texture of Bourdieu's conceptual thought. For example, the idea of habitus, which is crucially important to this book, depends for its meaning on its relation to the ideas of field, of capital, and of trajectory—and this group of ideas constitutes the "context of significant use" Moi refers to. In order for habitus to be a useful concept, it must be described in terms of the varieties of capital that compose it, those varieties of capital have value in specific fields of endeavor, and, in addition, habitus is shaped by its trajectory through those fields. As Moi argues, for Bourdieu's work to be useful in literary scholarship, his ideas must be used in concert to describe and analyze well-defined objects of study.

This study will examine the notion of profession in the modern and postmodern eras as a necessary first step toward understanding specific "professions" in the early modern period, the period in which the modern professions were taking shape. In a discussion of the value of a double object in historical research, Bourdieu writes:

> I strongly advised researchers to study at least two objects, for instance to take, in the case of historians, besides their principal object . . . the contemporary equivalent of this object. The study of the present has *at least* the virtue of forcing the historian to objectivize and to control the presuppositions that he is likely to project onto the past, if only by the fact that he uses words of the present to name past practices, such as the word "artist" which often makes us forget that the corresponding notion is an extraordinarily recent invention.[85]

The method wards against the anachronistic application of contemporary assumptions to past practices by forcing the researcher more fully to historicize both objects of inquiry in their differing particularity. In addition, attention to the "contemporary equivalent" of the object of study encourages an awareness of continuities in both the history of that object and the constellation of fields in which it exists.

The "totality of the social field" is necessarily historical and Bourdieu's method demands that attention be paid to the diachronic—historical—forces that contribute to a social structure at any given moment. His theory strives to reunite history with sociology, arguing that *"the separation of history and sociology is a disastrous division*, and one totally devoid of epistemological justification: all sociology should be historical and all history sociological. In point of fact, one of the functions of the theory of fields that I propose is to make the opposition between reproduction and transformation, statics and dynamics, or structure and history, vanish."[86] In the pursuit of this goal, Bourdieu advocates a "genetic sociology," a structuralism that looks for developmental linkages between different stages of a field's historical development without teleological bias or without eliminating differences between those stages in the interest of a tidy narrative: "What we need, in effect, is a form of structural history that is rarely practiced, which finds in each successive state of the structure under examination both the product of previous struggles to maintain or to transform this structure, and the principle, via the contradictions, the tensions, and the relations of force which constitute it, of subsequent transformations."[87] A genetic sociology demands analysis of specific social practices and phenomena in the context of an investigation of the historical transformations in the same set or sets of practices. Fields, in other words, can only be properly understood by combining closely focused sociological studies with a broad focus on history. This genetic sociology, a kind of genetic structuralism as Bourdieu sometimes calls it, offers a means to elucidate the ways in which the early modern fields of administration, law, theater, and playwriting gave rise to an embracing professional field, a field whose parameters and expectations continue to play a major role in the constitution and reconstitution of modernity.

IV

The following chapters will examine four related professions in an effort to establish the outlines of what I will term the professional field. Early modern England saw the establishment of durable patterns of behavior in the three professions I survey, patterns that have a major effect on the struggles that define subsequent developments in the system of professions.[88] I focus on these professions because the population contributing to their membership had much in common; all four are focused on London, which was the most "modern" of early modern English cities; and because they are close together in social space and therefore influence each other in direct and indirect ways.[89] For example, the Crown's administrators strove to control the production of plays and this effort involved lawyers who also attended the theater produced by professional playwrights. This kind of interlocking of direct and indirect influence makes these professions a logical constellation for study. It is also characteristically professional.[90]

In an effort to engage in a Bourdieuian literary history, the chapters below combine a focus on literary texts with an examination of legal manuals, handbooks for administrators, and contemporary social description, while also making use of twentieth-century historiography. Each chapter takes one or more plays as a starting point for more detailed examinations of the manner in which particular groups responded to a changing society and economy. This book relies on literary and specifically dramatic evidence for its discussion of early modern responses to social change because the drama represents playwrights' efforts to represent that change to their audiences. Examining dramatic representation of professionals, in other words, enables this book to complement its historical discussions with examples of contemporary cultural responses to historical changes such as the fragmentation and reorganization of traditional forms of acculturation, of work, of "self," and of rank. The groups of agents surveyed below responded to this fragmentation by asserting the role and dignity of their occupations.

Chapter 1 examines changes in the ideas of profession and vocation in early modern England. Profession and vocation are both terms deriving from Christian theology, the one referring to the declaration of faith, and the other to one's divinely ordained calling in life. The tension between the religious sense of vocation and its increasingly powerful secular alternative definition contribute to professional self-definition. I suggest that early modern England saw the beginnings of a professional ecology, an ecology in which changes in one discipline affect others with related interests or areas of competence. Faustus's career trajectory in Christopher Marlowe's *Doctor Faustus* serves as a literary illustration of these social and historical developments. Chapter 2 discusses the emergence of professional administrators in the secretariats of the Tudor Privy Council. The different treatments of the character of the Bastard Faulconbridge in Shakespeare's *King John* and in the roughly contemporary anonymous play *The Troublesome Raigne of John, King of England* suggest a transition between two models of royal service. Shakespeare's Bastard actively chooses a "career" as a royal servant by choosing to avow his illegitimate descent while the Bastard of *The Troublesome Raigne* is forced to lay claim to his royal ancestry, against his better judgment, and in this involuntary manner enters the aristocracy, and from thence comes to royal service. Shakespeare's Bastard chooses his profession while the Bastard of *Troublesome Raigne* is chosen by his. I argue that Shakespeare's Bastard Faulconbridge can be seen as a representation of the professional administrators who worked in the staffs of Elizabethan Privy Councillors such as William Cecil, Lord Burghley, and Sir Francis Walsingham. These administrators gained their places more by talent and training than by birth and preferment. By examining manuscript handbooks and administrative history, I argue that recognizably professional patterns of training existed for such men.

Chapter 3 examines the emergence of the law as a large and increasingly powerful profession in the course of the sixteenth century. Stage lawyers become increasingly threatening figures as the real-world legal profession becomes more and more powerful and more and more autonomous. Representations of lawyers reveal concerns about the social changes attending that transition. Legal practitioners, the apparatus of legal practice, and legal texts pervade the city comedies discussed in this chapter, much as they pervaded London, and the theater responds to both the professionalization of the law and its enormous growth in early modern England. Legal professionals became lightning rods for concerns about social change not only because of their role in those changes, but also because they were professionals and thus somewhat distanced from traditional categories of rank and, more importantly, because they exercised control over an increasingly powerful discipline. The chapter examines Shakespeare's *Merchant of Venice,* Jonson's *Volpone*, Middleton's *Michaelmas Term* and *The Phoenix*, the anonymous *Honest Lawyer*, and Massinger's *New Way to Pay Old Debts*—all of which treat aspects of English legal culture.

My fourth chapter investigates the emergence of the professional theater as an institution in early modern England. By reading records from the Office of the Revels, the *Diary* of theater producer Philip Henslowe, and antitheatrical tracts, I describe the institutional context within which playwriting developed into a profession. The chapter argues that the professionalization of the theater extends beyond the playwrights and actors who are the usual subjects of investigation to include craftspeople whose influence on the emerging profession of playwriting is considerable. Robert Greene's *James IV* and Francis Beaumont's *Knight of the Burning Pestle*, plays that juxtapose different kinds of dramaturgy, illustrate the way that craft practices are refracted into the drama at disparate stages of its professionalization. Greene's play stages a debate over the *ends* of drama by representing a conflict between *kinds* of drama. What emerges from the contest is less a resolution of the conflict between a didactic and a spectacular theater than a sense of the representational capabilities of the theater. Beaumont's play, written about seventeen years after Greene's, parodies generic and staging conventions in an effort to produce novelty, a play carrying the "privy mark of irony." Beaumont's parody has as much to do with literary convention as with physical theater. Both playwrights are concerned with novelty, both make use of technical resources to create it, and both write at transitional moments in the profession. The chapter also contributes to recent reevaluations of the importance of London's civic drama to the development of the theater of Shakespeare and his contemporaries.

Chapter 5 looks at professional playwriting by examining plays associated with the 1598–1601 Poet's War among Ben Jonson, John Marston, and Thomas Dekker. Beneath the invective and personal recrimination that pervade Jonson's *Poetaster*, Dekker's *Satiromastix*, and Marston's *Histriomastix*, the war was a debate about the definition of the writer, his possible social roles, and the relative value of different styles (here, the various modes of satire). That this struggle works itself out in terms of personal conflicts has as much to do with genre as it does with the combative dispositions of the writers. Along with having significant personal differences, Jonson, Marston, and Dekker occupied distinct positions in the profession, and the plays' invective serves to identify and contest these positions. The stakes of this conflict were the right to define the nature and structure of the emerging professional field of writing. Positions in the war thus depend both on individual dispositions and structural positions in the evolving field. As a debate about the nature and structure of the field of professional writing, the Poetomachia participates in the definition of the emergent category of "literature" by developing categories of evaluation that structure the field.

The final chapter combines the historical work of the preceding chapters with a return to the methodological questions of the introduction in an effort to accomplish two goals. First, it aims to describe a mode of historical scholarship that avoids avoid the impasses of both the Old Historicism and the New. The chapter argues that the kind of work I am describing here is one way to produce historical scholarship that is not a formalism in disguise (a common critique of the New Historicism), nor a purely archival and backward-looking "recovery" of the past, nor an anachronistic finding of the present in past texts, but a constructive engagement with and understanding of a past that is always already with us. My work argues for the necessity of a historical project that depends on the creation of a narrative within which it is possible to investigate both specific events and broader developments. Using Hayden White's work on historiography, historical interpretation, and narrative as well as Lutz Niethammer's *Posthistoire*, which surveys recent thought on the so-called "end of history," I suggest that historical narrative is both necessary and inevitable. Second, I argue that the kind of historical scholarship represented by *Representing the Professions* can help describe and critique the shape of the totality of the social field over broad spans of time and that this can form the basis of claims for the continuing relevance of Shakespeare studies and literary study more generally. In the course of the so-called "culture wars" of the '80s and '90s, the social role of literary study has been debated repeatedly, at varying levels of stridency. Michael Bérubé's *Public Access*, Bruce Robbins's *Secular Vocations*, Stanley Fish's work on professionalism, Gerald Graff's *Professing English*, Cary Nelson's work on the changing profession, Guillory's *Cultural Capital*, and many other books have raised questions about the place and function of English studies in the university and the culture as a whole.[91] Many of these analyses have identified the source of the crisis in functional terms—as English loses its original role of promoting and inculcating a national literature, it also loses its arguments for its place in the university. Claims for the relevance of the professional study of literature must thus find new grounds, and it is my hope that the kind of historical scholarship this book represents can contribute to the establishing of those grounds.

1
"To sound the depths of what thou wilt profess": The Professions in Early Modern England

> While the structure of the social field is defined at each moment by the structure of the distribution of capital and the profits characteristic of the different particular fields, the fact remains that in each of these arenas, the very definition of the stakes and the trump cards can be called into question. Every field is the site of a more or less openly declared struggle for the definition of the legitimate principles of division of the field.
> —Pierre Bourdieu, *Language and Symbolic Power*

THIS CHAPTER HAS A DOUBLE OBJECT: TO DISCUSS THE RISE OF early modern professions while raising questions about contemporary uses of the term profession in social theory. This double project has the salutary aim of guarding against anachronism and, more importantly, of outlining a genetic sociology of the professions.[1] Pierre Bourdieu argues that categories of perception are the product of historical struggles over the right to define "the legitimate principles of division" of fields, for the right to name social realities. "Profession" and "professional" are categories of perception with a great deal of symbolic power—the efforts of various more or less low-status occupations to claim professional status evidences this—and research into the process of professionalization demands analysis of the conditions that underwrite that symbolic power. In addition, if the current definition of what constitutes a profession is the product of historical struggle, then that struggle must be examined in order to gain a more objective view of the origins of the professions. My primary focus will be on four professions: administration, law, theater, and playwriting. All four show attributes defined later as professional, and, more importantly, all three are close in social space. Writers, lawyers, and administrators had much in common in the period and the developing structures of professional competition particular to each influenced the others. By describing the early modern redefinition of profession, I hope to outline the structure of an emerging professional field in early modern England.

I

> In this Bursse, or Exchange of humane affayres, which consisteth (as it were) altoegather in Marchandize, bargayning, buying and selling, it is very meete and necessary that there shoulde be men of all manners, conditions, and callinges: as the Princes or Potentates, Dukes, Earles, Barons, Knightes, Esquires, Gentlemen, Yeomen, Husbandmen, Taylor, Tanner, and Tinker, Cowper, Carter, and Cobler, with men of all other estates, degrees, and professions, summoned upon forfayture of 10 l. in Issues to appeare, with money or ware always ready, to maintain this Mundane market.
> I. M., *A Health to the Gentlemanly Profession of Servingmen* (1581)

I. M. describes human affairs as a great exchange—an image that recurs in later pamphlets—which consists wholly in buying and selling.[2] It is fitting, he avers, that in such a marketplace there should be all kinds of men occupying all manner of social, political, and economic positions. This passage also imagines itself as a summons to be honored by all on pain of a £10 penalty. He does not differentiate between those summoned—all are responsible to appear bearing either money or wares to offer on the marketplace. The social categories here lump together noble titles and professional ones suggesting that differences between them are not so much of kind as of degree. The list suggests that all of these are callings or professions—manners, conditions, and callings are grammatically parallel as are estates, degrees, and professions, which indicates a certain rough equivalence between them. All estates, degrees, professions, manners, conditions, and callings are equally subject to the summons of the Burse of Human Affairs, which demands that they maintain it. I. M.'s imagination of the social world as a great marketplace figures social interaction in terms of transactions between members of different callings in a space where they are formally equivalent. The dominant labels for human occupations here derives from the discourse of vocation and profession—terms whose meanings undergo considerable change in the period.

I. M.'s 1581 tract characterizes the work of servingmen as a profession with its own particular dignity, giving evidence of the availability and importance of the idea of profession in the later sixteenth century. In this tract, I. M. uses terms such as profession, calling, and vocation promiscuously and the lack of differentiation among the three anticipates the modern confusion of these terms.[3] Twentieth-century usage still commonly regards these three words as virtually synonymous, and I. M. seems to have thought of them in much the same way. For example, after figuring his subject as a loaf of bread, I. M. writes: "This Loafe is the profession of Servingmen, not course for the calling, but in respect of the workeman, whose short time in his trade, hath gayned him so small experience, as he can hardly fathome a loaf of free Cocket. . . . This Loafe (as I sayd before) this state and profession of Servingmen.[4] The same brief passage refers to service as a profession, a calling, a state, and a trade. In the treatise, these terms are all but interchangeable and the same dignity inheres to all of them. I. M. defends the calling of servingmen as professional and worthy of more dignity than it receives. His text makes a clear link between the "ancientness" of the profession and its ostensibly high social status and an additional link between its professional nature and that status. He is careful to distinguish between the status a servingman receives by serving a gentleman and the status he has on his merits as a servingman. After detailing the origins, history, social composition, and current state of the profession, the treatise closes by praying that

> this companie of Servingmen, may eyther be better rewarded for their service, and better esteemed of among their superiors equals, and inferiors; or els that none of my friendes, or wellwillers, doe take upon them this trade and profession: (though for my owne part I cannot speake of any thyng of this, by my owne

> experience, as having tasted my selfe the gaule of this bittersweete: for since I was a Servingman, I have recyved to full measure of my desartes at my Maisters handes) least they should fall into the before-rehearsed inconveniences, which are very incident generally to the professors of this callyng.[5]

His final words demonstrate a sense of corporate identity, of a shared horizon of expectations, that, in the tract at least, defines the profession of servingmen as a group with specific skills and, more importantly, a specific social identity based on the exercise of those skills.[6] Whether or not servingmen in general really had this sense of identity is less important than the fact that such a thing was imaginable as early as 1581.

While modern definitions assert that professions are characterized by a rational division of tasks and an internal organization linked to that division, it is important to note that this is not necessarily true of the occupations in early modern England that could be (and often were) called professions. After listing the various tasks involved in running a theater company, William Ingram writes: "This list of differentiated activities is of course arbitrary, proposing modern distinctions where none may be needed: in the early Elizabethan period, finding a place to play and finding someone to take care of company business would have seemed natural extensions of the business of stage playing, without necessarily implying any new division of labor or of personnel."[7] In contrast to Ingram, this chapter contends that early modern England saw the growth of a professional "division of labor and personnel" that developed in response to changing social conditions not out of an abstract rationalization of professional labor as some later definitions contend.[8] As Ingram notes, a division of tasks may not be new in itself, but I will argue that it becomes professional—the distinction lying in the evaluation of the division, its social meaning. Profession, vocation, and calling gain new definitions in the period as theologians, actors, lawyers, adminstrators, and writers all struggle to define their specificity and the value of their particular brand of symbolic/cultural capital in what Christopher Brooks calls the early modern "calculus of social differentiation." This "calculus" hierarchized different occupations according to their distance from theoretically demeaning manual labor.[9] Claims for the gentle or noble tradition of an occupation serve as ways to distance their practitioners from base manual labor—even when, as in I. M.'s case, manual labor of one kind or another defines much of the work of the profession.[10] I. M.'s tract goes to great lengths to claim elevated status for the labor of servingmen—arguing that they prop up great houses and that therefore their work is essential to the good of the commonwealth.[11] Sixteenth-century assertions of professional status define particular kinds of work as valuable and claim positions in a rapidly changing social order on the basis of that value.

As many sociologists and historians have noted, professions and professionals occupy a special place in Western industrial societies.[12] The possession of expertise recognized as "professional" grants its possessor a heightened occupational status that translates, in many cases, to enhanced social status. Professional knowledge plays a major and increasing role in the structuring and restructuring of modern society. As Anthony Giddens argues, "expert systems," professions and the knowledge they produce, are a major component of the dynamism of the modern social order: "By expert systems I mean systems of technical accomplishment or professional expertise that organise large areas of the material and social environments in which we live today. Most laypersons consult "professionals"—lawyers, architects, doctors, and so forth—only in a periodic or irregular fashion. But the systems in which the knowledge of experts is integrated influence many aspects of what we do in a *continuous* way."[13] Giddens defines "modernity" as the social conditions that emerged in Europe in the seventeenth century, conditions that since have spread throughout most of the world.[14] In early modern England, expert systems such as the law were coming to exert a growing influence over "material and social environments" by virtue of their mastery of particular kinds of knowledge. The knowledge characteristic of the law is a particularly good example of this—possession of legal knowledge (acquired by residence in the Inns of Court and represented by the call to the bar) entitled the possessor to claim gentility. The lawyer's knowledge enables him to manipulate the social world and that ability allows the profession to claim a social prominence that increased as the profession became more professional.

Professions and professionalism were a vital part of the dynamism of the transitional culture and society of early modern England. According to Giddens, one of the characteristics of the transition to modernity is the breakdown of traditional models of social order and hierarchy.[15] One effect of this breakdown is the erosion or, more accurately, the transformation of the authority of traditional elites and the growth of new groups, like the professions, with claims to at least part of that authority.[16] These claims are often registered in representations of those making the claims—lawyers, for instance—whether or not the representation accurately characterizes the profession or its practitioners.[17] In a period of social, intellectual, and economic ferment the ancient professions of law and religion found new and broader horizons for their activities while at the same time new professions were developing. Professions helped drive social and cultural change at the same time they were changed by those same developments. More specifically, the professions exerted an ever-growing effect on the structure of the social field, generating new modes of self-recognition and principles of social order. As Jean-Christophe Agnew notes in *Worlds Apart*, early modern culture was transformed by the growth in importance of a placeless market in which everything could be exchanged.[18] He argues that as markets became free of traditional constraints of place, time, and ritual, and as they shifted from barter to a money economy in the later Middle Ages, social life came to be "imbued" with a "pervasive and ongoing sense of risk, a recurrent anticipation of profit and loss that lends to all social intercourse a pointed, transactional quality."[19] This "transactional quality" calls forth new strategies to cope with anxieties about the self and the society within which that self exists. Some of these new strategies derive from the development of the professions in early modern culture.

The specifically professional "economies" of governmental administration, law, theater, and playwriting that develop in the period have a complex relation to a changing social order.[20] A growing demand for trained administrators in the Queen's government led to the growth of an administrative profession. The legal profession is shaped by the explosion of litigation that made so many lawyers' careers. The ever-growing market for plays and other theatrical entertainments helped form the professional theater and playwriting. All of these shaping factors are "economic" and relate to what Agnew calls "the market" but not in any simple way. The sociology of the professions has tended to link the rise of professions to narrowly economic forces and this practice has led many studies to reduce professionalization to, for example, a mere reflex of the Industrial Revolution.[21] The professions have a more complicated and ambiguous relation to economic change than many of the classic studies allow. This book will not privilege economic transition as the primary agent of early modern change, but will treat economic change as one factor among many influencing the growth of the professions. Struggles for status and identity form as much a part of the process of "professionalization" as do economic changes.

Historians such as Lawrence Stone, Christopher Brooks, Ian Archer, and Keith Wrightson have shown that, despite the durability of hierarchy and the many strident defenses of the established order, early modern England saw a greater degree of social and geographic mobility than is visible in earlier periods.[22] Under the pressure of this increase in mobility, principles of status, once stably—if only ideologically—based in the estates system, eroded to some extent in the sixteenth and seventeenth centuries.[23] The erosion of traditional hierarchy, particularly the decline in numbers and influence of the old feudal magnates and the tenurial system they represented, led to the development of new principles of distinction, rank, and influence. Groups with various claims to embody these principles struggled not only to claim places in the social hierarchy but also to define and redefine the terms that structure their *internal* hierarchies: the principles of "vision and division" that are internal to particular fields and that structure the habitus of agents in those fields.[24] The professions of administration, law, theater, and playwriting were among the groups struggling for status in a changing social order. According to Christopher Brooks, professional learning became part of a "calculus of social differentiation" that linked professionals with the gentry on the ladder of rank.[25] The occupational groups in this study made their professionalism the basis of their claim to a role in social space.

To call an occupation a "profession" recognizes (and, in a sense, creates) its elevated status, and by the twentieth century, occupations make assertions of their professional status the primary focus of their public self-representations.[26] This vocabulary of distinction develops out of early modern struggles over the role, nature, and place of "professions" in society. Those struggles have genetic and structural connections to present-day struggles, in part because early modern conflicts set the terms that structure the debates and struggles that follow. One of Pierre

Bourdieu's recommendations about constructing a research project is to be wary about the dangers of using "sociological" concepts that are themselves at stake without engaging in a detailed examination of their history. Definitions carry with them a history of misrecognitions, misrecognitions that have much to do with the history of the fields they define. In light of my wariness of received categories, I will survey the long history of the terms "profession," "professional," and "professionalization" in an effort to avoid importing attitudes that are the product of a lengthy historical struggle into an investigation of an early stage of that struggle.

II

> It is necessary to write a structural history which finds in each state of the structure both the product of previous struggles to transform or conserve the structure, and, through the contradictions, tensions, and power relations that constitute that structure, the source of its subsequent transformations.
> —Pierre Bourdieu, *In Other Words*

Influential contemporary scholars from Magali Larson to Andrew Abbott to Stanley Fish generally treat professionalism as a phenomenon of the late eighteenth and nineteenth centuries, linking the professions to the rise of industrial capitalism and the modern system of higher education.[27] This bias in study treats the modern professions as if they are born new with the Industrial Revolution. Both history and sociology have until fairly recently labored under serious misconceptions about the development of the professions since the Middle Ages.[28] Historians have taken the sociology of the professions to task for positing an imaginary total break between the premodern professions and those of modernity. Early modern professions *are* professions, according to historians like Christopher Brooks and Wilfred Prest who base their arguments on the development of the legal profession. Other scholars have examined medicine, estate management, and teaching, and find that these occupations can usefully be characterized as professions.[29] Wilfred Prest's important and influential essay "Why the History of the Professions Is Not Written" demonstrates the paucity of evidence for much of the sociological work on the historical development of the professions, and particularly for the claim that the professions underwent an epochal change at the "point of industrialization, modernization, or 'great transformation.' "[30] Prest's 1981 essay cogently and thoroughly critiques scholarship in the history and sociology of the professions, and many of his criticisms are still valid today. He bases his critique primarily on what he depicts as the inadequacy of sociological theory and the reliance of historians on a "general theory" of the professions deriving from sociology. The following pages will discuss the study of the professions in general terms and then turn to a more detailed discussion of two important recent sociological studies in an effort to lay the groundwork for a preliminary model of how professions develop and function in early modern culture.

In a useful survey article, Michael Burrage and Rolf Torstendal assert that neither Marx nor Weber, the founders of modern sociology, paid serious attention to the professions. In fact, Marx and Weber provided: "two powerful and compelling concepts, class and bureaucracy, to analyze adjacent, or even the same social phenomena, which have overshadowed and diverted attention away from the study of the professions ever since."[31] They argue that ever since sociologists have acted as social taxonomists, classifying and sorting professions in an effort to define them in terms of one or the other of these categories rather than studying them on their own terms.[32] Elliot Friedson, himself a prominent figure in the sociology of the professions, supports this contention with the claim that much sociological literature begs the question of what defines a profession, or, more damagingly, shifts the ground of debate to vague and unhistorical discussions of "professionalism" and "professionalization." In basic accord with Burrage and Torstendal, Friedson argues that scholars often try to "treat profession as if it were a generic concept rather than a changing historic concept, with particular roots in an industrial nation strongly influenced by Anglo-American institutions."[33] Instead of striving to find absolute definitions of professions, research should focus on "how people in a society determine who is a professional and who is not, how they 'make' or 'accomplish' professions by their activities, and what the consequences are for the way they see themselves and perform their work."[34] Researchers need to treat profession as a contingent, historical concept that is subject to change as the society changes and to offer changeable, context-derived definitions that reflect both the constitution and role of professions in a given culture.

Studies by Talcott Parsons and by coauthors A. P. Carr-Saunders and P. A. Wilson set the parameters of sociological inquiry into the professions.[35] Carr-Saunders and Wilson posited a series of basic characteristics that shaped many later definitions of professions: professions are elite bodies of experts who apply their specialist knowledge to "real world" problems.[36] They control the training of aspiring members of the profession and oversee their accrediting. Members of the profession also espouse and enforce an organization-specific code of ethics. This theoretical "public-spiritedness" has continued to be important to many later definitions. In other words, professions were held by Carr-Saunders and Wilson to offer their services more for the public good than for private gain. In their wake, searches for these basic characteristics dominated many studies of the professions. As Andrew Abbott writes "The Carr-Saunders volume epitomized two methodologies characteristic of writing on the professions, combining naturalism and typology. Early articles on the professions would summarize the life history of their particular case, review the then-current essential traits of a true profession, and decide whether social work or nursing or whatever really was a profession."[37] This approach produced a large body of unrelated case studies of individual professions that varied as the prevailing "essential traits" varied. Consensus on what those "essential traits" of a profession might be was elusive and the body of work produced was an undifferentiated mass of empirical studies that, according to Abbott, reflected the authors' prejudices rather than theoretical rigor.

This state of affairs in the sociology of the professions continued into the postwar era and only fairly recently have the ruling orthodoxies been challenged. In the 1970s and '80s, scholars began to question many of the assumptions that guided the earlier empirical studies. For example, Magali Larson's *Rise of Professionalism* looked at the professions more in terms of their place in the market (and their ability to control the exercise of their expertise) than as autonomous bodies operating at some distance from the economy. Despite this break with sociological tradition, she echoes the sociologists that preceded her, defining the professions as "occupations with special power and prestige . . . they have special competence in esoteric bodies of knowledge linked to central needs and values of the social system, and are devoted to the service of the public above and beyond material incentives."[38] She goes on to argue that this definition best suits professions like medicine, law, and technical occupations (such as engineering or architecture). It best applies to the "fully developed" professions of nineteenth-century America and England.[39] She links professionalization to a modernization defined as the "advance of science and cognitive rationality and the progressive differentiation and rationalization of the division of labor in industrialized societies."[40] According to this analysis, professionalism had to wait to mature until the great efflorescence of industrial capitalism in the mid-nineteenth century, and Larson does not deal extensively with antecedent developments.

Larson argues vigorously that the emergence of the professions is tied to an emergent social order, locating this emergence in the birth of industrial capitalism. She writes: "From dependence on the power and prestige of elite patrons or upon the judgment of a tightly knit community, the modern professions came to depend on specific formal training and anonymous certificates."[41] The rise of formal training and certification begins earlier, though the full development of accrediting institutions does come well after the sixteenth century. Early modern lawyers in particular qualify for practice by completing formal training, and while call to the bar is not an anonymous certificate, it is more formal than the "judgment of a tightly knit community." *The Rise of Professionalism* is very much an analysis of the professionalism arising in the nineteenth century and thus does not deal thoroughly with early and premodern antecedents. In her narrative, modern (i.e., fully developed) professions are defined by their markets (understood as populations that purchase a particular professional service), and, because of this, the struggle to control their markets is the constitutive force in their formation and it seems that these markets, like the professions themselves, are a product of modernity.[42] She treats professional training as an effort to enable students to provide recognizable products on a professional market. Larson grants this relatively undefined "market" (there is some slippage between what she describes as professional markets and a more general market) the power to determine the structure of both professional practice and training.[43] According to Larson's model, all professions operate in this manner: "The structures that emerged were analogous beneath the surface: insofar as they were modern, all levels of the new educational systems were spawned by capitalist industrialization."[44] These homologous structures are the basic structures of the professions that develop under market capitalism.[45] The relationship between changes in professional training and self-understanding is, I would argue, not restricted to the Industrial Revolution and similar changes occur in early modern England as its economic and social system underwent profound change. Larson's focus on the way that professions define themselves in terms of their actual (and potential) clienteles moves beyond the typologies she critiques and offers a useful way to think about early modern developments as well.[46]

Larson and other scholars of the 1970s and '80s develop a critique of professional ideology that unmasks the alleged disinterestedness of professionals as intense interest in both material gain and social power. After Larson, the high social status of, for example, medical professionals seems less a just reward for the services they provide than the goal of a professional group intent on achieving social power or authority.[47] Notwithstanding her focus on the historical nature of professionalization, Larson's account still depicts professionalism as developing across society, affecting occupations with professional aspirations in a more or less similar fashion over the course of the nineteenth century. She treats professionalization as a process whose broad characteristics remain constant across the whole spectrum of professions. Despite its sophistication and the undeniable advance it represents, Larson's account still oversimplifies the history of the professions. This oversimplification is a result of four related assumptions:

1) That professions underwent an epochal change with the advent of the Industrial Revolution.
2) That professions did not function in a market before capitalism's ascendancy.
3) That professional training did not aim at producing "adequately trained and socialized" people before the dominance of the market.
4) That "professionalization" was a phenomenon operating evenly across society as a whole.

All four of these assumptions have been aggressively questioned by later historians and sociologists. As Burrage and Torstendal note, historians demolished some of the cherished notions of the sociology of the professions:

> Some, such as the supposed "natural history of the professions," or the distinction between the "status" professions of the pre-modern world and the "occupational" professions of the modern world, were not great losses since they had never persuaded many sociologists. However, it was somewhat more unnerving when historians began to question assumptions which virtually all sociologists had accepted: namely that there was a marked difference between a rather static pre-modern dark age and a modern dynamic one, or that there was some intimate and therefore causal relationship between the rise of the professions and the rise of capitalism.[48]

Sociology had depended on a theory of rupture between widely divergent historical social forms, a rupture that transformed institutions, practices, and, most relevant here, professions. Under the influence of aggressive historical scholarship, sociology examined some of its assumptions—recognizing, for example, that, in practice, professions often do not resemble the sociological picture of them—and began to rework many of the underlying concepts of what Abbott terms the "professionalization story."

Responding to Larson and the "power theorists," Andrew Abbott's *System of Professions* offers an alternative to Larson's model of historical development by analyzing the professions according to a system model. Abbott does not focus exclusively on any particular profession, nor does he offer any kind of reductive unitary definition of what constitutes a profession. Abbott's book focuses on *relations* between professions in an effort to make sense of the way they develop by acting on each other as well as by refining and theorizing their own particular areas of expertise.[49] Abbott argues against Larson, Parsons, and Everett Hughes, who portray professions as developing either in isolation or as part of one general process called professionalization, arguing that professions develop through complex interactions and conflicts that the professionalization model cannot account for adequately.[50] In the wake of a thorough historical and theoretical critique of this model, he writes that "the evidence argues for a new approach to professional development that replaces the general professionalization concept."[51] Abbott's book describes relations between the microsystem of the individual profession and the macrosystem in which the professions compete in ways the general professionalization concept cannot. Abbott's relational model is able to account for particular developments in specific professions while not losing sight of the developing shape of the general system.

Abbott's discussion of the ecology of the professions not only demonstrates that professions cannot be understood in isolation, but also shows that "professionalization" was not a singular, structural phenomenon applying to all professions. Professions and professionalization developed as part of an interlocking system of occupations that, as they developed toward public recognition as professions, were engaged in a constant struggle over what definitions and practices made one profession distinct from another as well as what separated a profession from a mere occupation.[52] For Abbott, the crucial issue defining professional struggles is the control of professional work rather than organization, as in earlier models:

> The central problem with the current concept of professionalization is its focus on structure rather than work. It is the content of the professions' work that the case studies tell us is changing. It is control of work that brings the professions into conflict with each other and makes their histories interdependent. It is differentiation in types of work that often leads to serious differentiation within the professions. By switching from a focus on the organizational structures of professions to a focus on groups with common work we replace several of the problematic assumptions at once.[53]

In Abbott's model, professions compete for the legitimate control of kinds of work, for what he calls jurisdiction, and in the process they define themselves and influence their competitors' self-definitions.[54]

To give a brief example, Abbott discusses the rise of psychiatry in the early nineteenth century. Working on what Abbott describes as the hazy border between "bodily and mental ailments," early psychiatrists claimed jurisdiction over those who were later to be called the mentally ill. As is well known, "madmen" had fallen previously under the jurisdiction of legal authorities.[55] Psychiatry made a claim that "madness" was an illness subject to cures by suitable professionals: "Madmen are sick, they said; give them to us and we will cure them. A new theory and therapy justified the shift, and private bodies and state legislatures were soon dotting the countryside with insane asylums. Psychiatry was the profession of the superintendents of these institutions."[56] Psychiatry based its claim for professional legitimacy on its newly claimed medical jurisdiction over the newly named mentally ill. At the same time, other developing professions were "exploring" the same territory. Neurologists "took from other physicians any patient whose otherwise untreatable illness could somehow be attributed to 'nerves.' "[57] This put them into close contact with psychiatry and for a time they shared jurisdiction over the mentally ill. Then, the professions divided with neurologists coming to be "organic physicians working in hospitals" while psychiatrists "took over the neurologists' old position as the outpatient border guards of the medical profession, handling the symptoms and diseases that seemed not quite real" to other doctors and the broader society.[58] This example shows that professions do not necessarily follow a regular pattern of establishment and organization, that the content and structure of a profession's work changes over time in relation to its context, and that a full theory of professionalism must deal with the complexities of interprofessional competition and cooperation seen within a context of social change.

Abbott actively situates professions in a dynamic social context (not simply in a market) that has profound influence over the shape of professional work, training, and organization. The context of that work has as much of a constitutive role in defining a profession as the profession's expertise does, and Abbott argues that professionalization only makes sense in these terms. Neither particularist empirical nor "power literature" studies account for the way that developments specific to one profession affect and are affected by developments in another and by the effects those individual changes have on the whole system. Both models ignore the complex interconnections that structure the professional field, if for different reasons. Particularist studies focus so narrowly on particular professions that the system disappears, while the "power literature" tends to reduce the structuring forces in the system to a struggle for market control. Abbott strives to avoid both of these pitfalls by studying professions as part of a broad system. He argues that

> the professions make up an interacting system, an ecology. Professions compete within this system, and a profession's success

reflects as much the situation of its competitors and the system structure as it does the profession's own efforts. From time to time, tasks are created, abolished, or reshaped by external forces, with consequent jostling and readjustment within the system of professions. Thus, larger social forces have their impact on individual professions through the structure of within which the professions exists, rather than directly. . . . Professions are never seen alone, but they are also not replaced by a single encompassing category of "the professions." They exist in a system.[59]

Changes in one profession necessarily affect the other professions, to a greater or lesser degree as they are nearer or further apart in social space. Abbott describes a vacancy model of the "ecology of the professions" in which professions compete for position within a semiclosed set of jurisdictions.[60] In such a system, change in one profession's claimed area of expertise necessarily demands a response from other professions upon whose jurisdictions that claim impinges. Those responses themselves demand responses until the system settles into a new equilibrium: "Whether begun by vacancies or bumps, the changes lead to chains of disturbances that propagate through the system until absorbed either by the professionalization or de-professionalization of some group or by absorption within the internal structure of one or more existing professions. At every step of these chains occur jurisdictional contests."[61] In this model, professions close to each other in social space, as law and writing were in early modern England, necessarily, if not directly, influence each other's success patterns, training, expectations, mechanisms of distinction, and definitions of professionalism and professional conduct. For example, as lawyers develop a sense of themselves as serving the "freedom of Englishmen," writers begin to stress their educative role in the culture. Sir Philip Sidney describes poetry as his "unelected calling" and makes an argument for the usefulness and worth of writing in his 1583 *Apology*.[62] Defining the poet, he writes, "that it is not rhyming and versing that maketh a poet—no more than a long gown maketh an advocate who though he pleaded in armor should be an advocate and no soldier. But it is that feigning notable images of virtues, vices, or what else, with that delightful teaching, which must be the right describing note to know a poet by."[63] Sidney's comparison of poet and advocate is not mere coincidence, in Abbott's view, but serves as an example of the way that the discourse and status of one occupation affects those around it in social space. The poet's work is as immutable a principle of identity as that of the lawyer who even in armor would still be a lawyer. Law was becoming increasingly important in early modern culture and Sidney's comparison suggests that writing ("poetry" is not just verse) shares in that importance.[64] Abbott's definition is more dynamic and situational than that of earlier scholars; he defines profession simply as an aspect of the division of "expert labor," not in terms of some abstract list of essential qualities necessary for an occupation to qualify as a profession. Professionalization is less an overarching developmental pattern common to all professions than, as Abbott argues, the product of ongoing interactions such as those between law and writing.

Abbott's professional ecology articulates links between the professions' context and their inner workings, explaining professional change in terms of mediated responses to external stimuli, but does not make the mechanics of that mediation explicit. He argues for the situatedness of professions but does not offer a thorough explanation of the effects of that situatedness on particular professions. Abbott treats the effects of the professions' social context in terms of rational responses to social changes, calculated strategies objectively designed to achieve determinate ends.[65] However, the responses Abbott describes are often conditioned by the institutional and individual histories of agents involved in various professions rather than resulting from rational choices made on the basis of objective knowledge of the shape of the system.[66] Pierre Bourdieu's theory of fields offers a way to describe these kinds of choices in specific terms. If these choices do not derive from objective reason, neither are they random or irrational; according to Bourdieu: "Individuals do not move about in social space in a random way, partly because they are subject to the forces which structure this space . . . and partly because they resist the forces of the field with their specific inertia, that is, their properties, which may exist in embodied form, as dispositions, or in objectified form, in goods, qualifications, etc."[67] The professions provide some of the properties that structure social space. Abbott's theory pays less attention to the "forces which structure" social space, choosing rather to focus on conscious strategy. This is not to devalue his insights but to argue that his work can be supplemented by Bourdieu's social theory. If Abbott's theory is an ecology of the professions, Bourdieu's is an ecology of social practice.

Pierre Bourdieu's social theory depends on an interlocking set of concepts that together offer a working description of social life. The two most important of these categories for my discussion are habitus and field.[68] In what follows I will apply these concepts to a discussion (and definition) of profession and I will offer a description of the early modern history of the professions in the next section.[69] Bourdieu states that the work of definition is critical to any construction of an object of study and that without careful attention to definitions sociological and historical work cannot hope to produce anything like "objective" knowledge of social space. Speaking specifically of profession, he writes:

> "Profession" is a folk concept that has been uncritically smuggled into scientific language and which imports into it a whole social unconscious. It is the *social product* of a historical work of construction of a group and of a *representation* of groups that has surreptitiously slipped into the science of this very group. . . . The category of profession refers to realities that are, in a sense "too real" to be true, since it grasps at once a mental category and a social category, socially produced only by superseding or obliterating all kinds of economic, social, and ethnic differences and contradictions which make the "profession" of "lawyer," for instance, a space of competition and struggle.[70]

Bourdieu points out that "profession" is a category that tends to elide conflict and contradiction with a convenient and often unexamined label. For example, the " 'profession' of 'lawyer' " is defined by competition and struggle over, among other things, the terms by which success will be measured and these competitions and struggles are often obscured by uncritical uses of the term "profession." Elliot Friedson makes a similar point about the imperative of defining the object, but unfortunately fails to question the effects that accepting profession as a "folk concept" has on research. He writes: "If 'profession' may be described as a folk concept, then the research strategy appropriate to it is phenomenological in character. One does not attempt to determine what profession is in an absolute sense so much as how people in a society determine who is a professional and who is not, how they 'make' or 'accomplish' professions by their activities, and what the consequences are for the way they see themselves and perform their work."[71] Friedson argues for the value of contextualization and historicizing, but still approaches "profession" as an already-defined object of study. Friedson's functional, and more importantly, synchronic definition of profession makes reference to history, but does not seriously engage with the effect that historical conflict and struggle has on a particular definition of profession. He does not suggest that profession as an object of study itself needs study and this limits the explanatory power of the definitions he argues for. The "folk concept" of profession that he accepts seemingly without question carries with it a history and a "whole social unconscious" whose effects obfuscate historical struggles over the definition of "lawyer," "writer," or "administrator," to use my examples. Bourdieu argues that this is why defining the object is crucial to any research project: without the labor of definition one can easily fall into patterns of thought and investigation conditioned by the "social unconscious" embedded in the categories one uses to describe the object.

This discussion of the sociology of the professions explores some of the presuppositions and conventions that have determined the study of professions in modern culture. These presuppositions have generally excluded the pre- and early modern professions from significant attention.[72] Twentieth-century usage of the term associates professionalism with the Industrial Revolution and the birth of capitalism, tending to ignore the precapitalist history of the occupations we call professions. At the same time, both contemporaries and moderns call precapitalist occupations "professions" and no scholar denies that law, for example, was a profession in early modern England.[73] If "profession" is to be a useful term, it must be more narrowly (and historically) defined. Bourdieu's theory offers a rigorous framework for definition, contrasting the unquestioning use of the concept of profession to "taking it seriously": "Everything becomes different, and much more difficult if, instead of taking the notion of "profession" at face value, I take seriously the work of *aggregation* and symbolic imposition that was necessary to produce it, and if I treat is as a field, that is, as a structured space of social forces and struggles."[74] Treating professions as fields helps to free research from the preconceptions built into the received terminology. Rather than accepting the definition that the professions themselves have promoted, Bourdieu argues that the researcher must investigate the development of that definition at the same time that he researches the group that promotes it. As Abbott and Larson rightly note, there are tangible benefits for groups that are socially recognized as professions, and those benefits are the product of a history of struggles that the idea of a monolithic profession works to obscure. Viewing professions as fields also forces the researcher to examine how the definition of the field becomes a stake in struggles over legitimacy, certification, and success that are internal to the field in question but also have an important effect on its public image: "The very notion of writer, but also the notion of lawyer, doctor, or sociologist, despite all efforts at codification and homogenization through certification, is at stake in the field of writers (or lawyers, etc.): the struggle over the legitimate definition, whose stake—the word definition says it—is the boundary, the frontiers, the *right of admission*, sometimes the *numerus clausus*, is a universal property of fields."[75] From this perspective, the sixteenth- and seventeenth-century jurisdictional conflict between barristers and solicitors was, in part, a dispute over which group had the more legitimate claim to the professional title of lawyer. That conflict eventually resulted in the formation of upper and lower branches of the legal profession, each of which functions within strict boundaries and areas of expertise.

Treating professions as fields also avoids one of the theoretical pitfalls of empiricist studies. As Abbott notes, to embark on an empirical study of, say, social work as a profession already recognizes social work as a profession; in other words, it colludes in the profession's efforts to secure recognition as a legitimate profession. This becomes an important tactic in professional competitions where public recognition of professional status is crucial for successful jurisdictional claims.[76] Bourdieu calls this the "theory effect" of social science: "Social science must include in its theory of the social world a theory of the theory effect which, by helping to impose a more or less authorized way of seeing the world, helps to construct the reality of that world."[77] Thinking of professions in terms of fields requires an examination of how this "theory effect" is a stake in the struggles that define the field. It does not allow an investigation of profession to become a mere taxonomy that legitimates a group's claim to a particular status.[78] The concept of profession has to be as much of an object of inquiry as the groups who claim to be or are recognized to be professions.

III

> A vocation or calling is a certaine kinde of life, ordained and imposed on man by God for the common good . . . whatsoever any man enterpriseth or doeth either in worde or deede, he must doe it by virtue of his calling, and he must keep himselfe within the compasse, limits, or precincts thereof.
> —William Perkins, *Treatise on the Vocations and Callings of Men* (1603)

Professions in early modern English culture can be characterized as occupations that develop an internal structure whose structuring principles—the terms of distinction—become a stake in internal struggles for status that translate, through a series of mediations, into claims for the status of the occupation in the broader society. According to Abbott, occupations operate within a broader macrosystem that they both affect and are affected by. I suggest that the macrosystem these individual occupations operate in is the professional field; a field that takes its shape from the individual professional fields that comprise it as well as its place in social space. As Bourdieu argues, the field of power provides overarching terms of success and distinction that influence agents within, for example, individual professions. Bourdieu defines the field of power as "the relations of force that obtain between the social positions which guarantee their occupants a quantum of social force, or of capital, such that they are able to enter into the struggles over the monopoly of power, of which struggles over the definition of the legitimate form of power are a crucial dimension."[79] In other words, the field of power is the site of struggles over the legitimacy of various claims to exercise legitimate power in society. It is made of up of the relations between agents and groups of agents (such as professionals) with varying "quanta" of social force and who struggle to increase that force by defining their specific form of capital as the legitimate form of power. In early modern England, the field of power, and social space more generally, was in transition from a more or less traditional structure toward one that is recognizably modern. This transition put considerable strain on English society, which responded with a series of adaptations including the professionalization of activities that had previously operated in accord with older models of practice.⁸⁰ Occupations once guided by traditions derived from an earlier state of the field were forced to adapt to new social and economic pressures.⁸¹ Contemporaries recognized these changes, responding to them in treatises, manuals, and in conflicts over the definition of what came to be seen as the profession.

"Profession" and "vocation" had a variety of widely divergent definitions in the sixteenth and seventeenth centuries but religious uses dominate until the eighteenth century. Changes in the usage and definition of these terms register changes in public perceptions of the role and nature of "occupations" in early modern England. Profession refers to the "declaration, promise, or vow made by one entering a religious order," in other words, a profession (public declaration) of faith.⁸² Nevertheless, our modern sense of profession as referring to one's chosen occupation is extant, if not prevalent, in the sixteenth century.⁸³ According to the *Oxford English Dictionary*, the earliest usage of profession as referring to a secular occupation dates as far back as 1541 in an English translation of Galen: "The parties of the art of Medycyne . . . can not be separated one from the other without the damage and great detriment of all the medycinall profession."⁸⁴ Vocation, an older and more common term, is defined by the *Oxford English Dictionary* as "the action on the part of God of calling a person to exercise some special function, especially of a spiritual nature, or to fill a certain position; divine influence or guidance toward a definite (esp. a religious career); the fact of being so called or directed toward a special work in life."⁸⁵ In *Distinction*, Bourdieu describes vocation as "the proleptic assumption of an objective destiny that is imposed by practical reference to the modal trajectory in the class of origin."⁸⁶ Vocation, in other words, leads agents to select occupations in accord with the history of their class fraction but causes them to experience that selection as an imposition, a calling from somewhere outside the self. Where profession implies a degree of volition on the part of the professor, vocation does not necessarily imply any agency on the part of the person called. This is an important distinction: the transition from premodern divinely ordained vocations to modern, at least apparently, self-chosen professions involves precisely the redefinition of vocations as professions. By the late fifteenth century, vocation could refer to "the particular function or station to which a person is called by God" (1487 in Caxton's *Book of Good*

Manners) and by the mid-sixteenth century, vocation is used to refer to "one's ordinary occupation, business, or profession" (1553 in Wilson's *Rhetoric*).⁸⁷ This last definition points to the slippage between the terms. Earlier in the fourteenth century, Chaucer uses profession exclusively in the religious sense and never uses the term vocation.

Chaucer uses the term "professioun" three times in his poetry. All three of these uses are in the *Canterbury Tales*.⁸⁸ The *Summoner's Tale* uses one sense of profession to refer to specific groups of monastics:

> I ne have no text of it, as I suppose,
> But I shal fynde it in a maner glose,
> That specially oure sweete Lord Jhesus
> Spak this by freres, whan he seyde thus:
> "Blessed be they that povere in spirit been."
> And so forth al the gospel may ye seen,
> Wher it be likker oure professioun,
> Or hirs that swymmen in possessioun.
> Fy on hire pompe and on hire glotonye!
> And for hir lewednesse I hem diffye.
>
> (*SumT* 1919–28)

Here, "professioun" is used in the context of a hypocritical debate over who is nearer to the gospel's ideal of poverty. The friar claims that those of his profession are closer to the gospel than those that "swymmen in possessioun" even as he attempts to secure a donation. Later in the same tale, Chaucer uses the definition of profession as the promise made upon entering holy orders as a way to secure an oath to fairly divide a "bequest" among all the brethren of a convent:

> "Now wel," quod he, "and somwhat shal I yive
> Unto youre hooly covent whil I lyve;
> And in thyn hand thou shalt it have anon,
> On this condicion, and oother noon,
> That thou departe it so, my deere brother,
> That every frere have also muche as oother.
> This shaltou swere on thy professioun,
> Withouten fraude or cavillacioun."
>
> (*SumT* 2129–36)

Part of the joke depends on the fact that the friar swears on what the tale suggests is a false profession and in return receives a worthless donation.[89] The tale seems both to depend on this idea of profession and to render it ridiculous at the same time. The *Shipman's Tale* uses profession as security for an oath as well:

> I clepe hym so, by Seint Denys of Fraunce,
> To have the moore cause of aqueyntaunce
> Of yow, which I have loved specially
> Aboven alle wommen, sikerly.
> This swere I yow on my professioun.
> (*ShipT* 151–55)

Both of these tales are fabliaux, satirizing a variety of fiscal and physical transactions, and both use the same sense of profession to criticize the false professor. That profession can be used in ways that depend on spiritual connotations to refer to and (however ironically) secure secular transactions points to the ambiguities characteristic of the idea of profession even as early as the fourteenth century.

In the 1590s, Shakespeare's *King John* treats this ambiguity of definition in greater detail: in the play, the Bastard's career represents the choosing of a profession rather than the recognition of a vocation. The anonymous *Troublesome Raigne of John, King of England*, composed at roughly the same time as Shakespeare's play, serves as a useful counterpoint. In that play, the Bastard receives a literal call to service and his volition is never at issue.[90] Both definitions are extant at the same time and neither one seems to be dominant. Paul Marshall writes:

> In looking at sixteenth- and seventeenth-century views we find that there were in fact few systematic elaborations of the doctrine [of calling or vocation]. After the 1550s, apart from the better-known treatises of William Perkins, George Swinnock, and Richard Steele, there is only the exposition of Bishop Robert Sanderson. Nevertheless, the concept is widespread in these centuries: many people consistently worked with the notion without having a very clear notion of what they were saying nor what it might imply.[91]

Marshall gives early modern culture perhaps less credit than it deserves; people had a functional notion of what calling, vocation, and profession meant and used these terms to position themselves in a changing society. The religious senses of profession and vocation derive from a more traditional model of society; they are inclusive and holistic concepts that bind agents into a structured and hierarchical whole. Moreover, if vocation or profession are divinely sanctioned, their pursuit can only serve the greater glory of God. Rather than competing with central authority, this notion of vocation and profession buttresses it. The orderly and hierarchical model of society suggested by this definition, already idealized by backward-looking Tudor writers, was becoming more and more manifestly inadequate as an image of early modern society.

In the sixteenth century, several occupations began to develop into what Pierre Bourdieu calls autonomous fields with their own structuring principles and legitimacy outside of divine or temporal authority—hence their disruptive effect on traditional ideas about social order.[92] The development of increasingly autonomous fields disembedded subjects, to use Giddens's terminology, from their places in traditional society and eventually reembedded them in a recognizably modern one. The conflict-ridden redefinition of "profession" in the period is one response to this shift.[93] For example, William Perkins's *Treatise on the Vocations and Callings of Men* provides a religious framework in which to understand the increasing importance and flexibility of "professional" activity in the period. It would be both easy and foolhardy to conclude that Perkins's tract "proves" that "professions" exist in early modern England, despite the fact that he never uses the term. Instead, I will suggest that the *Treatise* documents a shift in the definition of vocation and calling in response to changes in what would come to be called professional practice. Anxious about instability and the pernicious results of ambition, Perkins argues that vocations are given by God, and that one must persevere with "constancy" in the profession God has chosen for him: "The . . . thing required, in doing the workes of a mans calling, in a good manner, and which ferues also for a good continuance in the calling, is Constancie. . . . For euen as the fouldiour in the field, muft not change his place, wherein he is placed by the Generall, fo muft the Chriftian continue and abide in his calling, without change or alteration."[94] Arguing from scripture, Perkins also states that "whatfoever any man enterprifeth[95] or doeth, either in worde or deede, he must doe it by vertue of his calling, and he muſt keep himself within the compaſſe, limits or precincts thereof."⁹⁶ This in spite of the fact that he later admits that there are legitimate reasons for a man to change his calling. Allowable reasons to change one's calling are private need (where the calling cannot support a person's needs) or public good (as being elected or chosen a magistrate). He nevertheless strives to put firm limits on the freedom to choose and change calling. Perkins's treatment of vocation is a response to a perception of disorder in his society—his stress on the need for men to stay within their vocation, once chosen, attests to this—and attempts to keep individual willfulness under control while still insisting that the choice of vocation is free.⁹⁷ It is this freedom that makes Perkins's work important as a document of a developing professional field. Vocation is both God-given and human-chosen in his work, and thus his use of the term is far closer to our modern definition than other contemporary usages.⁹⁸

Perkins describes the vocations and callings of men as falling under two broad rubrics, one of which is more important than the other. The first is the general calling to be a good Christian that is common to all men and women. The second is what Perkins calls a "personal" calling, of which he writes: the "execution of that particular office wherein a man is placed, is his perſonal calling."⁹⁹ Theoretically, the general calling informs an individual's personal calling and, more importantly, dignifies that calling, however base it may be. He asserts that "the workes of euery calling, when they are performed in an holy manner, are done in faith and obedience, and serve notably for Gods glorie, be the calling never so base."¹⁰⁰ The work itself is not at issue, what matters is the *manner* in which that work is done.¹⁰¹ Constancy, honesty, and diligence in the pursuit of a calling mark its possessor as virtuous and by implication ennoble the work itself. This ennobling goes so far as to enable Perkins to assert, in an age when the ownership of land signalled wealth and success, that "occupation is as good as land, becauſe land may be loſt, but skil and labour in good occupation is profitable to the ende, because it will help at need when land and all things faile."¹⁰² Perkins claims that one's personal calling, one's occupation is as good as land and more secure as a source of "help at need." He elevates the holding of an occupation to the economic, if not social, status of landholding; recognizing that occupations are easier to come into than land and that in the late sixteenth century land did not necessarily represent the same degree of economic or social security it did in previous centuries.[103] This change contributes to changes in the status of occupations, changes that turn law, administration, and letters into something resembling "modern" professions. Perkins's definition of occupation as "as good as land" points to his position as a cleric as well as to a fundamental change in an early modern economy of status.[104]

The traditional marker of a family's status was its ownership of land and landownership was therefore held to be the goal of any ambitious man. Several Jacobean city comedies have wealthy Londoners of common birth attempting to erase their base origins by buying land in the country so that they or their children can live the life and, more importantly, enjoy the status of the gentry. However, R. G. Lang argues that London merchants tended not to retreat to the countryside to live the lives of the gentry, nor did they necessarily provide means for their offspring to do so.[105] An awareness of the new fragility of landed wealth arguably underlies the practice of placing the sons of wealthy members of London's livery companies in apprenticeships, the university, or the Inns of Court rather than relying on land bought with mercantile profits to insure the gentility (and financial security) of later generations.[106] Michael and Baptist Hickes, for example, were sons of a successful mercer who provided for their training but did not leave them much in the way of landed wealth. Michael parlayed his legal training into a position in Lord Burghley's secretariat while his brother took over the family business and became a very wealthy man. Both men relied on their training, not a bequest of land, and this seems to have been more typical than not among the London citizenry. Successfully placing a son in an occupation "as good as land" was the primary ambition of many Londoners, regardless of their wealth.[107]

Christopher Brooks argues that the early modern professions were a common resort of the middling and better sorts of people seeking secure futures for their children. Even families in the minor gentry placed sons in apprenticeships with members of London's livery companies, suggesting that the benefits of security outweighed whatever social stigma might be attached to "trade." According to Brooks, there was "a significant, and increasing, degree of mobility between the gentry and trade during the sixteenth and seventeenth centuries."[108] Most gentle apprentices were likely not the sons of major gentry families (there was a great deal of status inflation in the period); instead, many came from the "mere" or parish gentry. In addition, it is possible that up to a fifth were sons of rich townsmen or professionals. Gentle families of modest means seem to have felt no compunction about apprenticing their sons, despite the fact that apprenticeship automatically ended one's gentle status.[109]

Apprenticeship was a common means of entering a "profession," and the model of apprenticeship structured professional training across a broad range of occupations and for a broad range of people. Writing of the bar, Christopher Brooks asserts that "before 1640, the practising bar was drawn just about equally from gentry and non-gentry backgrounds. Moreover, the much more numerous 'lower branch of the legal profession' were recruited from the same social groups which provided entrants to the more elite retail and mercantile trades, and clerkship, apprenticeship in all but name, was the standard mode of training."[110] Even the training of lawyers in the "upper branch" resembled apprenticeship in its exercises, its living arrangements where students lived with "masters," and its emphasis on practical knowledge over theory, despite their protestations to the contrary.[111] Recent research findings "locate professional occupations within the social world of the merchant, the artisan, and the yeoman farmer, as much as that of the aristocracy and the gentry."[112] Apprenticeship gave apprentices the technical training, habits of mind, and the social skills necessary to compete in their fields as well as serving as a bridge between usually separate social groups. This position between the gentry and the urban middling sort is an important facet of early modern professions. It helps account for their relative autonomy from external influences as well as the perceived need on the part of the Crown or city oligarchy to regulate them.[113] Brooks treats the professions as semiautonomous groups of people, standing on the borders between different ranks, and able to articulate ideas that had a profound influence on public discourse.

Brooks makes a strong case for the importance of "professional" ideas and discourse in the history of sixteenth and seventeenth century society: "By 1628, the rights of all landholders, large and small, with respect to the most powerful lord in the realm, the king, were being defended in a language which arose partly from professional jurisprudence and partly from the conflicts between tenants and their landlords. There is no better single example of the influence of a group within the middling sort on professional discourse, and indeed, political ideology more generally."[114] Lawyers, by virtue of their relative autonomy, developed a specifically professional body of knowledge and a vocabulary that was able to influence public debate on the most serious of questions. Lawyers provide a strong and obvious example of the influence early modern professionals were able to exert on their culture. More subtle effects arising from the development of professions include shifts in the status hierarchy that recognized merit as well as birth, the development of a professional theater, and the recognition of professional status itself as a valid principle of authority.[115] Brooks attests to the presence of groups in early modern social space that can be recognized as professionals, groups that exerted considerable influence over the shape of that space.

That early modern England had "professions" seems clear from contemporary representations and from changes in the definition of profession and vocation. Contemporaries differentiated "professions" from crafts by the nature of their learning and, in some cases, their public utility. Brooks writes,

> Learning of the sort which was associated with the professions became an important element in a calculus of social differentiation which united the professions and the gentry. Professional occupations successfully claimed a special status because of their education and learning. Physicians and barristers were regularly described as esquires. Attorneys are difficult to identify as such in contemporary records because they invariably have "gent" written after their names, and so are indistinguishable from minor country squires and the upper reaches of the urban elite.[116]

The professions fought to make their learning a stake in this "calculus of social differentiation" that aligned them with the ruling elite.[117] If there is a single characteristic most clearly joining the fields discussed in this study, it is that all of them stress the virtue, difficulty, and public worth of their particular knowledge.[118] Lawyers make frequent reference to the difficulties attendant on learning the law, and law manuals assert that legal learning is both as complicated and as beautiful as the classics. Sir Thomas Smith's *De Republica Anglorum* praises the administra-

1 / "TO SOUND THE DEPTHS OF WHAT THOU WILT PROFESS" 67

tion of the Queen's government, and Robert Beale's treatise intends to preserve and advance the knowledge of the Privy Council's secretariat. Writers like Ben Jonson, Robert Greene, and John Marston make their learning and moral intent part of both their work and their public self-representations. Civic pageants routinely praise the art of the craftsmen engaged in producing the shows in language that emphasizes design rather than handiwork, and Sir George Buc refers to a College of the Revels in his appendix to Stowe's *Annals*. As Brooks suggests, these professions base their claims to distinction on the idea that their knowledge is theoretical, like that of the universities, and not mechanical, like that of the crafts.

Professions, as Bourdieu notes, are occupations that have fought to be recognized *as* professions and the title of profession becomes the chief stake of the professional field. The outlines of this field appear, for example, in the struggles between attorneys and barristers that, in a sense, produce the legal profession. The division of the modern legal profession into upper and lower branches derives from a struggle between fractions of the legal field over their places in the field's internal hierarchy as well as in social space as a whole. The "professional" field in early modern culture, what Abbott calls the system of professions, develops out of the various internal conflicts of "professionalizing" occupations as they struggle for public recognition. The title of profession itself is the product of a struggle to differentiate "higher" occupations from "lower." The chapters below argue that early modern administration, law, theater, and playwriting are fields and describes their internal struggles over the right to impose the legitimate definition of the field (in law and playwriting), to claim and maintain jurisdictions (law and administration), to constitute the proper function and training of a practitioner (law, administration, theater, and playwriting), and to establish the place of professions in early modern culture. Taken together, the chapters below show how a major subset of the "professional" field begins to develop in early modern England.

2
"I mean to learn": Status and Service in the History Plays

> Have thou the ordering of this present time.
> —William Shakespeare, *King John*

TUDOR ENGLAND SAW A SERIES OF CHANGES IN THE NATURE AND shape of the Crown's organs of government. Professional lay administrators increasingly took the place of the clerical hierarchy in filling the great offices of the realm. Wolsey was the last ecclesiastic to hold the office of chancellor in the period and other offices underwent a similar process of secularization as the century went on. At the same time, the Crown strove to achieve a monopoly of power in England, systematically limiting the influence and number of the great magnate families. The history of the Percy Earls of Northumberland serves as a particularly good example. Once the unquestioned deputy rulers of the north, by the end of the Tudor period, Percy power was broken and "new men" ruled the north of England. Under Henry VII, "no strong and independent royal interest existed in the Marches which could confront the clienteles of the great lords, there was no alternative to the indirect rule of the latter."[1] Henry VIII's policy, promulgated by Wolsey and Cromwell, was to create an alternative to the rule of the regional courts, to administer the north with "new men" loyal to the Crown. James writes that after the execution of the "rebel earl of Northumberland at York in August 1572" the Percy influence disappeared and "thereafter the bureaucrats Hunsdon, Scrope, and Sir John Forster ruled, men whose authority had its root not in the soil of the Marches themselves, but in London. . . . The future lay with the 'new men.'"[2] These new men were administrators loyal to the Crown, men who owed their position and authority more to the Crown than to any local source of legitimation.

Henry VII, settling the realm after his victory in 1485, ruled vigorously through the traditional medieval offices and officers of the kingdom. It took his son's reign, the English Reformation, and the agency of Thomas Cromwell to change the regime from an essentially medieval household government to an increasingly "modern" national government. G. R. Elton's seminal work *The Tudor Revolution in Government* argues that "the years 1471–1509 saw a vast revival of the household potential in financial administration, at the expense of the national organization."[3] Elton writes that "the great restoration of government after the civil wars of the fifteenth century, the work of Edward IV and Henry VII, represented a restoration of medieval government at its most efficient" and all the developments of the Yorkists and Henry VII "marked the triumph of household methods in administration."[4] Household methods worked well for Henry VII because he was, to use an historical commonplace, a businessman, but Henry VIII's relative lack of interest in the day-to-day operations of the Crown demanded changes in the royal administration.

Under the pressure of a series of social, educational, political, and economic developments, England saw the growth of a nascent, if not fully formed, professional civil service.[5] This "civil service" operated under the auspices of the Privy Council, its officers were still selected by birth as well as ability, but ability was coming to be the most important qualification. Thomas Cromwell, himself an administrator selected for his talent not his relatively obscure birth, began the sixteenth-century process of centering the bureaucracy on the Privy Council and its staff of bureaucrats, which culminated in the Elizabethan Privy Council's executive ascendancy at the close of the century. The "bureaucrats" who did the work of governing, the men who, like the Bastard in Shakespeare's *King John*, had "the ordering of this present time" under Queen and Council will be the focus of this chapter.

Elton argues that under Henry VIII English government changed from the medieval household government of Henry VII to what he calls a modern form of national government. Where household government treated the kingdom as the personal estate of the King to be governed by the King's personal servants, "national government" governed through a national bureaucracy staffed by bureaucrats who were not necessarily personal servants of the King. Cromwellian reforms shaped the administrative structure inherited by later Tudor monarchs and accelerated the centralization of power in London. Elton makes Cromwell the central figure of the "administrative revolution" of the 1520s and '30s, seeing him as the original modern bureaucrat engaged in rational reform meant to enhance the efficiency of the national government.[6]

Cromwell's reforms and later developments under Elizabeth point toward the "professionalization" of administration in the period. Elton's body of work posits a bureaucratic revolution in London that as it expanded into the provinces transformed the Tudor polity from a medieval political society into a modern one. Mervyn James's *Society, Politics, and Culture* argues that in the course of the sixteenth century the Crown gained more effective control of the northern Marches by placing men whose power and position derived more from the Crown's favor than from local sources in charge of provincial government, replacing men like the Percy Earls of Northumberland whose authority was traditional and thus more or less independent of the Crown. The common theme of all these developments is the gradual replacement of the traditional elites whose status depended on noble heritage by "new men" trained up in the universities or the Inns of Court who did not necessarily have a noble pedigree. Conyers Read, B. W. Beckingsale, and A. G. R. Smith have all produced biographies that point to the development of coherent career patterns and models of training for administrators, developments that lend credence to Elton's (and James's) argument about the professionalization and modernization of governmental administration in early modern England.[7]

Administrative historians agree on the increasing education and ability of men entering what amounts to the civil service in the period. Part of the purpose of humanist education was to encourage men to seek out means of serving the commonwealth and this kind of public service came to be seen as a means to social advancement.[8] In the character of its Bastard, Shakespeare's *King John* (1594–96) depicts an early form of the increasingly professional administrator whose "real-life" analogues include Thomas Cromwell, Roger Bacon, William Cecil (Lord Burghley), his son Robert Cecil, and the secretariat that supported them.[9] As W. J. Jones notes in the context of the Court of Chancery, the history of administration and the "civil service" is intimately linked to "the political core of Tudor England."[10] With governmental administration developing into a professional occupation rather than a semidivine vocation in Elizabethan England, the Bastard's career trajectory—from obscurity to a high place in King John's administration due to his initiative and ability—has wider resonances. A significant proportion of Elizabeth's most powerful servants exhibit a similar trajectory: Burghley rose from his family's country obscurity and Bacon's background was still more humble. Thomas Cromwell's rise provided an important precedent for these and other men's careers. Shakespeare's Bastard actively chooses a "career" as a royal servant while the same character in *The Troublesome Raigne of John, King of England* (a contemporaneous play on the same topic) is forced to avow his ancestry by his blood, against his better judgment, and thus enters the aristocracy and only from thence to royal service. Shakespeare's Bastard chooses to be a servant of the Crown—that choice and his demonstrated ability grants him his authority as well as his identity.[11]

Shakespeare's *King John*, standing between the two tetralogies, marks a transition in his treatment of political and historical questions. This argument has been advanced by critics like Sigurd Burckhardt, Virginia Vaughan, Michael Mannheim, and Marsha Robinson (among many others).[12] Vaughan, for example, writes that the play "demonstrates Shakespeare's experimentation with more sophisticated dramaturgical techniques to convey political complexities, techniques he perfected in the Henriad."[13] Most of the criticism focuses on Shakespeare's changing treatment of *political* questions to the exclusion of *social* considerations; if *King John* marks a transition in Shakespeare's treatment of politics and history, it also marks a change in his depiction of the social issues attendant on that history and politics.[14] The Bastard is arguably the central player in the action, and represents the play's engagement with expressly social concerns: issues of class, rank, and vocation distinct from the explicitly political issues that have been discussed elsewhere.

Despite the lack of historical records concerning a Bastard Faulconbridge in John's reign, both Shakespeare and the anonymous author of *The Troublesome Raigne of John, King of England* make him a major player in the "history" of King John's reign.[15] The different treatments of the same figure in these two plays represent different understandings of service to the crown. In *The Troublesome Raigne*, Philip Faulconbridge claims royal ancestry (after direct supernatural prompting) and proceeds to behave as a person of noble descent. He goes off to war in France, pursues and kills Austria, receives lands, and woos Blaunch, all as though he had always been a member of the aristocracy. By contrast, Shakespeare's Bastard Faulconbridge exhibits a very different relationship toward his rise in status. In one of many notable contrasts, he does not engage in chivalric heroics to the same degree as his counterpart in the *Troublesome Raigne*. Shakespeare's Bastard is more a royal servant than a warrior. His status as adopted Plantagenet is treated by the play as a vocation in our modern sense of "employment." By the end of the play he administrates the royal succession to the throne without any real opposition from the hereditary nobles around him. Shakespeare's Bastard actively chooses a "career" as a royal servant in choosing to acknowledge his bastardy while the Bastard of *The Troublesome Raigne* is forced to avow his ancestry, against his better judgment, and in this involuntary manner enters the aristocracy, and from thence comes to royal service. The two plays exhibit alternative conceptions of identity—one chosen, the other essential—which are linked to the ability of each character to serve his King.

I

Both *King John* and *The Troublesome Raigne* contain a recognition scene—each play's Bastard finds out the truth of his birth in the public and legal context of a land (or succession) dispute. In *King John*, the Bastard and his brother "come from the country" (1.1.44) for judgment and in *The Troublesome Raigne* they, having "committed a riot" (l. 67–68), appeal to the King on the issue.[16] In both plays, Robert Faulconbridge accuses his elder brother of being illegitimate and thus barred from inheriting the family estate.[17] The basic claim is identical but details of its presentation vary considerably.[18]

In *The Troublesome Raigne*, Philip (the Bastard) presents himself as the victim of his younger brother's slander and greed: "the wrong is mine; yet wil I abide all wrongs, before I once open my mouth to unrippe the shamefull slaunder of my parents, the dishonour of myself, & the wicked dealing of my brother in this princely assembly"(ll. 86–90). He refuses even to address the "shamefull slaunder" in the best tradition of wounded honesty. Robert, Philip's younger brother, then speaks, making his case in the face of his brother's silence. In the initial encounter the Bastard presents himself as slandered and offers no hint that he might know or believe his brother's accusation to be true. In *The Troublesome Raigne*, then, the Bastard believes he is the legitimate heir and desires his inheritance; it is only as a result of external intervention that he resigns his claim.[19]

Shakespeare's *King John* treats this scene differently. In *The Troublesome Raigne*, when King John demands who the brothers are and what their business is, only Robert makes reference to the Bastard's dubious parentage; in *King John* the Bastard himself raises the question. "What men are you?" asks the King, and Shakespeare's Bastard replies:

> Your faithful subject I, a gentleman,
> Born in Northamptonshire, and eldest son,
> *As I suppose*, to Robert Faulconbridge,
> A soldier, by the honour-giving hand
> Of Coeur-de-lion knighted in the field.
> (1.1.50–54, my italics)

The "as I suppose" puts the matter into question from the very beginning of the encounter. The Bastard presents himself as uncertain of his parentage, immediately lending credence to his brother's accusation and eliciting wonder from the King and his attendants. Shakespeare's Bastard undercuts his own claim to the Faulconbridge land, suggesting that his actual desires run toward other goals. His specific desires can be inferred from his other speeches in this first scene. He noticeably fails to mention the inheritance in his first speech while making a point of referring to honor and status. His "supposed" father was "a soldier, by the honour-giving hand / Of Coeur-de-lion knighted in the field" and he himself is a "gentleman." Both these rank markers are discursively (if not actually) separate from direct dependence on land and inheritance. The Bastard thus appears to be more interested in status, soldierly virtue, and honor than in a regular annual income, however large and respectable.

The difference between the Bastards of *The Troublesome Raigne* and *King John* becomes even more clear in the actual recognition scenes. Both plays show the brothers submitting to royal arbitration, but the confrontation between the brothers in *Troublesome Raigne* culminates with an appeal from the King to Philip (the Bastard) in order to settle the dispute.

> John: Say who was thy father?
> Philip: Faith (my Lord) to answer you sure he is my
> father that was neerest my mother when I was got-
> ten, & him I thinke to be Sir *Robert Fauconbridge*.
> John: *Essex*, for fashions sake demand agen,
> And so an ende to this contention.
> Essex: *Philip* speake I say, who was thy father?
> Philip: *Philippus atauis aedite regibus*. . . .
>
> (ll. 231–41)

In what appears to be an aside, Philip ventriloquizes Latin speech which is said to come from the air (and the river and the land and the trees), and this Latin reveals that he is the son of Richard I and thus of glorious birth:

> Birds in their flight make music with their wings,
> Filling the ayre with glorie of my birth:
> Birds, bubbles, leaves and mountaines, Eccho, all
> Ring in mine eares, that I am *Richards* Sonne.
>
> (ll. 252–55)

Despite this information, which he immediately accepts as fact, Philip still recalls his position among the country gentry:

> How are thy thoughts ywrapt in Honors heaven?
> Forgetfull what thou art, and whence thou camst.
> Thy fathers land cannot maintain these thoughts,
> These thoughts are farre unfitting *Fauconbridge*:
> And well they may; for why this mounting minde
> Doth soare too high to stoupe to *Fauconbridge*.
> Why how now? knowest thou where thou art?
> And knowest thou who expects thy answere here?
> Wilt thou upon a frantick madding vaine
> Goe loose thy land, and say thyself base born?
> No, keepe thy land, though *Richard* were thy Sire,
> What ere thou thinkst, say thou art *Fauconbridge*.
>
> (ll. 257–68)

Philip evinces a highly sensitive awareness of the order to which he belongs in this speech. Lines such as "Thy fathers land cannot maintaine these thoughts / These thoughts are farre unfitting *Fauconbridge*" reveal his awareness of the economics of his position. He simply cannot support what Harrison calls the "port, charge, and countenance" of a Plantagenet on his income; and, more importantly, he recognizes the inappropriateness of a claim to royal blood by one born to his minor rank. Regardless of his having royal blood, he was not born a prince but the son of a country gentleman, and that fact outweighs his being a royal bastard.[20] "Why how now? knowest thou where thou art? / And knowest thou who expects thy answer here?" he asks himself. Reminding himself of who he is (a country gentleman), where he stands (in what amounts to a court of law), and in whose presence (the King's), he claims Fauconbridge as his father and thus claims the land while denying his royal parentage.

Philip voices received notions of order and degree in this speech (an impression further reinforced by the denouement of the episode). He is born to one place in the hierarchy and will not *willfully* transgress the bounds of his ordained place: "Wilt thou on a frantic madding vaine / Goe loose thy land, and say thyself base born?" Obeying both economic and social pressures, *The Troublesome Raigne*'s Philip wisely chooses to abjure his royal father and claim a merely gentle one. The final lines of his speech—"keep thy land, though *Richard* were thy sire / What ere thou thinkst, say thou art *Fauconbridge*"—evidence this decision to remain, as he says, "what thou art, and whence thou camst." The voices of the wind, birds, and "bubbles" make him briefly "forgetfull" of his place "ywrapt in Honors heaven." However, he comes back to earth and, despite the fact that he now somehow knows himself to be Richard's son, he decides here to say he is "Fauconbridge" and keep his land rather than admit he is "base born" in bastardy. In essence, he chooses landed gentility over landless nobility.

Philip conducts an internal debate over the merits of his options and settles on the one that seems the most practical. Weighing the merits of the cases made by two different voices— one that speaks from the rocks, streams, and winds telling him of his royal birth and another that speaks practically of economics and established order—Philip strives to choose the best course of action. The conflict of these voices dramatizes Philip's thought, his strategic weighing of options, and it bears witness to what Bourdieu would call his sense of the game of social status. In an apparently un- or half-conscious reverie (John and Elinor see him as being in a "traunce" or a "dreame"), Philip examines the positive and negative outcomes of his possible decisions and comes to one with the greatest chance for success and gain. The fact that the speech presents itself as a vision, outside of normal time, suggests that this is a representation of prereflective strategizing within the structures of the serious "game" of social status that produces a logical and practical action.[21] Bourdieu writes that the player "decides in terms of objective probabilities, that is, in response to an overall, instantaneous assessment of the whole set of his opponents and the whole set of his team-mates, seen not as they are but in their impending positions. And he does so 'on the spot,' 'in the twinkling of an eye,' 'in the heat of the moment,' that is, in conditions which exclude distance, perspective, detachment, and reflexion.[22] No dramatist could show the workings of this kind of instantaneous decision making without recourse to devices that appear to show "distance, perspective, detachment, and reflexion," and this is what the writer of *Troublesome Raigne* is forced to do. Philip's momentary trance, which ends with the King's command "Speake man, be sodaine," allows the play to show Philip's "on the spot" response to the "objective probabilities" for profit determined by his position in the game of social distinction.[23]

Against his immediate inclinations, the decision predicated on his assessment of his position in the social structure, Philip is subsequently forced by what he calls "honors fire" to "sweare" that King Richard was his father, thus relinquishing his claim to the Fauconbridge land. Blood tells, and Philip's blood tells him to claim royal parentage despite his conscious intention. The intrusion of a force he recognizes as external to his will shapes his speech:

> Please it your Majestie, Sir *Robert*
> *Philip*, that *Fauconbridge* cleaves to thy jawes:
> It will not out, I cannot for my life
> Say I am Sonne unto a *Fauconbridge*.
> Let land and living goe, tis honors fire
> That makes me sweare King *Richard* was my Sire.
>   (ll. 270–75)

In line 270 he begins to answer "Sir Robert Fauconbridge" but breaks off, unable to pronounce "Fauconbridge" and finishes the whole speech with "Please it your grace, I am King *Richards Sonne.*" Philip is *physically incapable* of saying he is the son of a mere knight; his royal blood speaks for itself, claiming its royal nature. Philip's physical incapacity reaffirms the power of order and degree but in a different way than in lines 257–68 quoted above. Philip both is and is not born to gentry status. His blood is royal though his breeding is not. Sir Robert, his ostensible father, was a local gentleman and Philip would have been bred up in that rank, thus he feels as though he belongs among the local gentry. However, his blood is that of Richard I which places him in another rank altogether—in terms of the play at least. Philip's individual choice to remain on the land is transcended and obviated by this royal blood that forces him to claim "so greate a Sire" as Richard the Lion-hearted.[24] His body refuses to speak the words that would deny its royal provenance; his "choice" of bastardy is determined for him by the powerful dictates of "honor" and facilitated by his body's refusal to be anything but what it is: Plantagenet.

In contrast to *The Troublesome Raigne*'s Philip, whose attempt to choose gentility over nobility fails before the power of his blood, the Bastard of *King John* chooses nobility over gentility, landlessness over landed status. Shakespeare's Bastard puts his legitimacy in question from the moment he first speaks, suggesting dissatisfaction with his social status from the very beginning. Unlike *The Troublesome Raigne*'s Bastard who speaks and carries himself much as any of the other aristocratic characters, *King John*'s Bastard demonstrates his difference and distance from other characters. He is more clearly individuated from his first appearance onstage than the Bastard Fauconbridge ever is. He speaks familiarly with the King and Queen Eleanor, without the more elaborate honorific language used by his brother.[25] His decision to claim bastardy and relinquish the land and its considerable income thus appears motivated by his personal desire—not by the influence of some force recognized as external to his will. The Bastard's choice is his own.[26]

As in *The Troublesome Raigne*, the dispute is over the Faulconbridge land, and the claim made by Robert, the younger brother, is the same. When King John asks Robert who he is, after getting the Bastard's ambiguity-laden answer, Robert responds "the son and heir to that same Faulconbridge" (1.1.56). The Bastard, like Philip in *Troublesome Raigne*, describes Robert's claim that he is illegitimate as a slander having nothing to do with him:

> That [allegation of bastardy] is my brother's plea, and none
>   of mine;
> The which if he can prove, a pops me out
> At least from fair five hundred pounds a year:
> Heaven guard my mother's honour, and my land!
>
> (1.1.67–70)

The Bastard's attitude toward the debate is, however, far less serious than Philip's in *The Troublesome Raigne*. Robert's accusation becomes the source of a joke in the next few lines:

> Compare our faces and judge yourself.
> If old sir Robert did beget us both
> And were our father, and this son like him,
> O old sir Robert, father, on my knee
> I give heaven thanks I was not like to thee!
>
> (1.1.79–83)

This joking tone pervades the Bastard's speeches in this scene, so much so that Queen Eleanor herself remarks "why, what a madcap hath heaven lent us here!" (1.1.84). The Bastard affects a devil-may-care attitude about the inheritance that contrasts Philip's serious demeanor in *Troublesome Raigne*. Where *The Troublesome Raigne*'s Philip wants (and tries) to claim legitimacy and thus keep title to the estate, Shakespeare's Bastard seems more or less uninterested in legitimacy and title. His jocular treatment of the dispute demonstrates his lack of serious interest in the land. He would, at this point, like to keep it but only because it provides him with a stable income. He could be said to be waiting for something better to come along, and it does in his "adoption" by Eleanor.

Robert, however, *is* interested in it and makes his case to the King in that light. He argues, in basically the same terms used in *The Troublesome Raigne*, that his elder brother was conceived while Sir Robert was on an embassy for Richard I, an assertion proven by the fact that the Bastard "came into the world / Full fourteen weeks before the course of time" (1.1.112–13). In addition to this proof of bastardy, Robert claims that Sir Robert made a deathbed will bequeathing the lands to him. However, all his arguments do no good, for the law, as John presents it, clearly makes the Bastard the legal heir. Wills had no force in John's England, nor could any child be "bastardized" who was born in wedlock. Thus in Shakespeare's play, as in history, the Bastard's title is legal and unassailable. This legal situation is quite different from that in *The Troublesome Raigne* where at the moment Philip involuntarily claims Richard as his father his claim to the land evaporates—which further demonstrates *The Troublesome Raigne*'s identification of position with blood. From the moment Philip asserts that his blood is Plantagenet and not Faulconbridge, he loses any right to claim the Falconbridge land. In Shakespeare's play, the Bastard deliberately relinquishes his legal right to inherit.[27]

Robert responds petulantly to the fully legal succession King John mandates, objecting "Shall then my father's will be of no force / To dispossess this child which is not his?" (1.1.130–31). This show of incredulity prompts a joking riposte from the Bastard: "Of no more force to dispossess me, sir, / Than was his will to get me, as I think" (1.1.132–33). The Bastard's joke constitutes his most direct acknowledgment of his illegitimacy and leads Eleanor to pose a hypothetical question. She asks:

> Whether hadst thou rather be a Faulconbridge,
> *And like thy brother*, to enjoy thy land,
> Or the reputed son of Coeur-de-lion,
> Lord of thy presence and no land beside?
> (1.1.134–37, my italics)

Essentially, she asks whether, if given the choice, he would stay on the land with the name and countenance of a Faulconbridge or leave it and take the name of Plantagenet.[28] Would he risk losing an income of £500 a year for the doubtful prospects of a landless royal bastard? The Bastard's incessant jokes about his brother's face (see act 1, lines 78–83, 92–94, 138–47), some of which lead to John and Eleanor's recognition of a resemblance to Richard I in the Bastard's "large composition" (1.1.88), make the basis of his recognition external or physical, rather than internal or spiritual as it is in *The Troublesome Raigne*.[29] Shakespeare's Bastard responds by saying "I would give it [the land] every foot to have this face: / It would not be Sir Knob in any case" (1.1.146–47). His response, like Eleanor's question, turns on the question of physical resemblance instead of innate abstract qualities. In other words, the Bastard claims a face, an appearance, rather than landed status. Eleanor then offers to take him into her service.

The Bastard's acceptance of this proposed service represents several key shifts in his social position. First, by accepting Eleanor's offer the Bastard relinquishes the land that is legally his and takes up a much riskier calling as a courtier-soldier. "Brother," he says, finally resolving the dispute, "take you my land, I'll take my chance" (1.1.151).[30] This act earns him a new name and rank. King John asks him to kneel and dubs him "Sir Richard, and Plantagenet" (1.1.162). He enters the ranks of the nobility as a knight and also, more importantly, is acknowledged as royal kin. He kneels as a mere gentleman of Northamptonshire and arises, to use the King's words, "more great." This is radically different from the treatment of events in *The Troublesome Raigne,* where the Bastard *intends* to choose to retain his land but is forced to relinquish it by supernatural intervention. *The Troublesome Raigne*'s Bastard, upon rising to his feet after being dubbed Sir Richard prays "Graunt heavens that *Philip* once may shew himself / Worthie the honour of a *Plantaginet,* / Or basest glorie of a Bastard's name" (ll. 302–5). He proclaims an essentialist idea of identity in which his acts will show the preexisting worth of his blood. *King John*'s Bastard, on the other hand, merely shakes his half-brother's hand in farewell and goes off to France in service to the king. "Well won is still well shot / And I am I, howe'er I was begot" (1.1.174–75), he says, disregarding any essentialist concerns like those worries about acting in accordance with birth that are voiced by his counterpart in *The Troublesome Raigne.* In *King John,* the Bastard makes a conscious choice about his destiny rooted in his own well-articulated desires, making what might, however anachronistically, be called a career decision. He makes this more explicit in the famous speech which follows: "this is worshipful society / And fits the mounting spirit like myself; / For he is but a bastard to the time / That doth not smack of observation; / And so am I, whether I smoke or no" (1.1.205–9). His is a "mounting spirit," willing and eager to trade financial security and stability for a thirteenth- or sixteenth-century version of upward mobility.

The dissatisfaction of Shakespeare's Bastard with his social status, apparent from the first, evidences his desire to move from a secure place in the local gentry to a more glorious, prominent, powerful, and potentially lucrative position in the aristocracy. Despite the stigma of bastardy, he anticipates a gain in "honour" at the very least and, given the workings of the patronage system, might expect more tangible rewards than that. J. E. Neale, Conyers Read, and other historians of the Tudor era discuss this system and their analyses suggest that Eleanor's adoption of the Bastard promises access to her patronage—a potentially lucrative source of income. Furthermore, Shakespeare's depiction of the Bastard's subsequent progress suggests that the playwright had the contemporary political scene in mind rather than that of the thirteenth century.[31]

The Bastard occupies a recognizable position in John's government, serving as a military organizer, a diplomat, and a kind of tax collector. All of these functions have analogues in Elizabethan officials' activities. Taking only Burghley as an example, early in his career he was sent to Scotland on a successful military expedition (1547), where he gained much useful knowledge of military administration. He was also instrumental in Elizabethan foreign policy and diplomacy and eventually became the Queen's leading adviser on this as many other issues. Though Burghley was at odds with the Queen on some policy questions early in his career, B. W. Beckingsale writes that by 1572, "Burghley had come closer to the Queen in his apprehension of the virtues of the negative and the ambiguous in diplomacy," and his staff played an important role in foreign policy.[32] The Bastard exercises all of these functions, if not at the level of recognized authority occupied by a Burghley. More typical figures would include the young Nicholas Bacon or Thomas Cromwell, and Michael Hickes (one of Burghley's secretaries). The Bastard's activities are typical of an Elizabethan administrative functionary.

In *The Troublesome Raigne,* the economic motivations of the Bastard Fauconbridge's "choice" are far more clearly defined. He does not show the same kind of ambitions toward service that Shakespeare's Bastard evinces in his actions. Elinor adopts *The Troublesome Raigne'*s Bastard Fauconbridge in these words: "I will not see thee want / As long as Elinor hath foote of land; / Henceforth thou shalt be taken for my sonne" (l. 294–96). In that play, the Bastard becomes Duke of Normandy—a further foregrounding of the "living and land" (l. 952) available to one of his rank. This never happens in Shakespeare's play. Shakespeare's Bastard becomes an important councillor of the King's but not a landed one; his rewards are those of office, not land. The Bastard's "Brother, take you my land, I'll take my chance" gambles everything he possesses on this "chance." All the changes in his fortunes, his language, and his social position depend on this gamble, on his choice of royal service over his right to his "father's" land. A physical resemblance to Richard I makes this professional choice possible and thereby grants him access to higher rank—but his success in occupying that position has less to do with his birth than his talent.[33]

II

The Bastard's social trajectory can be traced through developments in his speech as he moves through the play. His choice of "career," a choice made when he avows bastardy and thus enters the ranks of the attending nobility, takes him from a relatively low position in the hierarchy of rank—that of a country landholder resident on the land—to the much higher one of trusted royal servant. A crucial element in the Bastard's changing character is the fact that instead of being claimed by a mystical nobility, he claims, or professes, nobility, acquiring his rank simultaneously with taking on the profession of servant to the crown. Eleanor does not merely recognize him as Richard the Lionhearted's son, she offers him a job and the offer actually precedes formal recognition of his royal parentage: "I like thee well, wilt thou forsake thy fortune, / Bequeath thy land to him and follow me? / I am a soldier and bound to France" (1.1.148–50). He accepts the job and only then does the king dub him "Sir Richard, and Plantagenet" (1.1.162). His social rank, his rise to greater "honour," is contingent upon his choice of occupation.[34] It is in this spirit that he takes on his project of acquiring the noble linguistic habitus.[35]

In the first scene, the Bastard speaks in language more appropriate to Falstaff and Pistol in the Henriad than to the nobles who surround him in *King John*. In this initial scene the Bastard speaks in language appropriate to one of his status. He belongs, however tenuously, to the local gentry of Northamptonshire and his ostensible father, knighted on the field, was not born to the upper gentry but was elevated to it. Keith Wrightson writes of this group in his *English Society 1580–1680*, arguing that the gentry stood between the yeomanry and the "titular nobility" in a hierarchy of rank which placed the nobility at the top, knights and esquires second, "mere gentlemen" (which is how the Bastard initially identifies himself), and all others below them. Faulconbridge and his family historically belonged to the "mere gentlemen" level of this structure and had only recently risen to the next higher rung. Wrightson writes that gentility "derived from a degree of landed wealth sufficient to afford a certain lifestyle, which in turn gave rise to local recognition,"[36] which might, on rare occasions, grow into national recognition.[37] Gentlemen such as Faulconbridge (and by definition his sons) were locally recognized; their importance was limited to that local context and did not extend to the court or to the national political scene. Accordingly, the Bastard's language reveals a *lack* of urbanity and conventional "noble" rhetorical sophistication (a quality which marks all of the characters from the titular nobility in this scene) and thus his distance from the aristocracy.[38] Michael Mannheim writes that "the Bastard we see and hear in the first act is an Elizabethan soldier-of-fortune.... He is a mixture of chivalry, intelligence, surface cynicism, brilliance, arrogance, egotism, personal charm, and almost total indifference to the uglier realities of the world around him."[39] Mannheim goes on to characterize the Bastard's speech as "calculated to suggest that he . . . is of the blood royal."[40] While the Bastard is all the things Mannheim suggests he is, his use of colloquial expressions, lurid images, and so on seems less a calculated attempt to prove an affinity with the "blood royal" than a sign of his difference. His "madcap" language and reliance on colloquialisms have more in common with the speech patterns of the country than with those of the court.[41]

The Bastard's long speech at line 182 hinges on questions of utterance and the kind of language available to him now that he is a member of the aristocracy. He shows himself to be aware of a change in the power of his words as well as its basis in his new rank:

> A foot of honour better than I was,
> But many a foot of land the worse.
> Well, now can I make any Joan a lady.
> "Good den, Sir Richard!"—'God a mercy fellow!'—
> And if his name be George, I'll call him Peter
> For new-made honour doth forget men's names.
> (1.1.182–87)

His "foot of honour" enables him to change "any Joan"—any ordinary woman—into a "lady" as well as to change any George's name to Peter.[42] In other words, by virtue of his "new-made honour" the Bastard's language becomes performative,[43] endowed with power he formerly lacked. The change in his "honour" makes him "forget men's names" because " 'tis too respective and too sociable / For your conversion" (1.1.188–89). His new status—his conversion—is too aware of itself as new to recall the names (and thus share the society of) those who were formerly his peers. Interestingly, the Bastard seems to hypostatize his rank, to personify it, and locates the agency of forgetfulness in that hypostatized rank. What speaks and renames the people it encounters is not so much the Bastard himself but his "new-made honour." This is a crucial distinction; in these early scenes, the Bastard's consciousness is distanced from his rank, affording him the space from which to speak of "tickling Commodity," to discuss objectively the social practices of the class he has just entered (see the rest of this speech especially lines 190–204), and to make other apparently critical utterances. What happens later, as his project not "to practice to deceive" but "to learn" progresses, is that his learning project effaces that distinction, erases the space of the Commodity speech, and produces a very different speaker and mode of speech.

The Bastard, in describing the operations of his "new-made honour," describes socially contingent linguistic practices in ways that can be discussed further in light of Pierre Bourdieu's ideas about linguistic habitus, symbolic power, and their role in social relations. In the speech quoted above, the Bastard has just been made part of a class whose speech patterns he can describe with a measure of detachment and amusement. That he can do this at this point suggests that he is in possession of a different set of speech patterns derived from a different class. These speech patterns are markers or spoken objectifications of what Bourdieu calls linguistic habitus:[44] "dispositions which are impalpably inculcated, through a long and slow process of acquisition, by the sanctions of the linguistic market, and which are therefore adjusted, without any cynical calculation or consciously experienced constraint, to the chances of material and symbolic profit which the laws of price formation characteristic of a given market objectively offer to the holders of a given linguistic capital."[45] In the play, Shakespeare dramatizes shifts in linguistic habitus that would normally proceed far more slowly—sometimes taking generations—in the interest of showing the kinds of changes necessary for the Bastard to succeed in his social project. By telescoping this process, Shakespeare can also afford the Bastard the capacity to articulate, if not a critique, at least an analysis of two sets of dispositions because of his liminal position between two varieties of linguistic habitus.[46] Implicitly, his speech up to and including this point has instantiated one habitus: that of Philip Faulconbridge, ambitious country gentleman. This habitus predisposes him to use colloquial expressions, what E. A. J. Honigmann might call "rustic proverbs," in addressing his social superiors—an attempt to play up his wit and thus what he would see as his "courtliness," a strategy designed to draw attention.[47] The habitus he comments on, that of the courtier or minor noble (for lack of a better term), he characterizes as excessively polite, "cultured" (in the sense of liberal learning), and, at least potentially, deceitful.

The Bastard's ability to exercise power increases as he masters the idioms of the habitus he is working to assimilate. Two works used as handbooks for aspiring (and established) administrators, Sir Thomas Smith's *De Republica Anglorum* (first published in 1583 but circulated in manuscript from about 1565) and Robert Beale's manuscript "Treatise of the Office of a Councellor and Principall Secretarie to her Majestie" (ca. 1590) both emphasize the importance of language and habits of speech in the practices of the Queen's government. Those who serve in the government must know the language proper to their role as officers of the Crown and must develop a finely tuned awareness of the critical importance of specificity and accuracy in their use of that language. This language, like that which Smith refers to in his description of the workings of the Parliament, is highly formal and follows well-established, traditional patterns of presentation and exposition. Beale's work emphasizes the importance of a principal secretary's having a commonplace book filled with models of letters, proclamations, and other documents to use in his duties. In official correspondence, he must take care to avoid "any scholasticall, ambiguous or general phrase" by which "advantage may be taken."[48] Part of his responsibility is to watch carefully over his language as well as that of his staff. Beale's treatise goes on to discuss the importance of upright and circumspect behavior to the proper exercise of the office of principal secretary. Writing of "Thinges to be Done with Her Ma[jes]tie," Beale states that the secretary ought to:

> Use no peremtorie contestac[i]ons or replies but deliver your opinion simplie and the com[m]odities and inconveniencies that are like to ensue on both sides. Give no occasion that either her Ma[jes]tie or anie other doe thinke that you doe it as though you esteemed your owne witt better than theirs, but onlie of conscience and dutie, so as if thinges fall out otherwise, her highnes may conceive that you are not carryed, sometimes one waye sometimes another, to serve at private turnes, as perhappes she may be persuaded others have done.[49]

Beale insists that the secretary must present his position and his advice with at least the appearance of humility, impartiality, and steadfastness. "Give no occasion that either her Ma[jes]tie or anie other doe thinke that you doe it as though you esteemed your owne witt better than theirs," he writes, pointing to the fact that despite the councillor's superior knowledge of the issues at hand, he must be humble in presenting that knowledge.[50]

The officer's willingness to comport himself in a manner that will win the approval and assent of the monarch is essential to getting things done. Beale makes several references to the importance of careful behavior and circumspection:

> Be not one in speach and another in action. . . . Be cleane handed, and although it weare a hard matter to abbridge one that shall occupie that place of all takinge of that wh[i]ch will be offered, yet it is utterlie to be voided in matters wh[i]ch concerne either the honor of God or Justice. The Lord will blesse you otherwise sufficientlie and your Ennemies shall have lesse occasion to seeke your discreditt and overthrow, who most com[m]onlie in the supplantac[i]on of men, looke rather to some parte of the spoile or praie than eyther to iust matter or the service of God, Prince or Countrie.[51]

Beale's treatise ends with this advice on the central importance of moral behavior and religious piety to maintaining position in the government. These are not merely pious protestations, but are valid and valuable advice for a man navigating the perilous seas of Elizabethan power. Prudence, careful speaking, honesty, and respectful bearing—all these norms of behavior are as important a part of office holding as the purely administrative details Beale discusses in the early pages of the treatise.[52]

Smith's discussion of Parliament points to the importance of traditional language patterns to Parliament's functioning. For example, he writes that after the Commons choose a Speaker he presents himself to the Lords and:

> first praiseth the prince, then maketh his excuse of unabilitie, and prayeth the prince that he would command the commons to choose another. The chancellor in the princes name doth so much declare him able, as he did declare himself unable, and thanketh the commons for choosing so wise, discreete and eloquent a man, and willeth them to go and consult of lawes for the common wealth. Then the speaker requireth certaine requests of the prince in the name of the commons, first that his majestie would be content that they may use and enjoy all their liberties and priviledges that the common house was wont to enjoy.[53]

and so on. The Speaker comports himself humbly before the Lords and thus receives the approval of the upper house. The Commons and the Lords, as represented by the Speaker and the Chancellor, enter into a ritually patterned set of challenges and responses that authorize their delegation as representatives of their constituents.[54] The satisfactory completion of the dialogue legitimizes the Speaker who then makes ritual requests for the customary privileges of the lower house, requests which serve the additional purpose of recognizing the upper house's power. Both parties working together reinstate the workings of Parliament and, in a sense, recognize the other's role in the government of England. The exchange—what the Bastard would call a "dialogue of compliment"—is essential to the opening of Parliament and Smith's report suggests that it proceeds almost verbatim as he describes it. Rhetorical patterns like this one play an important part in the operation of the government and government demands that its functionaries be fluent in them.

The Bastard's evocation of the courtier's "dialogue of compliment" serves two purposes; first, it ridicules that dialogue by caricature but second, and more importantly, his speech shows the Bastard's awareness of and willingness to adopt the speech patterns he pokes fun at:

> Ere Answer knew what Question would
> Saving in dialogue of compliment,
> And talking of the Alps and Apennines,
> The Pyrenean and the river Po,
> It draws toward supper in conclusion so.
> But this is worshipful society,
> And fits the mounting spirit like myself;
> For he is but a bastard to the time
> That doth not smack of observation.
>
> (1.1.200–208)

His caricature of the excessively polite conversation of "Question" and "Answer" closes with the interjection "but this is worshipful society, / And fits a mounting spirit like myself."[55] He halts the critique with a reminder that this is the kind of conversation that fits his "mounting spirit" now that he belongs to "worshipful society." He claims that "he is but a bastard to the time / That doth not smack of observation." In other words, he is only a bastard (i.e., outside the pale of society) insofar as he does not "observe" the demands of the time.[56] The following lines offer a program for the inculcation of what amounts to both a new linguistic habitus and a new class habitus.[57]

The Bastard's bastardy "to the time" only lasts so long as he "doth not smack of observation." To truly move beyond his bastardy he must suit not only his outward appearance but also his "inward motion" to the age's requirements. His theoretical knowledge of the practices of his new class must be transformed into practical reflexes:

> He is but a bastard to the time
> That does not smack of observation.
> And so am I, whether I smoke or no.
> And not alone in habit and device,
> Exterior form, outward accoutrement,
> But from the inward motion to deliver
> Sweet, sweet, sweet poison for the age's tooth:
> Which though I will not practice to deceive,
> Yet, to avoid deceit I mean to learn;
> For it shall strew the footsteps of my rising.
>
> (1.1.207–16)

What the Bastard is saying is that he must make the practices he has just caricatured his own, unconscious parts of his habitus, if

2 / "I MEAN TO LEARN"

he is to succeed in his rising and do so in good faith: "Yet, to avoid deceit, I mean to learn; / For it shall strew the footsteps of my rising" (1.1.215–16). He "means to learn" in order to avoid deceit (and to avoid being deceitful) as he rises in rank and power—a rise in rank and power that takes the form of increasing administrative responsibilities.

The Bastard, as the representation of a changing linguistic habitus, rises up the social ladder and his language changes to mirror increasingly that appropriate to the rung he stands upon.[58] The space from which the Bastard makes his critical remarks on the practice of his new peers, exists in the lag time between his elevation to a degree of power at 1.1.162 and the point at which his language catches up to that power in the final scenes of the play where he acts as John's chief minister. The Bastard's awareness of the new performativity of his language (in lines 182–89 of act 1) bears witness to his consciousness of the power of his newly ennobled language, a power he believes derives from his new rank, not from the language itself.[59] He still speaks in the idiom of the madcap rustic gentleman at this point in the play—only later does he pick up more "elevated" verbal habits. His development of a "noble" linguistic habitus coincides with his recognition that the form of language *does* matter.[60]

The Bastard's speeches at the walls of Angiers represent his experimentation with the "noble" linguistic habitus and lay the groundwork for his increased responsibilities in the rest of the play. He uses three distinct vocal registers in his battlefield speeches. First, he speaks in the same "madding vein" he uses in act 1, scene 1 daring Austria to combat (2.1.135–40 and 290–293) and harps on bastardy in that voice during King John's address to the citizens of Angiers (2.1.275, 279). Second, he uses the high rhetoric of the kings' speeches:

> Ha, majesty! how high thy glory towers
> When the rich blood of kings is set on fire!
> O, now doth death line his dead chaps with steel;
> The swords of soldiers are his teeth, his fangs;
> And now he feasts, mouthing the flesh of men,
> In undetermin'd differences of kings.
> Why stand these royal fronts amazed thus?
> Cry "havoc!" kings; back to the stained field,
> You equal potents, fiery kindled spirits!

> Then let confusion of one part confirm
> The other's peace; till then, blows, blood, and death!
> (2.1.350–60)

This trumpeting call to violence, a speech that would fit Hotspur as well as the Bastard, seems appropriate to the moment in the Bastard's mind, but it fails to produce the desired result of renewed armed conflict and the kings engage in further dialogue with Hubert.[61] In his third speech, the Bastard changes tactics and engages in what he thinks of as Machiavellian "policy." He suggests that the kings attack the city, destroy its walls, and,

> That done, dissever your united strengths,
> And part your mingled colors once again;
> Turn face to face and bloody point to point;
> Then in a moment, fortune will cull forth
> Out of one side her happy minion,
> To whom in favor she shall give to day,
> And kiss him with a glorious victory.
> How like you this wild counsel, mighty states?
> Smacks it not something of the policy?
> (2.1.388–96)

The kings "like it well" (2.1.398) and after another appeal in the language of the honor culture from the Bastard, the armies plan to separate for the bombardment of the town. The Bastard's speech here is effective and he is well aware of it: "O prudent discipline! From north to south / Austria and France shoot in each other's mouth: / I'll stir them to it. —Come away, away!" (2.1.413–15). The rhyme in these lines and the Bastard's gleeful "come away!" suggest his pleasure in the efficacy of his speech—one of his goals is, as discussed above, to master the use of the performativity of noble language—and that glee heightens the contrast of his amazement at Hubert's performance in lines 423–54. Hubert's successful proposal of a dynastic marriage to end the conflict astounds the Bastard.

Hubert's speech overpowers the oratorical efforts of the kings and the Bastard. He manipulates the interests and preoccupations of the warring parties masterfully, and his words have better effect than all the cannon of the armies surrounding his town. Where the initial battle between the English and the French ends inconclusively, Hubert's speech ends the dispute conclusively. As the Bastard says:

> He speaks plain cannon, fire, and smoke, and bounce;
> He gives bastinado with his tongue;
> Our ears are cudgell'd; not a word of his
> But buffets better than a fist of France.
> Zounds! I was never so bethump'd with words
> Since I first called my brother's father dad.
>
> (2.1.462–67)

The Bastard recognizes that Hubert's rhetoric works as well as any physical weapon and learns from the example. Hubert's language is more effective than any of the Bastard's speeches thus far, which all focus on encouraging *physical* violence. Hubert's violent language, a form of what Bourdieu calls symbolic violence, has real political effects that the fighting before the walls of Angiers could not achieve. Where the Bastard's speeches advocate real physical violence, Hubert promises that all that violence will be fruitless:

> The sea enraged is not half so deaf,
> Lions more confident, mountains and rocks
> More free from motion, no, not death himself
> In mortal fury half so peremptory,
> As we to keep this city.
>
> (2.1.451–54)

This promise of stalwart resistance to all the violence the Bastard and the kings propose is linked to his proposal of a way to avoid it and altogether ends the threat of war. Hubert meshes his utterance with a specific linguistic market in a way that demands assent from the participants in the exchange. Bourdieu writes that "the conditions of reception envisioned are part of the conditions of production, and anticipation of the sanctions of the market helps to determine the production of discourse."[62] Hubert's speech anticipates "the sanctions of the market" in which it functions by combining the peace proposal with a promise of resistance and his words gain the almost immediate assent of Eleanor, John, Philip of France, and the couple to be wed, despite strong reasons not to let the match go forward.[63]

The marriage contract ends the conflict and all the parties, save Constance and Arthur, leave the field satisfied. The Bastard is uncharacteristically mute, however, until all the other characters exit. The "Commodity" speech is the last of the act and reveals both the Bastard's stunned recognition of what he sees as the hollowness of the rhetoric he has been experimenting with and the progress, or lack thereof, of his learning project. He has yet to learn how to misrecognize the effects of what he calls Commodity as they structure the action of agents who theoretically eschew such things. None of the noble participants speak of the marriage contract in these terms, easily translating the work of "tickling Commodity" into the language of love and honor.[64] Even Constance puts her revulsion at the match into the language of honor:

> Gone to be married! gone to swear a peace!
> False blood to false blood join'd! gone to be friends!
> Shall Lewis have Blanche, and Blanche those provinces?
> It is not so . . .
> I trust I may not trust thee, for thy word
> Is but the vain breath of a common man;
> Believe me, I do not believe thee, man:
> I have a king's oath to the contrary.
> (2.2.1–10)

The "false blood" of France and England comes first in her complaint, and she returns again and again to Philip's being forsworn. She barely touches on the fact that the marriage and the broken oaths derive from an essentially financial transaction.[65] This is what the Bastard finds most disturbing in the contract:

> Mad world, mad kings, mad composition!
> John, to stop up Arthur's title in the whole,
> Hath willingly departed with a part,
> And France, whose armor conscience buckled on,
> Whom zeal and charity brought to the field
> As God's own soldier, rounded in the ear
> With that same purpose-changer, that sly devil
> (2.1.561–67)

is led from war to peace. The Bastard names this purpose-changing devil Commodity. Its entry derails his sense of the world—"mad world, mad kings, mad composition"—forcing him to analyze events in terms of the policy he half-jokingly refers to in his battlefield speeches. John gives up territory and a monetary dowry to secure a political gain, and Philip of France gives up a religiously sanctioned war in return. He sees how Commodity biases what is supposedly the smooth running of the world, how it changes courses of action, and structures the world according to its logic:

> Commodity, the bias of the world,
> The world, who of itself is peised well,
> Made to run even upon even ground,
> Till this advantage, this vile drawing bias,
> This sway of motion, this commodity,
> Makes it take head from all indifferency,
> From all direction, purpose, course, intent—
> And this same bias, this commodity,
> This bawd, this broker, this all-changing word,
> Clapp'd on the outward eye of fickle France,
> Hath drawn him from his own determin'd aid,
> From a resolv'd and honorable war
> To a most base and vile-concluded peace.
> (2.1.574–86)

His own momentarily effective rhetoric fails before it as well, and he is forced to acknowledge that he must learn how to work with it:

> Well, whiles I am a beggar, I will rail
> And say there is no sin but to be rich;
> And being rich, my virtue then shall be
> To say there is no vice but beggary.
> Since kings break faith upon commodity
> Gain, be my lord, for I will worship thee.
> (2.1.593–98)

This flippant remark shows a developing awareness of the relationship of position to perception. His "whiles I am a beggar" and "being rich" comments are shorthand for two habitus that view the same social phenomenon in totally different ways.[66] He remains focused on questions of language, but realizes that the effective use of noble language depends on a changed awareness of Commodity directly related to his changed social position.

The Bastard's quickly quelled outrage in this speech not only demonstrates his increasing awareness of the links between position and perception (or misperception), but also his awkward position between two models of social behavior. The first, which motivates his outrage, derives from the "noble" linguistic habitus that generates his battlefield speeches and the second derives from "the policy," a more Machiavellian attitude toward the world and to language. At this point in the play, the Bastard exemplifies a mixed attitude toward social change. On one hand, he embraces the possibilities of social mobility and on the other he laments what he depicts as the evacuation of traditional honor values that attends that same rise. As in *1 Henry IV*, honor becomes both merely a word and a powerful tool, but not a transcendent value.[67] The Bastard's response to this transition is to rail at it in ways that relate to his social position. In this scene, he is caught between his theoretical and critical knowledge of how Commodity changes the course of events and his knowledge of the necessity of developing ways to misrecognize it if his ascent is to be secure.

Theoretical knowledge, the kind the Bastard demonstrates in his early speeches, presupposes an objective distance from the object of knowledge, in this case the practices of the "noble" habitus. Purely theoretical knowledge of practice, the kind that the Bastard voices in act 1, destroys it and, more significantly, makes it impossible to grasp as anything but theory. Mastery of practice as a lived reality escapes theoretical analysis that locates schemes and regular systems that those engaged in practice do not consciously possess. "Real mastery of this logic is only possible for someone who is completely mastered by it, who possesses it, but so much so that he is totally possessed by it, in other words depossessed."[68] The Bastard says he wishes:

> from the inward motion to deliver
> Sweet, sweet, sweet poison for the age's tooth
> Which though I will not practice to deceive,
> Yet, to avoid deceit, I mean to learn
>
> (1.1.212–15)

He is speaking of just this mastery that is not mastery, this possession to the point of depossession. What we see in acts 3 and 4 is the progress of this shift from an imperfect mastery *of* (best exemplified by the Bastard's battlefield speeches) to mastery *by* the practice of the noble courtier (best exemplified by the patriotic speech closing the play), a shift manifested in the changes the Bastard's language undergoes.

In acts 3 and 4, his education in the behavior of the powerful advances, and Shakespeare shows him taking an ever more important place in King John's government. He learns to anticipate the demands of his market better and his speech is more durably effective in achieving his ends and, more importantly, he begins to master the system of misrecognitions that so astounded him in act 2. From being hushed like a fractious child at the beginning of act 2 for his rude interjections to Austria (John tells him "We like not this; thou dost forget thyself" [3.1.60]), he serves as the king's principal officer by the end of act 4. He serves as John's military lieutenant, mustering the troops for war with France in 3.1, despoils the monasteries on John's orders in 3.3, and is consistently addressed as "cousin" by all the nobles surrounding him. The "four voices" Michael Mannheim writes of subside into one marking his all but complete success in assimilating the habitus of his new status.[69] The Bastard comes to exercise considerable administrative authority as a consequence.

Shakespeare returns to the issue of the relation of linguistic habitus to the administrative ability in the Henriad. The Bastard's battlefield language returns with Hotspur's drowned honor speech and Hal's facility at changing linguistic registers is, in some ways, his defining characteristic. Late in the play, Hotspur declares the fundamental difference between Hal and himself in the course of ignoring vital intelligence about the upcoming Battle of Shrewsbury. Interrupted by a messenger announcing the King's approach, Hotspur thanks him:

> I thank him, that he cuts me from my tale,
> For I profess not talking; only this—
> Let each man do his best: and here draw I
> A sword, whose temper I intend to stain
> With the best blood that I can meet withal
> In the adventure of this perilous day.
> Now, Esperance! Percy! and set on.
> (*1 Henry IV* 5.2. 90–96)

Hotspur prefers the action represented by the sword he draws to speech and vows to stain his weapon with the "best blood" he can find. In this play, Hotspur's failure to profess talking marks him as a heroic anachronism doomed to fall to Hal who assumes his vocabulary as Hotspur delivers his death speech.[70] Hotspur and the dispositions associated with him (battlefield valor, bravery rather than policy, and high rhetoric) are thus represented as objects of nostalgia. Shakespeare represents the loss of the old chivalric ideal *as* loss, while at the same time representing and praising its successor. Hal, unlike Hotspur, professes talking, and in this represents the rise of the new men, new men who broke the power of Hotspur's family under Henry VII. In *King John*, Shakespeare's Bastard embodies both of these positions—the chivalric and the politic—and, in his Commodity speech, laments the ascendancy of policy even as he embraces it.

The Bastard's rise offers an instructive resemblance to the fortunes of the Cecil family. The Cecils grew from a cadet branch of an obscure family of minor gentry on the Welsh border under Henry VII to great importance and honor under Elizabeth I. Their rise to prominence was dependent on their service to the crown. David Cecil, Burghley's grandfather, linked his family's fortunes to those of the Tudors. His small contribution as a yeoman of Henry VII's guard established a family connection that was the basis for Lord Burghley's service to Henry VII's granddaughter Elizabeth I.[71] Royal service, beginning with relatively minor posts, provided the Cecil family with what was eventually to be a vast income, elevation from the gentry to the peerage, and a position as chief advisers to the Queen.[72] The Bastard's service to the Crown begins with mere soldiering for Queen Eleanor but ends with his role as sole determiner of King John's burial and young Henry's coronation. The Bastard does everything from mustering armed forces to raising taxes by dissolving monasteries and settling the succession. These are roles played by Tudor ministers like Burghley or Bacon who were responsible for a similarly wide range of administrative duties. Robert Beale's treatise speaks of the breadth of an official's professional duties.[73] The fact that, as suggested above, the Bastard's job duties parallel those of figures like Burghley suggests less that Shakespeare was creating a deliberate allegory than that the Tudor functionary was a recognizable type with publicly recognized tasks.

In the final scene all defer to the Bastard's judgment; Salisbury and the Prince both wait on his ordering of the "business," in a notable contrast to earlier reactions to the Bastard's rise. Salisbury, for example, goes from calling the Bastard a "misbegotten divel" (5.4.4) to obeying his suggestions in the play's final scene.[74] His rise, from the Northamptonshire countryside to the heights of the court, depends on his choice of job, which amounts to choosing the profession of nobility. The play's final scene, which presents the king's death, the end of the French invasion, and the settling of the peace, also contains the Bastard's apotheosis as administrator. In the final lines the duty of disposing the "business" of state falls to him as King John wills it in one of his last speeches: "Have thou the ordering of this present time" (5.1.77). And the Bastard does just that:

> *Sal.* Many carriages he hath dispatch'd
> To the sea-side, and put his cause and quarrel
> To the disposing of the cardinal:
> With whom yourself, myself and other lords,
> If you think meet, this afternoon will post
> To consummate this business happily.
> *Bast.* Let it be so: and you, my noble prince,
> With other princes that may best be spar'd
> *Shall* wait upon your father's funeral.
> *P. Hen.* At Worcester must his body be interr'd;
> For so he willed it.
> *Bast.* Thither *shall* it then:
> And happily *may* your sweet self put on
> The lineal state and glory of the land!
> To whom, with all submission, on my knee
> I do bequeath my faithful services
> And true subjection everlastingly.
> (5.7.89–105, emphasis mine)

Throughout most of the play, the Bastard's language has been couched in conditional phrases. This speech marks a dramatic shift. Someone whose origins are, as the first act reveals, at best ambiguous, now wields great rhetorical and actual authority. The Bastard's "let it be so," his shalls, and his odd "may"[75] all demonstrate his authority, as does the fact that the prince and Salisbury, both of whom outrank him by birth, defer to his judgment. He and the "other lords" will settle the terms of the peace while Prince Henry and "other princes that may best be spar'd" will "wait upon" King John's funeral.[76] The Bastard is clearly in charge here; he is in full control of the performative power of his language. The last lines quoted above demonstrate this control in that they cement the Bastard's position as royal servant and, implicitly, as trusted administrator: "With all submission, on my knee / I do bequeath my faithful services everlastingly."⁷⁷ His offer does not admit of refusal—one does not refuse a bequest of service—and thus in the act of making it he assures its acceptance.⁷⁸ This speech represents the fullness of his assimilation to the ranks of the nobility.⁷⁹

The Bastard initially sees language as a strategic tool, viewing the acquisition of a noble linguistic habitus as essential to the advancement of his "career," an awareness wholly lacking in Philip. If the Bastard is to be an effective and successful member of the class he so suddenly joins, he must assimilate himself to its practices; he must, in a sense, become more noble than the nobles. This point is made clear by his battlefield speeches, which outdo any of the other nobles' speeches in the rhetoric of honorable war. This awareness points to another change in the understanding of the elements of social power: the Bastard's distinction derives from his linguistic mastery, and his power follows from that distinction. The play shows the operations of these elements in ways *The Troublesome Raigne*, with its traditional honor culture ideological structure, does not. In *King John*, power and social distinction are available to the capable few who choose to pursue them, and the play shows how the mastery of the aristocracy's social practices can lead to distinction, even if the mastering agent does not belong to the nobility by birth.

The professionalism of the Bastard's choices, for lack of a better term, becomes clearer when juxtaposed to the "choices" made by *The Troublesome Raigne*'s Bastard. As shown above, Philip Fauconbridge chooses to acknowledge his parentage only because he is forced to do so by the burning of "honour's fire" within his veins. If given a free choice, he would remain on the land, secure in the possession of a landed income and some degree of local influence. Instead, his royal blood, of which he is apparently unconscious until his brother's accusations of bastardy, forces him to relinquish that land and take up a place in the court as bastard son of a king. *The Troublesome Raigne* gives the impression that this is what Philip was born to; his destiny is to become Sir Richard Plantagenet and accompany King John in his French wars regardless of his personal will. Among the indicators of this are the recognition scene itself, his rapid transformation into the glory-hungry soldier presented in the scenes where he chases and kills the Duke of Austria, his wooing of Blaunch (a detail absent in *King John*), and, most interestingly for my argument, the lack of change in his language from the beginning to the end of the play.[80] Philip's diction remains relatively constant—unlike that of Shakespeare's Bastard. Where Shakespeare's Bastard's language is commented upon by Eleanor and the king, Philip's never is. Philip speaks with all the same pronouns, verb forms and idioms as his royal kin, and the tone of his speech remains at an essentially constant level of seriousness. This makes him unlike Shakespeare's Bastard whose tone shifts from satirically self-conscious to deadly serious by the end of *King John.* Philip represents one who is "to the manor born" even if he does not know it, while Shakespeare's Bastard can be seen as a parvenu seeking (with amazing success) to become such. This distinction reflects the difference between rank and "career" as preordained or destined, and rank and "career" as personal choice. The Bastard chooses his destiny rather than having it chosen for him. Because of his being born to his rank, Philip does not need to learn in the way that the Bastard does; he *is* what he is and the kind of service he provides expresses that essential being.

King John represents a changing understanding of service and of legitimacy in government.[81] This play presents the history of one character's movement up the social ladder and describes the mechanisms of that rise. The Bastard's movement from rural landholder to the administrating voice that closes the play depends more on his personal choices and his talents than his birth. A comparison of the two plays suggests that *The Troublesome Raigne* holds to a more naturalized or traditional notion of noble status than *King John*. It is in Philip's *blood* to be royal while this status is more ambiguous in *King John*. *King John* seems to suspend two definitions of nobility: the Bastard does after all have royal blood even if it does not burn with "honour's fire" to make him speak, while inclining toward a less "natural" or inborn notion of nobility. In essence it is the Bastard's *talent* not his blood that ennobles him.[82] If *The Troublesome Raigne*'s Philip is not the strategist Shakespeare's Bastard is, it is because Philip, being essentially noble, has no need for conscious strategy while the Bastard clearly does.

Where *The Troublesome Raigne* presents rank and distinction as inborn or preordained by forces explicitly external to individual persons, *King John* presents them as available to those with the ability to take them. Personally chosen profession begins to succeed divinely ordained vocation, a succession also beginning to take place in early modern England. The Bastard remains, in a sense, born to the rank he accedes to, but his ability and his desire have more influence on his successful occupation of that rank than does his dubious birth.

III

> Wherefor this being as a project or table of a common wealth truely laide befor you, not fained by putting a case: let us compare it with common wealthes, which be at this day in *esse*, or doe remaine discribed in true histories, especially in such pointes wherein one differeth from the other, to see who hath taken the righter, truer, and more commodious way to governe the people aswell in warre as in peace. This will be no illiberall occupation for him that is a Philosopher and hath a delight in disputing, nor unprofitable for him who hath to doe and hath good will to serve the Prince and the common wealth in giving counsell for the better administration thereof.
> —Sir Thomas Smith, *De Republica Anglorum* (1565)

Sir Thomas Smith, writing in the middle of the century, intended his *De Republica Anglorum* as a "project or table" presenting England as it was actually governed: "so as Englande standeth and is governed this day the xxxviij of March *Anno* 1565 in the vij yeare of the raigne and administration thereof by the most vertuous and noble Queene *Elizabeth.*"[83] I quote his comments at length because they indicate the depth of his preoccupation with describing accurately how "Englande standeth and is governed" for the purpose of edifying a reader "who hath to doe and hath good will to serve the Prince and the common wealth." Smith's book was written as a handbook of sorts for aspiring and active administrators in the Queen's government and, if Robert Beale's 1592 treatise on the office of principal secretary is any indication, that is precisely the use to which it was put. His other major political work, *The Discourse of the Common Weal of England* (printed 1581, written much earlier), was structured in the dialogue form common to educational works in the period.[84] It provides a detailed explanation of and proposes remedies for the price inflation England suffered in the sixteenth century. These works, and others like them, were part of the working libraries of Tudor administrators. Robert Beale asserts, "It is convenient for a Secretarie to seeke to understande the State of the whole Realme, to have Sir Thomas Smith's booke, althoughe there be many defects, which by progresse of time and experience he shalbe able to spie and amende."[85] Smith's book and Beale's treatise are both practical manuals for statesmen akin to the legal manuals which proliferated in the period.[86]

Beale's work opens with an explicit avowal of its purpose as a practical document. He asserts that his intention is to discuss the "practise of the place of the Secretarie, which consisteth partlie in dealieng with her Majestie and partlie with the rest of highnes most honourable Privie Councell"[87] and proceeds to do so in precise detail. Beale's focus is on the "practise of the Prince's secretarie" and his treatise makes absolutely no comment on the kind of person who ought to occupy that place. He writes "my meaninge is not to speake any thinge of such qualities as are fitt to be in one that shoulde be a Prince's Secretarie or Councellor. That argument hath been handled by others, and whom her Ma[jes]tie shall call to that place my simple Judgment must thinke sufficientlie qualified."[88] This position, written out by a clerk of the Council, accepts the Queen's prerogative to fill places in the Council as she pleases, a prerogative that was not always so calmly accepted.[89] It expresses the disposition of an Elizabethan "man of business," a bureaucratic professional who had served the council for sixteen years. A reading of the treatise and what can be reconstructed of the working process of the Queen's administration will illuminate the outlines of this disposition.

The Bastard's disposition, his willingness to learn, and his ability to master the intricacies of power, mirror the disposition required of Elizabethan servants of the Crown. Tudor functionaries often had to learn "on the job," particularly as the business of office changed and developed over the course of the century. Many of Cromwell's ad hoc and supposedly interim reforms made under the pressure of current events served as models for later administrative changes, particularly in the reform of royal finances and the centralization of the government's authority.[90] The "ad hoc-ness" of Cromwell's reforms was the precedent for the later practice of making reforms as needed, but only as needed. Officers learned and decided on courses of action as they took them with reference to the precedent recorded in the commonplace books Beale writes of, but without reference to a preexistent code of conduct. Beale's treatise attests to the "on-the-job" training required of Tudor ministers, lamenting that no regular means of training existed at the time he wrote: "Of late yeares . . . thinges have been made more private than weare fitt for her Majesties service and no meanes used of instruccion and bringinge up of others in Knowledge to be able to serve her Majestie, yet those rememberances may serve as Notes and heades whereto a Secretarie may referre such thinges as he may gett and be acquainted with in the time of his service."[91] The "rememberances" Beale refers to are commonplace books, notes, and other "memorials" that provided the basic manuals for those in the royal service. Beale states that the secretary must record "such thinges as he may gett and be acquainted with in the time of his service" in such memorials and notes and these records are to help him in choosing courses of action. From the evidence of Beale's treatise, it seems that this was the main means of training for administrator, and it required the predisposition toward learning and imitation demonstrated by the Bastard's career in Shakespeare's *King John*.[92]

The treatise contains detailed descriptions of the duties required of a secretary to the Privy Council and provides copious details about the kind of information a secretary (and, by extension, any important functionary) must have ready access to. Beale emphasizes the importance of the secretary maintaining what he calls memorials of necessary tasks, in the interest of efficiency in managing Council business. Beale's treatise describes the secretary as the chief facilitator and manager of the Privy Council. His instructions repeatedly stress the necessity of the secretary's need to document everything; to have records of all documents that pass through the hands of the councillors and to ensure that those records are kept up to date and accurate: "The Secretarie must have a care that the Clercks of the Councell keepe a perfect book of the Lordes sittinges of the place, daye, and numbre likewise of lettres signed."[93] This practice facilitated the keeping of a "Calender" by which the secretary can find old letters should they be asked after. Managing and controlling the access to information was a large part of the secretary's job, and the principal secretaries were responsible for the part of the Council's staff that did this work.[94]

Beale goes on to discuss the kinds of information the secretary must have ready to hand in the conduct of daily business. He asserts that the secretary must have knowledge of every detail about England's population, legal system, social structure, trade, cities, resources, roads, and so on. The secretary needs this encyclopedic array of knowledge and sources of knowledge for the proper and effective exercise of the office.[95] All of this data is designed to keep the secretary informed of all things at all times so as to make the best decisions. Beale writes that the secretary must have a secret cabinet for "signetts, cyphers, and secrett Intelligences" to keep such things secure, "a coppie of the bookes of the Justices of peace, of all commissions" detailing the legal apparatus in the provinces, a list of all judges and gentlemen ready for government service of whatever kind, contacts with the gentry in all "shires, Citties, and principall Townes," "the affeccion of the Gentry," an understanding of the state of the realm in fine detail, and so forth.[96] Beale tailors his message to a candidate for the office of principal secretary, but the admonitions are as applicable to lesser offices. Beale's own papers contain many of the same kinds of materials he discusses here which derive from his work as a clerk of the Council.

Beale's papers in the British Library contain a large number of commonplace books, registers of correspondence, copies of memoranda, and other such collections of documents, most with autograph notations in Beale's hand.[97] These were the working library of his profession and the very bulk of his papers suggest their importance to the exercise of his office as clerk. Other figures of similar rank kept even larger manuscript libraries which, in another indication of their importance, were contended over after their deaths. B. W. Beckingsale and Conyers Read record that there was much intrigue over the disposition of Burghley's vast stores of state papers and correspondence upon his death. Lesser figures like Burghley's secretary Michael Hickes also maintained large files which his heirs and successors in office preserved. All of this attests to the central importance of such manuscript collections to the functioning of government as well as their role in educating officeholders in the exercise of their offices.

The above discussion does not intend to suggest that no educational program existed for potential bureaucrats; there was an accepted, if not explicitly stated, series of educational steps budding administrators and public servants followed. There may have been no course of study in the day-to-day details of the work, but general educational expectations did exist and the universities and Inns of Court provided ways to satisfy them.

Hickes, Burghley, and Bacon's educational trajectories outline this program of study. Recent biographies of important Elizabethan administrators and their servants, Thomas Cromwell's eventual successors in the world of administrative reform, describe a common pattern of education on the parts of the major figures in the Queen's government. Read and Beckingsale's books on Lord Burghley, the patriarch of the Cecil family, are useful discussions of an administrator's training and career and A. G. R. Smith's *Servant of the Cecils* describes the life and career of one of the Cecils' principal secretaries, an important functionary in the central administration by virtue of his position in the family's secretarial staff.

Hickes was attached to the Burghley-Cecil household for most of his life and served in the royal administration as part of Burghley's personal staff. By the end of his life, Hickes held several lucrative offices in the government and was a very important financier, loaning large sums to the Crown as well as to merchants, nobles, and others. Hickes's education and training were directed toward public service and shared many characteristics with those of his employers Lord Burghley and, later, Robert Cecil. Hickes was the son of a London mercer who had only recently moved to the city from the county of Gloucestershire. His family seems to have been ambitious and both Michael and his brother Baptist were educated at Cambridge. Michael entered Lincoln's Inn in 1564 and was called to the bar in the 1570s.[98] The *Dictionary of National Biography* records that "at an early age he seems to have been received into the household of William Cecil, afterwards Lord Burghley, and ultimately became one of Cecil's two chief secretaries. The position gave give him much influence at Elizabeth's court, and being 'very witty and jocose' he was popular in society."[99] He seems to have absorbed Robert Beale's precepts on comportment and competence without perhaps having read the treatise. His legal training served him well in his later position as one of Burghley's personal secretaries. This kind of educational trajectory was common among Elizabethan bureaucrats from those of Hickes's relatively minor rank to such figures as Sir Nicholas Bacon and Lord Burghley. The educational and career pattern of what could be called gentleman-bureaucrats was relatively fixed by the middle sixteenth century.[100] More importantly, these men saw their lives in terms of a career pattern and shaped their affiliations, learning, and habits in light of that pattern.

Sir Nicholas Bacon, the father of Francis Bacon, was another bureaucrat raised up from humble origins to the heights of Elizabethan power. Bacon was born in East Anglia, the son of an ambitious yeoman farmer in or around 1510. The family seems to have intended Bacon for a career in law and public service. His early education was at the Abbey school at Drinkstone. Robert Tittler writes that "both the Abbey and its school had moved well into the forefront of the English ecclesiastical reform movement."[101] His time there provided an early introduction to Reformation thought and his later life demonstrates the formative influence of this early training.[102] Bacon went to university at Cambridge's Corpus Christi College (then Benet College), which was a hotbed of Reformist intellectual activity. In 1532, after leaving Cambridge, Bacon was admitted to Gray's Inn. Tittler describes the Inn as "a whirlpool of intellectual activity by the turn of the sixteenth century."[103] Bacon remained engaged in intellectual pursuits throughout his life, spending the years of Mary's reign out of public service but engaged in several academic projects, and kept close ties to Cambridge until his death. All of this demonstrates his possession of a disposition inclining him toward learning, and he might have been a great Tudor academic intellectual had he not also possessed dispositions that led him into public service.

Bacon entered the royal service early, having begun searching for a patron and an office as early as the late 1530s. Tittler asserts that Bacon (because of talent and ambition) turned from a purely legal career toward one affiliated with the court. This was in keeping with the Reforming and humanist ideas he would have been exposed to in the course of his formal education. He became Clerk of the Court of Augmentations in or around 1538 (he became Solicitor of the Court in 1540) and it is likely that he was brought in by Thomas Cromwell.[104] As solicitor, Bacon would have been responsible for a great deal of the day-to-day work in the court and also provided "legal counsel in the hearing and determination of cases" to the chancellor and other officials of the court as needed.[105] Bacon was highly successful in Augmentations and his experience there prepared him for his highest office—that of Lord Keeper, the official head of the Court of Chancery: "It was as head of the Court of Chancery that Bacon had the greatest opportunity to apply his particular training and expertise. It was there that he left his most enduring mark as a jurist."[106] Bacon oversaw changes in Chancery that tended to turn "time-servers into bureaucrats" and instilled "some sense of professionalism" in the court's personnel. Tittler's biography suggests that Bacon's willingness to learn and ability to adapt administrative practice to current needs were the basis of his enormously successful career.

William Cecil, Lord Burghley, Bacon's colleague and ally on the Privy Council, was trained in much the same manner as Bacon. He attended Cambridge, the Inns of Court, and demonstrated an aptitude for both learning and adaptation that made him the great political survivor of the Tudor era. B. W. Beckingsale writes that Burghley's "attributes were not those of a courtier or a soldier but those of a scholar and administrator."[107] He had an extensive education, was learned in law and court procedure, and was capable of adapting to rapidly changing circumstances. Attached to Northumberland's staff under Edward VI, Cecil survived his fall and Mary's accession largely because of his reputation, skill, and experience as an administrator: "Survival was the normal fate of the skilled bureaucrat."[108] Cecil's "reputation was that of a hard-working administrator and a moderate politician of more than usual integrity."[109] This explains his value to succeeding monarchs and his ability to survive. Robert Beale may have modeled his prescriptions for an aspiring Privy Councillor on Burghley's real accomplishments.

As G. R. Elton argues, the ancestor of all these figures was Thomas Cromwell, principal minister of Henry VIII, who presided over the greatest political and religious changes of the century. As vicegerent of the church, Cromwell oversaw the enforcement of the Royal Supremacy proclaimed in 1534. As secretary, he transformed that office into the leading office of state, a position it remained in for the rest of the century. As overseer of the Court of Augmentations, he managed the increase in Crown revenue due to the dissolution of the monasteries, the transfer of payments of first fruits and tenths from the Pope to the King, and laid plans for the Court of Wards that Burghley and Bacon were later to realize and enhance. Cromwell stands at the center of the administrative history of the Tudor monarchy. His background and training are, in a way, paradigmatic for his successors in office.

Cromwell was the son of an aspiring artisan (his father was a brewer and a fuller) who left England for the Continent where he was a soldier and a merchant in Italy and Holland. Personally ambitious, he learned much about business, commerce, and international affairs while he was in Italy and the Low Countries. After his return to England, he was a merchant, studied the common law, and eventually entered Wolsey's service as legal counsel. As with all of his successors in high office, Cromwell had a legal education that was particularly important as English government operated through courts of law. Legal knowledge was all but a prerequisite for government service. He entered Henry VIII's service as a consequence of Wolsey's fall, surviving the political destruction of his great patron, and officially entered the King's service in 1530 seeing it as his road to wealth and distinction. He was sworn to the Council in the same year.[110] G. R. Elton describes Cromwell as a studied man despite his lack of a university education. The catalog of interests from scripture to translation that Elton gives in his *Reform and Renewal* indicates the range of Cromwell's interests and attests to the fact that "he employed the mind of a reader and a student" in tackling his political tasks.[111] He stood at the center of a network of patronage not only of "politicians" but learned men as well—he appears to have had a "reputation as a patron to such men"—and met them not only as a patron but as a scholar himself.[112] His learning stood at the core of his work as a politician and guided his action in the public arena.

Elton's *Tudor Revolution* argues that Cromwell selected his appointees for talent, a point argued further in his *Reform and Renewal*. He argues that Cromwell, in addition to dispensing patronage to various and sundry applicants—particularly those with an eye toward public service—seemed interested in acquiring "a body of recruits from the Universities, to augment and continue the kind of advisory group that had collected around him."[113] Cromwell believed that the royal government ought to include such individuals. He maintained relations with individuals formally outside of the government who might be of use to the King, organizing them into a kind of department of his staff. "Cromwell came to see the need for bureaucratic organization even in his unsystematic relations with people who could be useful as intellectuals in government service."[114] He surrounded himself with people of similar disposition, all of whom were engaged in learning and willing to put their abilities at the government's service.

Shakespeare's Bastard, though clearly not the product of humanist training at the universities, nevertheless evokes something of the training that qualified those who entered the service of the Privy Council. For example, his attention to the courtier's dialogue of compliment refers to the training manuals and formularies that provided some of the training necessary for the exercise of the office of secretary.[115] His awareness of the need to weigh utterances carefully and to suit words to occasions also partakes of early modern rhetorical training. One action in particular links him to early Tudor officials—his despoiling of the monasteries in order to help fund John's resistance to the French. Like Cromwell, the Bastard inventories and seizes the revenues of the monastic establishment.

> KING JOHN.   [To the BASTARD] Cousin, away for England!
>   Haste before,
>   And, ere our coming, see thou shake the bags
>   Of hoarding abbots; imprisoned angels
>   Set at liberty; the fat ribs of peace
>   Must by the hungry now be fed upon.
>   Use our commission in his utmost force.
> BASTARD.   Bell, book, and candle, shall not drive me back,
>   When gold and silver becks me to come on.
>   I leave your Highness.
>   (3.3.6–13)

While he does not preside over the dissolution of monasteries, the Bastard does appropriate monastic wealth in order to serve the king's needs. The "imprisoned angels" are set at liberty to defend England from attack by a Catholic-supported French invasion.[116] This associates the Bastard with both the Reformation and with the Tudor officials who presided over Henry VIII's similar actions. His education and career, abbreviated though they are, represent a dramatic refraction of the skills and practices necessary for a Tudor bureaucrat.

IV

I mean to learn.
—William Shakespeare, *King John*

Shakespeare's play focuses on the career of the Bastard, the one character in the play who avows his intention to learn, and that career is homologous with, not identical to, the bureaucrats whose positions and dispositions he refracts. The Bastard is a conflicted figure, standing between two models of the social world, whose ambiguous status as a landless noble professional administrator positions him at the cusp of a transition from a late feudal to an early modern social order. His status as a landless noble affiliates him with new peers like the Cecils—Burghley's estates were largely a product of his service, not the reverse—and his profession—administration, for lack of a better term—is both newly professional and newly secular. His social location thus resembles that of his counterparts in the Tudor administration and though he lacks the formal qualifications that mark his real-world analogues, he does engage in an educational project throughout the play. This project, the learning he mentions after being dubbed Plantagenet, bears a resemblance to the practices described in Beale's handbook for administrators and in conduct manuals more generally. Moreover, the Bastard provides service of the kind offered by figures such as Thomas Cromwell, Michael Hickes, Nicholas Bacon, and other more and less important civil servants. At the same time, however, he espouses (if somewhat cynically) the values of a warrior nobility (even responding to Hubert's oratory in terms from the battlefield) and in the first acts of the play rejects the bias of "tickling Commodity," one of the principles of a new political world.

Tudor bureaucrats shared an educational trajectory, from grammar school, usually to university, and then to the Inns of Court. They tended to pursue similar private interests (many engaged in translation for example) and generally held moderate Protestant religious positions. Most of these figures had an interest in humanist intellectual activity and those who could extended some degree of patronage to writers and thinkers. These men were often both intellectuals and civil servants; they felt an obligation to put their learning at the service of the state.[117] As civic humanism spread through the culture of early modern England these attitudes became more common among the educated. For example, G. R. Elton and Mervyn James argue that the highly educated and trained men engaged in reformist intellectual activity desired entry into public office as a means of demonstrating their virtue in service to the state.[118] "Commonwealth, Protestantism, and Christian humanism have been jumbled together in a splendid porridge of reformist yearning, and I want to stress that in my opinion this crossplay of beliefs, weighing differently in different men strikes much more convincingly than a distinction of categories which turns individuals into representations of abstract ideals."[119] The so-called Commonwealth-men were less a "party" organized around "Erasmian" principles than a group of like-minded individuals who shared in the prevailing intellectual culture of the time.[120] This was the population that provided the government with many of its servants.

As the Tudor state moved away from the somewhat dispersed authority of the medieval monarchy, it required more and more officials capable of running an efficient central government. The Privy Council stood at the center of this developing governmental machinery and was staffed by the best examples of professional administrators in the period. The examples discussed above suggest that servants of the Crown who worked in their offices (rather than farming their duties out to deputies) shared certain educational and intellectual characteristics. The demands of a modernizing and centralizing government coincided with educational and philosophical developments to produce a new professional habitus. To use Bourdieu's terms, humanist-trained Tudor men found in the developing field of secular governmental administration a place where their skills could be profitably employed.[121]

Tudor intellectuals, highly educated, armed with Reformist ideals, and desirous of demonstrating their virtue in public life found in administration a social space where their particular combination of educational and social capital carried great value. Bourdieu writes, "the value of a species of capital (e.g. knowledge of Greek or of integral calculus) hinges on the existence of a game, of a field in which this competency can be employed: a species of capital is what is efficacious in a given field, both as a weapon and as a stake of struggle, that which allows its possessors to wield a power, an influence, and thus to *exist*, in the field under consideration, instead of being considered a negligible quantity."[122] Men like Bacon or Smith transformed their educational capital into a kind of bureaucratic capital that secured their places in the government and gave them entry to the highest levels of late Tudor society. The field was in an early state of development in early modern England, its boundaries still in the process of definition, and the capitals "efficacious" in the field are still not fully defined. Early Tudor bureaucrats brought a wide range of educational capitals to the field and most were able to exploit various elements of that capital in the course of their careers.

As the field developed, the range of viable capitals seems to have narrowed. As the century progressed, the educational pattern of government officers became increasingly homogenous. The shared educational trajectory of men occupying offices from the lower ranks of the administration to the highest offices of state suggests that the field had come to require such an education as an unofficial condition of entry as early as the 1560s. For example, the recommendations in Robert Beale's treatise demand that the councillor be well-educated before taking on the added responsibilities of high office. This educational requirement seems to have applied to the Council's staff as well, most of whom were Inns of Court trained or university graduates or both.[123] Councillors' personal staff seem also to have been expected to have similar qualifications. Michael Hickes, Burghley's secretary for patronage, was Cambridge and Lincoln's Inn–educated, a trajectory that fits the pattern exactly. The development of an unofficial and generally unacknowledged educational pattern for aspiring administrators is an effect of the development of the field:

> The field as a structure of objective relations between positions of force undergirds and guides the strategies whereby the occupants of these positions seek, individually and collectively, to safeguard or improve their position and to impose the principle of hierarchization most favorable to their own products. The strategies of agents depend on their position in the field, that is, in the distribution of the specific capital, and on the perception that they have of the field depending on the point of view they take *on* the field as view taken from a point *in* the field.[124]

Men like Burghley or Bacon who entered the field in the 1530s and 40s capitalized on the "specific capital" they possessed and, more importantly, tended to recruit men with similar capital. This practice helped to secure their own positions by defining their talents and training as essential. It also helped to establish a pattern of training for the profession of administrator.

The development of the field from the time of Thomas Cromwell and the rise of the secular bureaucracy to the Stuart era coincides with the development of an early form of professionalism on the part of those engaged in it. Michael Pulman argues that the Privy Council's operating procedure, while not bureaucratic in a modern sense of the word was nevertheless moving in that direction: "Modern bureaucracy was still undreamed of, but its procedures in a basic simple form, were already in existence, and it is as meaningful to assert that twentieth century departmental practices are the children of sixteenth century conciliar ways of doing things as it is to say that the cabinet of the Prime Minister is the direct descendant of the Privy Council of the Sovereign."[125] The councillors and their staffs had an established procedure for conducting business, compiled guides to that procedure, and had recognized and stable functions in the daily operations of government. Pulman perhaps overstates the case, but the conciliar government of the later Tudors was more modern and professional than its medieval household predecessor.

One of the great complaints of aristocratic dissidents was that their traditional place in the government of the realm was being usurped by newcomers without family or name. This was at least slightly disingenuous because the Privy Council still included men of old noble families.[126] However, the anxiety points to a change in the practice of government that is relevant to this discussion of the professionalization of administration in the period. The Privy Council came to guard the right to advise the Queen jealously, making counsel its exclusive province. Pulman states that there was an "unwritten convention that the sovereign should discuss 'matters concerning the public estate of government' only with her councillors."[127] The old great council consisting of all the major magnates in the kingdom had disappeared by this time as an advisory body and had been replaced by a Privy Council staffed mostly by recently created nobles like Burghley or talented commoners.

Essex's complaints at the end of the century of being "trodden underfoot" by upstarts were echoed by many of his followers who found their old families challenged by newcomers. James writes, "many of the latter had similarly experienced the competitive pressure of parvenu elements, and had seen their long-established place in the county hierarchies challenged by new families enriched most commonly by lawyer or courtier fortunes."[128] These traditional elites were being replaced at the county level as well as at court by men like those who staffed the Privy Council. The shift away from the medieval notion of the ancient nobility's right and duty to advise the monarch to what was perceived to be their marginalization under the Tudor regime is another effect of the "professionalization" of government in the period.

Shakespeare's Bastard, as noted above, stands between the old and the new men—he is a son of a king, but is illegitimate; he is enabled to choose a position in government by virtue of birth but advances by merit—and this ambiguous status allows him to mostly avoid the kinds of criticism mounted by members of old noble families. The Bastard's uneasy combination of high (if not legitimate) birth and talent thus refracts both the emergence of a newly professional administrative cadre and the loss of a traditional model of noble service. The Bastard's birth aligns him with the older model, but his practice and specifically his self-education ties him to the new men. I stress this here to emphasize the transitional nature of Shakespeare's representation. Unlike the Henriad where Shakespeare uses separate characters to embody warrior and managerial attitudes, *King John* combines them in one character and this in turn emphasizes the conflicted, awkward, and difficult emergence of an administrative profession.

The professional choice Shakespeare dramatizes in *King John* is homologous to the choice made by Tudor administrators. Rather than choosing to remain in their local communities, early modern administrators actively pursued government service and sought to gain the credentials necessary for entry into the field.[129] Shakespeare's Bastard gains his eventual high position not because he may or may not have royal blood, but because he pursues the "chance" (1.1.151) represented by Queen Eleanor's job offer and shows himself able to learn how to occupy his new position. Willingness to learn seems to have been the main requirement for government service. Robert Beale's treatise attests to its importance—the councillor (and his staff) must always be ready to learn and adapt to new situations—as does Sir Thomas Smith. Tudor administrators chose to join the profession and were able to do because the field was open to talented, educated, and dedicated men, not because they had noble blood to qualify them as worthy to serve the Queen.

3
"This! Why it outfrowns ink!": Social Conflict and the Legal Profession

> Still in law? I had not breathed else now; 'tis very marrow, very manna to me to be in law: I'd been dead ere this else. I have found such sweet pleasure in the vexation of others, that I could wish my years over and over again, to see that fellow a beggar, that bawling knave a gentleman—a matter brought e'en to a judgement today, as far as e'er 'twas to begin again tomorrow. O, raptures! Here a writ of demur, there a *procedendo*, here a *sursurrara*, there a *capiendo*, tricks, delays, money-laws.
> —Thomas Middleton, *The Phoenix*

Tangle, the pseudo-attorney in Middleton's 1603 play *The Phoenix*, rapturously describes his "sweet pleasure" in the law—in its endless productivity, its ability to transform knave to gentleman, its constant self-renewal, its texts. Like the titular phoenix, Tangle's law rises from the ashes of judgment to begin its argument again. His rapture here (and elsewhere in the play) centers on the vocabulary and documents of the early modern legal profession—the writs of demur, the procedendos, the sursurraras, the capiendos—and much of his speech consists of law Latin and the names of writs.[1] In Tangle's forty-five years as a "term-trotter," he has, phoenix-like, "been at least sixteen times beggared, and got up again, and in the mire again, that [he has] stunk again, and yet got up again" (*Phoenix* 4.126–30).[2] Tangle's fascinated entanglement with legal proceedings resembles that of many contemporary Londoners, not least Middleton himself.[3]

Trial scenes are a common feature of the early modern stage—inherently dramatic and agonistic as they are—and most of the plays under discussion in this book contain such scenes. *King John* opens with a hearing about a contested inheritance, *Poetaster*'s subtitle "His Arraignment" points to the trial scene with which the play concludes, *The Merchant of Venice* famously climaxes in a courtroom, Jonson's *Volpone* likewise ends in the court, and the city comedies discussed in this chapter contain various gestures at trials if not always actual ones. Legal metaphors, legal language, and legal instruments provide important resources to professional playwrights.[4] Shakespeare, Jonson, Middleton, and their peers may not have had the legal consultants that contemporary television and film writers have, but they did have extensive access to and experience with the law. In what follows, I will describe the emergence of the legal profession under the pressures of an increase in business, the relation of that emerging profession to broader social changes particularly as expressed in early modern city comedy. City comedy thematizes the use and abuse of the law as it becomes professionalized in ways that illuminate both the practice of the law and responses to that practice. Legal terms, concepts, and language become available to playwrights because of the professionalization and concomitant dissemination of the law in sixteenth- and seventeenth-century London.

In *The Phoenix*, Tangle's ability to dispense advice depends on legal knowledge derived from his personal experience of litigation and, by inference, from his absorption of legal terminology and techniques from one of the many legal handbooks published throughout the sixteenth and seventeenth centuries. When Tangle goes mad at the end of the play, his speech is even more laden with names of writs and forms of judgments drawn from such sources than it is early on. The cure for Tangle's law-madness, which revises Jonson's purge of the poetasters in *Poetaster*, is for him to expel the language that has driven him mad.[5] Quieto (the miraculously "unlawyered" and therefore quiet man) bleeds Tangle:

> *Quieto*: [Opens Tangle's vein over a basin]
> Now burst out,
> Thou filthy stream of trouble, spite, and doubt.

> *Tangle*: O, an extent, a proclamation, a summons, a recognizance, a tachment, an injunction, a writ, a seizure, a writ of praisment, an absolution, a quietus est
> [Holds up basin to Phoenix]
> *Quieto*: You're quieter, I hope, by so much dregs. Behold, my lord.
> *Phoenix*:: This! Why it outfrowns ink.
> *Quieto*: 'Tis the disease's nature, the fiend's drink.
> (*Phoenix* 15.312–21)

The blood that flows out of Tangle's arm at the same time this stream of names for written legal instruments flows from his mouth is blacker than the ink in which the writs and law books that afflict him are written, and the couplet associates legal ink with the devil's work: legal ink is the "fiend's drink." Tangle's cure is completed when Quieto baptizes him with the "oil of quietness," saying:

> Thou shalt give up the devil and pray,
> Forsake his works, they're foul and black,
> And keep thee bare in purse and back.
> No more shall you in paper quarrel,
> To dress up apes in good apparel."
> (*Phoenix* 15.329–33)

With Tangle's abandonment of "paper quarrels" and the "foul and black" written works of the devil, he finds a conscience and is transformed into an "honest quiet man." In Tangle's case, the effects of the law—here as "law-madness"—are intimately linked to its mode of circulation, to writing. Tangle's cure, *The Phoenix*'s final example of chastised corruption, offers a cautionary representation of the powers of the inky material of the law and its texts.

Despite such cautions, an increasing number of Londoners were focusing on the attractions of the law. Lawyers were members of a rising profession and legal training was seen by many as a means of ascending the social ladder.[6] Wilfred Prest writes that "by the beginning of Elizabeth's reign the law had virtually replaced the church as the career open to talents, the ladder on which young men could climb to power and riches."[7] At the same time, the London courts came to dominate England's legal world, drawing more and more business to the courts at Westminster, and with that business came more and more lawyers and their clients. Dekker and Middleton's 1604 plague pamphlet *News from Gravesend* records the wish of London's innkeepers, players, booksellers, drawers, tapsters, butchers, and "all the rest of the hungry commonalty of Westminster" that Nobody, Dekker and Middleton's putative patron, had left for Winchester in the 1603 plague instead of "all the judges, serjeants, barristers and attorneys" who did flee the city (*News from Gravesend*). Dekker and Middleton write that during the London courts' residence Winchester was much enriched by both lawyers and their clients, and, by implication, London was impoverished. The London courts brought more than legal business to the city and its suburbs as it drew litigants and other legal functionaries to London—filling inns and theaters as well as supporting many other businesses.

Legal jurisdictions abounded in London—and all occupied different courts. London was home to the three ancient common law courts at Westminster (King's Bench, Common Pleas, and Exchequer) as well as the Court of Requests, Star Chamber, Chancery, the Admiralty Court, various guild courts, the Lord Mayor's Court at Guildhall, and the suburban justices.[8] In addition, both houses of Parliament were courts of law as well as legislative bodies.[9] With all these courtrooms and their associated officials, it is no surprise that to contemporary eyes London appeared to be overcrowded with lawyers, plaintiffs and defendants of various degrees, and tricksters whose livelihood depended on the credulity of those going to law. Pettifogging attorneys, corrupt lawyers, and other legal functionaries appear throughout the drama of the period.[10]

Plays evidence the development of a division between abstract law and its particular, and often corrupt, incarnations that enhances the authority of "the law" as a social institution. Middleton's depiction of the law and lawyers in *The Phoenix* does not simply castigate legal practitioners. Responding to Tangle's appearance, Phoenix describes "sober Law" as an angel deformed by human abuse.[11] Those, he says, who are "near" to the angel Law do not "desire to have law worse than war, / Where still the poor'st die first; / To send a man without a sheet to his grave, / Or bury him in his papers" (*Phoenix* 2.222–25). Phoenix draws a careful, and common, distinction between the law as abstract justice (the law praised by common lawyers in published treatises throughout the period) and its practice (the viperous behavior of the pettifogger). The kinds of encomia for the law represented by Phoenix's speech are, paradoxically, rooted in the increasing presence of the paper it complains of. In the course of praising "sober Law" and its distance from "paper," Phoenix underscores Tangle's addiction to the law's textuality. While Tangle is fascinated and finally poisoned by the papers of the law, Phoenix holds that true justice would not want its suitors buried in paper. Nevertheless, as the sixteenth and seventeenth centuries progressed, the law became increasingly bound in paper and that paper becomes an ever-more prominent feature of early modern London.[12] Middleton makes the availability of legal language a target for satire at the same time that the drama makes increasing use of that same language—a language made available by the growth of legal publishing.

Early modern common lawyers tended to describe their learning as rooted in memory, and the central formal educational exercises of the Inns of Court were oral—whether they were the formalized readings, case-puttings, and moots or the less formal educational requirements of attending the courts and being resident in the Inns. Despite this self-described oral and memorial legal learning, the actual learning and practice of the law depended crucially on texts—manuscript commonplace books, handbooks, training manuals, reports, digests, etc.—that circulated throughout sixteenth- and seventeenth-century London.[13] Early modern stage representations of the law and lawyers depend as much on the new availability of printed legal texts (which become more and more common over the sixteenth and seventeenth centuries) as they do on literary conventions about the representation of lawyers.[14] These new forms of legal textuality owe their initial appearance to the convenience of printed works with their indexes and standard modes of citation offered to practicing lawyers and law students in their efforts at mastering, managing, and using the increasingly unwieldy and massive apparatus of the early modern common law. Law printing begins with the 1481 publication of Littleton's *Tenures*, a text that organizes and categorizes the often bewildering complexities of English land law. Subsequently, lawyers and printers produced endless volumes of law reports, legal manuals, precedent books, treatises, and massive commentaries such as Lord Chief Justice Coke's on Littleton. In addition to specifically professional texts such as these, a variety of less forbidding texts emerged, texts intended to be useful to a broader cross section of society than the relatively limited group of professional lawyers. The presence and circulation of these texts exert an important influence on legal education, the image of the professional lawyer, and the dramatic field of early modern London.

The normal practice of the law changed dramatically in the period as legal practice developed into a professional activity.[15] Lawyers developed regular, objective, and public standards of training and requirements for admission to practice. They developed a corporate identity based on their shared learning at the same time as their numbers and importance grew immensely. This prominence, combined with a developing professional identity, drew attention from the Crown as much as from the citizenry. The Crown imposed new regulations on practitioners and attempts were made to enforce old ones in an effort to control what was perceived to be the dangerous power of lawyers as individuals and as a body.[16] Responding to these anxieties, Jacobean city comedy commonly links lawyers to the threatening social mobility of the time. Their learning could serve to pit landlord against tenant, tenant against landlord, neighbor against neighbor, and even husband against wife. In the plays of the period, lawyers are often represented as unscrupulous, dishonest, inordinately ambitious, and greedy, in other words, as exhibiting all the qualities most threatening to good order in the commonwealth. Partly as a result of changes internal to the profession and partly as a response to external pressures, lawyers developed a legal habitus that structured and controlled the application of their learning in ways that served both their own interests and limited the danger legal practice represented (or seemed to represent) to the social order. Ironically, the development of this habitus, which translates into a corporate (professional) identity, is one of the changes provoking the anxiety that pervades city comedy. As lawyers developed ways to control themselves, this very self-control became perceived as threatening.

Despite the image of the law presented by Jacobean city comedy (and by earlier drama and pamphlets), legal practice was in fact more honest than not. Complaints about legal misdeeds are, obviously, rife in early modern culture, but evidence of actual and serious wrongdoing is far less common. Legal historians have found some examples of abuses of power by lawyers, but hardly enough to justify the outpouring of antilawyer rhetoric in the period.[17] In fact, many of the tropes and figures used in antilawyer writings derive from conventions in use since the ascendancy of imperial Rome and have little relevance to contemporary law or lawyers.[18] Lawyers were a convenient and traditional target for criticisms directed at the changing social, political, and economic structure of early modern England and became a natural focus for anxieties about change.

The city comedy of the early seventeenth century registers these worries in its representation of deceptive merchants with illegitimate aspirations, scheming legal tricksters, and victimized country gentlemen. Lawyers take a central position in many of these plays; their activities drive the plots, their knowledge serves the villains, their documents circulate through the action, and, often, their presence on stage provides an opportunity for comic stage business. E. F. J. Tucker writes, "Stage lawyers are often accompanied by flocks of suitors, tripping and tumbling over each other in their desperate quest for clarification and assurance, and are invariably fobbed off with curt, ambiguous answers, or ludicrously mollified by legal jargon."[19] Such scenes represent the pervasive concerns about the complexities of a legal system that was becoming comprehensible only to experts rather than the activities of real lawyers. Stage lawyers provide a conventional place to displace the opprobrium that might better be reserved for their employers who are typically members of the mercantile population: "Because he is the agent of the litigious client, the pettifogging lawyer is a personification of the client's greed. His aim is to profit from the avarice of others and fatten himself on their malice, yet greed and malice are the pettifogger's besetting sins."[20] The pettifoggers Tucker describes are, therefore, victims of their own avarice as much as they are tools of someone else's, and, more importantly, stand in for the avarice and ambition feared as destabilizing by early modern culture. Merchants and lawyers are tied together in many of these plays. Critics from L. C. Knights to Brian Gibbons to Susan Wells to Theodore Leinwand have argued that city comedy is a response to various social, ideological, and economic changes.[21] The plays discussed below exemplify the ways in which apprehensions about social change (real or imagined) were refracted by cultural production into images of lawyers that bear little relation to their actual practice.

Changes in the legal profession respond to developments in early modern culture. The Inns housed the largest concentration of learned people outside Oxford and Cambridge, and legal developments played a vitally important role in England's uneven transition from a feudal to a "modern" polity. The anxieties revealed by representations of lawyers respond to concern about the social changes attending that transition. Legal practitioners, the apparatus of legal practice, and legal texts pervade the plays discussed in this chapter, much as they pervaded London, and the theater responds to both the professionalization of the law and its enormous growth in early modern England. Legal professionals became lightning rods for concerns about social change not only because of their role in those changes, but also because they were professionals and thus somewhat distanced from traditional categories of rank and, more importantly, because they exercised control over an increasingly powerful discipline.

I

The medieval legal apparatus, staffed by what amounted to a guild of lawyers, changed in unprecedented ways in Tudor and Stuart England and those changes can best be characterized as professional. The dramatic change in the scale and nature of legal work, changes in legal training, the advent of printed legal texts (manuals, yearbooks, and reports), and the shift from a legal system dominated by provincial practitioners to one dominated by Londoners define the evolving early modern legal field.[22] These developments redefine a field that had followed traditions deriving from the twelfth and thirteenth centuries. The population of medieval common lawyers was small and stable, and its members were trained in largely informal ways. The common law itself had a stringently circumscribed jurisdiction generally limited to cases that failed to find resolution in other courts. This was all to change in the sixteenth and seventeenth centuries, and by the reign of James I, the common lawyers were members of a large, well-trained, and professional group. In what follows, I will describe the scope and effect of these changes on early modern legal education and practice as the law becomes a profession. Lawyers respond to their changed position by rationalizing legal training, developing patterns of practice, and, perhaps most importantly, developing what I will call a legal habitus that shapes and limits lawyers' professional activities.

One of the more influential of these changes was the explosion of litigation in the sixteenth and seventeenth centuries. Where the medieval common law courts heard relatively few cases, and judges often actively encouraged litigants to resolve their disputes in lower courts, the London courts of the sixteenth and seventeenth centuries heard thousands of cases a year and drew more and more business away from the provincial courts and from the lawyers attached to them. Christopher Brooks asserts that economic shifts, especially those related to the volatile English land market, contributed to this increase in litigation. The sixteenth and seventeenth centuries saw "a distinct centralization of the legal life of the realm, a shift from the provinces toward London" that paralleled the centralization of political authority.[23] As discussed in chapter 2, the law courts became increasingly important in the administration of government policy.[24] In addition, as litigation became economically accessible to a broad range of the population, the number of lawsuits grew exponentially.[25] At the same time as the law's place in early modern culture and society was transformed by the growth in legal activity, the legal profession's internal structure underwent immense changes.

Many scholars such as W. J. Jones, Wilfred Prest, J. H. Baker, Christopher Brooks, and Brian Levack have outlined the structure and function of the different courts and legal systems and the nature of legal training and practice.[26] These historians describe a legal system in the throes of reform and regularization. In the fourteenth and fifteenth centuries provincial courts heard almost as many cases as the London courts, but by the later sixteenth century the courts at Westminster (Chancery, King's/Queen's Bench, Common Pleas, and Star Chamber being the most important) saw the vast majority of business and held far greater authority and respect than local jurisdictions.[27] Under the pressure of this vast increase in business, all the Westminster courts underwent reforms in the sixteenth century. Jones describes changes in Chancery practice that were meant to enhance efficiency, record keeping, and speed, and thus to improve the court's ability to dispense justice.[28] Legal training responded to these reforms, which were also taking place to some degree in the other courts, by regularizing models of training and practice with the intention of producing a group of well-trained attorneys, clerks, and lesser court functionaries in addition to the barristers and judges.[29]

As the demand for legal services grew, so too did the population of legal practitioners, and under these twin pressures medieval lawyers were forced to revise their practice. Legal training in the fourteenth and fifteenth century was loosely modeled on medieval university lectures and disputations. Despite the academic origins of the exercises, they encouraged a practical rather than theoretical disposition toward the law. Early records of moots suggest that the learning exercises were more concerned with procedure than theory. This practical orientation is characteristic of a craft, and early legal training had far more in common with the crafts than with the universities, despite resembling the universities in the manner of teaching. This was to change in the sixteenth and seventeenth centuries. J. H. Baker notes that "the basic method of instruction, both in the universities and in the school of common law, was the lecture. A lecture, as the name implies (*lectura, lectio*), was originally a 'reading' of some text which required exposition—in the university law schools usually a part of the Digest or the decretals . . . Academical exercises were . . . split into two branches: the lecture, with accompanying questions, and the formal disputation, detached from lectures, in which the learner played a more active part."[30] Records of such oral exercises on the common law date as far back as the thirteenth century, before the Inns became recognizable institutions occupying a permanent place in London. Common law teaching naturally followed the dominant pedagogical practices of the time—practices exemplified by the universities and especially by their treatment of civil law. Educational practices were similar in the early common law and civil law "faculties" but the content was quite different.[31] Early "lecture series" seem to have consisted of discourses on courtroom practice rather than the more textually based lectures characteristic of civil law training in the universities. Because of the nature of the common law, its "teachers did not have texts to 'read' in the literal sense, until they took to reading on the statutes; but they used forms of writs and pleadings as the basis for their lectures, and they also lectured on procedure."[32] Moreover, the readings, the most formal academic exercises of the Inns, were not routine events—the majority of learning was through the less formal mootings, case-puttings, and private study discussed below. Once the Inns became established in the mid-fourteenth century, the learning exercises developed into a regular feature of their collegial life.

Despite the fact that the lawyers were trained in the Inns and that educational exercises were a normal part of their daily life, the four Inns were less colleges or academies of the law than large professional associations and residences. The Inns' educational role was an accidental effect of their function as the London offices of practicing barristers and attorneys. The early history of the Inns, insofar as it can be reconstructed, demonstrates that aspiring lawyers learned their law in a more or less informal way by attending court at Westminster Hall and living among practicing lawyers who, interestingly, were called "apprentices of the Bench" or "men of court."[33] Solid documentation of just what kind of "learning process" these students underwent is scant, but it is clear that it was informal and more concerned with practical matters of procedure than with theoretical jurisprudence.[34] Budding lawyers learned by immersing themselves in fourteenth-century legal culture, assimilating the practices and knowledge of those whom that culture recognized as legitimate practitioners. Apprentices in artisanal crafts also lived "among" the craftsmen from whom they learned, and the importance of being among lawyers to legal education remains high throughout the period. The title of "apprentice of the Bench" (which referred to those practitioners who were permitted to plead publicly but who were not serjeants-at-law, a position roughly equivalent to that held by barristers in the sixteenth century though the apprentices seem to have been more senior) points both to this method of training and to the practical, craftlike, nature of legal practice in the fourteenth and fifteenth centuries.

Admission to practice was governed less by explicit rules or the achievement of specific academic qualifications, than by satisfactorily assimilating a legal habitus.[35] Habitus, a set of predispositions to particular kinds of practice, predispositions that operate outside of conscious intention, derives from an agent's engagement with a field and its history, here that of law. Bourdieu writes that "the habitus, a product of history, produces individual and collective practices—more history—in accordance with the schemes generated by history."[36] The history of the discipline produces a specifically legal habitus that structures (and limits) the kinds of behavior available to particular lawyers. However, habitus is a "determining structure only in the sense that it determines limits for practice based on historical conditions of production."[37] It is a generative principle, but one whose products are structured by history. When Baker writes of the "common learning" of lawyers, he describes a legal habitus, habits of mind and body that could be applied to widely divergent problems in order to produce recognizably "legal" solutions.[38] Legal training inculcates this ability and the habitus on which it depends. In the fourteenth- and fifteenth-century Inns of Court, this inculcation happened as a product of the student's immersion in the legal culture of the day.[39]

The legal field imposes its own norms of perception and action on agents engaged in legal activity, creating a distinctive legal habitus. Acquiring this habitus, defined by what Bourdieu calls the "juridical sense," is the most important qualification for a lawyer. Bourdieu's description of twentieth-century law schools parallels early modern practice in that legal training seeks to familiarize students not only with the content of legal learning—precedent, statute, and procedure—but also to give them a legal disposition. Bourdieu asserts that "the 'juridical sense' or 'juridical faculty' consists precisely in . . . a *universalizing attitude*. This attitude constitutes the entry ticket into the juridical field—accompanied, to be sure, by a minimal mastery of the legal resources amassed by successive generations, that is, the canon of texts and modes of thinking, of expression, and of action in which such a canon is reproduced and which reproduce it."[40] Fulbecke and later manual writers argue strenuously that law students must relentlessly practice translating disputes into questions that can be resolved at law—a mode of thinking and expression structured by this universalizing attitude.[41] Baker compiles a broad range of *quaestiones* from the various Inns' moot-books, all of which require students to transform "real-world" problems into legal ones through habits of mind specific to the law—this is a hallmark of the operations of habitus. Portia's courtroom practice in *The Merchant of Venice* demonstrates some of these qualities. Besides upholding the law of contract to the letter, which allows Antonio to be spared (Shylock can have his pound of flesh, but nothing else), she finds a perfectly legal way to punish Shylock for what she construes (again through the mediation of the law) as his murderous intent.[42] The hold that Venetian law has on Shylock (4.1.343) depends on an act of legal interpretation that transmutes an unenforceable contract into attempted murder. Portia satisfies the real-world desire to punish Shylock by the represented exercise of a juridical sense. This sense depends on a rhetoric of impersonality and neutrality that "is the expression of the whole operation of the juridical field, and, in particular, of the work of rationalization to which the system of juridical norms is continually subordinated."[43] Portia's rhetoric in this scene partakes of this kind of neutrality—at least in the opening moves of the scene's legal game as she rationalizes and schematizes the legal questions at issue. Her status as "a young and learned doctor" (4.1.144), qualified to engage in this work, depends on her introduction as a youth who acquired "his" learning in Rome's law schools. In London's medieval Inns, traditional learning exercises and life among lawyers sufficed to produce this kind of learning as well as the habitus of a lawyer and proceeded without the need for explicit standards or regulation. This began to change in the sixteenth and seventeenth centuries.

The sixteenth century's legal habitus shifted as the demands on and positions of lawyers changed in response to the expansion of litigation, the centralization of legal and government business, and, not least, because the field itself changed. Still rooted in the need to inculcate a juridical sense in budding lawyers, legal training nevertheless was forced to change under pressures from within and without the profession. Developments in the legal habitus derive from confrontations with events or problems susceptible to solution by methods that emerge from that same habitus. The developing legal profession of the sixteenth century confronts events, in this case the enormous growth in litigation and the inadequacy of traditional legal training to meet the demand, and changes both training and practice in response.[44] However, these changes are limited by the logic of the legal field and "exclude all 'extravagances,' . . . that is all the behaviours that would be negatively sanctioned because they are incompatible with the objective conditions."[45] At a time when law and lawyers were exercising unprecedented power and influence in England, the legal habitus changed in ways that limited the uses to which legal knowledge could be put by excluding "negatively sanctioned" behavior. As one example, unspoken standards of behavior from medieval tradition were reinforced by a developing sense of lawyers' role in defending English liberties, particularly those of property.⁴⁶ In the changed context of sixteenth-century legal practice, older means of inculcating the legal habitus shifted from those appropriate to a small and closely knit craft to resemble those of a modern profession.⁴⁷

The legal profession in England before the Renaissance had many of the characteristics of a craft guild, including governance of practitioners by a body of "masters" who had some control over admission to practice.⁴⁸ The law was a social world—a community—as much as it was a discipline, and success as a lawyer required attention to both aspects. The public career of lawyers was fairly simple in the fourteenth and fifteenth centuries: lawyers went from students, to apprentices, to serjeants (the "order of the coif"), and finally became judges.⁴⁹ Senior lawyers did a wide range of work that would later become the province of the lower branch, acting as attorneys, conveyancers, and the like. The diverse and relatively undifferentiated nature of legal work determined the kind of learning that occurred in the Inns of Court and Chancery: lawyers had to be able to function in a variety of capacities. In addition, professional success (and, indeed, the ability to practice at all) also depended on the student's familiarity with and comfort in the highly formalized social milieu that was the legal field.

Prest argues that the most important requirement for call to the bar in the sixteenth century was simply that the aspiring barrister must have been "in commons" during the learning vacations for an average of seven years "The main academic elements were attendance at either four or six learning vacations immediately before call and participation in a given number of moots both abroad at the inn of chancery and within the parent house of court. The judges were content to leave the benchers free to determine the course of pre-call exercises, but did make some effort to standardise the length of membership necessary to qualify students for the bar."⁵⁰ During the "learning vacations," the student would have attended readings and case-puttings in addition to participating in moots, all of which comprised the formal learning exercises common to all the Inns. More importantly, he would have engaged in informal learning that ranged from the arguing of cases at dinner to solitary study of the law reports and yearbooks to socializing with practicing lawyers. The mealtime case-puttings and moots mimicked the conditions of practice in order to prepare the student for actual court cases. The fact that all four Inns required that a student be "in commons" (i.e., living, or at least taking meals, in his Inn) for a considerable length of time demonstrates the importance of the kind of informal learning typical of the Inns. Students were not only expected to attend the formal exercises, but to participate in the communal life of the Inns, and that participation was a necessary part of a lawyer's training. Lawyers practiced in courts staffed by their teachers, mentors, and fellow students, and the rules taught in moots or case-puttings had direct relevance to actual cases.

Aspects of the guildlike legal culture of the Middle Ages persisted through the sixteenth and into the seventeenth century, but, as the profession grew and the common law became more complicated, both students and teachers came to see the need for a more systematic and theoretical method of learning and teaching the law.[51] As David Seipp argues, common lawyers in the sixteenth century "had carried on for more than three centuries without a comprehensive, systematic treatise describing the whole of their law."[52] By the end of the century, he suggests, the need for such a treatise was apparent to many of them. Such a theoretical approach to legal learning had been made necessary by massive change in the nature, scale, and scope of legal business over the course of the second half of the century.[53]

As the law became more complex, the traditional oral exercises and manuscript commonplace books became increasingly inadequate by themselves as means of providing law students with all the knowledge they needed. In contrast to the fourteenth and fifteenth centuries, where the readings and exercises followed a set pattern and could cover the whole of the law, sixteenth- and seventeenth-century readings tended to become showpieces of reader's erudition on a narrow topic and made little pretense to covering broad areas of knowledge. The exercises remained tied to the old course of readings, a course that derived from a much earlier state of the field, and were less and less relevant to contemporary concerns.[54] Thus, the exercises were supplemented (and sometimes replaced) by printed texts.

Legal texts proliferated all though the later sixteenth and seventeenth centuries and mark a transformation in early modern legal culture. Because of print, legal learning became more and more readily available to both aspiring lawyers and interested lay people. For example, as early as 1543, *A Newe Boke of Presiden-*

tes in Maner of a Register (STC 1134) billed itself on the title page as comprehending "the very trade of makyng all maner euydence and instrumentes of Practyce, ryght commodyous and necessary for euery man to knowe." The later *Attourneys Academy* (1623, STC 20163) describes itself as being "intended for the publique benefit" (title page) of all Englishmen. This declaration of the general usefulness of such texts becomes a common feature of title pages. As Prest suggests in his essay "Lay Legal Knowledge in Early Modern England," a large market for legal texts aimed at a lay audiences emerges later in the seventeenth and eighteenth centuries.[55] Yearbooks, reports, and ancient treatises were all printed in the course of the century and new forms of legal writing reached print as well. Manuscript yearbooks, reports, and treatises had been the primary written resources for aspiring lawyers, and many barristers kept extensive notebooks that compiled useful precedents, models for pleading, notes from readings or arguments in court, as well as individual digests of the law that supplemented the aural exercises that formed the core of a lawyer's education. The advent of printed legal literature changed the traditional pattern:

> Within ten years of the introduction of printing into England in the 1470s, the London printers had found a market in the legal profession. The first printed English law book was Littleton's *Tenures* (1481), and by the end of Henry VII's reign a number of year-books were printed. The effect of printing the year-books was that in time the manuscripts were ousted from the practitioners' libraries. The printed version, with all its many defects, had the apparent advantage of providing the profession with a complete set of reports of accepted authenticity and having a standard method of citation.[56]

Printed records of precedent had obvious usefulness for practicing lawyers, and students were not slow to see advantages in such texts for their preparations for practice. Venerable manuscript treatises on the common law began to be printed in the sixteenth century: Britton was first printed in 1530, Glanvill in 1554, Bracton in 1569, and Fleta in 1647. These were supplemented by the Year Books (1481 and following and especially Tottell's editions following 1553) and Reports (1571 and following) which became the core of the standard reference library of the common law.[57] In addition to printed volumes of reports, the new printed literature of the law included handbooks, precedent books, recent treatises, and manuals designed to simplify or rationalize the formidable task of learning the law. The advent of such works marks an important stage in the professionalization of what still remained a craft.

Books such as Littleton's *Tenures* (1481), St. German's *Doctor and Student* (1528–31), Plowden's commentaries and reports (1578), Fulbecke's *Direction* (1600), Cowell's *Institutiones* (1605) and *Interpreter* (1607), Finch's *Nomotechnia* (Law French 1613, English 1627), Coke's *Institutes* (1628), Bacon's *Elements of the Common Laws of England* (1630, composed 1590s?), and Dodderidge's *Lawyer's Light* (1629) and *English Lawyer* (1631), to name only a few, all point to a field in the process of rationalization. As legal activity became a more important part of daily life, royal administrators, in concert with the judges and benchers, saw a need for standardizing requirements for admission to practice for both the upper and lower branches of the profession and focused primarily on ensuring the knowledge and competence of practitioners.[58] Learning the law became an ever-more arduous undertaking as the litigation boom continued. Not only did the student have to master the social and rhetorical skills of the legal community (as in the medieval model); he also had to master copious volumes of disorganized legal knowledge. The rapid development of legal publishing was, at least in part, prompted by the desire to organize that knowledge and thus make it easier to absorb. While the government focused on developing criteria for admission to practice, thereby hoping to encourage high pedagogical standards, practicing lawyers engaged directly with legal pedagogy.

Littleton's *Tenures* revised an earlier treatise on the forms of landownership under the common law. His book was, as many historians have noted, revolutionary in that it attempted to systematize knowledge that had only existed as disorganized lists and compendia of precedents.[59] Littleton's textbook was divided into two parts: the first dealt with the "estates" (the kinds of holding from freeholds to nonfreeholds) and the second with "tenures" (the means by which such estates are held). This organization simplified the confusing complexities of English land law into a comprehensible system. By the middle of the sixteenth century, publishers of Littleton included charts that laid out the estates on one axis and the tenures on another in order to illustrate points about land law. Baker writes, "from the date of its first publication in print in 1481 [Littleton] was seized upon by the whole profession as a faithful introduction to the common law of real property."[60] That the profession was in dire need of such introductions is further demonstrated by the publication history of Christopher St. German's *Doctor and Student* (1528–31), which was constantly in print throughout the sixteenth and seventeenth centuries.

Doctor and Student and other later manuals filled gaps left by traditional legal training. St. German's treatment of equity served not only as an introductory text on equity, but as a work of legal theory that provided a framework within which to understand the disparate rulings of the common law. For example, St. German writes that "Equytye is a [ryghtwysenes] that consideryth all the pertyculer cyrcumstances of the dede the which also is temperyed with the sweetnes of mercye. And [such and equytye] must alway be obseruyed in euery lawe of man and in euery generall rewle thereof & that knewe he wel that sayd thus. Lawes couet to be rewlyd by equytye."[61] St. German's definition of equity offers a means to understand both the extent and authority of chancery jurisdiction and a way to understand structuring principles of the common law.[62] William Fulbecke, writing after St. German, proposes methods of learning the law that are simpler and more "convenient" than the usual course of more or less disorganized solitary study punctuated by case-puttings, moots, and readings. Fulbecke addresses what Chief Justice Coke described as the surpassing difficulty of learning the law by offering a plan of study. He focuses on issues of conditioning, habitual practices, and the development of reflexes relevant to the practice of the law, paying particularly close attention to the importance of the student's linguistic dispositions and, more importantly, what Bourdieu would call his linguistic habitus. Fulbecke's *Direction* aims to lead student lawyers to internalize and reproduce the rhetorical and social norms that underwrite the linguistic and social authority of lawyers. Lawyers trade on the distinctive force of their language, a force that derives from its formal structure. The *Direction* makes the mastery of linguistic and social forms a central theme of its educational program and Fulbecke's deep awareness of the critical role of language in legal practice pervades his work: "Words if they be not vested with the substance of things, are of no force; rhetoric which is the artificer of persuasion, if it be severed from circumstances, and range without learning by a facile kind of sway, is called *Atechnia.*"⁶³ The legal content of his *Direction* derives mostly from other sources, demonstrating his concern with the *form* of learning rather than its *content.*⁶⁴ As Seipp notes, this emphasis is common to other seventeenth-century legal handbooks, most of which promote various logical methods of approaching the learning of the law. ⁶⁵

Seventeenth-century legal texts continue to combine theoretical jurisprudence designed for the dedicated law student with pragmatic programs of study, lists of writs, and briefs and pleadings to memorize, and continue to make legal learning more accessible to an ever-larger number of readers. According to the title page of Thomas Powell's 1623 *Attourneys Academy,* the volume is a comprehensive treatment of "the manner and forme of proceeding practically, vpon any Suite, Plaint, or Action whatsoeuer, in any Court of Record whatsoeuer, within this KINGDOME." Powell's book is one of those most commonly associated with attorneys and its popularity indicates both its usefulness and its ready availability. Moreover, Powell's "academy," unlike those of the Inns of Court and Chancery, is open to the entire literate population. The book begins with a treatment of the "manner of proceeding in the CHANCERIE" (B1r) and proceeds through all the London courts (Requests, Common Pleas, Exchequer, King's Bench, Star Chamber, Parliament, the Lord Mayor's and the Sheriff's Courts) in a systematic fashion. The book presents the rules of each court in great detail. Regarding actions of debt in the Court of Common Pleas, Powell writes:

> First you are to understand of what nature the Action which you would sue must be. If it be for Debt vpon a Bond, you must take a special care that your Originall doe agree with the Bond; For otherwise your proceeding will be erroneous. . . . If the Sheriffe do returne the Defendant sufficient: Then soon after the said Returne, when the Originall is fyled: The Plaintifs Attourney must goe to the Office of the *Phillozer* of the said County; and there search and be satisfied whether any Attourney haue appeared for the Defendant or no. (N3–N3v)

Powell continues step by step through the stages of an action for debt and, at each stage, states what both the plaintiff's and the defendant's attorneys need to do. Of Powell's work, Christopher Brooks writes that works like the *Attourneys Academy* are a common feature of attorneys' libraries and copies of similar works have been found that date back to at least the 1580s.[66] Brooks goes on to suggest that works of this kind were a typical means of acquiring legal knowledge for attorneys. Manuals such as this are common throughout the period—ranging from this kind of handbook for attorneys to collections of models of pleadings for barristers.[67]

The proliferation of legal handbooks of whatever description and derivation is a major feature of early modern legal culture. Where legal knowledge was once acquired and reproduced orally or in manuscripts, the sixteenth and seventeenth centuries saw legal training become increasingly dependent on printed sources. Because the law as practiced had much to do with precedent, law books tended to base themselves on preceding texts, creating a series of textually based models for presenting, learning, and deploying the law. Practices once structured primarily by speech come to be structured more and more by writing, and, specifically, by print.[68] These printed sources become ever more common and develop into a significant part of early modern textual culture more generally—law books are available to a broad population and legal language becomes an increasingly common feature of ordinary discourse, at least as that discourse is represented in early modern drama. At the same time this movement from manuscript to print in legal training was taking place, England saw an incredible increase in litigation. Between 1490 and 1640, cases in late stages in the two most important common law courts (King's Bench and Common Pleas) increased thirteen-fold from about 2,100 to almost 29,000.[69] This increase made litigation an unavoidable fact of London life.

Under the pressure of this increase, early modern lawyers saw their once medieval profession gradually transformed into something resembling a modern career. New career trajectories emerge as the structure of the legal profession changes. The change is homologous to that which I discuss in chapter 2: from the traditional, household administration of Henry VII to the professionalized, bureaucratic administration of Elizabeth I. Lawyers went from resembling a medieval guild in which there were few distinctions between the kinds of work different lawyers did to a modern profession in which different practitioners fulfilled very different functions. From a relatively undifferentiated population in the fourteenth and fifteenth centuries, barristers and attorneys became more and more distinct populations doing very different work in the sixteenth and seventeenth. New work inundated the central courts, as J. H. Baker notes, and "neither of the old branches of the profession had any monopoly on the new work which flooded into the King's Bench and conciliar courts in the sixteenth century."[70] The members of the old branches were few in number and were thus unable to keep up with the increased flow of business. This shortage of counsel forced the courts to relax some of the traditional restrictions on the rights of audience in the central courts. The ranks of the serjeants (and "apprentices" admitted to the ranks of pleaders) were supplemented by allowing senior students at the Inns to practice in the central courts, since attorneys were not permitted to plead in the central courts. Baker argues that before the sixteenth century, only the most senior members of the Inns (benchers or "apprentices") had been permitted to plead in the central courts, but in the sixteenth century their numbers were insufficient to the demand for counsel, and thus utter barristers (students who had been called to the bar of their Inn, i.e., permitted to participate in the formal learning exercises) were admitted to practice.[71] This change gave rise to a new branch of the profession: the barristers.[72]

Both Prest and Baker show that the rank of barrister began as a purely internal mark of a certain degree of learning on the part of a student and that only the increasing demand for legal services made it a public and professional degree. By the late sixteenth century the Inns had developed a three-tiered hierarchy of ranks. The benchers occupied the highest position—a self-selecting group of senior lawyers in charge of the Inn. The barristers came next and comprised the bulk of the practicing lawyers and beneath them were the inner barristers, only some of whom were training for a legal career.[73] Barristers came to be, as Prest puts it, "the main professional element" in the Inns and dominated the upper echelon of the legal field.[74] The barristers laid exclusive claim to the pleading in the central courts, relegating attorneys (and solicitors) to preparing cases for that penultimate stage and to handling the routine paperwork that surrounded lawsuits. Conflicts between attorneys and barristers center on conflicts over areas of practice; conflicts largely resolved in favor of the barristers. What was once a mark of a certain degree of learning on the part of the student became a professional qualification without which one could not plead in Westminster.

Regulation of those admitted to legal practice did exist in the thirteenth century, but the standards for admission were far less formal than they became later. Baker writes "the element of professional regulation was probably added later in the thirteenth century. In 1275 it was enacted that professional lawyers found guilty of deceit were to be punished; and in 1280 the city of London made regulations concerning practitioners in the mayor's court, for the administration of an oath to those newly admitted."[75] He goes on to assert that the judges selected and swore attorneys in Common Pleas, apparently at their own discretion. By the fourteenth century, the judges "could exercise their discretion by reference to an established standard, the status of an individual in the inns of court."[76] Such regulation as existed was self-imposed and no specific criteria beyond residency and "status" in the Inns were laid down until the sixteenth century when being called to the bar in one of the Inns became the minimum qualification required for practice in the courts at Westminster.

Once a lawyer entered the ranks of the barristers, he was able to provide a wide range of legal services. The common law judges, who were the primary regulatory authority for lawyers, put few restrictions on what a barrister could and could not do. As Prest writes, "Barristers still could and did deal directly with clients, drawing up briefs and pleadings themselves; attorneys had not lost all rights of appearance in the Westminster courts and students frequently worked as or for attorneys both before and after call to the bar."[77] Despite this, the rigid modern division between the work of barristers on one hand and that of attorneys and solicitors on the other that obtains today is a product of developments in professional practice that began in the sixteenth century.[78] As barristers gained exclusive rights to plead in the central courts, the work of attorneys became more concerned with the work that led up to the oral or written pleading.[79] Brooks argues that "on the whole, therefore, the learning of the attorneys was practical; it was concerned with the bureaucratic and procedural rather than the more theoretical aspects of the law."[80] Attorneys and solicitors were eminently qualified to initiate lawsuits, manage the cumbersome apparatus of writs necessary to legal process, and to act as intermediaries between clients and barrister: "From about 1550, it seems likely that attorneys and solicitors were increasingly the lawyers most commonly consulted by litigants in the first instance, and that barristers were only called in when necessary. By the 1630s, newly appointed serjeants-at-law were reminded by Lord Keeper Finch not to be overindulgent in their efforts to get attorneys to bring them work, and after the Restoration Roger North described a legal profession in which attorneys dominated contacts with clients."[81] This developing division of labor was underscored by a status hierarchy. Barristers, with their Inns of Court training and exclusive rights of audience, were the elite of the profession, while attorneys, often trained by apprenticeship, were the lower branch, the base of the pyramid at whose apex stood the serjeants-at-law and the judges.

The legal profession was thus defined by a series of oppositions between groups of practitioners, oppositions that shaped both training and practice. Prest, Baker, and Brooks argue that some early modern condemnation of attorneys derives from the simple fact that they served the middling and poorer sorts of people, not the better sort or the aristocracy. In contrast, barristers, who tended to serve the gentry or aristocracy, were able, more or less successfully, to lay claim to a higher rung on the social ladder. In other words, the rank of clients helped determine stature within the profession. In addition, the site of practice came to define a status hierarchy. London lawyers were the elite, serving the central courts and arguing in Westminster, while provincial attorneys were seen as less distinguished, less learned, and, therefore, less worthy than the London barristers.

Before the mid-sixteenth-century explosion in litigation, the vast majority of lawyers lived and worked in the provinces, usually serving the interests of local litigants. Litigation tended to remain in the area that it concerned and the structure of the legal system encouraged this localism.[82] Local lawyers handled local causes and seem to have used the superior courts as a somewhat rare recourse in cases not readily resolved in the locality. Christopher Brooks argues that many early Elizabethan practitioners had little or no connection to the London courts or the Inns.[83] These lawyers would have learned their law by clerking for other local practitioners and by following the local courts, not by undergoing the more academic discipline of the Inns.[84] Local jurisdictions eroded over the course of the century with more and more business being concentrated in the London courts.[85] At the same time, London-trained lawyers, trading off their credentials as Inns of Court men, gathered more and more legal business to themselves. Brooks continues, "there was a sense of vocational pride amongst the London lawyers which produced attacks on the unlearned and amateur lawyers who acted in the provincial jurisdictions, and this was reinforced by an awareness amongst landowners that they were likely to get more reliable legal services from 'professional' practitioners."[86] Brooks calls attention to landowners' belief in the greater reliability of London-trained professionals over locally trained lawyers. London lawyers traded not only on the distinction of Inns of Court affiliation but also on a developing sense that Inns of Court men received superior training—that they were more skilled than local attorneys. The quality of professional training becomes a tool in a jurisdictional competition (in Abbott's sense) between fractions of the profession. Along with the dominance of the central law courts and the increasing regulation of who could conduct business in those courts, the London lawyers' victory in this professional competition contributed to the decline of the provincial lawyer who had dominated the profession in the midcentury. By the end of the century, law and legal activity was firmly associated with London, not the provinces.

Because of the existence of a shared frame of reference, a shared structure of competition, and a shared system of training and practice, the early modern legal profession may best be described as what Bourdieu calls a field. A field, for Bourdieu, is a structured space of competition between agents seeking to gain the greatest profit, economic or symbolic, for their products:

> The field as a structure of objective relations between positions of forces undergirds and guides the strategies whereby the occupants of those positions seek, individually or collectively, to safeguard or improve their position and to impose the principle of hierarchization most favorable to their own products. The strategies of agents depend on their position in the field, that is, in the distribution of the specific capital, and on the perception that they have of the field depending on the point of view they take *on* the field as a view taken from a point *in* the field.[87]

Early modern legal practice partakes of all of these qualities. The structure of the courts, of the Inns, and of the legal hierarchy all serve to guide the strategies of agents holding positions in the structure. Lawyers sought to advance their careers, bring in a large income, and secure whatever position they may have achieved in the course of their careers. As Brooks notes, lawyers utilized different strategies in pursuing such goals. The divergence in practice between practitioners in the upper and lower branches provide the best examples. This divergence is the result of particular agents' different positions in the field: those in the lower branch have one set of strategies available to them and those in the upper have another. The coherence of the legal field—its ability to structure the practices of those who participate in it—came to define the self-perception of its members as well as their perception by the public they served over the course of the sixteenth century. In the following section I examine that public perception, arguing that city comedy recognizes an increasingly coherent and influential legal field by linking it to disruptive social change.

II

> 'Tis my glory, though I come from the city,
> To have their issue, whom I have undone,
> To kneel to mine, as bond-slaves.
> —Philip Massinger, *A New Way to Pay Old Debts*

Before the sixteenth century, most English people, if they had any contact with the law at all, would have encountered local attorneys and local courts that followed the customs of their shire or even of their manor.[88] Royal justice would only have appeared at the assizes or quarter sessions that were regular but not ordinary events in the life of provincial towns and villages. Brooks notes that "as late as 1628, Sir Edward Coke wrote that 'there be divers laws within the realm of England,' and then went on to list sixteen different varieties, only one of which he called the common law."[89] The common law, the law that most dominates our sense of English jurisprudence, was not recognized as the law of the land until much later. Local law courts (courts baron, or courts leet, and even ecclesiastical courts) still saw large numbers of cases, and efforts were made to keep litigation in the county of origin. Westminster justice became more attractive as its power to supersede local jurisdictions grew, as its efficiency improved, and as the social distinction attached to having suits in London grew. The dominance of the London common law courts was part of the increasing centralization of government (and of social distinction) in England. This centralization of legal practice and training contributes to popular (and elite) anxieties about the role and status of both law and lawyers, anxieties that pervade the period's cultural production.

Lawyers were, as they had been since classical antiquity, a target of satire and abuse in public pronouncements, plays, poems, fiction, and popular sentiment. Writing of early modern barristers, Prest asserts that "hostility toward common lawyers seems to have burgeoned precisely as the profession grew in size and social prominence during the sixteenth century, while the specific complaints mirror recent changes in its organization, as well as much older topoi."[90] E. F. J. Tucker's study of representations of common lawyers suggests that satirical representations of lawyers speak more to contemporary social dislocations than to actual contemporary legal abuses. Tucker argues that a "Ricardian upswing" in legal satire was linked to a series of social changes that lawyers were part of:

> The Black Death and the Peasant's Revolt (1381) had ushered in a period of economic change which struck at the very roots of feudal society, all this coinciding with the phenomenal growth of the middle classes. Although the value system associated with feudalism remained largely intact it was, nevertheless, the legal profession which introduced the most dramatic social changes and which fostered the growth of mercantile enterprise, not only in the expansion of commerce, but also in the all-important distribution of landed wealth.[91]

Lawyers were intimately related to similarly sweeping changes in the sixteenth century, and it is unsurprising to see a similar upswing in satirical portraits of legal professionals. More importantly for my argument, Tucker demonstrates that the content of legal satire does not necessarily mirror actual practice and that "lurid descriptions of legal corruption and severe criticism of lawyers should not . . . be taken as proof that satirists felt any real disaffection for the law per se."[92] Lawyers and the legal system, while guilty of some of the sins attributed to them, serve as convenient representatives of a changing society.

As figures identified more and more firmly with the urban world of London, lawyers were linked to social, political, and economic changes that were themselves rooted in London. As social historians like Keith Wrightson and Mervyn James note, the provinces were progressively marginalized and their autonomy eroded by the Tudor monarchs' successful effort to centralize government. Authority rested with the King or Queen's representatives in the counties, and the most visible representative of that authority was the legal system, which became almost completely focused on the courts at Westminster. Plays like Massinger's *New Way to Pay Old Debts* bear witness to an anxiety about the disruptive role of city figures in local society. Overreach and his legal staff actively seek to overturn the normal order of life and replace the old (i.e., legitimate) authority with a new and implicitly illegitimate authority that they represent.[93] Law becomes an agent of social disruption in these plays, not of cohesion as it is in the self-representations of actual lawyers.

Literary representations and demographic realities (as far as they can be reconstructed) also differ on the question of the social aspirations (and roles) of London merchants. Figures like Ephestian Quomodo in *Michaelmas Term* or Sir Giles Overreach in *A New Way to Pay Old Debts* seem to have been more the exception than the rule in Elizabethan and Jacobean England. Both express a desire to succeed as landed gentlemen that was not shared by the majority of their peers, most of whom did not retire to country seats in an effort to join the ranks of the gentry. R. G. Lang argues that London merchants tended to remain in the city and their descendants made up a large proportion of the next generation of successful merchants.[94] Lang suggests that the mercantile population of London was relatively stable and socially homogenous. They were also, more importantly, consistent in their social aspirations, placing sons in trade and passing businesses and connections down to their descendants. The linkage of mercantile ambition and legal trickery that appears everywhere in early modern literature bears only small resemblance to actual events. Merchants were, as Ian Archer notes, strictly governed by their livery companies, and it was in their best interests *not* to engage in chicanery that would discredit the trade nor did they typically retire to the country.[95] Nevertheless, they are consistently represented as having such ambitions and stage merchants' maneuverings toward this goal are also consistently linked to lawyers.

Despite this, the literary representation of figures like Giles Overreach and Ephestian Quomodo in city comedy is far more common than that of merchants like Baptist Hickes. As George notes in the *Knight of the Burning Pestle*, the plays performed at Blackfriars "still have girds at citizens" even seven years after the theater's opening. His demands for something "notably in honor of the city" are met with parody and jokes by the Beaumont's players who nevertheless offer a play that at least does not openly criticize the city. These plays criticize illegitimate mercantile aspirations, aspirations that are linked to the exercise of legal procedure. Where the plays show merchants to be interested in moving out of the city and into the country to join the ranks of the gentry with the assistance of corrupt and venal lawyers, Archer, among others, describes a *cursus honorum* that bound company members to the civic oligarchy that in turn helped promote the order that was such an important concern of both the oligarchy and the Crown.[96] Like lawyers, London merchants were discursively, if not actually, linked to what were often depicted as disruptive social changes. In both cases, writers responded to change by deploying stock representations—the bad and unscrupulous lawyer or the greedy and unscrupulous merchant—which do not necessarily reflect actual practices. The difference between what the plays represent and what seems to have been the case demonstrates an increasing level of anxiety over threats to hierarchy, an anxiety that seems unwarranted. I contend that the worries evoked by these plays derive from another source—the increasing availability of London lawyers to a wider range of the population.

Despite periodic riots and apprentice unrest, the civic order of London remained remarkably stable at the same time that city comedy was representing it as under threat. Still less were there significant numbers of citizens striving to take the places of the gentry, nor do such aspirations seem to have been a source of social disturbances. Lawyers too placed themselves on the side of established authority—many legal manuals depict the law as one of the primary supports of good order. Such disturbances as did occur were contained quickly and participants seem to have been less interested in challenging the authorities (or, for that matter, traditional notions of hierarchy) than in calling attention to the need for existing authorities to act.[97] For example, Archer writes that the targets of apprentice violence "all represented groups or activities marginal to city life. In normal circumstances, the elite escaped direct criticism."[98] The basic structure of civic government, the rule of the oligarchy, was not in question. Nor was the elite divided into conflicting factions, the Court generally supported the city and vice versa.[99] Thus, it appears that anxiety over the possibility of disorder and strife outstripped actual threats to the city's stability.

The conflicts apparent in urban life were contained and never seem to have broadened into a general disaffection with the established order. Despite the apparent absence of large-scale conflict between the gentry and citizens, dramatic representations of urban life in the period depict a world of conflict between status groups in which members of the lower orders struggle to climb up the social ladder.[100] Upward mobility was not uncommon within the ranks of the citizenry, with men of relatively obscure origins rising to high office in civic government.[101] Archer asserts that "most of the City's rulers were first generation inhabitants recruited from relatively modest provincial backgrounds.... The elite may therefore have been popularly perceived as open to men of talent."[102] R. G. Lang's research suggests that few of these men sought to leave the business of the city for lands in the country. Still fewer engaged in the vexatious and baseless lawsuits that appear throughout popular literature. City comedy, however, presents merchant characters attempting to gain the lands and titles of gentlemen; it presents characters of higher rank in danger of losing position to those of lesser blood, representing a world in which traditional criteria of rank are momentarily destabilized, often through the agency of the law.

That lawyers are linked to a perceived threat to the "natural" order of society is not, perhaps, surprising given the pervasiveness of antilawyer rhetoric in early modern culture. However, lawyers represented themselves as a force of order and good governance in Tudor-Stuart legal manuals and historical tracts. Tracts such as Sir Thomas Smith's *De Republica Anglorum* or Sir John Fortescue's *De Laudibus Legem Angliae* argue that the English common law is the best of all legal codes and that its practitioners are among the most learned and best qualified in the world. St. German's *Doctor and Student* never questions the authority and inherent goodness of the law it discusses, and Coke's massive work on Littleton speaks to the respect with which the law was held. The conflict these rhetorics—between the antilawyer language of plays and pamphlets and the laudatory language of legal manuals and political tracts—evokes the depth of the division between lawyers' self-perception (and self-advertisement) and the way early modern culture perceived them. Lawyers, ideologically committed to the rule of law, saw themselves and their work as shoring up the commonwealth and protecting the rights of Englishmen from arbitrary authority. Nonlawyers saw instead the power and abstruse knowledge lawyers possessed and viewed them, not unreasonably, as dangerous and possibly threatening figures.[103] Early modern cultural production refracts fears and anxieties about links between the law and lawyers and disruptive social change into, for example, plays that depict lawyers as rapacious agents of disorder and illegality and the courts as dupes of such tricksters.

III

Lawyers of one kind or another appear in large numbers in early modern drama and legal mechanisms drive many plots. As with Middleton's *Phoenix*, the picture of early modern law offered in these plays is fundamentally ambiguous. On one hand, the law is respected, even enshrined, while on the other its grubby practitioners are often castigated and where they are "good" they tend not to be active practitioners. This complex and contradictory picture is nothing new—E. F. J. Tucker's book on the history of representations of lawyers demonstrates that—but in early modern London the law being represented was rapidly changing as were its practitioners. Plays like Shakespeare's *Merchant of Venice*, Jonson's *Volpone*, Middleton's *Michaelmas Term*, S. S.'s *Honest Lawyer*, and Massinger's *New Way to Pay Old Debts* all make use of the dramatic possibilities associated with the law.[104] *Merchant* addresses the potential brutality of a common law free from the restraints of equity; *Volpone* calls attention to the way legal form—as argument—can overwhelm content and lead, at least potentially, to the law perpetrating injustices. *Michaelmas Term* shows the ease with which legal trickery can defraud the honest. *The Honest Lawyer* argues that in order for a lawyer to be honest, he cannot practice the law because the actual practice of the law is always corrupt and destructive. *New Way* allies London lawyers and upstart merchants in an effort to upset traditional patterns or rank and status. All these plays refract in various ways anxieties about the role of an increasingly autonomous legal profession in a period of rapid social change.

Shakespeare's *Merchant of Venice* and Jonson's *Volpone*, though both set in Venice, present legal matters with distinctively English resonances. The civil law jurisdictions represented in both plays (Portia is a doctor, not a barrister, for example) still speak more to English ideas, English fears, and English law than they do to an imagined Italy. Portia's legal cleverness in Shakespeare's play offers a clear representation of the ways in which legal reasoning can convert human action into "actions" in the legal sense.[105] Moreover, as MacKay notes, Portia also deploys the language of the equity jurisdiction of Chancery. One of the purposes of the law of equity was to soften the rigors of the common law by the application of conscience. For example, Chancery "looked askance at the harsh penalties granted at law and allowed recovery only for actual damages."[106] MacKay argues that the failure of Portia's equitable plea mirrors early modern practice at the end of the sixteenth century in that equitable remedies could not be applied in suits originating in common law courts. Original suits in equity were a different matter.[107] Faced with this impasse, Portia exploits the literalism of the common law of debt to hoist Shylock with his own petard. Where Shakespeare's play shows the ways that legal cleverness can be put, however ambiguously, in the service of justice or mercy, Jonson's *Volpone* depicts a legal system that is dangerously blind to more or less nefarious trickery.[108]

Lawyers and lawcourts figure prominently in Jonson's play. The closing action of the play occurs before a panel of judges, one of Volpone's many suitors is a lawyer, and Mosca's efforts to exploit Volpone's will, a legal instrument, lead almost directly to his fall and Volpone's with him. In act 1, Mosca offers an introduction to the nature of the legal profession as he explains why Volpone favors the lawyer Voltore:

> I, oft, haue heard him say, how he admir'd
> Men of your large profession, that could speake
> To euery cause, and things mere contraries,
> Till they were hoarse againe, yet all be law;
> That with most quick agilitie, could turne,
> And re-turne; make knots, and vndoe them;
> Giue forked counsel; take prouoking gold
> On either hand, and put it vp: these men,
> He knew, would thriue, with their humilitie.
> (*Volp.* 1.3.53–60)[109]

Speaking to Voltore, Mosca commends the lawyer's ability to speak to every cause, to argue contraries, and make everything he encounters into law. The abilities described here are an important part of legal training—the arguing of opposite positions on various causes (cases, actions) was as important to legal education as it was to rhetorical training more generally, if not more so.[110] Likewise, the corrupt practices listed (taking bribes from both parties in a lawsuit, giving "forked counsel") are common features of the antilawyer literature. The common thread in Mosca's commendation is the moral ambiguity of the lawyer's position. Men of this "large profession," Mosca says, are able to thrive because of their "agilitie" in moving from position to position, client to client, without regard for anything but "prouoking gold." The term "re-turne" has both the virtue of referring to the agility of the lawyer's dance from case to case as well as being a legal term referring to the response to the writs that constitute the lawyer's business.

Voltore's courtroom oratory demonstrates both his skill—his "agilitie"—and his lack of scruple about the niceties of truth. It also addresses the secondary aspect of anxieties over the law—the court's susceptibility to such oratory. Preparing the avocatori for Volpone's testimony, Voltore tells them:

> May it please the court,
> In the meane time, he may be heard in me:
> I know this place most voide of preiudice,
> And therefore craue it, since we haue no reason
> To feare our truth should hurt our cause.
> (4.5.214–28)

Asked to speak on, Voltore spins a tale about "the most prodigious, and most frontlesse piece / Of solid impudence, and trecherie, / That ever vicious nature brought foorth" (4.5.31–33). In this space "void of prejudice," Voltore's tale produces precisely that and none of Bonario and Celia's protestations make a difference to their condemnation, despite their truth. Jonson describes a law court where truth is wholly trumped by skillful maneuvering. In 4.6, the avocatori ask Bonario and Celia to "make good [their] report" (4.6.16), offering them a chance to tell their tales:

Avocatore 1: What witnesses have you,
To make good your report?
Bonario: Our consciences.
Celia: And heauen, that neuer failes the innocent.
Avocatore 4: These are no testimonies.
Bonario: Not in your courts,
Where multitude, and clamour overcomes.
(4.6.15–10)

Multitude and clamor do overcome here, at least temporarily. Conscience and heaven cannot act as witnesses, nor do they count as testimony. Only the deceitful words of the lawyer's plot carry weight in this courtroom. Voltore's performance owes much to the antilawyer tradition, but the duping of the court and the victimizing of the innocent also speak to anxieties about the operations of justice in Jonson's London.

In this play, the financial machinations of all the characters taint the operations of the law and blind the avocatori to all but the most spectacular confession. Even after Voltore's confession that his tale was false in 5.12, the court still fails to discriminate truth from falsehood. Mosca, the parasite whom most characters scorn in the rest of the play, appears in the garb of a clarissimo and Avocatore 4 recognizes him only as a "gentleman" and a fit match for his daughter. The court remains prejudiced until Volpone reveals himself and exposes the whole of the plot. Only then are Bonario and Celia's claims of innocence credited and this only comes through what the avocatori themselves call a "miracle" (5.12.95). The law and the lawyers called to serve it have all but nothing to do with the resolution of the trial, and the villains' fates are decided in accord with a logic of resemblances rather than legal reason—absent throughout the legal scenes in the play.[111]

Jonson presents the law here as neutral, neither good nor bad, but more susceptible to bad uses than good because of that neutrality. Voltore is able to profit from the court's putative lack of prejudice because, at least as Jonson stages it, that lack of prejudice is actually a lack of judgment. Easily manipulated by legal maneuvering and responsible to none, Jonson's scrutineo appears as a semiautonomous institution holding great power in the world of the play. No outside authority appears, not even the relatively ineffectual presence of the Duke as in Shakespeare's play, to sanction or condemn the proceedings. The court, abused as Avocatore 1 says (5.12.110), responds with revenge rather than reform. Voltore may be disbarred and banished, but as Mosca recognizes, he and lawyers like him "haue a gift" thanks to their "education" that will "neuer let [them] want, while there are men, / And malice, to breed causes" (5.3.89–91). Worries about that gift, its source in the specialist training lawyers received, and its relation to human malice and greed are not necessarily eased by the play's resolution that urges the audience to contemplate the rewards of vice. Avocatore 1 asserts that "mischiefs feed / Like beasts, till they be fat, and then they bleed" (5.3.150–51), but in Jonson's play and other city comedies the feeding all but outpaces the bleeding.

The plays of Middleton, S. S. and Massinger also treat law and lawyers as dangerously amoral tools that can be put to any use. All three plays turn on various kinds of legal trickery employed by the villains to further their venal goals as they strive to climb up the social ladder. As the character Michaelmas Term says in the induction to *Michaelmas Term*, the law terms are times of "silver harvest" for those engaged in the business of the law. Michaelmas Term claims to have "wealth enough to redeem beggary" (ind. 20) and goes on to reiterate how lucrative the legal terms are for him and his kindred throughout the induction. "What subtlety have we here?" Michaelmas Term asks on being presented with a dumb show: the first of the other three terms brings in "a fellow poor, which the other two advanceth, giving him rich apparel, a page, and a pander" (ind. 29.1–29.3). Michaelmas Term reads the show as demonstrating how the law terms are times when those who "shrug for life's benefits" can creep up from poverty to be "wrapt in silk and silver" (ind. 30–32).[112] The dumb show's narrative is very similar to the story of Andrew Lethe, described in the dramatis personae as "ANDREW LETHE, born ANDREW GRUEL, an upstart adventurer." Term time is the time for such upstarts to rise, in spite of their real origins in the lower orders, origins to which they must eventually own up and to which they must return. The culminating reinscription of social norms occurs, ironically, by the specifically legal agency of common law judges.

Michaelmas Term presents a world of incessant and destabilizing conflict between status groups that is at odds with the picture of a more or less stable London painted by historians. Merchants and gentlemen are shown to be in conflict from the first scene onward. In the first scene, the gallants Cockstone, Rearage, and Salewood avoid Quomodo, who enters plotting ways to exploit the gullibility of his gentle customers.¹¹³ Quomodo's deeper goal becomes clear as he discusses his desire to take the lands of an Essex heir with his two henchmen, Falselight and Shortyard. Shortyard asks, "What is the mark you aim at?" (1.1.101), and Quomodo replies:

> Why, the fairest to cleave the heir in twain,
> I mean his title; to murder his estate,
> Stifle his right in some detested prison.
> There are means and ways enow to hook in gentry,
> Besides our deadly enmity, which thus stands:
> They're busy 'bout our wives, we 'bout their lands.
> (1.1.102–7)¹¹⁴

Shortyard approves of this "revenge" and happily goes off to ensnare the unwary Richard Easy for his master Quomodo.¹¹⁵ The conflict between gentleman and tradesman is clearly laid out in this scene and Easy, the country innocent, becomes the victim of Quomodo's urban wiles. This conflict is all-pervasive in the world the play presents; tradesmen and merchants are constantly seeking ways to exploit and bring down gentlemen while the gentry seeks to defend itself against these unscrupulous upstarts. Quomodo's final line before his exit encapsulates his position and best expresses the kind of antagonism the play depicts in gentry/merchant relations: "Gentry is the chief fish we tradesmen catch" (1.1.132).¹¹⁶

The hook Quomodo uses to catch gentry is the law, specifically instruments of debt. Easy is convinced to enter into a bond as security for his "friend" Shortyard. Shortyard asks for a loan of £200 in cash and Easy stands as surety for the loan. However, rather than the cash they ask for, they receive a quantity of cloth supposedly worth the same amount. Easy puts his land up as a surety for the bond, and thus risks losing it to Quomodo should Shortyard default on the bond. Through the collusion of Quomodo and his agents, the cloth is sold back to Falselight for a mere £60, placing Easy's lands in hazard should Shortyard be unable to raise the remaining £140 he owes to Quomodo. This kind of swindle was, at least in literature, not uncommon.¹¹⁷ Upon its success, Quomodo exults: "First I have caught him in a bond for two hundred pound, and [now have I] my two hundred pound's worth of cloth again for three-score pound. Admire me, all you students at Inns of Cozenage" (2.3.439–42). Quomodo's mention of the Inns of Cozenage, a joking reference to the Inns of Court, links legal practice with cozenage and transforms them into the Inns of Cozenage, of which he is master. Law, for him, is merely a species of trickery which enables him to disinherit Easy.

Quomodo's exploitation of the practices of debt law to capture Easy's lands is intended to enhance his status among his peers.[118] His secondary purpose is to pass the lands down to his son, securing a place for him in the gentry: "for the thrifty and covetous hopes I have in my son and heir, Sim Quomodo, that he will never trust his land in wax and parchment, *as many gentlemen have done before him* . . . I will honestly discharge you, and receive it in due form and order of law, to strengthen it forever to my son and heir, that he may undoubtedly enter upon't without the let or molestation of any man, at his or our pleasure whensoever" (4.1.39–47, my italics).[119] Quomodo here asserts that Sim is a gentleman and ought not to engage in the same kind of folly as Easy. Sim Quomodo, the inheritor of Quomodo's knavery, has been trained at Cambridge and is a student at the Inns of Court.[120] In Quomodo's mind, Sim *is* a gentleman by virtue of his education, and the land will seal his gentle status. It is unclear whether Quomodo expects Sim ever to practice law, but he is certain that legal training will assure gentle status. Thus, *Michaelmas Term* figures the legal profession as both an agent of social disruption and an ennobling and refined discipline that ensures gentility. Sim's legal acquirements are to be more like those of the gentleman "students" at the Inns of Court than the professional students. Many sons of gentlemen attended the Inns, acquiring social graces (dancing, fencing, etc.), as well as a smattering of law.[121] Harrison describes the Inns as a kind of finishing school for the gentry. Furthermore, Quomodo's "thrifty and covetous hopes" are that his gentleman son will possess the land "forever," implicitly leaving his city origins behind and ennobling the name of Quomodo. Quomodo's plots fail due to his own overly clever faking of his death and, more importantly, through the agency of his servant Shortyard. Quomodo loses the land in much the same manner he gained it. In addition, his shop and fortunes are also lost through a piece of Quomodo-like trickery.

Posing as a beadle, Quomodo comes to collect funeral fees from the supposed widow Quomodo. She requests a "discharge," a receipt, which he signs his own name to as a joke. Easy exploits the contractual language of the memorandum later to claim ownership of Quomodo's business. The memorandum reads: "that I have received of Richard Easy all my due I can claim here in the house, or any hereafter for me. In witness whereof I have set to mine own hand: *Ephestian Quomodo*" (5.1.104–6). Quomodo's one-time servant Shortyard defrauds Sim out of his ill-gotten inheritance, conveying it back to Easy thus punishing Quomodo's deceit and inappropriate ambition. Justice, in the person of the judge, is satisfied with this resolution, and Quomodo receives no further punishment than his pronouncement: "Thou art thine own affliction, Quomodo" (5.1.164). The agents of corruption, Shortyard and Falselight, are banished "that all error from our works may stand" (5.1.167) and the play closes with order restored.[122]

Michaelmas Term testifies to the power that the legal profession held in the popular imagination. Law is here both a tool for cozenage and the final arbiter that restores the natural order. The play also demonstrates the way in which the power of the legal profession translates into a developed sense of social identity. Legal training can make a student gentle. The very pursuit of legal knowledge carries social distinction; merely attending an Inn of Court made people seem more distinguished. All of Quomodo's legal machinations seek to acquire land that will underwrite and make permanent his son's claim to gentility, a claim initially made on the basis of his university and legal education. Anxieties about the power of the law to change the principles of social distinction appear in this play in the way the final scene insists on restoring all the characters to their proper places. Easy resumes title to his land and, as compensation for Quomodo's attempted theft, gains Quomodo's fortune as well as his wife.[123] Unlike Jonson's play, the subversion of normal order represented by Quomodo's temporary successes is contained in such a way as to underline the authority and durability of that order.[124]

The play's ambivalent relationship to the law derives from the tension between the law's perceived ability to disrupt traditional social order and its actual role in upholding it. The judge who appears at the play's conclusion and his actions resolve all the conflicts of the play and restore the normal order. In a sense, the judge banishes the "familiar accidents" of term time through the power of the same institutions that Quomodo and his henchmen pervert in the course of the play. Interestingly, the play puts no lawyers on stage—other than Sim the law student the closest figure to a legal professional we see is the scrivener who draws up the bond—and the authority of law as such is never challenged. Law is figured as a powerful, regrettably value-neutral tool available for the use of good and evil men alike. What condemnation of legal activity there is in the play focuses on individual misuse of the law; in other words, the law's morality depends on its practitioner, not the law itself. This, as Tucker's study demonstrates, is typical of representation of law and lawyers in the period. The distinction between a neutral, or even good, law and corrupt (or moral) practitioners is taken up by the author of *The Honest Lawyer* and it underlies much of the action in Massinger's *New Way to Pay Old Debts*.

IV

The Honest Lawyer (1616) is, like *Michaelmas Term*, set in the urban world of merchants and citizens. The playwright, S. S., sets up an elaborate conflict between Vaster, a gentleman, and Old Gripe, a usurer who holds bonds secured by Vaster's estate. Gripe has secured mortgages from many debtor-gentlemen through the exploitation of debt law, much as Quomodo exploits Easy in *Michaelmas Term*, and the play follows Vaster's efforts to regain his lands and take revenge on Gripe. In addition to this main plot, one subplot deals with the chicanery of Griffin, an attorney, as he fleeces clients by advocating needless suits and then acts as attorney to both sides in the disputes he foments. Both plots are resolved through the agency of Old Gripe's son Benjamin, who is the "honest lawyer" of the title. The play depicts the conflict between an honest and a dishonest lawyer purely in terms of a moral conflict between a good man and a bad man. The play represents legal activity as being almost completely bound up in advice and the writing and signing of legal documents—which, aside from trials, is not an inaccurate portrayal of the operations of the law. The play's trial scene is presided over by an abbot who appears at the play's close to render judgment—a far from typical resolution in the real world, but not uncommon in these plays.

The subplot of Griffin, Sager, and Bromley provides the best illustration of stereotypical attitudes toward legal practitioners. In the subplot, lawyers and the law are depicted as greedy agents of dissension among neighbors. Griffin creates a dispute over a lease between Bromley and Sager, who had previously lived as peaceful neighbors.[125] Protesting loudly that he loves peace, Griffin plots to fleece both men by drawing up a "composition" that would resolve the dispute he himself seems to have created. "Nay sir," he declaims, "Ile bind no man: but if I could perswade you—to be fleeced both, so I might be kept warm in your wooll—How say you neighbor *Sager*?" (C4^v). Bromley hires him and thus aligns himself with legal corruption, but Sager refuses, voicing conventional critiques of lawyers as creators of dissension, claiming not to have ever met any lawyer that "loues peace."[126] Valentine, the ex-soldier, likens lawyers to his kind of rogue and coney-catcher, underscoring the dishonesty of legal practitioners in the world of the play. In fact, it seems that the reason Benjamin Gripe is called the "honest lawyer" (B1^v) is simply because he does not actually practice law.

Griffin's work results in Bromley's murderous rage when his suit against Sager is lost.[127] Benjamin Gripe brings Sager the news of his legal victory: "Good newes; friend *Sager*, the day's yours" (E3^v). But, he also tells Sager that:

> *Bromley*'s growne mad with rage: I'm iealous of him. You know the hopes of your posteritie dwell on your present fortunes: all which burne with the short Taper of your singular life, Say he should quench it.
> Sag.   How Sir? murder me?
> Ben.   I cannot tell, it's but my ielaousie.
>   Tis not amisse, to keepe preuentions eye
>   Open and wary, Instruments of death
>   Stand ready prest to a malicious arme,
>   And policie, like a cunning Iesuite,
>   Slips behind the arras for a call.
>   The dead once done, helpe it who can, or shall.
>   (E3^v–E4^r)

Bromley's avarice, enflamed by Griffin's promises of an easy victory in the courts, drives him to the point of murder. Fortunately, Benjamin warns Sager and they trick Bromley into stabbing a decoy, thinking it is Sager asleep in a field. After the "murder,"

Bromley plans to enter into the estate immediately.[128] Griffin is here associated with the rigors of the law, rigors that deny charity and what Benjamin describes as true justice. Bromley confesses to Griffin as Benjamin steps aside and, threatening to reveal Griffin as a "forgerer," forces him to swear to be silent. Griffin accedes readily:

> Our guilt shall bind our secrecie; who liues
> An unsuspected villaine, winks at others
> Unlawfull deeds, to teach their eye-lids how
> To wink at his.
>
> (H1ᵛ)

Both characters collude in the legal seizure of Sager's land—it is later revealed that they share the land—and in the concealment of each other's crimes. This portrait of the lawyer as criminal pervades the play and Benjamin Gripe's honesty only serves to underscore the dishonesty of his profession.

Benjamin Gripe, the honest son of the usurer Gripe, acts as the sole effective agent of justice in the play. All the other characters are either ineffectual (like Vaster in his disguised attempts to verify his wife's infidelity at the same time he pursues vengeance on Gripe) or corrupt. He is a lawyer, but the only professional activity he engages in is the offstage drafting of a deed returning Vaster's lands to his family, and the majority of his activity in the play is better described simply as the exercise of virtue. Despite this, Anne inexplicably praises him thus:

> Oh pure quintessence of thy profession.
> How many hast thou robd, thus to make up
> Thy perfect goodness! as if wiser nature
> Had made an extract of ten thousand Lawyers,
> And thrice refin'd in with immortal fires:
> Then set it like a sanctified Lampe
> On th'Altar of thy soule; to give exemplar light,
> In the dull darkenesse of this sinne-borne night.
>
> (E3ᵛ)

His lawyerly virtue, as Anne's speech emphasizes, is meant as an example to a profession composed entirely of men like Griffin who exploit the law for personal profit, not to serve the good of others. *The Honest Lawyer* depicts a wholly corrupt legal profession whose corruption is only made clearer by the presence of its title character.[129]

The pettifogging lawyer Griffin is the only practicing lawyer in the play and his corrupt machinations are halted by the actions of the nonpracticing "honest lawyer" Benjamin Gripe. Tucker writes that "the honest lawyer is a constant presence upon the stage, often as a rather characterless or semi-allegorical figure serving as the continual reminder of those enduring values by which the villainous lawyers must eventually be judged"[130] In *The Honest Lawyer*, Benjamin's actions in helping the Vaster children, in foiling all the corrupt schemes around him, and finally by redeeming his father appear to present a standard for lawyers to aspire to, but very little of his activity is actually like that of a practicing lawyer. The play, like *Michaelmas Term*, figures the law itself as neutral or even good, and its practitioners as corrupted by the power it offers. The urban world of *The Honest Lawyer* is dominated by a legal profession that lacks any kind of moral scruple or professional ethics. Benjamin's "sanctified Lampe" distills the essence of "ten thousand Lawyers" to make one good lawyer, demonstrating the low esteem the play holds for the legal profession. Essentially, he is the "quintessence of his profession" because, in terms of the play, he does not act like he belongs to it at all. In this play, the power of the legal profession is both undeniable and destructive.

A New Way to Pay Old Debts depicts a quite different world than that of *Michaelmas Term* or *The Honest Lawyer*. The action is set in the country, though city characters do occupy it, and is concerned almost exclusively with the gentry. Despite this fundamental difference, the three plays are similar in that they examine the aspiration to rise from one estate to another and both are driven by the conventions of city comedy. The values expressed by the villains are similar, as are the tactics they use to achieve their essentially similar goals. All exploit the law, all seek to gain the lands or money of the gentry, humbling them in the process, and all revel in the seeming downfall of their social superiors. All are likewise punished. The denouement of Massinger's play offers an unambiguous endorsement of traditional order, with the truly gentle characters triumphing over the upstart Sir Giles. Lord Lovell offers this sententious statement as Sir Giles is carried offstage raving: "Here is a precedent to teach wicked men / That when they leave religion and turn atheists /

Their own abilities leave 'em" (5.1.379–81). Lovell goes on to assert that he will be the "umpire" of the settlement of the land questions raised by Overreach's fall. Overreach's criminal ambition is harshly punished and Lord Lovell, as a representative of true nobility, presides over the restoration of the order Overreach had overturned.[131]

The play is saturated with legal language, much more so than *Michaelmas Term*. Overreach and his corrupt attorney Marrall exploit their superior knowledge of legal procedure and Overreach's immense cash resources to engross the lands of his neighbors in an effort to transform Overreach into the leading figure in local society, the man all must bow to, even those whose blood is more honorable than his.[132] Overreach discusses his usual means of engrossing the land of a neighbor who is reluctant to sell in the second act:

> I'll . . . buy some cottage near his manor,
> Which done, I'll make my men break ope his fences;
> Ride o'er his standing corn, and in the night
> Set fire on his barns; or break his cattle's legs.
> These trespasses draw on suits, and suits expenses,
> Which I can spare, but will soon beggar him,
> When I have harried him thus two, or three year,
> Though he sue *in forma pauperis*, in spite
> Of all his thrift, and care he'll grow behindhand.
> (2.1.34–42)

The well-known and much discussed costs and delays of legal actions become Overreach's tools here and work to impoverish and weaken his neighbors to the point where he can purchase their land at a discount. His neighbors can ill afford the costs of pursuing lawsuits and the delays all but ensure that judgments against Overreach will not come in time to prevent the necessity of selling the land. "With the favor of my man of law," Overreach continues:

> I will pretend some title: want will force him
> To put it to arbitrement: then if he sell
> For half the value, he shall have ready money
> And I possess his land.
> (2.1.44–48)

Overreach seems to have a legal staff dedicated to just this sort of practice. He employs a London lawyer to "pretend . . . title" for him and keeps a local attorney, Marrall, with him to pursue matters in the neighborhood and drum up trouble for Overreach's victims.

Indeed, the legal profession, at least what the play shows of it, seems to collude willingly with Overreach in his quest to engross all the land he can find. The only actual lawyer depicted in the play, the attorney Marrall, is presented as an amoral, duplicitous agent of Overreach's project. In the last act, as Overreach's plans fall apart, Marrall turns on his master and reveals some of his tricks, tricks that Marrall presents as innate to the profession of solicitor:

> Was it not a rare trick
> (And it please your worship) to make the deed nothing?
> I can do twenty neater, if you please
> To purchase and grow rich, for I will be
> Such a solicitor, and steward for you,
> As never worshipful had.
>
> (5.1.322–27)

Here, Marrall, the agent of the law, reveals that much of his work depends on "rare tricks" to enable his master (whoever he might be) to "purchase and grow rich." The play presents the legal practices of solicitors as dedicated to enabling the purchase of land, by whatever means, honest or dishonest, so that the attorney's employer can grow rich. The "tricks" themselves are a secret of the trade, "mysteries / Not to be spoke in public" (5.1.329–30). This language suggests that the methods Marrall speaks of are the core of the trade, its mystery, and thus presents the profession of attorney as one rooted in deceit.[133] In *A New Way to Pay Old Debts*, legal practice is also linked to the kind of inappropriate aspirations possessed by Overreach.[134] The two are bound together in the world the play represents.

Massinger sets up an opposition between innate gentle virtue and an equally innate common baseness. He marks Overreach's aspirations as inappropriate and his position in local society is seen as illegitimate by other characters throughout the play. Overeach's fondest dream, the aim of all his machinations, is for his daughter to be able to cast off her "humble title" and become known as "right honorable" and have her served by "ladies of errant knights decay'd" (2.1.79). He says " 'tis my glory, though I come from the city, / To have their issue, whom I have undone, / To kneel to mine as bond-slaves" (2.1.81–83). Margaret Overreach, daughter of one who comes "from the city," will enact her father's triumph over the true gentry by having them as her servants. Overreach himself acknowledges a difference between "true gentry" and his own position at several points in the play.[135] For example, in the scene cited above, he explains his position to Marrall: " 'Tis a rich man's pride, there having ever been / More than a feud, a strange antipathy / Between us, and true gentry" (2.1.87–89). He expresses here much the same sense of conflict between gentry and citizen as Ephestian Quomodo does in *Michaelmas Term*.

Overreach's plans for his daughter are the core of his threat to the natural distinction between status groups. If he can marry Margaret into a peer's family, he will have triumphed:

> All my ambition is to have my daughter
> Right honourable, which my lord can make her.
> And might I live to dance upon my knee
> A young Lord Lovell, borne by her unto you,
> I write *nil ultra* to my proudest hopes.
>
> (4.1.99–103)

As he says earlier in the play, Overreach's main goal is to have his daughter bowed to and served by gentlefolk of higher rank than she. His victory in the struggle, the "strange antipathy," between true gentry and those like him, will be to mix his blood with that of the nobility. Overreach goes so far as to offer to put all his possessions and abilities in service to Lovell, to "supply your riotous waste" so that the "scourge of prodigals, want, shall never find" him, stereotyping Lovell as a profligate simply because he is noble.

Characters of gentle origin such as Alworth, Lady Alworth, Lovell, and Welborne engage in a similar rhetoric of difference and conflict. The play finally endorses their superiority; their discourse delineates a clear division between the legitimately gentle and the commons. Welborne condemns Overreach as base, Lady Alworth's servants scorn Overreach almost as much as they do his servant Marrall, and Lord Lovell disdains to marry Overreach's daughter stating, "I would not so adulterate my blood / By marrying Margaret, and so leave my issue / Made up of several pieces, one part scarlet / And the other London-blue" (4.1.223–26) regardless of how rich her father might be.[136] Lady Alworth makes the nature of the distinction between gentle and common quite clear in conversation with Lord Lovell:

> I dare say then thus;
> As you are noble (howe'er common men
> Make sordid wealth the object, and sole end
> Of their industrious aims) 'twill not agree
> With those of eminent blood (who are engaged
> More to prefer their honours, than to increase
> The state left to 'em, by their ancestors)
> To study large additions to their fortunes
> And quite neglect their births: though I must grant
> Riches well got to be a useful servant,
> But a bad master.
>
> (4.1.179–89)

Common men make "sordid wealth" their object while noblemen prefer maintaining their "honours" to making "large additions to their fortunes." This is precisely the difference between Overreach and the gentry characters in the play: he makes wealth his primary object regardless of the way it is gained, while the gentlemen, though not averse to wealth, prefer it to be "well got" and are not, at least rhetorically, consumed by avarice. As discussed above, the play goes to great lengths to assert the essential difference of gentle and common blood, a difference the play presents as under threat from characters like Overreach.

A New Way to Pay Old Debts makes the alliance between the legal profession and illegitimate social aspirations more explicit and deeper than either *Michaelmas Term* or *The Honest Lawyer*. In the earlier plays, the law is a value-neutral tool wielded by self-serving lawyers, but its disruptive effects are not integral to law or the legal profession. In contrast, Massinger's play shows a legal profession actively pursuing social disruption. Massinger draws a stark opposition between the goodness of the law itself and the malice and cupidity of its practitioners. Massinger overwrites the ambiguity and complexity of the represented legal field in *Michaelmas Term* and *The Honest Lawyer* in the interest of his play's basic conservatism and emphasis on order and degree. Here, lawyers stand on the side of aspiring commoners seeking to inveigle their way into the gentry by tricky, urban, and legal means—in other words, on the side of disorder. The law, on the other hand, at least intends to restrain such abuses by its practitioners even if it is finally powerless to control them. Marrall, rather than repenting and serving the law properly, offers to put his services at the real gentry's disposal. He is punished only by local authority and by his association with Overreach, not by the law. What this depiction suggests, then, is that by the time Massinger wrote his play legal professionals had achieved such a degree of autonomy that they could be represented as outside of the normal bounds of behavior and, implicitly, of authority. Institutional autonomy represented a threat to traditional hierarchy, and fears about this threat are refracted by cultural production into representations of lawyers as wholly rapacious and irresponsible agents of greed and disorder.

V

The picture of Jacobean society laid out in these plays is of a conflict-ridden and seemingly fluid society where traditional categories of rank and degree are subject to change. Characters of humble origin are capable, even if only temporarily, of competing with their betters, exploiting what the plays depict as gentlemen's naiveté. However, struggles of this sort were the exception rather than the rule these plays suggest. Historians have seen few signs that the kind of ambition Quomodo and Overreach express was common. What these plays demonstrate is that concern over such ambitions was high in the period. Characters akin to Overreach appear in many other plays, suggesting that the normative order was perceived as being under threat by newly powerful social groups.

These plays locate a large part of that threat in professional legal activities. All share a concern with the disruptive possibilities inherent to the growing power of the law courts in government and in daily life. Lawyers, as discussed above, were both more numerous and more visibly powerful than ever before, and their new position did not fit well into traditional notions of rank. As with administrators, and, to a lesser degree, writers, their authority was rooted in their professional qualifications, qualifications that were independent of birth, rank, or even in some cases wealth. Lawyers drew so much attention and criticism not because they were incompetent, unprofessional, corrupt, or poorly trained, but because they represented a social group whose power depended solely on themselves. The virulence (and inaccuracy) of the charges leveled against lawyers in these plays points to the autonomy of the field, an autonomy that seems to have been viewed as threatening.

Lawyers drew much the same kind of criticism that other professions were to draw in later periods. Their self-governance, their power, their elitism, and the arcane nature of their knowledge and practices all drew attacks. The autonomy of late Tudor and early Stuart common lawyers can be seen in their dissidence, in the internal debates over royal authority and the law, and in their willingness to support the cause of the parliamentary party.[137] Despite their political (and legal) support of the Commonwealth cause, lawyers were condemned and the legal system radically (if temporarily) reformed. Under the Protectorate, the courts and their officers came under strict government control, and the Inns' educational role suffered setbacks from which they never recovered. As Bourdieu argues, autonomy is the chief characteristic of a field and autonomy is best expressed in the degree to which the field translates questions into the terms of debate within the field. Lawyers in early modern England did precisely this as is demonstrated by the language of legal manuals and by the perceptions of lawyers in popular literature. As Tucker's book shows, the common lawyer was often ridiculed for his unrelenting conversion of life into law.[138]

That legal professionals had a recognizable public persona and that lawyers could and did found great landed families is well documented as is the fact that the legal profession drew on a wide range of the population from the sons of the upper gentry to those of the yeomanry and tradesmen. The implications of these facts are less clear. Ian Archer's argument about office-holding as an integrating and stabilizing force in London society can be applied to the law as well. Archer suggests the growing unwillingness of citizens to serve in the lower offices in city government is a product of a growing degree of social stratification and, more importantly, status conflict. This breakdown of traditional ordering principles contributes to the anxiety about stability that pervades the cultural production of late Elizabethan and Jacobean London. Changes in the legal profession contribute to this anxiety as well and for similar reasons. As Baker, Prest, and Brooks have shown, lawyers and the legal system more generally became increasingly autonomous in the period. Where the great common law courts were once strictly subordinated to the Crown—for example, suits at common law once could only be had by royal consent—by the middle years of the sixteenth century the three courts were coming to be relatively autonomous institutions only ostensibly regulated by the Crown. At the same time, the legal profession was becoming more and more self-regulating and self-authorizing. J. H. Baker writes, "when we contemplate lawyers as a whole, we are bound to wonder whether these diverse men of law can properly be regarded as constituting a single profession."[139] The unifying factor is the legal Inns in London; the vast majority of practicing lawyers were in some way affiliated with an Inn of Court or Chancery. As early as 1450, lawyers were defined by their association with an independent institution: the Inns of Court. Baker continues "Membership of an inn was probably conceived, by 1450, as being the clearest indicator of professional status and as a warrant for claiming the vague qualification 'learned in the law' which afforded protection against the stringent laws of maintenance."[140] Maintenance is the tort of meddling in another man's litigation, and until 1967 "the ancient crime and tort of maintenance confined the conduct of litigation to a professional class."[141] This professional class was identified by membership in one or another of the Inns, none of which were under the direct control or supervision of the Crown or of London's government.[142] By 1600, the legal profession was largely self-authorizing, was governed by a self-selected judicial oligarchy, and, as litigation grew, was ever more important to the government of England. That the institutional autonomy of the legal profession was anxiety provoking is demonstrated by the depictions of law and legal activity in the city comedies discussed above. In the plays, the law and lawyers are dangerously free of the conventional constraints of hierarchical morality. This anxiety recognizes the developing professional autonomy of lawyers, but fails to recognize that at the same time as lawyers became autonomous they developed a professional habitus that helped control and restrict the application of their potentially dangerous learning.

4
"The Art of Revels Hath a Settled Place in the City": The Revels, Civic Drama, and the Theater Professions

> The poet's eye in a fine frenzy rolling,
> Doth glance from heaven to earth, from earth to heaven;
> And as imagination bodies forth
> The forms of things unknown, the poet's pen
> Turns them to shapes, and gives to aery nothing
> A local habitation and a name.
> —William Shakespeare, *A Midsummer Night's Dream*

THESEUS'S DISCOURSE ON THE IMAGINATION IN *A MIDSUMMER Night's Dream* privileges the poet's pen in the embodying of "aery nothing," crediting the pen with the ability to make the intangible tangible. Writing, in Theseus's view, is sufficient to give shape to "the forms of things unknown." However, as Shakespeare and his contemporaries knew, the local habitation for those forms was not the result of solitary creation, emanating from the writer's pen, but was a collaborative project occupying quite tangible spaces and requiring equally tangible bodies and properties to produce the shapes Theseus describes and, as the lines are delivered on a stage, embodies. It has become something of a commonplace that playwriting was a collaborative process in early modern England.[1] Writers, we know, did not generally work alone and revision was the rule rather than the exception. However, another area of collaboration has received less attention—the collaboration between the playwrights, the actors, and those who provided the playing places, the costumes, the properties,

4 / "THE ART OF REVELS HATH A SETTLED PLACE IN THE CITY"   163

and the other physical elements necessary to theatrical production. These craftsman collaborators influenced the emergent profession in profound ways.

Playwriting, like the other professions under discussion here, emerged out of a long history. In England, the writing of dramatic entertainments stretches back at least to the medieval liturgy; however, as a specifically professional practice, the writing of plays takes its modern form only in the post-1576 world of London's theaters. That world—comprised of players, managers like Henslowe and Langley, writers, and audiences—exerted a necessarily formative influence on the developing profession of playwriting; shaping its concerns, its subject matter, and the self-perception of those engaged in it.[2] This is not news, as a large body of scholarship indicates, but the theater world was also inhabited by a large number of craftsmen whose influence on the plays and playwrights is less well documented and certainly less well discussed.[3] As with the writing of drama, the staging of drama has a long history and both histories are mutually constitutive.

Period discussions of the Revels—broadly understood to encompass theatrical performance, dance, music, and other forms of entertainment—point to an awareness of the importance of craft traditions to the production of entertainments and indeed sometimes downplay the role of the writer in favor of the designer or artificer.[4] In his description of London's educational institutions, Sir George Buc writes that he

> might hereunto adde for a Corollary of this discourse, the Art of Reuels, which requireth knowledge in Grammar, Rhetorike, Logicke, Philosophie, Historie, Musick, Mathematickes, & in other Arts (& all more then I understand I confesse) & hath a setled place within this Cittie. But because I haue described in, and discoursed thereof at large in a particuler commentarie, according to my talent, I will surcease to speake any more therof: blazing onely the armes belonging to it, which are Gules a crosse Argent, and in the first corner of the scutcheon, a Mercuries Petasus Argent, and a Lyon Gules in cheefe.[5]

Unfortunately, the "particuler commentarie" did not survive.[6] One striking thing about this description, brief and tantalizing as it is, is how many skills are combined under the umbrella of the art of the Revels. As Master of the Revels, Buc was familiar with many of the details of this art despite his profession of not understanding it very well. More importantly, Buc's comments point to the developed nature of "the Art of Reuels" in his London. He states that it comprises those disciplines usually associated with writing—grammar, rhetoric, history, philosophy—as well as music and mathematics. The "other Arts" mentioned here are likely to include such things as architecture, carpentry, lighting, and so on—the technical trades associated with the production of theater. Buc lists these skills as a theatrical trivium and quadrivium—as if there was a curriculum at a school of the Revels. Often attached to Stowe's Survey, Buc's *Third University* deals with London's educational institutions—making a claim that London is the third university—and the inclusion of the Revels in this work underscores the recognized institutional status of the Revels establishment. Not only is it important to the Crown, London chorography recognizes it as well. The traditional trivium of grammar, rhetoric, and logic is joined in this theatrical curriculum by a slightly revised quadrivium that substitutes history and philosophy for geometry and astronomy. In Buc's vision, the art of the Revels requires knowledge of these arts and these same arts have a recognized place in London.[7] His assertion derives from and reflects the regular and central part played by staged entertainment in his London—whether in the Revels Office proper or in the public theaters or on the streets, playing had a place in London and so too did the artificers supporting those entertainments. Stage production then as now demanded large numbers of technical professionals to provide the stages, props, lighting, and costumes essential to mounting a performance, and it is the influence of the early modern population of such theatrical artificers and their "art" on the development of early modern drama that is the subject of this chapter.

The records of the Revels Office suggest that the office's needs for stage carpenters, painters, tailors, designers must have had much in common with the needs of professional acting companies and theater managers. So too, the Lord Mayor's Shows employed a wide range of craftsmen, designers, and writers. An examination of various records of payments for "theatrical" services by the Revels Office and the City of London suggests the existence of a population who provided sophisticated carpentry, painting, costuming services to the Revels and to the city.[8] These skills are distinct from, though related to, those of traditional tailors, carpenters, builders, and other artisans. The patterns of employment and practice that emerge trace the activities of a group of technical professionals whose skills would also have been available to the professional theaters. Regrettably, the records are far scantier for the public theaters—for example, Henslowe's *Diary* provides little in the way of names beyond the Fortune contract with Peter Street—but the pattern still exists and Street's career is illustrative of the interconnections between craftsmen and the various kinds of theater.

A regular population of theater craftspeople emerges in the course of the sixteenth and seventeenth centuries—names recur in the extant records over long periods of time, sons inherit their father's roles, and so on—which points to the existence of a body of skills and techniques that actors, producers, and playwrights would have both known of and been able to depend on in their work. Moreover, as Buc attests, these skills and techniques were at least somewhat rationalized and thus teachable—having such a body of skills is one of the defining features of a profession. The passing down of skills suggested in the records has a strong resemblance to guild practices, but at the same time Buc's imagination of a school or academy for the Revels and its skills points to the existence of an at least somewhat rationalized set of skills possessed by Revels workers.[9] By paying attention to this group of artisans and the skills they brought to the theater, it is possible to establish a longer view of the professionalization of dramatic entertainments in the period that attends to both the more or less "literary" context of the emergence of professional playwriting and to usually underexamined aspects of the material conditions that shape it. I contend that professional dramatic writing owes as much to a body of stage techniques and design principles that derive from a usually underconsidered group of theatrical craftsmen as it does to a "literary" tradition.

The next chapter treats the emergence of canons of literary judgment in the theater; my concern in this chapter is with an emerging sense of and debate over the tools—scripts, props, costumes, or buildings—and capacities—representational, didactic, entertainment—of the theater. Robert Greene's *James IV* and Francis Beaumont's *Knight of the Burning Pestle*, plays that juxtapose different kinds of dramaturgy, will illustrate the way that craft practices are refracted into the drama at disparate stages of its professionalization.[10] Greene's play stages a debate over the *ends* of drama by representing a conflict between *kinds* of drama, and the kinds are signaled by reference to particular kinds of stagings. Neither side in the contest emerges victorious—Bohan's asceticism is contaminated by Oberon's aestheticism and vice versa—but what does emerge is a sense of the representational capabilities of the theater. Beaumont's play, written about seventeen years after Greene's, takes developed generic and staging conventions of the professional drama and parodies them in an effort to produce novelty, a play carrying the "privy mark of irony." Beaumont's parody has as much to do with literary convention as it does with physical theater. Both playwrights are concerned with novelty, both make use of technical resources to create it, and both write at transitional moments in the profession. Likewise, the professionalization of the theater extends beyond the playwrights and actors who are the usual subjects of investigation to include craftspeople whose influence on the emerging profession of playwriting is considerable.[11]

Most accounts of the emergence of writing for the theater in the sixteenth century focus on matters that can more or less comfortably be labeled literary—matters of education (with the appearance and subsequent decline of the University Wits), of competition between nonaffiliated playwrights (see Bentley or Shapiro), of stage language (Magnusson and others), or of influence of writer upon writer.[12] Theatre history has offered provocative accounts of what William Ingram calls the "business of playing" that point to the influence economic considerations have on the emerging professional theater and on playwriting.[13] Another context, the institutional context of what could be called the theater trades, is less often discussed. Books like Streitberger's *Court Revels* describe the changing structure of the Revels Office and Bergeron's *English Civic Pageantry* describes the City dramatic tradition, but the focus remains on the plays or masques and their writers without as much attention being given to the relationship between those masques and plays and the craftsmen called upon to realize the designs.[14] Dramatic possibilities, however, have much to do with technical ones—without the ability to build certain things (a flying chair, say) certain kinds of dramatic action are impossible if not strictly unimaginable—and developments in the one influence and structure developments in the other. As Andrew Abbott argues, professions interact in a complex ecology and to understand developments in one profession (here playwriting) one must understand its relations to professions close to it in social space.[15] In other words, the practices of a group of craftsmen who worked in the Revels Office and for civic entertainments such as the Lord Mayor's Show influenced the development of professional playwriting in early modern England. These craftsmen provided another part of the dramatic vocabulary employed by professional playwrights and the acting companies.[16]

Several important patterns emerge from an examination of the Revels, Works, and city records related to dramatic production. First, regular patterns of staffing can be discerned in the records of the Revels Office, the Works, and the Lord Mayor's Shows all through the period. The Revels Office tended to employ the same group of craftsmen year after year and each livery company tended to hire the same writers and designers from Show to Show. The Works' responsibilities at times overlapped with those of the Revels Office and at least some of the craftsmen worked for both and, at least once, the Works made use of Peter Street's skills.[17] It also appears that certain families tended to provide the same kinds of services for each office.[18] Second, the Revels and Lord Mayor's Shows employed a wide range of craftsmen doing specifically theatrical tasks. "Property-makers," painters, tailors, "other artificers," wiredrawers, and carpenters all provided various essential services to what amount to more or less permanent production companies.[19] Third, in the case of the Lord Mayor's Shows, production responsibilities shifted over time from being primarily in the hands of the livery company who had elected that year's mayor to being contracted out to individuals or groups who promised to provide the pageants in exchange for a lump payment that would cover the expenses of the production.[20] This may be an analogous phenomenon to the increasing reliance on professional players in the Revels Office after the 1580s.

The contracting out of these tasks by the livery companies and by the Revels Office to increasingly well-organized groups demonstrates the professionalization of these practices. Where amateur members of the livery companies once wrote, designed, built, and performed the Shows, by the end of the period all aspects of production save funding were the province of professionals—actors, stage architects, musicians, and so on. Many definitions of professionalization hold that professions are defined by the specialization of skills and the contracting out of tasks by the livery companies suggests that this was occurring in early modern London's theatrical trades. The example of "property-making," a term first used in the Revels records, underscores the specialization of skills that developed on the production end of the theater. This process occurs in tandem with the professionalization of writing. Both define the institutional context of early modern professional playwriting and professional theater more generally. In what follows, I will discuss the craft practices in the Revels establishment, in civic pageantry, in the public theaters, and then turn to an examination of the ways practices from these three sites of production inflect Robert Greene's *James IV* and Francis Beaumont's *Knight of the Burning Pestle*.

I

> In the mean time I will draw us a bill of
> properties such as our play wants.
> —William Shakespeare, *A Midsummer Night's Dream*

Records of craftsmen's work—bills for properties, to slightly distort Quince's line—can be found in a wide variety of printed sources, the most accessible being the various Malone Society *Collections* volumes dealing with dramatic records from the City, from the Chamber accounts, and from the Declared Accounts of the Office of Works, as well as Albert Feuillerat's twin volumes on the Tudor Revels Office.[21] These craftsmen's services could have been available not only to the Revels Office but also to the producers of the Lord Mayor's Shows and, it would stand to reason, to the professional theaters.[22] The Revels Office records transcribed by Albert Feuillerat give detailed accounts for the period from 1558 to 1589, covering the beginnings of the professional drama.[23] The records of the Lord Mayor's Shows in *A Calendar of the Dramatic Records in the Books of the Livery Companies of London* (Malone Society *Collections* 3) run from 1560 to 1640 providing a complementary look at the relations between the City and the Revels and between the City and the players, writers, and managers associated with the playhouses. References in the records of the Office of Works and in Henslowe's *Diary* provide instructive details about the particulars of stage building and, in the case of Peter Street, confirm that at

4 / "THE ART OF REVELS HATH A SETTLED PLACE IN THE CITY"   169

least one craftsman linked to theater was employed by the Crown for theatrical tasks. Taken together, these records describe the outlines of a theatrical field that extends from the writers and actors to carpenters, tailors, prop-makers, tirewomen, plasterers, wiredrawers, plumbers, carters, and a whole range of other artisans whose influence, though at times hard to see given modern scholarship's necessary focus on texts, is pervasive in the development of early modern drama.[24]

John Astington describes changes in the function of the Master of the Revels over the course of the sixteenth century in terms of a transition from acting as a "production co-ordinator" to becoming the licenser and censor we more usually imagine when thinking about the Office.[25] Until the 1580s, the Master oversaw a large and diverse group of workers who produced everything from costumes to large set pieces for the various royal entertainments during the Revels season.[26] An early Master, Sir Thomas Cawarden, Master from 1544 to 1559, was known for his ability to take designs from sketches to the stage and "presided over a production team which included skilled and sophisticated craftsmen and artists, with whom he was apparently able to communicate in an informed and knowledgeable manner."[27] Cawarden and his staff's success depended on a shared language concerning the demands of production.[28] This kind of interaction can best be described as professional—depending as it does on a collective sense of the project at hand—and indicates the importance of the craftsmen and artists Astington describes.

Cawarden's successors seem to have inherited a well-established cadre of theatrical craftsmen who appear year after year in the payroll records. For example, one tailor appears in all the accounts where craftsmen are named from 1558 to 1589. Thomas Clatterbook, whose first work for the Revels is as early as 1549–50, appears under the heading "Taylors and others" in 1558 as the second in the list (behind John Holt, Yeoman of the Revels 1550–70) and appears in almost every other account where workers are named for the next three decades. His forty or so years of work span the end of Henry VIII's reign, Edward VI's, Mary's, and well into Elizabeth's reign as well. As with Cawarden, his service survived changes in monarch, in religion, and in policy.[29] After Holt's death, Clatterbook takes the first place in the listings heading a more or less constant group of tailors and others who "attend" on the Revels for the Christmas to Shrovetide production season and the annual "airings" of the Revels stock through the period covered in Feuillerat's book. This suggests that these craftsmen enjoyed regular, year-round employment in theatrical production.

Painters, the other large category of Revels employees, follow a similar pattern of regular employment for a stable group of craftsmen. After 1558, Richard Bosum ("warden") George Bosum (Richard's brother), John Knight, Edmund and Thomas Bush, and a few others are routinely employed as painters and some of these people continue to serve after the Bosum brothers disappear from the records and the Lyzard family takes their place.[30] This kind of pattern also extends, though with more variations, to the mercers, haberdashers, boatmen, providers of "necessaries," ironmongers, and so on employed by the Office throughout the period covered by the detailed records transcribed in Feuillerat's Elizabethan volume. Aside from the obvious advantages of a reliably present group of artisans, such practices of hiring also are likely to have created an institutional memory about costumes, stages, set pieces, lighting arrangements, and other elements of production (such as how to transport large and fragile items), memories spanning most of the sixteenth century. The strong likelihood that such an institutional memory, a set of habitual practices, existed points toward the existence of a similarly well-established body of techniques of staging, of costume conventions, of design principles all linked to the production of spectacular theatrical events for an aristocratic audience.

Spectacular entertainments have a long history and a long institutional history as well. The Revels Office existed in one form or another at least from the reign of Henry VII and the Works has a considerably longer history. The Works was responsible for the construction of all royal buildings, including the temporary banqueting halls used for Tudor Revels. Many of these buildings resemble temporary theaters—some of the halls built on the Field of the Cloth of Gold were meant to house both banquets and to provide seating for entertainments. John Orrell's books on English theater design establish the existence of principles of what he terms "festive architecture," principles that he argues help explain the building of the Theatre in 1576.[31] Likewise, a body of techniques and design principles grew for the production of smaller elements—set pieces, properties, costumes. Feuillerat's transcriptions detail the names and occupations of the craftsmen, though, frustratingly, not much about their practices. Despite the lack of a work on scenic design not derived from classical or Continental sources or details in records of precisely what kinds of skills were involved, the Revels records do bear the traces of such skills in the way they list payees for services. The accounts are divided up by craft or task—tailors are paid separately from wiredrawers, for example. The specialist carvers, carpenters, and joiners responsible for building the grottoes or Castles of Love used in mock jousts are paid separately as well. Labor was necessarily divided in the Tudor Revels Office and that division of labor led to the development of specific skills.

One holder of such skills, John Carowe (a joiner and carver), appears in the Revels records for the first time in 1547 being paid for his work for Edward's coronation celebrations.[32] He appears repeatedly from this date until his death sometime in 1574. The account heading his name appears under varies from joiner to carver to, most often, "propertymaker."[33] The designation of propertymaker has very clear theatrical associations—all of the *OED* citations have to do with the theater—and points to a specific set of functions. In the records, propertymaking refers to both the manufacture of small items, like the heads, swords, and darts for which Carowe was paid in 1558, as well as the construction of large pieces of stage furniture and scenic devices that always have clear theatrical purposes. Carowe (sometimes spelled Carow or Caro) also oversaw other propertymakers. For example, the 1572 Christmas revels accounts read:

> Propertymakers: Iohn Caro, Iohn Rosse, Nicholas Rosse, Iohn Rosse Iunior, Thomas Sturley, Iohn Ogle, Iohn David for Caro.
>
> Propertymakers, Embroiderers, and Haberdashers: Iohn Caro, William Pilkington, Iohn Sharpe, Iohn ffarington, Iohn Tuke, Iohn Owgle, Iohn David for Caro, Ione Pilkington
>
> Propertymakers, Embroiderers, and Haberdashers: Iohn Carowe, William Pilkington, Iohn ffarrington, Iohn Tuke, Ione Pilkington, Thomas Tysant, Iohn David for Caro.

The payments are separated, likely to keep individual projects distinct. Carowe serves as a foreman of sorts for the prop-making crew on three separate occasions during the 1572 Christmas season. The placement of his name at the head of the list as well as his occasional extra payments for his "paines" indicates his position relative to his companions. John David's repeated payments here and elsewhere "for Caro" suggest some kind of connection between the two men—David may have been Carowe's apprentice or partner, but there is no confirming evidence for this.[34] The accounts link embroiderers and haberdashers to propertymakers, suggesting that the craft was polyglot, combining the skills of a variety of individuals in the production of the stage furniture required by the Revels production staff. Regardless of the particular content of any one property-making task, the same individuals tended to do them and thus developed a series of transmissible techniques applicable to a variety of tasks.

Clearer inferences about the passing on of skills can be drawn from the presence in these records of repeated references to John Ross and John Ross junior.[35] John Ross takes over from Carowe after his death in 1574 for at least one season ("Iohn Rosse after Iohn Carow his decease" and various Rosses continue being paid until the records become abstracts without detailed lists of payments. Ross and his workmen built large items for the Revels. In 1572, John Ross received payment "for mony to him due for making of A Chariott of xiiij foote Long & viij brode with a Rocke vpon it & A fowntayne therin with the furnishing and garnishing therof for Apollo and the Nine Muzes. by the composition & appoyntment of thaforeseide Iohn ffortescue esquier & Henri Sackford esquier."[36] This "chariott" is both large and complicated—twelve feet long, eight wide and carrying a "Rocke" with a working fountain—and seems to have represented Mount Helicon and the Pierian Spring. Constructing such elaborate "properties"—very like those built for the Lord Mayor's Show—demands a sophisticated group of craftspeople with a body of techniques of construction, decoration, and design that can be applied to varying demands from the writers and commissioners of the masques and plays that dominate the Revels calendar until the 1590s when detailed records disappear.

The "production values" of Revels shows were, in a critical commonplace, extremely high.[37] The bulk of expenditures in the earlier records are on elaborate costuming and settings for both plays and masques. In 1567–68, the Revels Office spent £643 on seven plays and six masques:

> the first namede as playne as Canne be, The seconde the paynfull pillgrimage, The thirde Iacke and Iyll, The forthe sixe fools, The fivethe callede witte and will, The sixte callede prodigallitie, The

4 / "THE ART OF REVELS HATH A SETTLED PLACE IN THE CITY" 173

sevoenthe of Orestes and a Tragedie of the kinge of Scottes, to which belonged diuers howses, for the setting forthe of the same as Stratoes howse, Gobbyns howse, Orestioes howse Rome, the Pallace of prosperitie Scotlande and a gret Castell one thothere side. Likwise for the altering and newe making of six Maskes out of ould stuffe with Torche bearers thervnto.[38]

The office was responsible for the building and "settinge forthe" of the plays and for the renewing of the costumes for the six masques.[39] These houses appear to have been purpose-built for each of these plays and must have been transported from the Revels Office's workshops to the place of performance. The complexity and difficulty of the task is demonstrated by the expense. Other records detail the high cost and corresponding splendor of the costumes devised for both masques and plays (a common formula states that the players had costumes and other necessaries out of the "Revels stuff"). In the process of producing such elaborate and spectacular shows, the Revels Office must have developed a body of techniques and a group of skilled artisans who employed those techniques. Both artisans and their skills would have been visible to the playing companies who became an increasingly significant part of the Revels schedule and those contacts would have exerted influence over the development of the professional stage.

II

> Like signiors and rich burghers on the flood,
> Or as it were the pageants of the sea,
> Do overpeer the petty traffickers
> That curtsey to them, do them reverence,
> As they fly by them with their woven wings.
> —William Shakespeare, *The Merchant of Venice*

Civic pageantry is more important to the development of the professional theater in terms of financial support, the development of technical resources, and the development of a theatrical rhetoric than often appears. Salarino's comment likening Antonio's ships first to seagoing burghers and then more properly to "pageants of the sea" registers the dignity and importance of such pageants—lesser ships "curtsey to them, do them reverence" as they sail past (1.1.11, 14).[40] His description would make little sense if the pageants were not both well known and well respected in Shakespeare's London. As David Bergeron argues in his *Practicing Renaissance Scholarship,* civic drama was far from a marginal form and commanded the talents of gifted writers and artificers.[41] Players and playwrights appear routinely in City records not only as objects of anxiety or criticism, but as payees for all kinds of services.[42] The close association of the livery companies with professional playwrights and theater craftsmen in the seventeenth century in what are among the single largest annual expenditures of the companies—the Shows—undermines the starkness of the traditionally perceived opposition between the City and the theater.[43] Civic pageants and other entertainments supported the writers and players from early on in the history of professional theater and that support plays an important role in shaping that theater.[44] The fact that the city oligarchs relied on professional playwrights (and, at various points, players) suggests a closer relationship between the city fathers and the theater business than often appears. Other records suggest that hostility to playing on the part of the City was far more ambiguous and situational than absolute and unchanging. The playwrights and the theater business offered services that the Companies found useful at least once a year. The employment of professional playwrights supports writers with substantial payments and exposes them to the mechanics of production at the same time. The links between civic pageantry and theater are close at the level of the writers, and, I would suggest, at the level of production.

The Lord Mayors' Shows records that appear in the Malone Society *Collections* detail payments for services similar to those recorded in the Revels accounts.[45] Tailors, painters, carpenters, and other craftsmen are all employed in the construction of the various pageants and water shows that accompanied the Lord Mayor's annual installation. The Shows became increasingly spectacular over the course of the sixteenth century and by 1600 the complexity and lavishness of the Lord Mayor's Show was at least equal to that of Revels productions.[46] Between 1540 and about 1600, the livery company from whose ranks the mayor was chosen appears to have produced and supervised the pageants itself. Routine mention is made of the selection of a committee to supervise the work and authorize the payments that are formally reported in the various account books transcribed in MSC 3. The shows included "pageants" to be carried along the parade route, fireworks and gunfire, speeches by both adults and children, and music. In 1561, for example, the Merchant Taylors' accounts include payments to the following:

1. Cabill, painter for drawing the pageant—5 s.
2. R. Drumslate and company—£3
3. Scutte, painter for the pageant—£5
4. Davys, porter for him and his co. who carried the pageant—26s 5d
5. John Tailor, master of the children of the late Monastery at Westminster for children who sang and played in the pageant—30s
6. Mr. More for hire of harps and his child playing in the pageant—21s
7. Ewen and Nicholas Hollonby for foist, shot, powder—£45
8. Matthew Sharpe for gunshot—£10
9. John Holt, mummer for attendance on children in the pageant—10s[47]

John Shutte was paid £12 to "make for this company ageynst the feaste of S & Iude next a pageant accordyng to suche a patterne as shalbe Devised to answer the speches also here devised & deliuered to hym and also he to fynde ij men to be woodhouses to cast sqwybes or wildefyer the morrowe aft' the seid feaste" (41). The speeches and the design of the pageant follow—David, Orpheus, Amphion, Arion, and Topas discourse on the hoped-for good government to come under the new Lord Mayor while standing on a pageant wagon (or platform carried by porters) decorated with the stories of each speaker.[48] No mention is made of the identity of the speechwriter or the designer of the pageant—it is conceivable that these tasks were carried out by members of the Company itself. The names and role of the writer and artificer become increasingly prominent in the Jacobean Shows and are almost never (with the exception of Munday) members of the livery companies. Early Shows do not demonstrate the kind of specialization in tasks that develops as they become larger and more elaborate. The largest expenditures in this early Show are for a foist and the pyrotechnics accompanying it (about a third of the total of £151).[49] Later Shows emphasize the pageants more, though fireworks remain important, and that emphasis complicates the task and may account for the turn to production syndicates.

A well-developed sense of the expected shape and form of the pageants emerges by the 1560s. Respecting such expectations, the Grocers decided not to have a barge for the Bachelors of the Company in the 1562 Show "for that there hath none thies many yeres paste neither of this Companie nor of any other companye / But onely A ffoyste and othr pleasure on the water as was vsed at the last tyme when sir Iohn Lyon was maior or at any other time syns" (45).[50] The elimination of the Bachelor's barge puts more emphasis on the spectacle, which now has no competition on the water. The Grocers show attention to precedent both from within their own company and from the practices of other companies; attesting to the existence of a collective expectation of what the Show should look like, at least in outline. These changing expectations are grounded in production techniques common to those engaged in designing, making, painting, and writing for the Shows.

Writers, first named in 1568, become an increasingly important part of the production of the Shows, especially in the seventeenth century. James Peele, father of the dramatist George Peele, is the first named writer in the MSC collection (1566), followed by Mulcaster (1568), and then by a succession of writers almost all of whom have close associations with the professional theater. George Peele, Anthony Munday, Ben Jonson, Thomas Dekker, Thomas Middleton, John Webster, and Thomas Heywood all wrote speeches for the Shows.[51] Interestingly, Munday's son Richard, a painter, was employed at least once to decorate banners for kettle drums.[52] This close connection between professional playwrights and civic entertainment provides some additional insights into the emergence of professional playwriting and professional theater more generally. Civic pageantry predates the building of theaters as does the Revels tradition and both practices made important contributions to the development of the early modern stage. The "literary" contributions of the Revels and pageant traditions have been well documented while the technical ones have received less attention.

The Shows themselves become increasingly elaborate, sophisticated, and expensive, and, most importantly, complicated entertainments over the course of the period. The array of skills needed to mount the Show increased and led to the development of a division of labor under a species of director. In 1609, the Show was called *Camp-bell, or, The Ironmonger's Fair Field* and honored the installation of Sir Thomas Campbell. The water pageant (provided by Robert Legg) included "a whale rounded close wthout sight of the boat to row with ffins / open for ffireworkes at the mouth and water vented at the head"; "a Mermaid wth her Combe stroking her hair and a Glasse in her other hand"; a sixty-foot-long foist with fireworks, and a galley with cannon in the bow and stern. The land shows (devised and provided by Munday who also wrote the speeches) include "two persons vpon a flyenge dragon and unicorne wth their speeches A bell field carried in A Chariott ... a greate pageant of A ball field guilt; wth an Ocean about wherein shall moove Mermaides, Tritons, & c playeng on instruments and singing."[53] Munday, John Grinkin, and Legg were paid large sums to provide the speeches, pageants, and water shows and appear to have acted as managers as much as artists. This kind of production demanded the services of a wide array of highly skilled craftsmen working under the direction of an equally skilled producer.

After 1600, the companies demonstrate a tendency to hire what sound like contractors to provide the pageant on behalf of the company from which the mayor had been elected. This shift makes sense in light of the ever-more spectacular nature of the performances—the livery of the company in question would likely have welcomed offers to do what must have become an increasingly complicated task—and is a sign of the professionalization of theater production. Rather than produce the shows themselves, the companies turned to experts. For example, in 1610 Anthony Munday (who also devised the pageant) and John Grinkin were paid £206 for "making, painting, gilding the pageant" and for "making and gilding more stuff" for Sir William Craven's installation as Lord Mayor. In 1612 Thomas Dekker and a Mr. Hemynge (who it is tempting to identify as John Heminge of the King's Men) were paid £197 for "the devise of the Land shewes being a Sea-Chariot, drawne by two sea-horses, one Pageant called Neptunes Throne, with the seaven liberall sciences, One Castle called Envies castle, One other pageant called vertues throne, and for the printing of the bookes of the speeches, and for the persons, and apparel; of those that went in them."[54] These large payments show that both sets of partners—Grinkin and Munday, Dekker and Hemynge—were acting as producers for the pageants—hiring craftsmen, producing scripts and what sound like commemorative books, arranging transport, and so on. In 1617, Thomas Middleton was paid the large sum of £282 for "the ordering overseeing and writing of the whole devyse for the making of the Pageant of Nations The Iland The Indian chariot The Castle of fame" according to a contract between Middleton and the Grocers.[55] The pageant was called *The Triumphs of Honor and Industry* (STC 17899) and closes with thanks to the painters Rowland Bucket (who also worked on the 1614 Show), Henry Wilde (painter for the 1604 Show), and Jacob Challoner. Middleton's name later appears routinely in collaboration with Garrett Christmas, a "carver."[56] Partnerships such as these between a playwright and a craftsman appear repeatedly in the accounts after about 1610 and become the dominant model of pageant production until the cessation of the Shows after 1640.

The growth of production syndicates in the seventeenth century provides more indirect evidence of the existence of group of craftsmen who were capable of providing specifically theatrical services to both the Lord Mayors' Shows and the professional theater. In the absence of more comprehensive records from the playing companies, it is hard to be definite about any of this, but the connections between Munday and Grinkin, between Middleton and Christmas, between the companies and (at least) the King's Men, suggest that theater professionals were a large and well-developed community in early modern London that extended beyond the players and their poets. The Christmas family's role in Jacobean and Caroline Lord Mayor's Shows indicates both the existence of such individuals and their connections to professional writers for the stage. As noted by David Bergeron in his 1968 essay, Garrett Christmas first appears in the City dramatic records in 1618 and "from this modest beginning he was to gain increasing importance in the overall production of the pageants."[57] For the next two decades, Christmas and his family dominate the production end of the pageants, acting as producers and general contractors for the majority of the Shows, regardless of who is writing the speeches.[58]

Bergeron describes the relationship between the writer and artificer as being largely harmonious and he notes that in many of the later pageants, the dramatist fades into the background as Christmas assumes more and more of the responsibility for negotiating with the various companies employing him.[59] While he notes this shift, he attributes it more to the "artistic talents and

4 / "THE ART OF REVELS HATH A SETTLED PLACE IN THE CITY"

apparently congenial personalities" of Christmas and his family than to what I take to be developing patterns of practice in the early modern theater professions.[60] In 1629, Christmas and Dekker produced the Show for the installation of Sir James Campbell as Lord Mayor. I cite the full text of the MSC 3 transcription of the record below in order to point to the nature of the collaboration between the men and to the kinds of negotiations they engaged in with the Ironmongers.

> 17 September Ironmongers' Court Books, iv. 4–5:
> Accordinge to an order of Courte made the xjth of August last. Theis p~sent treated and agreed wth the said Mr Crismas and Mr Decker conc'ning the making of the Pageants for the Shewe on the next Lord Maiors day after, the said xpmas and Decker pnted them wth a plott wherein was contayned 6 seuerall Pageants Namely
>
> > A Sea Lyon\
> > 2 Sea Horses/ for the Water
> > An Estridge
> > Lemnions forge
> > Tempe or the ffeild of hapines
> > 7 Liberall Sciences //
>
> ffor the accomplishing whereof they demaunded 200 li, wch theis present conceived to be an ouervalue, and thereupon offerred them 180 li wch they accepted of for the making and finishing of the said Pageants to be furnished wth Children and Speakers and their apparell and necessaries thereunto belonging. Landcariage by Porters; Watercariag by boats and Watermen as is accustomed. The Greene=men with their ffireworks; The Musicke for the Pageant; And to give the company 500 bookes of the declaracon of the said Shewe And the Comittees demaunded that
>
> > the Sea Lyon
> > the 2: Sea horses }be brought into the hall
> > & The Estridge
>
> (after the Solemnity) there to be sett vpp for the Companies vse, whereunto Mr Crismas excepted but was contented to deliuer backe the Sea Lyon and the Estrige, and desired to retaine the Seahorses to himselfe. All the rest he undertooke to pforme for the said some of 180 li effectually and sufficiently to the Compas Liking In witnes whereof they haue hervnto subscribed
>
> > Tho: Decker, Garett Chrismas [61]

The description here is characteristic of the late records of the Shows in both the level of detail (and is not unlike that given in many of the Elizabethan Revels records) and in the kind of operation being described. Christmas and Dekker contracted to provide "the Pageants for the Shewe" and presented the Ironmongers' Court with a "plott wherein was contayned 6 seuerall Pageants" including water and land shows.[62]

Notes about the presentation of the "plott" to committees established to evaluate them appear in many of the records—at times competing offers are recorded and the minute books detail bidding wars between rival production syndicates.[63] The various committees mentioned also have clear, if not articulated, expectations of what they want to see and how much it should cost. For example in 1619 the Skinners took proposals for the Show: "Anthonie Mundaie, Thomas Middleton, and Richard Grimston, poettes, all shewed to the table their severall plottes for devices for the shewes . . . itt is wholie referred to the Consideracon of the Comittees formerlie Appointed for business of the like nature and they are to make Choice of whome they shall best approve of."[64] The committees are appointed "for business of the like nature" and are wholly empowered to make decisions about the various proposals. The members of the committee evaluate the bids, bargain with the "proiectors," and make their choice. They exercise theatrical taste, judge the feasibility of the plots, and their decisions depend on their knowledge of previous shows and their requirements. Both sides of the negotiations share a language and that language is the language of the professional theater. There are a number of records where the company decides the bid is too high and offer a lesser payment. Some of the language in these records suggests that this too was customary practice and, more importantly, documents the existence of groups who could compete for the Lord Mayor's Show contract.

Returning to the 1629 Show, Christmas and Dekker demanded £200 for their services but were bargained down to £180. This sum was to cover all expenses associated with the Show, though on occasions the companies did grant extra funds to cover cost overruns. Negotiations over money are a recurrent feature of these transactions. The process of production as described places vastly more emphasis on the work of the artificer—Christmas's concerns and abilities take the forefront here. Christmas and Dekker accept the £180 for "the making and finishing of the said

Pageants to be furnished wth Children and Speakers and their apparell and necessaries thereunto belonging." The pageants are to be made, finished, and then furnished with children and "Speakers" to deliver Dekker's part of the pageant. Fabrication precedes writing and acting.[65] Christmas also wanted to retain the ostrich, sea lion, and sea horses for himself but settles for only the sea horses. Despite the fact that Dekker's name precedes Christmas's on the signature line, Christmas's role seems to be more important (he is constantly named first in the body of the record) and his requirements are those that are described and met by the company. "All the rest," the recorder writes, "he [Christmas] undertook to pforme for the said some"—"they" sign, but Christmas agrees to "perform" the contracted work.

Christmas's desire to retain the sea horses illustrates another important aspect of the field I am trying to outline here and one that contributes directly to pageant production and by extension to the writing of plays. Scenic properties, devices, costumes—all of the material of the theater was reusable in different circumstances.[66] *Londons Tempe* (the 1629 Show) opens with a "waterworke, prefented by *Oceanus,* King of the Sea (from whofe name the Vniuersall Maine Sea is called the Ocean) He, to celebrate the Ceremonies and Honors, due to this great Feftiuall, and to fhew the world his Marine Chariot, fits Triumphantly in Vast (but Queint) fhell of a filuer Scollup, Reyning in the heads of two wild Sea-Horfes, proportioned to the life, their maynes falling about their neckes, fhining with curles of gold" (*Londons Tempe* 1629). Dekker's text goes on to describe Oceanus's appearance in great detail and then finally turns to the speech Oceanus delivers from his "vast (but quaint)" chariot. The sea horses with their "maynes falling about their neckes, fhining with curles of gold" represent a major investment of talent, time, and expertise, and it is no surprise that Christmas wished to retain them. Moroever, the horses reappear in at least one later pageant. In 1632's *Londini Artium & Scientarium Scaturigo,* Arion appears with Oceanus, himself reappearing from the 1629 Show, and Amphretite "mounted vpon two Sea horfes, holding each of them a Staffe and a Banner."[67] The "Sea horfes" fabricated, it appears, for the 1629 pageants provide some of the material around which Heywood builds the speeches for the 1632 Show. Christmas's art, in other words, structures that of Heywood, and is connected to Dekker's script for the 1629 Show. The history of these horses, only one property out of what must have been a great many, is, in a way, like the history of the scripts and the playwrights who wrote them. The Show's structure is highly regular, following a fairly rigid pattern from year to year, and each set of speeches appears to have been intended to accomplish similar goals from year to year. There is, for example, always a water show with associated speeches. This encourages recycling of materials, speeches, and motifs—a recycling that structures Christmas's art in much the same way that Christmas's own work structures that of the writers.[68] Materials reappear in different contexts much as do scripts and their writers.

The circulation of writers, properties, scripts, and motifs characteristic of the Shows resembles the patterns of practice in the Revels establishment and offers instructive parallels to the professional stage companies whose records are so much more elusive and fragmentary. Plays like Thomas Preston's *Cambyses, King of Persia* blend materials from the diverse theatrical traditions circulating in the 1570s and signal some of those traditions by modes of speech and by properties associated with particular figures. For example, the vice Ambidexter speaks in a particular mode and carries physical signals identifying him as a vice—the dagger of lath and the language both being important indicators. Later plays parody this kind of strategy—see for example, Jonson's *The Devil Is an Ass* (1616) where the hapless devil Pug initially chooses an old-fashioned vice, Iniquity, as his assistant but is ridiculed by Satan as being hopelessly out of date:

> Had it beene but *fiue hundred*, though some *sixty*
> Aboue; that's *fifty* yeeres agone, and *six*,
> (When euery great man had his *Vice* stand by him,
> In his long coat, shaking his wooden dagger)
> I could consent, that, then this your graue choice
> Might haue done that . . .
> But *Pug*,
> As the times are, who is it will receiue you?[69]

Jonson's jokey introduction of Pug depends on reference to traditional stage markers of character, markers that are both aural and physical. The prop dagger marks the character as out of date just as much as the verse that Iniquity speaks when he appears. Jonson uses the same technique as Preston but by parodying it produces novelty. Despite having very different intentions, these

4 / "THE ART OF REVELS HATH A SETTLED PLACE IN THE CITY"

mutually reinforcing references in both plays recycle physical and aural elements in ways that resemble the ways that the producers of the Lord Mayor's Shows recycled motifs and props. These practices, shared in different contexts, point to ways in which the artificers and the playwrights and the actors influenced each other as the theater profession developed on London's public stages.

III

> Here's a marvail's convenient place for our rehearsal.
> This green plot shall be our stage, this hawthorn
> brake our tiring-house, and we will do it in action
> as we will do it before the Duke.
> —William Shakespeare, *A Midsummer Night's Dream*

Peter Quince finds marvelously convenient rehearsal space in Athens' woods, describing it in terms deriving the structure within which he delivers these lines.[70] Quince and his fellows understand their project by reference to the public stages even though their performance will be at court in a chamber likely to be without the apparatus of the theaters. Nevertheless, their efforts are structured by a sense of what drama is that is signaled by this reference to playhouses. Throughout 2.4, the mechanicals fret over what amount to questions of representation—Bottom's much-discussed anxiety about the ladies' reaction to the play's content turns on his faith in the power of representation—the same questions that Greene's *James IV* wrestles with in a slightly less comic register. The proposed solutions offered by Bottom and Quince are simultaneously literary and theatrical. Quince promises a prologue written in fourteeners to explain that no one really dies in the play and Bottom solves the wall problem by designing a costume. These solutions, laughable or not, mirror solutions playwrights and production companies found to similar, if less ridiculous, problems. For example, long set-speeches in plays like *The Spanish Tragedy* and *Tamburlaine* solve problems of time and space in ways not much different from the mechanicals'—Bottom and company may be silly, but they are part of a field and understand the parameters of that field.[71] *A Midsummer Night's Dream* meditates on imagination, on the bodying forth of strange shapes, but that imagination is structured by the parameters of the theater and specifically by those of the public stage.

The story of the building of the first London theaters has been told many times with an increasing richness of detail as more material is unearthed from the archives and from the archeological record. We now know more about the physical properties of the theaters of Shakespeare's London than at any time perhaps since they stood in Shoreditch, Southwark, and Blackfriars. This knowledge has, in the case of the Globe reconstruction, produced new thinking about the staging of early modern plays that has challenged influential accounts of performance practice.[72] A substantial body of work now exists on the physical properties of the theaters, on some of the individuals involved in their construction, and on the repertory of plays performed on their stages. Below, I will argue that the patterns of practice that existed in the staging of Revels Office productions and civic pageantry also contributed to the emergence of the theaters as well-understood and, to use Bruce Smith's term, well-designed "instruments" for the production of plays. Moreover, the craft tradition—the specifically professional skills of theater builders, propertymakers, and others—exerted a powerfully shaping force on the emergent profession of playwriting, an influence insufficiently remarked on in discussions of early modern dramatic writing.

Early modern dramatists worked in a field that took shape under a wide variety of literary, social, political, and economic influences. Much recent criticism has pointed out the extent to which the plays were shaped in response to a whole range of external conditions, both material and ideological, but less attention has been paid to the ways in which the institutional parameters of the theater business itself influences the development of professional playwriting. The above discussion of the elaborate and highly sophisticated production apparatus associated with the Revels and with civic pageantry demonstrates the range of professional skills available to the those engaged in theatrical endeavors in early modern London—even before the appearance of durable purpose-built theaters. The builders of theaters made use of those skills as the players, writers, and technicians moved back and forth between Court and City.

Under a series of economic pressures (chief among them the increasing expense of the elaborate staging of masques and other scenically demanding entertainments), the Revels Office began relying increasingly on the professional acting companies for its performance schedule after about 1580—professional players become the dominant performers after 1583 with the establishment of the Queen's Men—and production records get more and more attenuated until they become mere abstracts by the middle of the 1590s.[73] The tailors, carpenters, propertymakers, wiredrawers, haberdashers, and other artisans who had been employed by the Office, some for decades, may have found themselves without a reliable market for their skills, which, if descriptions of Revels shows are any indication, were considerable. In the absence of early documents with names of craftspeople, it is impossible to say if any of the Revels workers found their way to the acting companies, but the kinds of skills possessed by men like Clatterbooke, Carowe, Ogle, Holt, and the others were those needed by an emerging professional theater.[74] Moreover, the players were frequently at court and thus in contact with these craftsmen—at least with their props, lights, and costumes.

Given the paucity of records for tailors, carvers, and "propertymakers," in the *Diary* and other records, in what follows I will focus on larger carpentry projects—the building of the theaters. John Orrell argues that the construction of the playhouses of early modern London depends on the existence of a notion of what a playhouse should be "Beyond the practical needs of the actors and their audience lay a common sense of what they were about when they entered into that conspiracy of playing that creates the drama."[75] In Orrell's argument, that common sense of what "they were about" derives from the festive building tradition of the Tudor banqueting hall—a tradition closely associated with both the Office of Works and the Revels Office. Actors would have been almost as familiar with the form of the banqueting hall as builders and would have shared in this sense of the requirements of playing space. The practicalities of theater design derive from the physical demands of the need for a stage, for places for an audience to stand or sit, and for a way to control entry and to collect money.[76] However, as Orrell also notes, these functional requirements do not suffice to explain the building of the theaters—enormously complicated and risky ventures. One way to account for it lies simply in the idea that Brayne and Burbage may have, like Quince, imagined performing spaces in terms of what was visible in festive buildings that already stood.

The existence of production and construction techniques in the Revels Office are themselves some of the conditions of possibility for the building of the theaters. My interest here is not in the exact origins of the theory behind the design of the theaters, but with the implications of that "sense of what they were about" for early modern theater entrepreneurs and the playwrights who wrote for them.[77]

Peter Street is the best known and certainly the most discussed of the early modern theater builders. As the demounter and rebuilder of the Globe, the builder of the Fortune, and carpenter for many of Henslowe and Alleyn's entertainment projects, Street was instrumental in the development of the physical matrix in which early modern drama took shape.[78] Street's sense of design most likely derived as much from a kind of practical sense as from any kind of explicit theory of building. As William Ingram notes, Peter Street was the son of a London joiner named John Street who lived in the same parish (St. Stephen's) as James Burbage and his family. Also living in the same parish were a number of other people potentially connected to the theater, what Ingram calls "a remarkable collocation" (if his inferences are correct). One possible effect of this collocation is to put a group of theatrically interested or involved people in the same place at the same time—a serendipitous density of population that may have fomented ideas about whether and how to build a theater. Ingram goes on to speculate on who might have built the theater, doubting that William Sylvester, the object of Brayne's complaints about the Red Lion, would have taken on the job: "Let us not forget, the carpenter Robert Burbage, who in 1576 had been a freeman for three years, and now had just taken on as his apprentice his possible relative Henry Burbage, aged twenty-three. Peter Street is a candidate in only a technical sense, for in 1576 he was still finishing his apprenticeship. His master, Robert Maskall, might have been hired to do the job, in which case he would have gained his experience early; but my own feeling is that Robert Burbage is the likeliest candidate."[79] The suggestive pattern Ingram discerns, however cautiously he approaches it, does afford some room for speculation about potential contacts between the builders of the first theaters and Peter Street, builder of the Globe and Fortune. He may not have been part of the Theatre project, but did do his apprenticeship in close proximity to it and to those involved. Street was, as is well known, hired to dismantle the Theatre in 1599, some twenty-three years after its construction by some of his neighbors, and rebuilt it as the Globe. In 1600, Henslowe hired him to build the Fortune following the specifications of the Globe's stage.[80] Street also renovated the Paris Garden and worked on buildings around Alleyn's bear-baiting arena in Southwark.[81]

Street's work on these varied endeavors, contracted by different and competing theater enterpreneurs, signal his notoreity as a builder of performance spaces. How he came to dismantle the Theatre is, unfortunately, a matter for evidenceless speculation, but his later work on the Fortune and for other Henslowe projects most likely results from his reputation—a reputation that depended in large part on the Globe Theatre. Bruce Smith argues that the Globe (and by inference other theaters) offered playing companies spaces eminently suited to the propagation of sound: "In effect, the stage of the Globe acted as a gigantic sounding board: made of a reverberative material, it translated vibrations in the air above into standing waves in the air underneath, producing a harmonically rich amplification of the voices of the actors positioned on top."[82] The theaters, in other words, were well designed to suit the needs of performers who had no other means of artificial amplification. This kind of design derives, as Orrell notes, from a tradition of festive construction that is associated with the Revels Office. Street and the other theater builders, a small but not insignificant group, possessed a set of special skills whose application was predominantly theatrical.[83] Street's success in building such effective instruments both gives him an amount of notoriety and establishes a pattern of building that other theater entrepreneurs imitate—Henslowe has him build the Fortune stage to the exact dimensions of the Globe's.

Street's later career was dominated by construction related to the theaters and entertainment more generally, and this work appears to have gotten him into trouble with the Carpenters. Susan Cerasano notes that Street was an important member of the Carpenters' Company and only ran into difficulties with the Company around the time he turned to theater building.[84] Cerasano cites the Carpenters' attempts to regulate the trade in terms of the usual search regime—checking the quality of workmanship for example—but also in terms of the population admitted to the Company's ranks. The companies had, as noted above, a complicated relationship to the theater business, worrying about it at the same time they employed its services. Street may have represented a particularly uncomfortable confluence of worries for the Carpenters. He is a member of the Company, he is closely associated with the theater, he appears not to have paid as much heed to some Company rules as was necessary, and he was the holder of an increasingly specialized and recognizable set of skills. Cerasano suggests that what she calls his "professional downfall" with regard to the Carpenters is directly related to his theatrical work. While Cerasano appears to see his success in avoiding being ruined in terms of a chance connection with Alleyn and Henslowe and the theater industry, it appears that his reputation as a theater builder is just as important. Theatre building is a complicated thing and Street, more than any of his contemporaries, seems to have mastered it.[85] The Carpenters were jealous of their monopoly on the building trades in London and it is tempting to see Street and his specific skills as a developing threat to at least part of that monopoly.[86] This aspect of the theater business is difficult to investigate given that evidence is scarce, but Street's skills and the precedents set by the construction of the Globe and Fortune contributed to the development of the theater professions in a variety of ways—most clearly in providing a stable space in which to work.

Street's most famous building, the Globe, was well known for its structural magnificence and the lavishness of its ornament as were most of London's theaters. Neither of these features of the theaters is accidental and both have structuring effects on the drama produced on the Globe's stage. Evidence of these effects is as subtle as the acoustic evidence cited by Bruce Smith and as obvious as the mechanicals scenes in *Midsummer Night's Dream* cited above. The relationship between the actors' words and the theater is complex and the one always influences the other. Elizabethan and Jacobean theater was deeply metadramatic—concerned with its institutional status, its place, its role—and plays often profit from staged self-reference. Examples of this kind of self-reference like Jonson's parody of stage devils in *The Devil Is an Ass* rely on references to costumes or props associated with modes of theater to mark differences. Jonson's attack on the history plays in the prologue to the Folio *Every Man in His Humour* makes use of these kinds of allusions but also refers to the stage itself:

4 / "THE ART OF REVELS HATH A SETTLED PLACE IN THE CITY"

> As, for it, he himselfe must iustly hate
> To make a child, now swadled, to proceede
> Man, and then shoote vp, in one beard, and weede
> Past threescore yeeres: or, with three rustie swords,
> And help of some few foot-and-halfe words,
> Fight ouer *Yorke*, and *Lancasters* long iarres:
> And in the tyring house bring woundes to scares.
> He rather prayes, you will be pleas'd to see
> One such, to day, as other playes should be.
> Where neither *Chorus* wafts you ore the seas;
> Nor squeaking throne comes downe, the boyes to please;
> Nor nimble squibbe is seene, to make afear'd
> The gentlewomen, nor roul'd bullet heard
> To say it thunders; nor tempestuous drumme
> Rumbles, to tell you when the storm doth come;
> But deedes, and language, such as men doe vse:
> And persons, such as *Comoedie* would chuse,
> When she would show an image of the times.
> (pro. 6–23)[87]

Jonson ridicules specific material practices in this prologue in the name of his brand of comedy—and those practices that are tied to playhouses.[88] All of these techniques can be located in actual plays (Shakespeare's first tetralogy being only one) and are linked to the kinds of skills discussed above. In addition, the use of the tiring house to "bring wounds to scars" locates the plays criticized specifically on actual stages in the public theaters. Like Quince's recognition of a bush as a tiring house in *Midsummer Night's Dream*, the reference to the tiring house here understands a kind of drama in terms of the physical space it occupies and the material techniques it uses—the rolled bullets, the creaking throne, and the squibs. Jonson argues these methods are to be scorned for poetic reasons (in the name of comedy) and, more importantly (if bulk of comment is an indication) because they are silly or inadequate to represent the actions described (as with the drum signaling the arrival of a storm). Jonson desires a drama that would "use deeds, and language such as men do use" in order to show "an image of the times" and in order to achieve it, he derides an alternative mode by attacking its stage technique.[89]

Henry V's Chorus, the Chorus attacked in Jonson's prologue, constantly refers to the supposed representational inadequacies of the theater in ways that bear at least a surface similarity to the kinds of criticisms Jonson makes. The Chorus's comments have often been taken to underscore the importance of the words spoken and the audience's imagination rather than the spectacle seen in the Globe's wooden O. This is most certainly the case, but the Chorus is also archly underplaying the actual capacities of the theater to represent the events and scenes the play presents:

> Suppose within the girdle of these walls
> Are now confined two mighty monarchies,
> Whose high, upreared, and abutting fronts,
> The perilous narrow ocean parts asunder.
> Piece out our imperfections with your thoughts;
> Into a thousand parts divide one man,
> And make imaginary puissance;
> Think, when we talk of horses, that you see them
> Printing their proud hoofs i' th' receiving earth;
> For 'tis your thoughts that now must deck our kings.
> (pro. 19–28)

Peter Womack points out that the representational problems the Chorus alludes to have largely been solved: "The banal problems which seem to be troubling the company's spokesman . . . have been overcome many times over the previous decade."[90] Womack sees the Chorus as producing a "rhetorician's aporia" that enlists the audience's imagination in the project of imagining an English community. Both the aporia and the imaginative project Womack identifies draw at least some of their power from a series of technical expectations and capabilities the theater had established in the course of the previous decade.

English theaters, as the Chorus forcefully reminds us in the epilogue, have "oft" shown events of similar scope. In addition to doing the kind of political work Womack describes, the Chorus's false humility also calls attention to what the actors and their stage *can* do. For example, when the Chorus tells the audience that " 'tis your thoughts must deck our kings," he is being at least slightly disingenuous. The costumes that "decked" the actors were one of the most consistently spectacular of early modern theater's resources—as many have noted, costumes often came from the wardrobes of the aristocracy. Thus, in some ways, when the bishops of Canterbury and Ely enter in 1.1, they are "like themselves" at least in habit.[91] This is likewise true of 1.2 when

Henry appears for the first time. Indeed, the splendor the theater itself presents a vision of the magnificence of the court especially as the theaters in some ways at least resembled the great banqueting halls constructed by the Office of Works. While the "flat unraised spirits that [have] dar'd / On this unworthy scaffold to bring forth / So great an object" (*Henry V* pro. 7–10), protest their inability to present the fields of France, they do produce good representations of the magnificence of the court, a magnificence in part produced by the work of the Revels Office in conjunction with the professional theater.

Henry V's Chorus relies on two intimately related sets of practices. The first, and more important in terms of the actual speeches, are the practices of playwriting—practices Shakespeare repeatedly calls attention to as he refers to the pen and the author over the course of the play. The second, less remarked on, are practices related to the technical side of theater. From the repeated descriptions of the scaffold, the seats which move from London to Southampton to France, of the walls of the Globe itself, Shakespeare calls attention to the ways in which the play depends on the physical substance of the institution of the theater. Robert Weimann's recent *Author's Pen and Actor's Voice* describes a dialectic between playwrights and players in the development of the professional theater. Weimann's discussion of the relation between actors and authors links developments in genre and in modes of representation to a broadening set of relations between different parts of the theater enterprise. The craftsman's tools play as important a part as the actor's voice or author's pen in the development of the professional theater.

IV

> Changes as decisive as an upheaval in the internal hierarchy of different genres, or a transformation of the hierarchy within genres themselves, affecting the structure of the field as a whole are made possible by the *correspondence between internal changes* (themselves directly determined by the transformation in the chances of access to the literary field) *and external changes* which offer to new categories of producers . . . and to their products consumers endowed with dispositions and tastes in harmony with the products these producers offer them.
> —Pierre Bourdieu, *The Rules of Art*

Robert Greene's generic experimentation (witnessed by his prose romances as much as his plays) bears witness to the kind of generic upheaval Bourdieu describes. Generic upheavals, in Bourdieu's view, depend on the coincidence of changes in education and reading practices—"chances of access"—with changes in audience—audiences disposed to enjoy new products.[92] Greene (like Marlowe and Nashe) occupies an exemplary position in the changing field as an example of the new kind of producer Bourdieu refers to above. He was educated in the humanist moral tradition but found himself working for audiences whose dispositions did not necessarily match up well with the kinds of products he had been trained to produce. The success of Marlowe's plays influenced Greene's dramaturgy (his early works imitate the Marlovian "mighty line" and the spectacular sweep of *Tamburlaine*). Marlowe blended classical learning and popular dramaturgy in a way that transformed the Elizabethan playwriting. Greene's early plays reflect his searching for models in a radically changed (and radically unstable) professional theater. His work seems to have been intended to appeal to both learned and unlearned audiences in much the way that Marlowe's seems to have.[93] This effort, an effort to produce and respond to "external changes" depends as much on Greene's sense of the dispositions of the audiences for which he wrote as it does on his awareness of other changes, changes in the technical side of the theater in which he worked. The kinds of external changes Bourdieu describes depend both on educational shifts and a shifting and developing sense of what is possible in the theater—an awareness of the practical aspects of production helps audiences respond to new work at the same time that those changes help make that new work possible. An examination of Greene's work can serve as a useful way to explore this conjunction of social, educational, and structural changes as they relate to the emergence of the theatrical field.

Greene's play *James IV* demonstrates a sophisticated and ambivalent awareness of theatrical convention in the many metatheatrical comments that appear throughout the play (one character, Slipper, functions as an incarnate comment on the conjunction of the play world and that of the audience).[94] The play's generic hodgepodge (its mixture of romance, pastoral, and tragedy [finally undermined by the other elements] under the rubric of a history play), points to Greene's painfully self-aware dramaturgy. The play's literary self-consciousness—its pointing to the tradition of the Machiavel, its allusions to pastoral, and its announcement of itself as artifice—derive, at least in part, from Greene's academic training, which steeped him in a deeply allusive and imitative style of composition. This is a well-established feature of Greene's work overall but Greene's self-awareness in the play also points to the advent of a theatrical field in which playwrights work as part of a broad group of theatrical professionals. Greene is not only aware of a literary tradition, but also of a crafts tradition—of traditions of staging. Greene alludes to and exploits the resources of these craft traditions as much he does traditionally literary ones.[95]

Despite critical charges about the play's incoherence and the frame's irrelevance, the frame that describes *James IV* as a contest between Bohan's rigidly didactic aesthetic and Oberon's more playful and pleasure-loving art is an essential part of the play and offers a glimpse of Greene's fraught relations with the theater professionals for whom and with whom he worked. The opening chorus establishes that the "demonstration" of reasons to leave the world and live in a tomb that Bohan promises to present will be overtaken by a contest between two models of theater—one that delights and another that instructs. Bohan's didactic play occupies one extreme where didacticism takes over from drama while Oberon's dumb shows, music, and dancing occupy another where sumptuous display and beauty take precedence over content. Both extremes have literary and theatrical antecedents that are linked to particular stage practices. Greene's practice straddles these extremes and *James IV* represents a professional entertainer's accommodation to a moralist's desire to instruct mediated by the institution of the theater. This accommodation is specifically professional and points to the beginning of a contest over the profession's self-definition that shapes its development in profound ways.[96]

Greene's reputation as a dramatist has suffered due to readings of the play that fail to situate it in the context of theatrical production in the 1590s. To take a characteristic example, in an essay tellingly entitled "Robert Greene as Dramatist," Kenneth Muir writes:

> Although rash critics have compared Bohan to Shakespeare's Oberon and Prospero, the induction and choric interludes between the acts are tedious and unnecessary. It is absurd for

Bohan's sons to appear as characters in the play he is presenting before Oberon, especially as the events are supposed to have taken place in an earlier age; it is artistically confusing when Slipper is rescued from the gallows by the intervention of Oberon; and Greene does not explain how Nano, who takes service with Ateukin in the first act, should be in Dorothea's service in the second. It may be added that the scenes in which Lady Anderson falls in love with the disguised Dorothea are bungled, and nothing is made of Sir Cuthbert's jealousy. The debate between a Lawyer, a Merchant, and a Divine (5.4), which was presumably intended to illustrate the evil results of James IV's misgovernment, is never once brought into focus.[97]

Muir's reaction is typical of critics of this play and Greene's drama in general. He likes the story of James's temptation, fall, and redemption, but sees the frame and other "interludes" as tedious or unnecessary. Ironically, without the frame, the internal narrative makes almost no sense: the abrupt fairy-tale resolution is a direct result of Oberon's intervention in the didactic story Bohan attempts to tell. Muir also misrepresents the "problem" of Nano's service: Ateukin takes him into service intending to present him to Dorothea as his gift. Even the otherwise strange conversation among the lawyer, divine and merchant makes sense in the context of the frame's debate. All of the elements Muir castigates the play for are precisely those that make it interesting as theater, and, more importantly for my argument here, offer insight into the field of production of which it is a product. The play combines multiple genres (romance, comedy, dance, etc.)—making use of the multiple possibilities available to a dramatist at this early stage in the development of the professional theater—as part of Greene's attempt to instruct while entertaining. The combination is far from seamless, as Muir recognizes, and this reflects not only Greene's uncomfortable relationship with theater, but also the field's inchoate state.

James IV thematizes a dramatic contest, constantly reminding audiences that Bohan and Oberon are staging a struggle between what the play imagines as two kinds of drama, not least by keeping them onstage throughout the performance.[98] The resolution of Bohan and Oberon's contest is a kind of provisional synthesis of didacticism and aestheticism (for lack of a better and less anachronistic term). This stage debate between kinds of theater depends as much on these "literary" categories as it does on

4 / "THE ART OF REVELS HATH A SETTLED PLACE IN THE CITY"

the existence of recognized patterns of staging that derive from the practices of theater craftsmen. In other words, these patterns signal distinctions between kinds of playing practice. Where the Revels Office produced the kinds of shows Oberon's fairies perform, the itinerant professional acting companies of the earlier sixteenth century produced sparer shows more akin to that which Bohan strives to present. The aesthetic questions of the play depend on an awareness of the material conditions of different styles of playing. Greene strove to straddle what emerges in the play as the extremes of professional practice, and this straddling produces *James IV*'s often confusing blend of stoic *contemptus mundi* and luxuriant visual pleasure. Rather than synthesize what McCluskie terms a theater of spectacle with a theater of ideas or choose one above the other, Greene appears to have juxtaposed them, playing with already established visual and material languages, in an effort to call attention to various conventions of playing. This kind of attention to convention, a key feature of later drama like Beaumont's *Knight of the Burning Pestle*, is specifically professional and here depends on the existence of conventions of staging that derive from a combination of Court and City traditions. The uneasiness and problems inherent in staging the play bear witness to the difficulty of the project Greene and his contemporaries undertook.

Despite Muir's assessment of the play's framing fiction as an irrelevant excess, the various seemingly disparate elements of the play make sense *as a play* only in the context of the frame. Ironically, without the frame the charges Muir makes are accurate. In other words, the play makes no narrative sense without the constant presence of Bohan and Oberon. The best example of this is the all-but incredible resolution of what is set up as a tragic plot in a comic scene of reconciliation.[99] In the chorus after act 3, Bohan claims that the rest of the play will be "ruthful," but his claim is not borne out by the action:

> . . . it would make a marble melt and weep
> To see these treasons gainst the innocent;
> But since she 'scapes by flight to save her life,
> The king may chance repent she was his wife.
> The rest is ruthful, yet to beguile the time,
> 'Tis laced with merriment and rhyme.
> (chor. 3. 3–9)[100]

Instead, the play ends in reconciliation and feasting, not the "ruthful" tragedy Bohan promises. Merriment and rhyme take over completely by the end of the play, driving the action rather than being a palliative to the "ruthful" play Bohan promises here. In fact, the primary focus of the play turns from the narrative of James's corruption to the relationship between Bohan and Oberon whose details emerge through the contested staging of the play.[101] Bohan clings to his aesthetic even at the end of the play despite losing control of his narrative to Oberon. After the final scene, he tells Oberon:

> Mark thou my jig, in mirkest terms that tells
> The loath of sins and where corruption dwells.
> Hail me ne mere with shows of guidly sights;
> My grave is mine, that rids from despites.
> Accept my jig, guid king, and let me rest;
> The grave with guid men is a gay-built nest.
> (chor. 5. 5–10)

Bohan's "jig" does not, however, "in mirkest terms" tell a story of corruption and punishment.[102] The moral tale Bohan claimed would instead show why he hates the world becomes a pastoral, comic play that culminates in a mass reconciliation between couples, nations, and kings in which only the servants are punished. Oberon, not Bohan, has the final word and his antics sing and dance Bohan to rest.[103]

The play is thus less about the (totally unhistorical) fall and dubious redemption of James IV than about the current state of the field of cultural production, and more specifically of the subfield of writing for the theater. Greene worked in a theater that was fundamentally collaborative and his play reveals the signs of this collaborative field. Bohan's refusal to see how his play has changed in production—in the process of collaboration—is only one of these signs. The jigs, dumbshows, and other apparently extradramatic interludes are, as my colleague Kirk Melnikoff notes, the product of a theater that was "still in the early stages of professionalization [and] popular elements like jigs and hornpipes would have been seen as no more extraneous to a play than a good story."[104] Greene's innovation as playwright is to attempt to unify these popular elements with the plot of his play and, more interestingly, to do so in such a way as to make a point about the purpose of writing plays. The play thematizes a *dramatic* contest, constantly reminding the audience that Bohan and Oberon are staging a struggle between two kinds of drama not least by keeping them onstage, or, as in our show, just offstage, throughout the performance. The resolution of Bohan and Oberon's contest is a kind of rapprochement between didacticism and, for lack of a better term, aestheticism. It is not, though, a resolution that synthesizes or simply combines these modes. Instead, what Greene does is exploit the representational resources of disparate literary and stage traditions in the service of his argument about the purpose of playing and, more importantly, to make a good play.[105]

Several recent critics have pointed to Greene's conscious artistry in the play—calling attention to the way he plays with generic conventions, to the frame, and to Greene's staging of a kind of dramatic theory. A. R. Braunmuller writes that Greene "probes . . . the relation between dramatic illusion and the dual realities represented by the theater audience and the stage audience. . . . Greene has encircled the conventions of the internal play with another illusion having conventions of its own and dramatic aims necessarily different from those implicit in the internal play."[106] Braunmuller's attention is mostly given to "literary" aspects of the play—seeing it as a strong precursor to Shakespearean romantic comedy—and he stresses Greene's authorial experimentation. Likewise, Alexander Leggatt describes an internal debate in the play between the "satiric, moralizing, finally despairing" Bohan and the "festive, comic, life-affirming" Oberon. Leggatt argues that "the conflict between them is one familiar elsewhere in Greene's work . . . the conflict between a celebration of the pleasures of life and the impulse to repent and renounce those pleasures."[107] These concerns are literary and more or less biographical, focused on what Greene is doing with specifically writerly conventions. Finally, Clinton Crumley's discussion of the play as "historical romance" pays careful attention to the way the frame narrative works with history and romance to gesture "toward a domain somehow untouched by chronicle history."[108] All of these welcome reappraisals of the play, and of Greene's dramaturgy more generally, focus on what amount to philosophical questions about aesthetics, about history, and about genre.[109] These approaches to the play need to be supplemented by more attention to the material underpinnings of the questions the play asks—the aesthetics of Greene's play, in other words, are grounded in a theater where craft traditions, kinds of staging, were as subject to contestation as written traditions.

James IV begins this contestation by depicting Oberon's fairies dancing about the tomb where Bohan lives with his sons Slipper and Nano in stoical retreat from the corrupt world. After some dancing and stage business, Oberon questions Bohan about why he "dwellest in a tomb and leavest the world" (ind. 38–39). This question is the opening gambit in a Bohan offers a biographical explanation—he lived in the court, in the country, and in the city, but found all these ways of life wanting and thus has retreated to his tomb—but then offers to show Oberon why he hates the world "by demonstration" (ind. 106):

> In the year 1520 was in Scotland a king, overruled by parasites, misled by lust, and many circumstances too long to trattle on now, much like our court of Scotland this day. *That story I have set down*. Gang with me to the gallery, and *I'll show thee the same in action* by guid fellows of our countrymen; and then *when thou seest that*, judge not if any wise man would not leave the world if he could.
> *Oberon:* That will I *see*; lead and I'll follow thee. (ind. 109–14; my emphasis)

Bohan imagines his play as a visual demonstration—the enactment of a treatise on world loathing—and envisions his audience judging what they are shown after the demonstration ends. He introduces the play by talking about writing—setting down the story—and then stages it "in action" with good fellows who mysteriously appear to act the story. The opening scene of the frame stresses Bohan's authorial position, one of stoical remove and moralistic intention, while Oberon is represented as being a member of the audience—passively watching the demonstration of why one ought to forsake the world. Both Bohan and Oberon speak of seeing the play, placing emphasis on the visual impact of the action, but, as the play proceeds, the kinds of vision they imagine become increasingly distinct.[110] Bohan's "demonstration" is meant to show the reasons for his retreat "in action"—it is a thesis-driven show—where Oberon seems more interested in the visuals of the play as visuals, bracketing the thesis of the production as Bohan imagines it. The framing device calls attention to the artificiality of the play—its composedness—and, more importantly, initiates a debate over the form and intentions of its artifice.

Bohan's stark, world-forsaking aesthetic comes into conflict with Oberon's more luxuriant and visual one throughout the choruses, and those conflicts go some distance toward explaining the otherwise totally inexplicable happy ending of the play by demonstrating Oberon's increasing influence over the action. The Oberon-Bohan conflict also refracts what seem to be Greene's ideas about different kinds of staging. In one of the first of the choric interludes, Oberon recognizes Bohan's skill in depicting the way of the world: "Here see I good fond action in thy jig, / And means to paint the world's inconstant ways; / But turn thine eyen, see which I can command" (chor. 6.1–3).[111] What Oberon commands is a dumb show, a pageant of sorts, depicting *"two battles strongly fighting the one [led by] SEMIRAMIS, the other [by] STABROBATES. She flies, and her crown is taken, and she [is] hurt"* (chor. 6.3.1–3). The dumb show is introduced here as a demonstration of Oberon's skills—skills put into competition with Bohan's "jig."[112] Jig has a very specific theatrical meaning and both Bohan and Oberon consistently refer to Bohan's play by this term. Jigs are common features of the public stage—one of the things *Tamburlaine*'s induction claims to be distancing itself from—and Greene, influenced as he is by Marlowe, knew this as well as his audience. Oberon's dumb show—the performance *he* can command—is a very different kind of display. "Two battles" enter and fight leaving, Bohan tells us, "everywean ... betaint with bloud," and Oberon has to gloss the show's allegorical significance because Bohan cannot tell what it means: "What gars this din of mirk and baleful harm, / Where everywean is all betaint with bloud?" (chor. 6.4–5). Oberon explains that this shows "what is worldly pomp" by describing the fall of Semiramis "in her pride."

The "din of mirk and bloud" Bohan responds to is a spectacle that depends on visual effects for its force—how else is an audience to recognize Semiramis and Stabrobates but by some kind of visual cue—and Oberon's shows all depend on this kind of display. Bohan's appreciation of Oberon's skill is tempered by his desire to have Oberon "mark [his] talk and prosecute [his] jig" (chor. 6.14–15). The chorus calls attention to several distinct aspects of performance. First, by labelling Bohan's play a "jig" and linking its presentation to "talk," the chorus locates it firmly on the public stages and connects it to a particular kind of staging—one that relies on the spoken word and what Bohan calls action more than iconic staging or costume. Second, Oberon's show is pure spectacle—mystifyingly so—and requires explication from its creator. This type of display is characteristic of Revels production, and, interestingly, the pamphlets recording Lord Mayor's Shows include detailed explications of the meaning of the various figures and props in the shows. Finally, it opposes "talk" to vision—words to spectacle. Moments like these explicitly oppose one kind of performance to another—Bohan's jig versus Oberon's dumb show—and both kinds of performance emphasize different kinds of craft.

Oberon's dumb show may be illegible to Greene's onstage audience, but Bohan's "demonstration" is also unclear. Neither Oberon nor Bohan appears capable of easily interpreting the performance before them. In chorus 7, for example, Oberon expresses confusion about the importance of what he has just witnessed: "How should these crafts withdraw thee from the world?" (chor. 7.1).[113] Why, in other words, should the relatively innocuous events depicted have led Bohan to renounce the world and flee to the wilderness to live in a tomb? Prompted by the apparent inadequacy of Ateukin's "crafts" to explain Bohan's loathing of the world, Oberon presents a vision of "pomp" which presumably does give a reason to "withdraw . . . from the world" (chor. 6.1):

> Enter CYRUS, Kings humbling themselves; himself crowned by olive, that at last dying [is] laid in a marble tomb with this inscription:
>
> > Whoso thou be that passest, for I know one shall pass, know that I am Cyrus of Persia, and I prithee envy me not this little clod of clay wherewith my body is covered.
>
> All exeunt. Enter the King in great pomp who reads it, and issueth, [and] crieth, "Ver meum." (chor. 7.2.1–8)

Craft in this chorus most immediately refers to Ateukin's trickery, but by opposing it to Oberon's pomp, Greene draws an analogy between that craft and the play itself. In other words, the play's craft, its art, is at this point inadequate to explain Bohan's motivations, which calls forth Oberon's "pomp" in an effort to do what the play produced by Bohan cannot. Oberon supplements the Ateukin-as-Machiavel plot with this visual show that, by being seen, is meant to convey a meaning Bohan's play does not. Oberon's productions appeal to an audience trained in reading visual allegory, the kind of stage design Orrell describes as being one of the foundations of English theater architecture, a dramaturgy distinct from or, maybe, supplemental to the word-oriented drama Bohan strives to produce.[114]

Bohan's insistence on calling his play a jig—no matter how unlike a jig it is—locates his work in a popular tradition that, it could be argued, Bohan is trying to revise into a useful form. While *Tamburlaine*'s induction scorns the "jigging vein of rhyming mother-wits," Bohan embraces at least the label, appropriating the social and institutional capital associated with it, in order to revise it and attempt to produce a satire of courtly corruption. Likewise, Oberon's "pomp" and the series of dances, dumb shows, and tableaux that constitute it owe a great deal to the kind of visual spectacle characteristic of both the Revels and the Lord Mayor's Shows and put that immediately recognizable symbolic capital in service of an analogous agenda of demonstration, of entertainment, and finally, like Bohan after all, of instruction. Both presenters depend implicitly on the audience's awareness of and response to different traditions of staging, traditions which here, as elsewhere, are represented by quite specific technical elements—elements that derive from an established craft tradition that helped produce the theaters on whose stages Greene's play was produced.

Both stage traditions, curiously, fail here. Neither Bohan nor Oberon understands the other's show. The kinds of representations offered are insufficient to the task at hand, whatever it may be. Greene, unlike Bohan or Oberon, does not restrict himself to one or another kind of representational strategy—both Bohan's "jig" and Oberon's "pomp" are available to him for strategic use. Greene's juxtapositions of failed shows in *James IV* points to his own difficult relationship with the stage and to a larger and long-standing crisis in the field, a crisis that cannot be explained solely in literary terms. Nor can it be explained in craft terms. This crisis is a representational one—archly looked back on by *Henry V*'s Chorus—that Greene resolves by foregrounding it. In *James IV*, Bohan's thesis-driven demonstration founders at the same time that Oberon's spectacle does and out of that conjoined failure emerges the play. Greene's play makes itself out of a set of references to theatrical practices and thus comments on the state of the field while also offering itself up as a different kind of representation—a representation that also represents the professional theater. Greene's experiment may not be as successful as those of other writers, but his experimentation, like that of Marlowe or Shakespeare relies on an encounter between well-understood set of staging traditions and the body of skills the playwrights brought to the theaters.

The choruses engage in the kinds of debates that Braunmuller, Leggatt, and Crumley describe, but also, in their emphasis on distinct kinds of theater craft, represent an uneasy linking together of very different stage traditions in the service of Greene's dramaturgical intent. Moreover, the questions Greene appears to be asking have as much to do with fundamentally theatrical questions about communicating across the stage-audience divide as they do with philosophical questions about pleasure and renunciation, satire and comedy, and so on. The more abstract questions that Braunmuller, Leggatt, Crumley and others rightly discuss find their root in Greene's wrestling with the varied technical tools at hand in order to convey his meaning in the play. The conflict between the two aesthetics in this play refracts a struggle with what Greene found to be refractory materials. The illegibility of both Oberon and Bohan's productions at various times in the play and their ongoing mutual revisions of the performance raises questions about the didactic usefulness of drama by struggling with the material components of that drama—the struggle with the material precedes the questions and drives the kinds of resolutions Greene comes to, however provisional they may be.[115]

V

Francis Beaumont's 1607 play, *The Knight of the Burning Pestle*, depends for much of its comic energy on a conflict between the worldly sophistication of the acting company and its normal audience at Blackfriars and what is represented to be the backwards taste of the Citizen and his wife, members of the Grocers' Company. [116] In turn, this conflict depends on the assumed existence of two very different norms of theatrical presentation that are assumed to be related to different populations.[117] The urbane sophisticates to whom the arch commentary of the Prologue

Boy appeals expect a witty city comedy (*The London Merchant*) while George and Nell, the Citizen and his wife, desire an heroic tale of a grocer errant. However, the distinctions between these populations are far less rigid than often appears and that the play itself appears to be doing something other than simply poking fun at one or the other side of the conflict it stages. This is a point noted by many recent critics of the play—the intended play (*The London Merchant*) seems to many writers to be deserving of the parody offered by George and Nell and the play's relationship with its audience is more evenhandedly critical than was once allowed.[118] In what follows I will expand on these readings and argue that the play, like *James IV*, grapples with disparate dramatic elements—both "literary" and technical—at a transitional moment in the development of early modern drama.[119]

The play, as is well known, was not successful in its first performances. Whether this was due to the play's satire of almost the entire social spectrum or because of its generic strangeness is unclear.[120] The failure was of such a scale that Walter Burre printed an explanatory dedication to Robert Keysar, the manager of the Blackfriars theater where the play was produced, when the play was published in quarto.[121] Burre's dedication describes the play's "unfortunate" birth and lack of acceptance in a manner that stresses *Knight*'s novelty:

> Sir, this unfortunate child who in eight days (as lately I have learned) was begot and born, soon after was by his parents (perhaps because he was so unlike his brethren) exposed to the wide world, who for want of judgement, or not understanding the privy mark of irony about it (which showed it was no offspring of any vulgar brain) utterly rejected it; so that for want of acceptance it was even ready to give up the ghost . . . If it be slighted or traduced, it hopes his father will beget him a younger brother who shall revenge his quarrel, and challenge the world either of fond and merely literal interpretation, or illiterate misprision. Perhaps it will be thought to be of the race of *Don Quixote*: we both may confidently swear it is his elder by a year. (dedication 1–24).[122]

The "unfortunate" child was exposed and rejected soon after its birth, Burre speculates, because it is so different from its brethren among Beaumont and Fletcher's "offspring," further stressing the play's uniqueness. According to Burre, the play met with rejection because its audiences either lacked judgment or misunderstood the "privy mark of irony" the play bears. This too, suggests the novelty of the play—it did not, at least initially, find an audience predisposed to respond favorably to it.[123] A successor play, imagined by Burre, is to defend *Knight* against the various potential (and actual) offenses of the audience—misprision, foolish or literal interpretation—and assert its worth as a legitimate child of Beaumont's invention.[124] *Knight* did, of course, find its place with its other brethren, but only with the advent of an audience disposed to receive it. In Burre's eyes, this audience is a reading audience, one with the judgement and understanding to appreciate its privy mark of irony. All of the reasons Burre gives for the play's failure appeal to its reading audience's superior judgment—those who did not appreciate the play's irony in the theater are thus labeled as "wanting" judgment, as incapable of "understanding," as foolish, as either illiterate or overliteral. The reference to *Don Quixote* (published in Spanish in 1605 and not available in a printed translation until 1612) underscores Burre's effort to appeal to a self-recognizing elite audience who would have been familiar with the *Quixote* and asserts *Knight*'s priority to Cervantes' novel.

Burre's comments refer to a specific version of the play—the printed quarto that saves *Knight* from "perpetual oblivion"—and argues based on a reading audience. Burre's quarto is dedicated to Keysar, the manager/owner of Blackfriars, and the person who rescued the manuscript. Burre flatters Keysar, as is usual in dedications, commending his "judgement, understanding, and singular love to good wits" (dedication 11). Not coincidentally these are the qualities Burre sees as being necessary to appreciate the play's "privy mark of irony" properly, and they remove the play from the theater and relocate it in the library. For instance, at least some of Burre's commentary plays with the difference between a reading (literate, "discerning") and a theatrical audience (lacking judgment, vulgar) in ways that have been reproduced in modern receptions of the play that see it in terms of a clash between elite and popular culture. That clash typically assumes that where elite culture (the theater of the boy companies) is sophisticated, popular theater is not.

In an important reconsideration of the purpose of Burre's dedication, Zachary Lesser argues that Burre takes a calculated risk in printing the failed play. Burre, Lesser suggests, was confident "that he could exploit a new and important cultural division in the theatrical market. Print (as opposed to the stage) allowed him more precisely to target his imagined audience, and the techniques that enabled him to attract his buyers could turn a failed stage play like *The Knight* into a successful publication."[125] Burre's imagined audience is an audience capable of the judgment alluded to above. While usefully calling attention to this move as specifically related to print, Lesser underemphasizes the play's own attention to its audience and his argument reproduces the usual pattern that opposes the "poor taste, naïve dramatic sensibility, and ostentatious dispensing of money" of the Citizens to the tastes of the gentlemen (and implicitly the reading audience) the Prologue Boy constantly apologetically addresses.[126] Lesser's argument about Burre's marketing tactics for the printed version of Beaumont's play avoids the usual class-based distinctions between fractions of the reading audience, but, by imputing naivete to the Citizens, reproduces that distinction in terms of the onstage audience. The play complicates this picture consistently throughout and reveals the outlines of a more dynamic and self-conscious field. This is not to say that the play makes no distinctions, but that they are far more dynamic and unstable than Burre suggests. *Knight* may have failed in its early performances, but not because of a straightforward clash between a clever fraction of the audience and a less sophisticated one. Beaumont's play places at least two highly developed theatrical modes into contact in ways that highlight both the affinities and distinctions between them.

Combining styles like *James IV*, the play's induction and choruses break the frame of the narrative repeatedly, allowing Rafe, the Citizen's apprentice, to enter both the playworld and the acting company presenting that world.[127] Rafe's presence invigorates a highly conventional city comedy plotline by injecting different theatrical modes into what is in some ways a single-note production.[128] His interruptions, like Bohan's, derive from a different mode of theater, one that the players recognize as alien to their planned play. Rafe's "audition" in the induction serves as a good example of this. Told to "speak a huffing part" by Nell, Rafe produces a version of Hotspur's "drowned honour" speech from *1 Henry IV* and, as further evidence of his qualifications, George and Nell list his acting credits:

WIFE: Nay, gentlemen, he hath played before, my husband says, Mucedorus before the wardens of our company.
CITIZEN: Ay, and he should have played Jeronimo with a shoemaker for a wager. (ind. 82–85)

1 Henry IV (1596), *Mucedorus* (1598), and the hoary *Spanish Tragedy* (1588?), are all old plays linked to a "huffing" or bombastic style of acting and to the outdoor theaters.[129] Hotspur's speech, itself a species of parody, serves as a kind of stereotypical example of the style and synecdochally refers to a whole group of plays. Rafe's performances to this point have, significantly, been before the wardens of the Grocers' Company—part of the governing body of the company and thus linked to civic authority—a group theoretically hostile to theater but who are, in fact, sophisticated audiences of and patrons of drama.[130] Rafe, as his subsequent appearance in the play suggests, does indeed have a good deal of theatrical experience, it is just not of the same kind as that of the acting company he is inserted into by the Citizens. The Citizens' tastes are clearly aligned with the repertory of the outdoor playhouses whose writers and actors populated civic drama—George's list of favorite plays derives from his attendance of public theater plays that, in Hattaway's word "glorify" the city—not with the city comedies that, as George says, after seven years "have still girds at citizens" (ind. 8). Generic distinctions (history or romance vs. city comedy), associated theatrical ones (public vs. private), and what the play represents as homologous social distinctions (citizen vs. gentry) provide a large part of the play's comic energy, and a great deal of that comedy derives from the perceived (and actual) instability of these categories and oppositions.[131]

The distinctions that the play puts into conflict presuppose the existence of a variety of readily recognizable theatrical languages that depend not only on different playwriting conventions, but on different *staging* conventions. As noted above, Rafe's audition demonstrates his ability in "huffing" parts—parts linked to the outdoor theaters—but the chivalric narrative the citizens create piecemeal for him owes as much to the theater of display characteristic of both court revels and civic pageantry as it does to the language of the plays many of Rafe's speeches cite or allude to. For example, late in the play, a bored Nell and George desire Rafe to reappear in an exchange worth quoting at length:

4 / "THE ART OF REVELS HATH A SETTLED PLACE IN THE CITY" 207

CITIZEN: What shall we have Rafe do now, boy?
BOY: You shall have what you will, sir.
CITIZEN: Why, so, sir; go and fetch me him then and let the Sophy of Persia come and christen him a child.
BOY: Believe me, sir, that will not do so well. 'Tis stale; it has been had before at the Red Bull.
WIFE: George, let Rafe travel over great hills, and let him be very weary, and come to the King of Cracovia's house, covered in black velvet, and there let the King's daughter stand in her window all in beaten gold, combing her golden locks with a comb of ivory, and let her spy Rafe, and fall in love with him, and come down to him, and carry him into her father's house, and then let Rafe talk with her.
CITIZEN: Well said, Nell, it shall be so.—Boy, let's ha't done quickly.
BOY: Sir, if you will imagine all this to be done already, you shall hear them talk together. But we cannot present a house covered with black velvet, and a lady in beaten gold.
CITIZEN: Sir boy, let's ha't as you can then.
BOY: Besides, it will show ill-favouredly to have a grocer's prentice to court a king's daughter.
CITIZEN: Will it so, sir? You are well read in histories! I pray you, what was Sir Dagonet? Was not he prentice to a grocer in London? Read the play of *The Four Prentices of London*, where they toss their pikes so. I pray you, fetch him in, sir, fetch him in.
BOY: It shall be done.—It is not our fault, gentlemen.
(4.27–51)

The scene is laden with specifically theatrical references that emphasize the differing styles and production capacities of different theaters—capacities all the interlocutors acknowledge. Moreover, George and Nell display a knowledgeable taste for particular kinds of drama, making specific reference to plays both as performed (the "Sophy of Persia" idea) and as written. George's "read the play" command marks both his mastery of the material—he knows what he likes and can cite examples—and his (represented) literacy.[132] Not only does George like live theater—Nell complains that he's always going to plays but never takes her—he reads printed plays as well. Heywood, the playwright George cites as exemplary, becomes closely associated with the

Lord Mayor's Show, writing a number of them in the 1620s and '30s.[133] Beaumont shows George and Nell as more sophisticated than they appear on the surface. Rather than simply making the Citizens a butt of knowing jokes, they display a legitimate variety of theatrical taste, a taste rooted in London civic drama and in the plays of Dekker, Heywood, and the early Shakespeare. Here, the Boy's ignorance (or snobbishness) instead of the Citizens' hypothetical naiveté is held up to ridicule.

In fact, Heywood's *Four Prentices of London* evinces a striking degree of theatrical self-awareness and sophistication about its practice. In the prologue, Heywood introduces the play with not one, but three prologues who go on to debate the meaning and relevance of the play's title, content, and intention. Prologue 1 enters complaining about the presence of the two other prologues: "What meane you my masters, to appeare thus before your times? doe you not know that I am the Prologue? Do you not fee this long blacke veluet cloake vpon my backe? Haue you not sounded thrice? Do I not looke pale, as fearing to be out in my speech? Nay, haue I not all the signes of a Prologue about me?"[134] Prologue 1's complaint asserts his claim to be the "real" prologue to the play. The claim is based on a series of formal and theatrical markers the speech calls attention to. First, Prologue 1 wears a long velvet cloak—a sign of his position. Second, he appears after the third sounding—the usual sonic signal that the play is about to begin. Third, he shows signs of stage nerves—a sign of his readiness to speak. All of these, Prologue 1 avers, mark him as the true Prologue to the play despite the fact that the other Prologues bear the same signs. The colloquy that ensues demonstrates the sophistication of both the playwright and his presumed audience at the Red Bull. All three prologues discourse on the play's legitimacy—of title, of form, and of content. The debate here is humorous but that humor depends on the audience's willingness to engage in the kind of metatheatrical discourse being staged.[135] That discourse presents a dramatic theory by way of theatrical and technical signals that are far from naïve or unsophisticated.

When George asks for something the Boy believes to have been done before at the Red Bull, his request is dismissed as "stale" with what seems like a slighting reference to the status of the theater that also imputes a lack of sophistication to plays and audiences at the Red Bull. The Boy's refusal to produce an imitation of a Red Bull play points to the imagined acting company's sense of itself as committed to innovation, even though *The London Merchant* is a highly conventional play.[136] This voiced commitment—whether borne out by the action or not—in turn points to a sense of status—Red Bull material is not for this company, they are engaged in some other kind of project, one that may, by virtue of that same innovation, be superior to that of other theaters.[137] However, this representation (and this reading) depends on the audience's awareness of the variety of theatrical possibilities available on contemporary stages, and is itself the object of parody. These possibilities are also at issue in Nell's request for a spectacular courtship between Rafe and the Princess of Cracovia. Faced with this request for spectacle, the Boy is forced again to refuse, but this time for what appears to be a different reason.

The Boy tells her that the company cannot fulfill her request—at least not in full—because they are not equipped to produce such a show. The "house covered with black velvet, and a lady in beaten gold" Nell wishes to see is beyond his company's production capacities, and the Boy is forced to offer the speech she asks for, but not the show. The joke here, as elsewhere, relies on the apparent ludicrousness of the request and the way the citizens settle for what the Boy tells them they can have—a set of speeches.[138] However, the request would not be nearly as ludicrous, or perhaps not ludicrous at all, in a different context—that of a different theater or of a civic pageant. Civic pageantry, in fact, could and routinely did present such shows for the enjoyment of the city.[139] As an example, Heywood's own later *Londons Ius Honorarium* opens with a water show depicting Scylla and Charybdis: "Vpon the water are two craggy Rockes, plac'd directly opposite, of that diſtance that the Barges may paſſe betwixt them & theſe are full of monſters, as Serpents, Snakes, Dragons, &c. ſome ſpitting Fier, others vomiting water, in the baſes thereof, nothing to be ſeene, but the ſad relicks of ſhipwracke in broken Barkes and ſplit Veſſels, &c. The one is calld *Silla*, the other *Charibdis*, which is ſcituate directly againſt *Meſſana*; *Scilla* againſt *Rhegium*."[140] The rocks are occupied by the Sirens and Ulysses, the speaker of the water show's speech, sails between them to signify "wise and discreet" leadership. This is only one of many such descriptions that point to the elaborate and spectacular staging that was demanded by those sponsoring the Lord Mayor's Show. This is a relatively late (1631) Show, but is characteristic of the design of earlier Shows. A "house covered with black velvet, and a lady in beaten gold" would be well within the capacities of any of the producers of these pageants. Nell asks for a spectacle that is possible of presentation, only not in the theatrical space she occupies in the play. Thus, for the acting company onstage, the joke in this scene depends on what they can present as a vulgar and uninformed taste for spectacle, while for the Citizens, the joke depends on what they can present as the Boy's ignorance, allowing George and Nell to instruct the Boy about theater.

Much like Greene's *James IV*, the play concludes with what Merrythought rightly calls an unexpected reconcilement that closes with Nell's inviting the cast and audience home for a "pottle of wine and a pipe of tobacco." Merrythought's reconciliation refers to the settling of the differences between his family and Luce's, between himself and his wife, and, most importantly, between the various kinds of theater represented onstage in the course of the play. Act 5 begins with an interlude in which Rafe delivers a Mayday speech in old-fashioned fourteeners ("London, to thee I do present the merry month of May; / Let each true subject be content to hear me what I say: / For from the top of conduit head, as plainly may appear, / I will both tell my name to you and wherefore I came here" [int. 5.26–29]), which parodies part of Don Andrea's induction speech from the *Spanish Tragedy* and Mayday speeches more generally.[141] The play then brings the disparate elements of the plot together, along with the various theatrical modes associated with those elements, into a conclusion that unites Jasper and Luce and their families.

The reconcilement at the close of the play unites all the players—Rafe makes a literally final appearance to deliver a long and typically parodic death speech—and also unites a whole series of different theatrical modes.[142] Objecting to Rafe's death, the Boy complains that: " 'twill be very unfit he should die, sir, upon no occasion, and in a comedy too" (5.274–75). Appealing to comic decorum, the Boy makes a final (still unsuccessful) effort to silence the Citizens and is answered with an appeal to another set of principles: "Take you no care of that, sir boy, is not his part at an end, think you, when he's dead?" (5.276–77). Both the Boy and the Citizen are right—there is no reason for Rafe to die (and the manner is particularly absurd—an arrow through the head that

Rafe wears as he enters), but at the same time, Rafe's part *is* over when he dies and if there is to be closure for the *London Merchant* plotline there needs to be closure for Rafe's and death makes as much dramatic sense as anything else. Rafe, joining the rest of the company onstage, brings together three very different dictions—the historical, the tragic, and the comic—and two kinds of theaters—the public and the private. *Knight* marks the varied voices—from the early Shakespeare and Kyd's declamatory mode to city comedy's efforts to represented words "such as men do use"—as much by their respective staging histories as by their diction.

Beaumont's experiment in this play—the "privy mark" Burre misrecognizes as an effect of social distinctions—places many of the possible theatrical modes available to him on stage at the same time. Well-established patterns of staging drama come into contact in this play at a moment when new forms are emerging (tragicomedy, city comedy, comical satire). Those patterns depend equally on a written tradition and a trade tradition—Beaumont never attempts to separate particular dramatic voices from their associated sets of properties—and the hoped-for pleasure of the play, its innovation, depends on the juxtaposition and humorous use of all these sets of practices. Generic change, as with Greene's earlier play, relates to and is signaled by technical aspects of theater, technical aspects audiences respond to just as much as they respond to written or, better, spoken ones. The prologue can be read to say that the play is made from a combination of theatrical traditions:

> From all that's near the court, from all that's great
> Within the compass of the city-walls,
> We now have set our scene. Fly far from hence
> All private taxes, immodest phrases,
> Whate'er might show like vicious:
> For wicked mirth never true pleasure brings,
> But honest minds are pleased with honest things.
> (ind. 110–16)

The play draws "from all that's near the court"—the Revels tradition of song, dance, and spectacle—and "from all that's great / Within the compass of the city-walls"—the public theater, civic drama—to "set our scene." The speech places the court as parallel to all that's great within the city, not as identical. It does not set its scene outside the city, instead it uses the resources of court and city drama to produce a play that hopes to please with "honest things"—metaphoric things and actual ones.

VI

Taking "metadrama" seriously, as I think these plays require, demands that we extend our definition of the term to include elements that have typically been excluded from consideration.[143] These include the physical properties (of whatever description) that actors as much as playwrights made part of their craft. The artisans who made these things—whether property heads or entire buildings—were a significant part of the theatrical field and as part of the field influenced the profession of playwriting. As Abbott argues, professions exist in an ecology, a system of mutually influencing forces, and that ecology is as important to professions as the interior logic of each individual professional group. Playwrights were influenced by craft traditions as theater artisans were influenced by the demands of playwrights. Buc's vision, cited at the beginning of this chapter, of a school of the Revels points to the ways these disciplines interact. His imaginary curriculum links grammar, rhetoric, logic, philosophy, history, music, and "other Arts" under the umbrella of an "Art of Reuels."[144] This Art does not privilege particular aspects of the "curriculum" but brings them together. Buc's image is a useful reminder of the importance of understanding the emerging theater profession in terms of relations between its various constituents and constituencies.

Professional craftsmen aware of the needs of the theater were a key part of the early modern field of theatrical production. Traditions of theater building, propertymaking, scenic painting, and set building developed in tandem with traditions of acting and writing. The officers of the Crown in charge of entertaining the monarch were well aware of the specialized skills of theatrical artisans and, whether in the Revels Office or the Office of Works, made extensive use of their skills. The City oligarchy, despite their worries about the effects of playing, were also not slow to employ the skills of artificers like Garrett Christmas and his sons in the production of the civic pageants that made such an important contribution to the spectacular order of London life.

4 / "THE ART OF REVELS HATH A SETTLED PLACE IN THE CITY"

And, the public theaters depended on the buildings created by men with extremely specialized skills—skills most readily applicable to what John Orrell terms "festive" architecture. Playwrights thus operated in a field that is structured not only by competitions between writers—such as the Poet's War, the subject of the next chapter—but by a series of well-understood habitual practices directly related to practical matters of staging. Whether consciously as in the many metadramatic moments in the plays discussed above, or unconsciously as the parameters of the possible in imagining Theseus's "forms of things unknown," craft traditions had an important role in shaping the emergent profession of playwriting.

Greene's play enacts a contest between kinds of drama by testing the representational capacities of two kinds of theater. Appearing through a contest between spectacle and action, this contest works out "literary" questions by using all the means available at the time Greene wrote. Those resources are literary, deriving from Greene's education, and artisanal, deriving from the craft of the theater in which he was working. In *James IV*, both sets of practices, of resources, are mutually dependent and the play as a whole emerges out of Greene's use of both. The craftsman's artifice is no more a means to his artistic ends (a notion that in terms of the period makes little sense) than Greene's script is a means to the ends of the craftsman. Theatrical artifice in all senses of the word is both the form of Greene's play and, in a sense, the content.

Beaumont's later play takes up similar issues, but instead of staging a contest between what Greene sets up as opposed poles, *Knight* puts various modes of artifice onstage at the same time, drawing on all the tools available to Beaumont and the Children of the Revels. The play has often been read as an effort to appeal to what are imagined to be elite audiences at Blackfriars. Walter Burre's dedication plays to a self-identifying reading elite but the play itself engages in a different project. Both the acting company and the interrupting Citizens demonstrate sophisticated dramatic tastes that Beaumont playfully juxtaposes and in the juxtaposition produces a novel play—one that didn't find a stage audience until the 1630s. Nell and George, far from being naïve or unintelligent, represent one variety of theatrical taste, a variety that is as legitimate as the implied one the players claim to be playing to. However, in order to recognize this, it is necessary to pay attention to the care with which Beaumont depicts the technical aspects of what the Citizens want. Nell's request for a velvet-covered house does not come from nowhere—it derives from and represents the kind of show staged every year at the installation of the Lord Mayor (and, incidentally, is quite similar to the performances Oberon presents to Bohan in *James IV*). Beaumont's dramatic experiment thus depends on careful and accurate to existing staging techniques—not only to styles of writing or of acting.

The playwrights discussed above—Greene, Shakespeare, Jonson, Heywood, Beaumont—recognize and make use of the technical skill of theatrical craftsmen and that recognition is one of the hallmarks of a profession—a profession that provided the "goodly frame" within which the playwrights who are the subject of the next chapter outlined the limits of the field of dramatic writing.

5
"Honesty and Vulgar Praise": The Poet's War and the Literary Field

IN WORKS SUCH AS *DISTINCTION*, *THE FIELD OF CULTURAL PROduction*, and *The Rules of Art*, Pierre Bourdieu argues that the determination of the value of an artwork is structured by a series of paired oppositions—high, low; avant-garde, bourgeois; popular, elite; interested, disinterested; vulgar, refined; and so on— and that in the literary field the shape of these oppositions and the value attached to one or another pole emerges in the context of historical struggles between writers, between writers and their audiences, between writers and publishers (however defined), and between publishers and audiences.[1] The structure of the field is therefore a product of these struggles over the right to determine the principles by which works will be judged. The specific content of these oppositions vary over time, but struggle over that content remains a more or less constant feature of the literary field and the field of cultural production more generally. At the same time, the field depends on the development of a relative autonomy from external categories of evaluation—in other words, in order for the literary field to exist as a field it must develop its own canons of judgment.[2] Conflicts over canons of judgment thus play two roles—they determine the shape of the literary field, its hierarchies and terms of evaluation, and they declare the independence of the field from categories that do not derive from within the field.[3] Bourdieu's ideas suggest ways to historicize the development of a recognizably modern literary field over the course of the later sixteenth and seventeenth centuries.

I

Early modern professional writing developed in a social world characterized by conflict and dissension between writers and stationers, writers and dramatic companies, writers and audiences, and writers and writers—as well as all the permutations of these groups—and those conflicts defined the shape and structure of the emerging literary field.[4] The Parnassus plays (performed at Cambridge between 1598 and 1601) and the roughly contemporaneous Poetomachia are only two manifestations of this larger conflict; however, I will argue that the terms they put into play are terms important to the subsequent structuring of the literary field.[5] As a final statement in the Poetomachia, Ben Jonson's *Poetaster* (1601) takes as its central subject the nature and function of the writer and makes an argument for the ascendancy of a particular kind of writer and writing—conveniently, one represented by Jonson himself. As such, the play is not only an intervention in the Poetomachia, but also functions as an attempt to shape the developing field of professional writing. The Parnassus plays lament the passing of an older, patronage-based model of the writer's social role because of the rise of the professional writers whom Jonson strives to shape in his own image.[6] This group of plays provide particularly vivid examples of an ongoing conflict, a conflict that structures both the literary field and the profession of writing.

As has often been noted, professional writing developed in the wake of the printing press during the slow transition from a feudal to a capitalist economic order.[7] However, the profession of writer did not take shape solely or even primarily as a result of the development of print and a market for books, nor did it arise from more or less purely "literary" pressures. Neither did the profession develop from some simple combination of the two, as a blend of literary and economic concerns, but it also developed in the context of a more general movement toward professionalization in early modern culture. The transformation in the literary field in early modern England occurred in tandem with economic and social transformations. The ranking of genres shifted decisively and drama took a new position outside the civic and liturgical context of its early history. The social composition of the population of writers changed dramatically at the same time as the audience for plays, poems, and literary prose grew immensely. The populations of producers and consumers changed in the course of the sixteenth century as humanist educational ideals spread through English society, as literacy rates rose, and, perhaps most importantly, as the business of printing made "learning" accessible to a much wider public.[8] As the market for cultural products broadened, so did access to a formerly more restricted literary culture. This broadening enabled new categories of producers to develop and find an audience for their writing.[9] The primary site of this development was the theater, which saw the advent of explicitly professional writers who came into competition with the university-trained writers who had supplied much of the demand for new scripts in the 1580s and earlier.

The anonymous Parnassus plays (*The Pilgrimage to Parnassus*, *1* and *2 Return From Parnassus*) were performed at Cambridge between 1598 and 1601. These student plays depict a world in which the skills gained at Mount Parnassus (Cambridge) find no recognized outlet in the world—characters complain about their lack of opportunity, the travails of competition for patrons, and their conflicts with the emerging professional writers associated with the presses and theaters in London. The plays lament the passing of an always at least somewhat imaginary patronage system that, to the characters' minds, ought to have provided places for university-educated men. The student-playwrights nervously depict the advent of a commercial system that does not value the cultural capital represented by a Cambridge MA as much as did the patronage system whose passing the plays lament.[10] Characters such as Ingenioso, Furor Poeticus, Phantasma, Philomusus, and Studioso recognize the advent of a system that fails to recognize them and retreat from it—leaving the field, in a sense, to the writers they criticize.

The Poetomachia, a "stage-quarrel" among writers who were emerging as leading professional dramatists, was at its height from 1598 to 1601. The most important participants were John Marston, Thomas Dekker, and Ben Jonson.[11] In what follows, I prefer the term Poetomachia to War of the Theatres (the other common name for the conflict) for two reasons. First, it was the term used by contemporaries (Dekker refers to the "terrible Poetomachia" lately fought out on the stages of London in his dedication to *Satiromastix*) and, second, it makes the fact that this was a conflict among writers, not theaters, clear. In fact, theaters as such seem not to be in conflict here at all except insofar as they compete for audiences. The professional conflict among writers represented by the Poet's War is not characteristic of rivalries among theaters. Beneath the invective and personal recrimination that pervade these plays, the war was a debate about the definition of the writer, his possible social roles, and the relative value of different styles (here, the various modes of satire). That this struggle works itself out in terms of personal conflicts has as much to do with the genre of the plays as it does with the combative dispositions of the writers. Along with having significant personal differences, Jonson, Marston, and Dekker occupied distinct positions in the field and the plays' invective serves to identify and contest these positions. Because of the biographical interest of the conflict, relatively little attention has been paid to the war's role in the professionalization of writing in late Elizabethan England. Nevertheless, the stakes of this conflict were the right to define the nature and structure of the emerging professional field of writing. Positions in the war thus depend both on individual dispositions and structural positions in the evolving field. As a debate about the nature and structure of the field of professional writing, the Poetomachia participates in the definition of the emergent category of "literature" and the terms the Poet's War puts into play exert a powerful influence over that emergence.[12]

II

> It is the field of production, understood as the system of objective relations between these agents or institutions and as the site of the struggles for the monopoly of the power to consecrate, in which the value of works of art and belief in that value are continuously generated.
> —Pierre Bourdieu, "The Production of Belief"

Pierre Bourdieu argues that the value of art (and the success of its creator) in whatever genre depends crucially on the shape and hierarchical structure of the field in which that work of art is produced. The field of production comprises the relations of writers, readers, and publishers; relations that are "the site of struggles for the monopoly of the power to consecrate," to declare one work rather than another to be legitimate and valuable.[13] The power to consecrate is the most valuable prize in the struggles that structure the field of production since it establishes the categories of value that determine success or failure for writers. In the 1590s, the field of literary production (for lack of a less anachronistic term) was divided among gentle amateurs, university-educated writers, and an emergent group of professionals working for London stationers or for the acting companies.[14] The institutional context of the "power to consecrate" poetry and other written works of art was, as will be discussed below, shifting from a patronage model measuring success in the esteem of "virtuous" (i.e., noble or gentle) readers to one in which success was measured in terms of the market.[15] Control over this power was at least momentarily up for grabs, and interested parties (writers, stationers, the Crown, the church, and so on) struggled to define the categories of evaluation for "literary" art. In the course of these struggles "literature" was gaining its modern definition.

Literature as a category of cultural production did not exist in the same way in early modern England as it does today in our technologized and specialized society.[16] According to the *Oxford English Dictionary*, literature did not acquire its modern definition until the eighteenth century. The older sense was "acquaintance with 'letters' or books; polite or humane learning; literary culture." Playtexts, pamphlets, novels, and so on had to fight for recognition as "polite or humane learning." Literary production was divided among gentle amateurs, "professionals" of whatever rank, anonymous writers, lawyers, preachers, and others. All of these writers produced texts we would recognize as "literature," but those texts and their writers would have looked different to readers in the sixteenth century.[17] "Poesy" was a highly contested sphere at least partially defined by struggles and negotiations within it. Works like Sidney's *Defense of Poetry* or, in an indirect manner, George Puttenham's *Art of English Poesy* take on the question of the nature, usefulness, and social position of writing and writers in the context of a debate about the moral effects of poetry.[18] Professional writers themselves struggled, more or less explicitly, to define their place in a series of negotiations with these generic hierarchies claiming positions within existing structures and, sometimes, transforming them. Texts and their authors were engaged in a complicated and ongoing competition for audiences, patrons, and economic success.

The anonymous Parnassus plays (1598–1602) portray conflicts between a set of expectations rooted in a patronage model and the realities of the developing market for written products. Despite being written and performed in Cambridge, the plays are painfully aware of the London market for intellectual products—the London printers and players are both the only option for the characters and no option at all. In *The First Part of the Return from Parnassus*, Ingenioso, a scholar and poet, gets only two groats for a series of verses commissioned by Patron and, recognizing that this is likely to be all he will receive, decides to go off to London and live "by the printinge house" (375). Ingenioso, Philomusus, and Studioso, all impoverished scholars, "goe to the press" (1474) as a response to the failure of the traditional patronage economy to support them. This turn to publication and the print market recurs throughout both parts of the *Return from Parnassus*. Characters comment repeatedly on the flood of printed works inundating the churchyard of St. Paul's. Ingenioso and Iudicio describe a proliferation of publications of dubious value—the presses produce many "draughty" inventions of unqualified writers (i.e., non-"scholars")—that crowd out the worthy works of writers such as themselves.[19] The principle of value operating in this market is whether or not something will sell, not whether or not a work is valuable for its artistic merit or moral usefulness. Traditional paths of reward—noble or gentle patronage or service to Crown or Church—are represented as insufficient, debased, unavailable, or all three.[20] The final Parnassus play ends with all the scholar characters retreating from London—Philomusus and Studioso go off to become shepherds; Ingenioso, Furor Poeticus and Phantasma move to the Isle of Dogs and write satires complaining about their fate; and Academico goes back to Cambridge.[21] In the face of the debasement of all traditional markets, the Parnassians retreat from London. The play closes with no note of merriment because of the economics of scholarship and the lack of positions for qualified men. Ingenioso says that those

> Who kenne the lawes of euery comick stage,
> And wonder that our scene ends discontent.
> Ye ayrie witts, subtill, [Iudiciuous],
> Since that few schollers fortunes are content,
> Wonder not if our scene ends discontent.
> When that your fortunes reach their owne content,
> Then shall our scene end here in merriment.
>
> (2202–8)

Ingenioso's last words include the members of the audience, Cambridge men all, in the "scene" promising that only when their "fortunes reach their owne content" will the play actually be able to end in merriment. By pointedly violating generic convention, the speech drives home the point that "few schollers fortunes are content" and that it would be dishonest to pretend otherwise. The play assumes an audience familiar with "the lawes of euery comick stage" and it recognizes both the authority of those laws and justifies violating them. The appeal here to the "lawes" suggests the the criteria of evaluation are understood in "literary" terms—in terms of the field of production. University men are in competition for places in the writing field with men who lack formal qualifications—the Parnassus plays come from the perspective of the placeless educated—and the Parnassians' final rejection of the world of professional writing represents a despairing recognition that those qualifications no longer provide guarantees of success in an increasingly open and contentious market.

The theaters provided a reasonably lucrative source of income for writers but their presentation in the Parnassus plays suggests that they were not seen as an appropriate venue for the talents of the educated.[22] The humanist ideal that the educated should be of service to the commonwealth had no place for writing for the professional theater. As E. H. Miller writes in his book on nondramatic writers, " 'Profite,' or utility, was an obsession with English humanists, a yardstick which precluded theory and abstract speculation and minimized aesthetic experience."[23] Writers working in genres whose apparent primary focus was entertainment were therefore suspicious figures and had a conflicted relationship to themselves and their work. The pattern of Robert Greene's career as discussed in Helgerson's *Elizabethan Prodigals* typifies the kinds of accommodations writers made with their difficult position. Helgerson sees a pattern of youthful prodigality in the careers of writers born between 1545 and 1560. All of them were gentlemen whether by birth or by education.[24] Most of these writers began their careers writing works for pleasure but express repentance and regret for such youthful folly later in life. For example, Greene's early work was dominated by prose romances, written to entertain, while his last pamphlets were elaborate confessional warnings not to follow his path. For Greene, theater was the most destructive waste of God-given talents. His *Groatsworth of Witte Bought With a Million of Repentance* (1592) describes "making plaies" as "peeuish follie."[25] He continues:

> I would sweare by sweet S. George, thou art vnworthy better hap, sith thou dependest on so meane a stay. Base minded men all three of you, if by my miserie you be not warnd: for vnto none of you (like mee) sought those burres to cleaue: those Puppets (I meane) that spake from our mouths, those Anticks garnisht in our colours. Is it not strange, that I, to whom they all haue beene beholding: is it not like that you, to whome the all haue beene beholding, shall (were yee in that case as I am now) bee both at once of them forsaken?[26]

This passage is followed by the famous "Tyger's hart in a Players hyde" attack on Shakespeare and closes with a final admonition to "seeke . . . better Maisters; for it is pittie men of such rare wits, should be subiect to the pleasure of such rude groomes."[27] Greene presents theater as a base realm filled with ungrateful exploiters of God-given "wits," and writing plays contaminates and curses the writer as Greene portrays himself having been cursed. He warns his colleagues against wasting their excellence in such mean pursuits (and by association with such mean persons).[28] Another part of Greene's warning, not as obvious perhaps, is that the players' support of writers is doubtful and that his impoverishment should stand as a warning not to rely on them for their livelihood, much less support in sickness or age.

Where the Parnassians and the University Wits (especially Robert Greene) often railed despairingly over the changing markets and criteria for their work, other writers took advantage of the transition from a patronage to a commercial metaphor for writing.[29] In Dekker's *Guls Horn-Booke* (1609) the print market is understood through a patronage metaphor: "The theater is your Poets Royal Exchange, upon which their Muses, ([which] are now turnd to Merchants,) meeting, barter away that light commodity of words for a lighter ware then words, *Plaudites*, and the *breath* of the great *Beast* ; which . . . vanish into air . . . when your *Groundling*, and *gallery-Commoner* buys his sport by the penny, and, like a hagler is glad to utter it againe by retailing."[30] The Muses now operate in the marketplace—once the inspirers of manuscript verse dedicated to patrons, now the factors of a new mercantile venture. The Muses are still present but operate within an utterly changed context. Value, once thought to be conferred by moral or social usefulness and the appreciation of an elite audience, now could derive from an alternate and competing source in theatrical performance and, not insignificantly, in books. The category of "patron" expands enormously in this conceptualization—in the largest sense, the market itself is the patron of writers—and moves some distance toward the modern definition of patron as customer—as buyer of goods or services. This emerging market for cultural goods complicates the question of value by making the loci of judgment multiple. The plays associated with the Poet's War are examples of negotiations with these complicated and tangled questions of value.

These shifting loci of value for intellectual or cultural products in early modern England point toward the development of a literary field—a subset of a more general intellectual field, itself in the process of change. Arguing that the intellectual field as we know it today took form in the early modern period, Bourdieu writes "intellectual life was dominated, throughout the Middle Ages, during part of the Renaissance . . . by an *external* legitimizing authority."[31] When this external authority, as noble, royal, or clerical patronage for example, becomes a less important source of legitimacy, "the intellectual field becomes an increasingly complex system, increasingly independent of external influences . . . a field of relations governed by a specific logic: competition for cultural legitimacy."[32] As Bourdieu outlines it, the transition is from a patronage economy toward one increasingly based on internal struggles for success and legitimacy. Bourdieu sees the stage as being at the forefront of this development: "The dependency of writers on the aristocracy and its canons of taste persisted for longer in the domain of literature than in the theater"[33] because the theater depended less on the goodwill of particular noble patrons for economic success than on "entrance fees paid by a public of increasingly diverse origins."[34] Drama thus becomes relatively autonomous and struggles within the theater tend to be seen as struggles within the theater.[35] Theatre's autonomy, of course, is only relative. The licensing function of the Revels Office and the necessity of royal or noble patronage for acting companies limited theatrical autonomy in significant ways. These limitations, however, operate at some remove from properly "theatrical" issues: debates over style, genre, and, most importantly, the function of theater happened within the theater, not as the result of external pressures.

Such struggles within the dramatic field, exemplified by the Poetomachia, outline the shape of part of the field of cultural production in early modern England. Fields function as relatively autonomous areas of human activity operating according to internally coherent rules of practice that determine value, success, and power within that field. Professional writing for the theaters in late Elizabethan and Jacobean England had begun to take on these characteristics. Writers argue amongst themselves about questions of value, representation, and conduct. Bourdieu writes: "If the literary field (etc.) is universally the site of a struggle over the definition of writer (etc.), then there is no universal definition of the writer, and analysis never encounters anything but definitions corresponding to a state of the struggle for the imposition of the legitimate definition of the writer."[36] The Parnassus plays depict this struggle in the commentary the Parnassian characters make on other writers. The *Second Return* contains a long critique of contemporary writers—both positive and negative—for example, Iudicio makes fun of Marston as "a Ruffian in his stile, / Withouten bands or garters ornament" (268–69). The most exemplary descriptions are those of Marlowe, a Parnassian, and Jonson, the citizen-playwright.

> *Marlowe* was happy in his buskind muse,
> Alas unhappy in his life and end.
> Pitty is it that with so ill should dwell,
> Wit lent from heaven, but vices sent from hell.
> (286–89)

While Marlowe's God-given gifts are not sullied by being lodged in a vice-ridden body, Jonson's wit is limited by his being a bricklayer.[37] Iudicio dismisses him as "the wittiest fellow of a Bricklayer in England" (293). Ingenioso insults Jonson because of his slow composition, his imitation of classical models, and so on.[38] Iudicio's insult emphasizes his tradesman status in opposition to the gentility of other writers. Jonson, it is implied, writes like an artisan while a writer like Marlowe has a "buskind muse" who enables him to write with the ease and grace denied to Jonson.[39] The author(s) of the Parnassus plays argues for a definition of the writer that is based in the traditional social order, an order that denies men of common origin or those without educational qualifications access to the glories of learning.[40] In many ways the Parnassus plays represent an earlier state of the field in which gentility (however acquired) was understood to guarantee access to and, to some extent, success in the field.[41] Lack of gentle status or education automatically excluded players from the game. This was no longer true by the late sixteenth century and the struggle the Parnassus plays depict was already lost by the time they were written and performed. The Cambridge-trained writers in the *Second Return* seem to know that they will have to accommodate themselves to a system that does not recognize their legitimacy as readily as it did even ten years earlier.[42] Dekker's comment on the theater as the Poet's Royal Exchange vividly illustrates the transition from the model of aristocratic patronage and stable expectations lamented by the Parnassians toward a new system where multiple new constituencies have a role in determining a work's success or failure, and, more importantly for writers like Dekker, Jonson, and Marston, its *merit*. The Parnassians recognize the passing of one model without presenting a new one, while the generation of writers represented by Jonson, Marston, and Dekker struggle to define new criteria of evaluation in an equally new cultural terrain.

The Poetomachia depicts struggles over the nature and shape of that terrain as it develops into a recognizably literary field. Authorial remarks in prologues, epilogues, and elsewhere in plays all designate the opposition as being between "poëtasters" or "playsters" and authors or poets, not university men and tradesman writers. The class conflict described by Greene and the Parnassus plays—between gentle and nongentle writers—is transformed into a battle within a profession whose participants recognize the debate in terms of writerly skill, not of rank.[43] This terminological transformation suggests that writers were engaged in an effort to forge a corporate identity *as* writers in the late sixteenth century.[44] Thomas Dekker's *The Wonderful Year* (1603) shows signs of this effort in its dedication to Walter Thuresby, London's water-bailiff. He writes that "I have clapped the cognizance of your name on these scribbled papers; it is their livery. So that now they are yours, being free from any vile imputation save only that they thrust themselves into your acquaintance. But general errors have general pardons: for the title of other men's names is the common heraldry which all those lay claim to whose crest is a pen and inkhorn."⁴⁵ Dekker asserts that writers have a heraldry and a crest of their own: the "heraldry" of the writer is the name of his patron, and the "crest" of the writer is a pen and inkhorn. Dekker places his work under the protection of his putative patron by virtue of the dedication, and his language suggests that this practice is a common one ("general errors have general pardons"), a practice understood by both writer and dedicatee. Dekker's dedication to the reader is even more revealing. He describes the reading practices his work is likely to be subjected to by the mass of book buyers who would have been its primary audience. It opens with a description of the "scurvy fashion" of addressing readers: "To maintain the scurvy fashion and to keep custom in reparations he must be honeyed and come over with 'gentle reader' and 'learned reader' though he have no more gentility in him than Adam had, that was but a gardener, no more civility than a Tartar, and no more learning than the most arrant stinkard that except his own name could never find anything in the horn-book."⁴⁶ The dedication continues in the same vein, asking rhetorical questions (why write?, why do readers do as they do?, etc.), and offers insight into the writing profession. Readers appear to have wanted "honeyed" addresses that flatter their learning or gentility and writers (prompted by the economic concerns of publishing) catered to this desire.⁴⁷ Dekker both observes and critiques the "scurvy fashion" of flattering the reader in the *Horn Book* demonstrating the authority of "fashion" and his desire to be free from such external pressures. Writing of being "pressed to death—that's to say, to be a man in print," he states that the writer must not be surprised by "the stinking tobacco breath of a satin gull, the aconited sting of a narrow-eyed critic, the faces of a fantastic stage monkey, nor the 'Indeed-la!' of a puritanical citizen."⁴⁸ And given that people like this are his audience, he ought not expect praises from them. Only an "ass" "would entreat as players do in a cogging epilogue at the end of a filthy comedy that, be it never such wicked stuff, they would forbear to hiss or to damn it perpetually to lie on a stationer's stall? For he that can so cozen himself as to pocket up praise in that silly sort makes his brains fat with his own folly."⁴⁹ Dekker describes an established pattern of production and reception with its own terms of success or failure that will be recognized by "wise men" who will see in the condemnation of the mass of readers a confirmation of value.⁵⁰ Recognizing the impor-

5 / "HONESTY AND VULGAR PRAISE"

tance of the market, Dekker addresses booksellers as the "factors to the liberall sciences" and, more than a little disingenuously, treats publishing as a regrettable but necessary part of the act of writing.[51] Dekker's work points to the establishment of a set of norms for writers, their writing, and their reception. The norms of a literary field are as much the product of struggles within the population of writers as they are of negotiations between writers and their audiences. The Poetomachia, as a kind of crystallization of such a struggle, offers access to the fraught beginnings of the transition from a market dominated by patronage and external legitimating authorities toward an internally coherent and self-legitimating field of cultural production.

III

> *I care not much if I make description ... of that terrible* Poetomachia, *lately commenced betweene* Horace the second, *and a band of leane-witted* Poetasters. *They have bin at high wordes, and so high, that the ground could not serve them, but (for want of* Chopins*) have stalk't upon stages ...* Horace *hal'd his* Poetasters *to the* Barre, *the* Poetasters *untruss'd* Horace: *how worthily eyther or how wrongfully,* (World) *leave it to the Iurie.*
> —Thomas Dekker, "To the World," *Satiromastix* (1602)

During the years of the Poet's War Dekker, Jonson, and Marston were all relative newcomers to the writing of plays. Jonson's first plays were performed in 1597-98, Dekker's in 1598, and Marston's in 1599.[52] Not only were they starting their careers, they were also experimenting with the genre of comical satire that was in fashion at the same time as the Poetomachia raged. The Bishops' Ban on satire in 1599 closed the market for verse and prose satire and Marston, for one, turned to the stage to find an outlet for satirical commentary. Jonson had already been working out a stage language for satire in his *Humour* plays and was coming to align himself with the legacy of Horatian satire. Dekker appears as a dramatist in Henslowe's diary in 1598 and his prose work begins to appear after the turn of the century. As David Riggs notes, Jonson and Marston (and, I would add, Dekker) were more alike at the turn of the century than they were different and this similarity bred conflict.[53] In contrast to

Riggs's position that the resemblance and thus the rivalry is personal, my contention is that the intensity of the conflict has more to do with these writers' professional need to differentiate their plays from each others' early in their dramatic careers than with specifically personal rivalries. The intensity of the conflict points to the closeness of the competitors' positions in the field and drives the escalating rhetorical violence of the war as the combatants strive for distinction within it. This struggle for differentiation characterizes the developing field of professional writing and the Poet's War is only one of the more public and historically resonant of these struggles.[54]

The plays associated with the Poetomachia employ a series of opposing terms—poet to poetaster, original to ape, priest to the Muses to play-dresser, author to plagiary, speedy or slow, deliberate or hasty—that mark one writer as valuable and others as pretenders, fakes, or hacks.[55] Jonson valorizes these terms in ways that are readily recognizable to a modern audience—being original is good, slow and careful is better than hasty and sloppy, aping is bad—but these value judgments would not have been self-evident to an early modern audience, an audience that would have contained a significant number of people trained to take pleasure in imitation and in the development of traditional themes and plotlines. Jonson's attacks on "plagiaries" points to his careful definition of imitation and its distinction from mere aping. As Richard Peterson notes, imitation is crucially important to Jonson's writing. He argues that for Jonson "to imitate in the true sense is to assimilate and remake in a spirit of admiration that inevitably shades over into active emulation and rivalry."[56] This is not the "aping"—mere copying—that the poetasters are guilty of. Part of what Jonson does in the course of the Poetomachia is propose (with some success) a novel value system in which to evaluate writing that ranks originality over traditionalism, independence over clientage, professionalism over amateurism. The primary opposition in the structure Jonson sets up in the course of the Poetomachia is between the poet and the poetaster.[57] Poets are "priests to the Muses," respected by the state, and possess a legitimate voice in both the sphere of poetry and in the court. That this system of oppositions emerges in the context of a professional contest between playwrights is no accident. Title to the designation of "poet" becomes a stake in a struggle for audiences.[58]

Jonson's effort to redefine the nature and role of the "poet" changes the terms of the debate by changing the criteria by which works are evaluated. Jonson makes his satire an integral part of his play's action—the subplot of Ovid's fall works in close tandem with the main plot about Horace's eventual victory over the poetasters Crispinus and Demetrius in a battle over the nature and purpose of writing and writers. Jonson shifts the satire to matters of vocabulary, of style, and of decorum rather than being wholly bound up in caricature.[59] Marston's recognition of Jonson as "Most refined and serious poet, and his sincere and wise friend" in the Latin dedication to *The Malcontent* (1604) points to both Jonson's victory in this war and his opponents' acceptance of that victory and its terms—Marston praises Jonson as a "serious poet," the very title Jonson strove for in the Poet's War. The Poetomachia's staging of a contest over categories of value occurs within a highly competitive professional marketplace in which playwrights sought commissions from acting companies and acting companies sought scripts. Jonson, Marston, and Dekker are only three representatives of a much larger category of producers all of whom were in competition for the attention of the acting companies.

In addition to this competition among playwrights, public and private acting companies competed for the same London audience at the turn of the century. The Children of the Queen's Revels had just begun playing at Blackfriars and necessarily found themselves in conflict with the established adult companies. This conflict has often been simplified into an opposition between high and low culture or between types of theater. Jonson and Marston have been traditionally aligned with the child companies and elite culture with Dekker on the side of the adult players and a more popular mode.[60] However, Dekker and Marston appear (at least in Jonson's representations) to be allied in their attack on Jonson and his style. The plays and playwrights, however, cannot be divided easily into opposing camps with tidy borders. Jonson and Dekker wrote for both adult and child companies and Marston seems to have debuted either with Henslowe or with the Children of Paul's.[61] The lines of battle in the Poet's War have more to do with professional struggles within a broader institutional context than with divisions between adult and child companies, much less elite or popular culture.[62] None of these writers showed any kind of exclusive affiliation with one company or kind of company—Shakespeare being an exception—and their careers are those of freelance writers seeking work from whoever would pay.[63] Under such circumstances, popularity and public success were crucially important stakes in the struggle for commissions. The conflict represented in these plays is thus less one between different types of acting companies than it is between different kinds of playwrights.

As Shakespeare notes in *Hamlet*, the contention between the "poets and players" seemed to be on all the stages of London at the turn of the century. According to Rosencrantz's account, the "little eyases" of the child companies "so berattle the common stages" that fashionable theater goers fear to attend the public theaters and for a time the only successful plays were those in which the child and adult companies attacked each other.[64] Despite Rosencrantz's comments, these plays he describes are more concerned with conflict between poet and poet than between "the poet and the player."[65] Hamlet himself notes the folly of a conflict between child actors and the adult actors they will grow up to become: "Will they not say afterwards, if they should grow themselves to common players—as is most like, if their means are no better—their writers do them wrong to make them exclaim against their own succession?" (2.2.345–49).[66] Being more insightful than Rosencrantz, Hamlet sees that the responsibility for the war lies with the writers, not the actors. The writers have more of a stake in these exclamations and their interests are necessarily different than those of the players—especially of the child actors who "exclaim against their own succession" in these plays.[67]

Plays associated with the Poetomachia were popular successes, apparently occupying a significant portion of the market for plays at the turn of the century. This popularity translates to economic success for the acting companies, and, indirectly, into professional success for the playwrights. The conflict among these three writers has much to do with this fundamentally economic struggle, a struggle mystified into a conflict over standards of quality for plays. In *Poetaster*, Jonson advocates a particular kind of diction, simple and direct, which he opposes to the fustian of some of Marston and Dekker's work and seems to believe that this diction would be more attractive to (as well as morally better for) audiences.[68] It is not by accident that the pill Horace administers to Crispinus in *Poetaster* forces him to vomit up fanciful words drawn from Marston's satires and early plays. Jonson's play attempts to purge such vocabulary and, by extension, such works from the profession. *Poetaster* criticizes both Marston and Dekker as bad writers and holds up Horace and Virgil as the standard to which all writers should aspire. Jonson strives to establish his kind of play as a standard—which would ensure both his status as poet and his marketability as playwright.

Marston's *Histriomastix* (1599, Q 1610) seems to have been written for a child company and the play is less a unified satire than a series of loosely related episodes tied together by a double subplot—one of which is a transparent attack on the common players with whom the Children of Paul's were competing.[69] *Histriomastix*'s main narrative demonstrates the pernicious effects that Peace and Plenty have on a slothful populace. Each act is presided over by a different ruling passion that dominates the action of all the characters in that act. Marston sutures the subplot of the players (Posthaste and Sir Oliver Owlet's Men) and Chrisoganus's educational program for the courtiers of the "ill-nurs'd age of *Peace*" onto this allegorical material (which is often discussed as an older play Marston was revising) and these subplots represent Marston's intervention in the Poet's War.[70] The subplots layer a kind of pseudorealism over the highly conventional and moralistic primary plot of the play. Sir Oliver Owlet's Men form as a result of the plenty attendant on Peace's ascendancy:

> Incle: This *Peace* breeds such Plenty, trades serve no turnes.
> Belch: The more fooles wee to follow them.
> Posthaste: Lett's make up a company of Players,
> For we can all sing and say,
> And so (with practise) soone may learne to play.
> (250)

The players' original trades (beardmaker, fiddle-string maker, and peddler) "serve no turnes" and they therefore turn to playing. Belch, Incle, and Gut seem greedy rather than unemployed and readily assent to Posthaste's proposal.[71] Marston spares no effort in making them appear ridiculous. Posthaste, the company's playwright, is a buffoon with pretensions to gentility and his play is a poor retelling of the story of Troilus and Cressida. The actors in the company are incompetent drunkards who mangle Posthaste's already-mangled lines. Such a depiction—played as it was by the Children of Paul's—could only have been a challenge to the established adult companies and, more importantly, their playwrights.

At the turn of the century, Marston was writing verse satires for an elite audience of Inns of Court men, classically educated courtiers and bureaucrats, as well as the broader book-buying public. Philip Finkelpearl argues that his primary audience would have been at the Inns, an elite audience of budding lawyers, sons of gentry attending the "noblest nurseries of humanity and liberty," and administrators in training.[72] After the banning of satire in 1599, Marston turned to drama and wrote for the Children of Paul's, a company performing in one of the private houses near the Inns of Court, finding there, Finkelpearl argues, an audience he saw as fit for his work.[73] *Histriomastix* owes much to this context—Marston was striving to make a name for himself in a new (for him) genre—and Marston's targets in this play have much to do with the new market in which he was working. The newly reconstituted boy companies would have been in competition with the well-established adult companies playing at the public theaters, and Marston's picture of adult players doubtless owes much to this competition. By criticizing the adult companies and their playwrights as buffoonish incompetents, Marston proclaims the superiority of his new employers and of his own work. In the words of *Histriomastix*'s Landulpho, adult actors dare with:

> Most ugly lines and base-browne-paper-stuff
> Thus to abuse our heavenlie poesie,
> That sacred offspring from the braine of Jove,
> Thus to be mangled with prophane absurds,
> Strangled and chok't with lawlesse bastard wordes.
> (264)[74]

Landulpho's "our" makes "heavenlie poesie" the rightful possession only of gentlemen like himself, not players and playwrights. Ugly, base, and bastard words conspire in Landulpho's speech to abuse "poesie" which is defined as sacred. The status language here seems calculated to appeal to the "elite" sensibilities of his audience and alludes to the superior quality of Marston's own work and medium. The "lawless bastard words" Marston claims are choking "heavenly poesy" are ironically the target of Jonson's ire in *Poetaster*—the Marston character vomits up what Jonson characterizes as precisely this kind of vocabulary. This element of the play is a direct intervention in a highly competitive dramatic marketplace, a marketplace seeing the rapid rise of Ben Jonson.

Chrisoganus appears to be the play's version of Jonson, and it has been accepted that this was the origin of Marston's quarrel with him.[75] However, as James Bednarz notes, Chrisoganus is hardly an uncomplimentary portrait. He is universally admired as a learned and upright man, is able to attract students (at least at the beginning and end of the play), and is the only character untainted by the various passions that infect other characters in the play. He serves almost as a choric voice of reason in the chaos of the play's action. An example of this is his remarks in 2.1:

> That common-welth is never well at ease,
> Where Parchment skinnes, whose use should beare records,
> Must head their brawling Drummes and keep a coyle,
> As if they threatened *Plenty* with a spoyle.
> (257)

This speech is followed by a short dialogue on the comparative value of sport and learning in which Chrisoganus tries to convince the others that learning is better: "What better recreations can you find, / Then sacred knowledge in divinest things?" (257). Mavortius insults him for his belief in the right of the learned to teach (and chastise):

> How you translating-scholler? you can make
> A stabbing *Satir*, or an *Epigram*,
> And thinke you carry just *Ramnusia's* whippe
> To lash the patient; goe, get you clothes,
> Our free-borne blood such apprehension lothes.[76]

Chrisoganus' response—"Proud Lord, poore Art shall weare a glorious crowne, / When her despisers die to all renowne" (258)—typifies his stoical virtue in the face of the progressive corruption he observes around him throughout the play. However, Marston presents him as essentially ineffectual, his good advice goes unheeded, his moral pronouncements command no assent and still less observance, and he can only wait for the inevitable arrival of Astraea that restores good order.

James Bednarz argues that this depiction of the poet as irrelevant is what Jonson took umbrage at in *Histriomastix*.[77] He presents the opposition in the Poet's War as essentially philosophical, between Marstonian skepticism and Jonsonian faith in the moral role of the poet: "As a struggle to establish literary reputations, the Poet's War was consequently both as playful and as serious as the game of literature itself. The stage quarrel thus afforded Marston and Jonson a vehicle for aggressively expressing the differences that were already present in their divergent approaches to literary theory."[78] That *Histriomastix* presents Chrisoganus's position as irrelevant is arguable, he effects no real change and his teaching gains few adherents—but characters do recognize his wisdom and, at the end of the play, pledge to follow him:

> *Mavortius*: How might we tread the path's to happy ends,
> Since foes to Learning are not Vertue's friends.
> *Chrisoganus*: First entertaine submission in your soules
> To frame true concord in one unity . . .
> Your lawes appoincted to be positive,
> (By *Warre* confounded) must be brought againe.
> For law is that which Love and Peace maintaine.
> *Philarchus*: Thou sonne of knowledge (richer then a man)
> We censure thy advise as oracles.
> *Chrisoganus*: Follow, and Ile instruct you what I can.
> *Mavortius*: We followed beasts before but now a man.
>
> (296)

Both Mavortius and Philarchus reverse the positions they have held throughout the play and now decide to follow a "man" rather than the "beasts" who dominate the bulk of the play. Bednarz's position is persuasive, especially in that it offers an explanation for Jonson's taking offense at his depiction as Chrisoganus, but it hides the fact that the Poet's War is primarily a professional conflict by labeling it a philosophical one.[79]

Jonson never explicitly responds to Marston's "skepticism" and his *Poetaster* attacks Marston (and Dekker) not for their literary theory but for their lack of literary skill.[80] Demetrius

5 / "HONESTY AND VULGAR PRAISE"

(Dekker) is labeled a "play-dresser and plagiary," Crispinus (Marston) is called a "poetaster and plagiary," and both are taken to task for libel and calumny. Demetrius admits that the reason he maligns Horace is "that hee kept better company (for the most part) than I; and that better men loved him than loved me: and that his writings thrived better than mine, and were better liked and graced" (5.3.449–53). Demetrius envies Horace his company, which he earned through his writing, and, more importantly, he resents the fact that Horace's work was more successful than his own. The play links moral and literary quality but places more emphasis on writing. Demetrius and Crispinus vomit up outlandish *words* after taking Horace's pill, not ideas or moral positions. In *Poetaster*, Jonson presents himself as a better writer, not the possessor of a superior philosophy, and it is in these terms that the battle is fought.[81]

Proclaiming from the outset that the Poetomachia is about other writers' envy of his work, Jonson's *Poetaster* begins with envy personified rising up from below the stage in an effort to gain allies for an attack on the author. The Prologue enters as Envie sinks down "againe" having found no one to "helpe [it] to damne the Author" (ind. 46) telling the "Monster" to stay and let the Prologue tread on its neck in victory:

>So spight should die,
>Despis'd and scorn'd by noble industrie.
>If any muse why I salute the stage,
>An armed *Prologue*; know, 'tis a dangerous age:
>Wherein, who writes, had need present his *Scenes*
>Fortie-fold proofe against the coniuring meanes
>Of base detractors and illiterate apes.
>
>(prol. 3–9)

The Prologue is, of course, describing the Poetomachia where the writer must be wary of attack and fortify his work against potential lurking enemies. The speech puts several key Jonsonian terms into play even before the action begins. First, Envy is despised and scorned by "noble industrie"—a virtue Jonson consistently claims for himself.[82] Noble industry triumphs over the calumnies of Envy, as Jonson believes his work as a product of such industry must triumph over that of his rivals. Jonson's industry is noble even if his background is not—this is a hierarchy based on merit, not external categories of rank. Jonson's claims here oppose the Parnassus plays' dismissal of him as a mere bricklayer by making his origins irrelevant. Second, he sets up an opposition between "who writes" and the "base detractors and illiterate apes" who populate this "dangerous age." This dichotomy characterizes the kinds of oppositions the play envisions as existing among various classes of writers. The epithets imply a specific hierarchy of evaluation and privilege a particular mode of writing. Jonson uses the language of social rank to criticize his critics—they are not merely detractors, but *base* ones—which places him on a higher rung of a writerly social ladder.[83] By calling his opponents "illiterate apes," Jonson asserts the value of writers who are literate originals—again, writers like himself. However, in such a dangerous age these values are not self-evident and therefore the Prologue must therefore go armed.

Despite the envy and calumny of his attackers, the Prologue asks that the "Author" not be blamed for separating himself from them:

> He doth implore,
> You would not argue him of arrogance:
> How ere that common spawne of ignorance,
> Our frie of writers, may beslime his fame,
> And give his action that adulterate name.
> Such ful-blowne vanities he more doth lothe,
> Then base dejection: There's a meane 'twixt both.
> Which with a constant firmenesse he pursues,
> As one, that knows the strength of his owne *muse*.
> (prol. 15–24)

Jonson places himself above the "frie" of writers who have libeled him in an effort to take the high ground in the conflict. Imploring the audience not to think him arrogant, Jonson describes his course as a "meane" between the extremes of arrogance and "base dejection," a course appropriate to his sense of his place in the poetic hierarchy (he knows the "strength" of his muse). Casting himself, however ironically, as an icon of restraint and probity (and, bizarrely, modesty) in the closing lines of the prologue he declares: "this [his work] he hopes all free soules will allow; / Others, that take it with a rugged brow, / Their mood he rather pitties, then enuies: / His minde is above their iniuries" (prol. 25–29). Jonson separates himself from what he describes as the rabble, elevating himself and denigrating his detractors in one and the same move while disavowing that this is his goal.

The prologue situates Jonson in the midst of what he portrays as an acrimonious and unfair (to him) theater world. His tactics here, as within the play proper, are attempts to distinguish himself from his most immediate competitors in the field. This distinction, allegorized in the play by the contrast between the poetasters Crispinus and Demetrius and the poets Horace and Virgil, represents, straightforwardly enough, an attempt to mark himself as a poet worthy of the attention of discerning patrons (Horace and Virgil's relations to Mecoenas and Augustus being homologous). Jonson exploits the cultural capital still associated with the patronage system—by associating himself with Horace, a writer with a noble patron, Jonson makes a claim for his own talent—in order to win a professional conflict. By aligning himself with what he defines as noble virtues, he lumps his opponents into the rabble of commoners.[84]

In the 1616 Folio, Jonson prints an apologetical dialogue he asserts was suppressed "by authority" when the play was first performed. The dialogue rehearses the claims made by the Prologue, dramatizes Author's stoic and reasonable response to the libels cast against him, and reinforces the image of Jonson/Horace/Author as reasonable, just, and virtuous. For example, in response to queries about why his work drew all the libels it did Author says that:

> I never writ that peece
> More innocent, or empty of offence
>   My Bookes have still beene taught
> To spare the persons, and to speake the vices.
>   ("To the Reader," 74–85)

In language reminiscent of his epigram "To My Book," Jonson asserts that *Poetaster* was "empty of offence," deserving none of the opprobrium heaped upon it by "enemies tongue." The play is hardly "empty of offence," containing as it does a large amount of personal satire and criticism. Nevertheless, this is precisely how he speaks of his epigrams, and such language characterizes Jonson's effort to shape his public persona into that of a sage and moral critic of contemporary abuses.[85] This effort, never particularly successful, intends to separate Jonson from the rabble by asserting his distance from those who fail to "spare the persons." Jonson articulates this as a position (whether or not he actually holds it) in the context of an effort to distinguish his plays and poems from those of other writers. It mystifies the various economic, personal, and artistic interests at work in the Poetomachia into a more abstract debate about the morality of satire.

In addition to this, the dialogue refers to Jonson's work as "bookes," not plays. In the Folio *Works*, itself a massive intervention in Jonson's ongoing definition of himself as an author, *Pöetaster* becomes a book—a literary artifact—rather than a play.[86] By printing this apology, Jonson revives a dated (and factitious) defense in order to mark himself as a dignified or noble poet and not a base poetaster in permanent form. He describes the effect of his writing as an indelible mark on the foreheads of his enemies—"my prints should last, still to be read / In their pale fronts" when the things written against him "shall like a figure, drawne in water, fleete" ("To the Reader," 169–71). Like his competitors, Jonson depicts the action of his satire in terms of writing, the terms of the field in which the debate takes place. *Poetaster*'s Folio publication reinforces the sense that the contest represented in the plays of the Poetomachia is a literary one, a contest between modes of writing.[87]

Dekker's *Satiromastix* (1602) responds to Jonson's intervention in the Poetomachia and describes itself as an attempt to "untruss" the "humorous poet." *Satiromastix* grafts a series of scenes depicting an impecunious and dishonest Horace clearly modeled on Jonson onto a play with few, if any, other links to the Poetomachia. Structurally, this is similar to the way the players' subplot functions in *Histriomastix*. Dekker makes use of one of Jonson's own characters to conduct the untrussing: Jonson's Captain Tucca reappears in Dekker's play to attack Horace. In other words, he appropriates Jonson's literary weapons for use against him. Rather than create his own critic or appeal to an external authority, Dekker one-ups Jonson by co-opting his own creation. Like Jonson, he uses specifically literary tools to fight a literary battle. Moreover, the dedication "To the World" expresses Dekker's position on the war in explicitly writerly terms.

Dekker addresses the printed version of his play "To the World"—to the whole world of readers—in much the same way that Jonson addresses his audience in the suppressed dialogue that closes *Poetaster*. Where Jonson staged his position statement, Dekker pointedly *writes* it as part of the published version of the play. He opens by disingenuously stating his quondam resolve to "bee round with thee (the world)" ("To the World," 1)—namely, the audience. "Yet because thou wilt sit as Iudge of all matters . . . I care not much if I make description (before thy Universality) of that terrible Poetomachia, lately commenc'd betweene Horace the second, and a band of leane-witted Poetasters" ("To the World," 3–9). Dekker is engaging in essentially the same tactics as Jonson in his apologetical dialogue by claiming that he would rather not indulge in the conflict, but is forced to by circumstance. His second paragraph makes this clear:

> I could heere (eeven with the feather of my pen) wipe off other ridiculous imputations: but my best way to answer them, is to laugh at them: onely that much I protest (and sweare by the divinest part of true Poesie) that (howsoever the limmes of my naked lines may bee and I know have bin, tortur'd on the racke) they are free from conspiring the least disgrace to any man, but onely to our new Horace; neyther should this ghost of Tucca, have walkt up and downe Poules Church-yard, but that hee was raiz'd up (in print) by newe Exorcismes. ("To the World," 40–47)

This echoes some of the language in Jonson's dialogue, a dialogue Dekker likely would have seen, if Jonson's claim about it being performed on stage is true. Dekker writes that he could "wipe off" the indelible blots Jonson would have stamped in his forehead with his pen's feather. The attention Dekker gives here to materials—his pen, ink blots—moreover foregrounds the practice of writing. Like Jonson, Dekker casts the conflict in terms of writing, but unlike Jonson he admits to conspiring disgrace to at least one person: "our new Horace."[88] He casts at least part of *his* response as being prompted by "newe Exorcismes" which call up Tucca "in print," suggesting that the printed version of *Satiromastix is* responding to Jonson's own quarto.

Dekker's rhetoric points both to his engagement with Jonson's own language—an effort to use Jonson's tactics against him—and his involvement in the developing literary field. A field is defined by the practices common to it—common struggles, shared rhetoric, common rules of "the game." Dekker writes in language well-suited to this kind of debate—he uses similar rhetoric in the *Guls Horn Book* among other pamphlets—abusing those he regards as fools in flip and vivid language.[89] "To the World" attacks Jonson's pretensions and imagines a literary court presided over by Apollo as the final arbiter of poetic value and the justice of such claims to superiority. In Apollo's court, Dekker says Jonson would have been the loser.[90] Dekker's epilogue, spoken by Tucca, recognizes that poetic strife will continue: "If you set your hands and Seales to this, *Horace* will write against it, and you may have more sport: he shall not loose his labour, he shall not turne his blanke verses into wast paper: No, my Poetasters will not laugh at him, but will untrusse him agen, and agen, and agen" (epilogue 20–24). This strife, fought in terms that, as they are repeated and recycled, become specific to this literary struggle, points toward the constitution of a dramatic (and by extension a literary) field with practices that guide both the production of plays and the competition for distinction among playwrights. Dekker's "agen and agen and agen" makes this kind of competition a structural feature of the field. Horace's efforts will not be wasted, he "shall not loose his labour," but will produce an ever-expanding body of responses and counterresponses. Perhaps the best evidence of this is the persistence of the term "poetaster" in discussions about good and bad poets—Dekker sarcastically adopts the term, but in that adoption he accepts the shape of the opposition between poet and poetaster Jonson is striving to establish. In the Poetomachia, both sides share a rhetoric that focuses attention on the participants as writers.

IV

Marston and Dekker graft their ctitique of Jonson onto the main plots of *Histriomastix* and *Satiromastix*. The "untrussings" they engage in act more or less transparently as attacks.[91] Jonson's play, on the other hand, makes the critique of Marston and Dekker an integral part of the plot and denouement of *Poetaster*. Unlike the essentially limited critiques Dekker and Marston offer, Jonson's play is a thoroughgoing effort to define the proper role, subject matter, and deportment for writers and as such raises the stakes of the entire debate. Where Marston and Dekker seem content to critique Jonson for what they depict as self-importance, Jonson measures his attackers, and, by extension, all of his fellow writers, by standards he portrays as given and immutable. From

Marston and Dekker's personal attacks, Jonson turns to abstractions about good and bad writing. This movement, a reformulation of personal attack into a kind of statement of principles, represents both a straightforward mystification of those attacks (Jonson still engages in the kind of attack he claims to be disavowing) and an effort to win the contest by shifting its grounds. *Poetaster* is thus part of Jonson's effort to redefine the field, an effort that culminates in the publication of the 1616 Folio.

Poetaster lines up five examples of writerly personas in three groupings for the audience's examination: first, Demetrius and Crispinus, second, Ovid, and last Virgil and Horace. Demetrius and Crispinus are workmanlike writers described as "poetasters," "plagiaries," and "play-dressers." They are mere imitators, revisers, artisanal writers rather than poets. They are obsessively envious of Horace's preferment and do not recognize that that preferment is wholly contingent on Horace's superior skill as a poet. Stung by an accusation that he had borrowed from Horace, Demetrius cries: "Alas, sir, HORACE! hee is a meere spunge; nothing but humours and observation; he goes vp and downe sucking from euery society, and when hee comes home squeazes himself dry. I know him, I" (4.3.104–7). Demetrius attacks Horace as an imitator, a "spunge" sucking up words and ideas everywhere he goes, which is precisely the charge Jonson levels against both Marston and Dekker. Apish imitation, even in the mouth of a villain, is something to be criticized. Captain Tucca, who acts as a sympathetic advocate for the poetasters, chimes in, stating that "what he once drops vpon paper against a man, liues eternally to vpbraid him in the mouth of every slaue tankerd-bearer, or water-man" (4.3.111–13). Horace's satires seem to be popular where Demetrius's and Crispinus's work is scorned. Gallus even prefers Horace's company to that of Deme-trius and Crispinus saying "O, that HORACE had staied still, here" (4.3.130) when faced with the prospect of dining with the two poetasters. Their motives in attacking Horace derive from envy of his success and that envy helps to doom them in their trial at the end of the play. Jonson suggests that envy of another's gifts leads to bad poetry.

Jonson treats Ovid as a kind of middle term in the continuum between the poetasters and himself. Ovid typifies the position of the gentleman amateur, spending his talents in the service of poetry rather than the state. Accused of frivolity and, worse yet, playwriting, by his father, who had planned for him to study the law, Ovid responds:

> I am not knowne vnto the open stage,
> Nor doe I traffique in their *theaters*.
> Indeed, I doe acknowledge, at request
> Of some neere friends, and honorable *Romanes*,
> I haue begunne a *poeme* of that nature.
> (1.2.63–67)

Ovid may be writing a play, but defends his work by asserting that it is not destined for the "open stage," instead it is a "poeme" commissioned by some "honorable Romanes." Jonson refrains from directing outright criticisms of the kind he makes of Demetrius and Crispinus at Ovid, but his position is shown to be compromised by a kind of moral laxity. His poetic talents, great though they be, are being directed at base entertainments—Ovid is exiled for participating in a feast where the diners impersonate the gods—not elevating the populace. The play condemns Ovid on both moral and literary grounds (not by accident is he caught at the feast by Horace, Caesar, and Mecoenas) for his wasting his poetic gifts in this manner when they should be placed in service of the state.

Horace and Virgil, the final pair of writers, stand at the top of the hierarchy and represent the ideal to which all poets should aspire. They unite talent and moral probity, thus escaping the fate of Demetrius and Crispinus who are merely bad writers, as well as the fate of Ovid, who is a good writer but lacks firmness of character. In the final scene, Caesar asks Horace his opinion of Virgil:

> What thinke you three of VIRGIL, gentlemen,
> (That are of his profession, though rankt higher,)
> Or HORACE, what saist thou, that art the poorest,
> And likeliest to enuy or to detract?
> (5.1.75–78)

Caesar asks Horace and his fellow professionals to evaluate Virgil's work, allowing poets to criticize or praise a fellow poet, before he makes any final determination about the work. This is an important point—Caesar asks Horace and the others for their *professional* opinion, implying that they are more qualified than he to judge the work of a fellow poet. The principle of peer judgment is one of the defining characteristics of a field—here Caesar recognizes the autonomy of the "literary" field by deferring judgment to those he deems best suited to make a fair evaluation: other poets. Even as the play dramatizes patronage—Mecoenas, after all, is the traditional figure of the generous patron—it attempts to obfuscate the financial aspect in favor of a spiritualized notion of poetic value. By dramatizing an act of professional judgment and maintaining the image of patronage, the play executes a double move: Jonson asserts that the judging of poetry is best done by poets while at the same time valorizing the judgment of Caesar and patrons more generally. Caesar recognizes Virgil's virtue and seats him in the throne. Horace responds to the idea that he is "likeliest to envy or detract," asserting that "he that detracts, or enuies virtuous merit, / Is still the couetous, and the ignorant spirit" (5.1.92–93) making the primary category of evaluation the quality ("virtuous merit") of the work and disclaiming a role for personal feeling in the matter. Caesar applauds this sentiment and asks the question again prompting Horace to describe Virgil as a "rectified spirit," a learned man, and as a poet whose work "shall gather strength of life, with being, / And liue hereafter, more admir'd, then now" (5.1.137–38).

Poetaster concludes with an elaborately staged trial scene that allows Jonson to present the opposition between the writerly persona he espouses and that which he attributes to his rivals Marston and Dekker in a particularly graphic manner. The trial begins with a reading of the charges against Demetrius and Crispinus. They are charged with calumny—depraving Horace, "taxing him falsely of selfe-loue, arrogancy, impudence, rayling, filching by translation, etc" (5.2.231–32).[92] The indictment names Crispinus as a "poetaster and plagiary," Demetrius as a "play-dresser and plagiary," but Horace is a "poet, and priest to the Muses" (5.2.216–28). The trial is judged by Virgil, speaking from Caesar's throne, who orders Tibullus to read samples of both Demetrius's and Crispinus's work. Crispinus's comes first:

> *Rampe up my* genius, *be not retrograde:*
> *But boldly nominate a spade a spade.*
> *What, shall thy lubricall and glibberie Muse*
> *Liue, as she were defunct, like punke in stewes?*
> (5.2.275–78)

The poem Tibullus reads is laden with vocabulary typical of Marston's early poems—lubrical, glibberie, snotteries, and so on—a vocabulary Jonson scorns as fustian and willfully obscure. A libel by Demetrius follows that almost quotes *Satiromastix*:

> *Our Muse is in mind for th'vntrussing a poet,*
> *I slip by his name; for most men doe know it:*
> *A critick, that all the world bescumbers*
> *With satyricall humours, and lyricall numbers:*
> *And for the most part, himselfe doth aduance*
> *With much selfe-loue, and more arrogance.*
>
> (5.2.302–8)

Jonson caricatures Marston and Dekker's diction in these verses in order to position himself as the true possessor of the poet's voice while at the same time defining that voice. Virgil reacts scornfully to these verses, and he tells Caesar they are "strangely worded," going on to say of Demetrius and Crispinus that "if they should confidently praise their works, in them it would appeare inflation" (5.2.297, 360–61). In other words, they are criticized for their poor writing.

Virgil and Horace exact a telling form of justice as the play closes. Horace administers an emetic that causes Crispinus to vomit up the words that offend the true poets. The pill administered, Crispinus begins spewing forth the words Jonson finds so objectionable:

> Crispinus: *O—retrograde—reciprocall—incubus.*
> Caesar: What's that, HORACE?
> Horace: *Retrograde, reciprocall,* and *Incubus* are come vp.
> Gallus: Thanks be to IUPITER!
> Crispinus: *Glibbery, lubricall,* and *defunct.*
> Horace: Well, said, here's some store.
>
> (5.2.468–73)

The vocabulary Jonson purges here is that associated with the early work of Marston leaving behind what he depicts as the more measured tones of his own "plain" style. Virgil prescribes a strict diet of Cato, Terence, Plautus, and the "best Greekes." Virgil asserts that this will cure Crispinus by making his work like that of a true poet's—measured, decorous, learned, and wholesome—like Jonson's self-representation. Jonson, however disingenuously, aligns himself with these traits of moderation as a way of claiming victory in the Poet's War, a war effectively ended with this play.

V

> It will be looked for, book, when some but see
> Thy title, *Epigrams, and* named of me,
> Thou shouldst be bold, licentious, full of gall
> Wormwood, and sulphur, sharp and toothed withal;
> Become a petulant thing, hurl ink, and wit,
> As madmen stones: not caring whom they hit.
> Deceive their malice, who could wish it so.
> And by thy wiser temper, let men know
> Thou art not covetous of least self-fame:
> Much less with lewd, profane, and beastly phrase,
> To catch the world's loose laughter or vain gaze.
> He that departs with his own honesty
> For vulgar praise, doth it too dearly buy.
> —Ben Jonson, *Epigrams* 2 ("To My Book")

Ben Jonson's admonition to his book at the opening of his *Epigrams* is part of an ongoing effort to reconfigure and control the reputation of his work. Jonson asserts that these poems, despite their origins and genre, will not be full of license, gall, or lewdness, but will be honest, decent, and worthy of serious praise. Nor are they directed toward the "vulgar," or interested in "self-fame," but rather they are intended for an audience that will "understand" them and justly praise them. The tension Jonson articulates here between "honesty" and "vulgar praise" is one of the structuring principles of the way he imagines the field. In practice, the distinction is blurry—particularly since Jonson is a relentless self-promoter—but its articulation represents a strategic intervention in the discourse about poetry. The project represented by this epigram is not restricted to the epigrams, but extends throughout all of Jonson's work. The plays become "dramatick poems" and, at least in the case of *Sejanus*, accrete a massive scholarly apparatus as they enter print. It is a commonplace to discuss Jonson's 1616 *Works* as an effort to assert the literariness of plays—a kind of clearing of the way for the Shakespeare folio and the subsequent recognition of drama as a legitimate "literary" genre—but Jonson's intent in pronouncements such as the epigram quoted above, in his publications, and in his plays is not merely a claim for a genre's legitimacy (or for the value of his own work). Jonson's published works do make explicit claims for the value of his own work, but, more importantly, his assertions and self-positionings in the contentious literary marketplace of early modern London have lasting effects on the definition of the writer's role and on the shape of the literary field more generally. Throughout his career, Jonson strives to define his work and, by extension, his role as a professional writer as honest and, more importantly, worthy of respect.

The "terrible poetomachia" discussed above is a refracted representation of the struggles that define the field of cultural production—a field whose paradigms govern the production and reception of the work of art. Jonson, Marston, and Dekker's relation to each other's work and to the broader market for cultural products outlines part of the vexed transition from a "literary" field more purely governed by external concerns to one increasingly dominated by struggles and considerations recognized in terms of the field itself. The profession was thus coming to be defined on its own terms at the same time that playwriting was gaining a precarious legitimacy, as demonstrated by the increasing resort of gentlemen to it as a career. The Poetomachia demonstrates that playwriting was recognized by its practitioners as a profession with its own criteria of judgment, criteria which were the stakes of the war played out in *Histriomastix, Poetaster*, and *Satiromastix*. Jonson turns the Poetomachia into a struggle over the definition of a good play—his style being portrayed as superior to that of his rivals. This response, a response that becomes more common in later literary struggles, is both innovative and structured by the field itself.

The Poet's War ends, in part, because it produces an always-contestable image of the professional playwright. Jonson's *Poetaster* criticizes his rivals for failing to measure up to an authorial standard he himself defines. Whether or not Jonson (or Marston, or Dekker, or any other playwright) measures up to this standard is less important than the fact that such a standard was articulated and thus made contestable. Marston and Dekker are content to satirize elements of their rival's personality and poetic practice but only incidentally attack him as a *writer*. In response to these attacks, Jonson espoused a particular kind of professionalism—one defined by a kind of rhetorical restraint and, if the structure of *Poetaster* can serve as evidence, a commitment to a unified action on the stage.[93] Neither Marston nor Dekker made any such gestures; they contented themselves with criticizing what they depict as the pretensions of their rivals and did not take the additional step of articulating a position.[94] By espousing these stylistic standards, Jonson defines his work as distinctive, worthy of attention, and thus makes it marketable to both the acting companies and the paying audience.[95] Jonson's professionalism was thus not merely an effort to defend himself from what he saw as slander, but was also a claim for and defense of the marketability of his plays. Jonson's version of professionalism thus emerges in the context of the field—as an effect of a struggle for position—and his stress on standards (painfully clear in *Poetaster*'s trial scene) derives from his individual disposition—his classicism, his contentiousness, his commitment to Horatian poetics—as well as the developing structure of the field. A social agent's actions are always structured by a combination of individual history and position in a series of fields, and Jonson's declarations in *Poetaster* result from the confrontation between his immediate sense of being threatened and his location in the emergent professional field.[96]

Rather than offer a straightforward response to the charges laid against him, Jonson chooses to engage in a struggle to define the shape of the field of dramatic writing. *Poetaster*, instead of relying for its effectiveness on the kind of libels and comic personations of Marston and Dekker's plays, offers a picture of what Jonson views as the proper shape of a specifically literary hierarchy. The criteria for evaluating status in this hierarchy are literary (for lack of a better and less anachronistic term)—poetic quality wins over sensationalism—and the judges are writers, not patrons, buyers, or, as various outbursts in Jonson's later career show, audiences. All three playwrights respond to attacks on their professional stature by reference to writing and their skills, but Jonson turns what could have been a relatively minor professional conflict into a position taking in the field of cultural production. The impetus behind this position taking remains professional, and Jonson is nothing if not a professional, but the conflict is refracted into a debate about standards of quality for plays—the refraction has long-lasting effects. This early modern struggle and the terms it introduces exert a profound influence on subsequent struggles and on the development of professional writing—contributing to the origins of a self-judging and self-authorizing "literature."[97]

6
Conclusions

> By forcing one to discover externality at the heart of
> internality, banality in the illusion of rarity, the common
> in the pursuit of the unique, sociology does more than
> denounce all the impostures of egoistic narcissism,
> it offers perhaps the only means of contributing,
> if only through awareness of determinations, to the
> construction, otherwise abandoned to the forces of
> the world, of something like a subject.
>
> Pierre Bourdieu, *The Logic of Practice*

BOURDIEU'S ARGUMENT IN *THE LOGIC OF PRACTICE* ATTEMPTS TO find a way out of the impasses of subjective and objective approaches to understanding human agency. For Bourdieu, the objectivist approach (typified by structuralism) "tends to constitute the model constructed to account for practices as a power really capable of determining them" and thus fails to account for the ways that the regularities it describes are actually produced in practice.[1] It misrecognizes the model as the cause or explanation of practice rather than investigating how it is that practices are often regular enough to be capable of being modeled. More significantly, the objectivist approach to understanding the subject "ignores the dialectic of social structures and structured structuring dispositions through which schemes of thought are formed and transformed"—it ignores what Bourdieu elsewhere calls the work of time.[2] The "subjectivist" side represented in its strong form by rational-actor theory asserts that practices result from a self-transparent subject's rational choices. This theory of practice, the obverse of objectivism, excludes the possibility that though an agent's decisions might be reasonable they are not fully accessible to reason and still less can they be fully ascribed to a wholly rational choice. It is "unaware that practices can have other principles than mechanical causes or conscious ends and can obey an economic logic without obeying narrowly economic interests."[3] Here, as elsewhere, Bourdieu suggests that "the principle of practices has to be sought instead in the relationship between external constraints which leave a very variable margin for choice, and dispositions which are the product of economic and social processes that are more or less completely reducible to these constraints, as defined at a particular moment."[4] This idea, that understanding the principle that guide agents' practice has to be found in the complex interactions between individual choice and the constraints of constructed dispositions, has guided my work in this book, which has been concerned with developing an account of the emergence of the professions in early modern England. The professions are one of the forces that constrain or preempt the construction of a subject and hence my interest has been to attempt to find some of the "externality at the heart of internality, banality in the pursuit of rarity, the common in the pursuit of the unique" whose discovery can help bring determinations to light.

This project emerged from a desire to write about the advent of modernity—a quixotic and all but impossible task—and in the process of defining the scope of this work into something manageable, the book became a social and literary history of professions linked by their concern with the effects and uses of writing. My wish, however hubristic, to provide an account of modernity as emergent in sixteenth-century England participated in the 1990s academy's investment in big theory, big ideas, and big books. Since then, in the aftermath of theory and the more or less full establishment of an historicist orthodoxy in literary studies, scholars have begun to move away from the grand narratives of the history of the subject (or of capital or other large categories) in favor of more narrowly defined objects of study. Heeding the cautions of postmodern critics of metanarratives, early modern studies has focused attention on smaller areas in the interest of avoiding the perceived dangers of teleology, anachronism, or generalization. While there are real risks of distortion in *grands récits*, it is likewise risky to avoid the project of constructing a subject—riskier, I would argue—because to relinquish the history of the subject surrenders that history to the "forces of the world." This danger is far greater than the more or less avoidable dangers of totalization or reduction that recent theory has pointed to and thus made more avoidable. This book, therefore, offers both a contribution to the construction of a "something like a subject" and suggests ways to produce historicist scholarship that can avoid the pitfalls of metanarratives while producing smaller narratives that suggest connections between social, historical, and literary phenomena over time.

Much scholarly work in literary and cultural studies in recent decades has been concerned with the "history of the subject," offering accounts of the emergence or dissolution of the modern subject, of various versions of subjectivity whether dominant or dominated, of the historical or economic forces driving changes in the subject, or, more radically, of the nonexistence of the subject now or in the past. Many of these accounts appear to have in common a desire to contribute to an increasing awareness of the range of determinations that construct individual agents' experience of subjectivity in order to make change either possible or, in stronger forms, inevitable.[5] Bourdieu's work often disavows investments in direct or broad transformations out of a suspicion that a focus on individual transformations (such as those characteristic of certain versions of psychoanalysis) tends merely to reproduce the same determinations under another name. From a Bourdieuian perspective, then, many versions of the "history of the subject" substitute one set of impostures for another rather than contributing to "the construction of something like a subject."[6] A focus on more general categories of determinations—such as those deriving from the professions discussed in this book—agitates against the narcissism implicit in more "individualistic" treatments of "inwardness" or subjectivity in the period. An awareness of the "impostures of egoistic narcissism" can thus afford a more adequate account of the ways that agents construct subject positions in a social field characterized by social, economic, and historical constraint. This book has striven to make a contribution to this construction by describing the emergence of a set of professions in early modern England—professions that continue to be important in contemporary society—and by characterizing some of the more general features of the idea (and ideals) of profession at the same time.

The professions are deeply involved in the "impostures of egoistic narcissism" that Bourdieu describes in the opening pages of *The Logic of Practice* as agitating against the construction of a subject position. Practitioners suggest, for example, that their privileges derive not from institutional sanctions or the kinds of historical developments discussed above, but from the individual deserts of the practitioner whose guiding principle is service.[7] These mystifications both enable professions to construct themselves—claims for the significance and usefulness of an occupation are crucial to professionalization—and also allow them to make public assertions that justify the privileges that usually accompany recognition as a profession (monopoly over an area of work, for example).[8] Early modern administration, law, theater, and playwriting are also deeply involved in representing English society to itself—whether by reorganizing government so as to concentrate authority in a monarch served by an increasingly professional and secular bureaucracy or by adjusting legal training and practice in response to political, economic, or social change or, most centrally for this study, by presenting dramatic representations of such changes in a theater that was making claims for its value as a social force.

I have argued that, despite prevailing sociological positions, a group of early modern occupations developed into recognizably professional endeavors in the sixteenth and seventeenth centuries. Beginning with a survey of the history of the ideas of profession, calling, and vocation, this book has demonstrated the emergence of patterns of training and practice that can best be understood as professional. The professions emerge partly as a response to changing social conditions—the "legitimation crisis" of the estates system being one example—and offered agents means to secure positions as well as to represent them as legitimate.[9] As the chapters have shown, representation occupies a central position in the development of these four fields—whether directly as with the theater trades and playwriting or indirectly as with the law and administration—and careful attention to the ways these representations refract, shape, and are shaped by social change has been essential to this book's argument about the literary and social history of profession. My analysis of administration, law, theater, and playwriting has also been concerned to establish some of the factors that make the identification of sixteenth- and seventeenth-century England's culture as "early modern" plausible. These strands of argument complement each other and derive from methodological preoccupations related to but distinct from those of the New Historicism.

6 / CONCLUSIONS

This concluding chapter combines the historical disposition of the preceding chapters with a return to the methodological questions of the introduction in an effort to accomplish two goals. First, I take up the "crisis of the humanities" as a way of introducing the current centrality of historical scholarship in literary study generally and early modern studies specifically. In the second section of this chapter, I discuss the current ascendancy of historicism in early modern studies in order to suggest that current preoccupations with history and materiality can have the effect of turning literary history into an antiquarian activity. In the course of this discussion, I argue that one way to assert the continuing relevance of Shakespeare studies and literary study more generally in face of doubts about its purpose lies in a historical scholarship that, rather than engaging in an antiquarian recovery of the past, strives to construct an awareness of the determinations that structure social change, determinations whose force extends beyond their immediate historical context. My book represents a mode of historical scholarship that is not a formalism in disguise (a common critique of the New Historicism), nor a purely archival and backward-looking "recovery" of the past, nor an anachronistic finding of the present in past texts, but a constructive engagement with and understanding of a past that is always already with us. This book argues, therefore, for the necessity of a historical project that depends on the creation of a narrative within which it is possible to investigate both specific events and broader developments.[10]

I

> Many objections have been made to a proposition which, in some remarks of mine on translating Homer, I ventured to put forth; a proposition about criticism, and its importance at the present day. I said: "Of the literature of France and Germany, as of the intellect of Europe in general, the main effort, for now many years, has been a critical effort; the endeavor, in all branches of knowledge, theology, philosophy, history, art, science, to see the object as in itself it really is." I added, that owing to the operation in English literature of certain causes, "almost the last thing for which one would come to English literature is just that very thing which now Europe most desires—criticism"; and that the power and value of English literature was thereby impaired.

> More than one rejoinder declared that the importance I here assigned to criticism was excessive, and asserted the inherent superiority of the creative effort of the human spirit over its critical effort.
> —Matthew Arnold, "The Function of Criticism at the Present Time" (1865)

Arnold's nineteenth-century meditation on criticism articulates one of the founding oppositions in literary studies—that between "creative effort" and "critical effort"—an opposition that still structures the discipline.[11] Moreover, Arnold registers the importance that questions of method had and continue to have in the field. What Arnold describes as the European effort to "see the object [of study] as in itself it really is" arguably remains the agenda of both theoretical and historical criticism of literature.[12] The counter position likewise remains remarkably similar—valuing the aesthetic or moral effects of literature and eschewing interest in demystifying the means by which those effects are achieved. Arnold, widely recognized as an inaugural figure in modern professional literary criticism, thus articulates some of the principles of vision and division that structure the game of literary studies.[13] Arnold's argument that the lack of a criticism interested in seeing literature "as in itself it really is" impairs the "power and value" of English literature also serves as one of the early justifications for the study of English as an academic discipline.[14] This aspect of the profession—its engagement in the elucidation and transmission of a national literature—has diminished in importance in recent thinking about literary study, but remains institutionally fundamental.[15] It also expresses a division between two models—one that encourages research into what "it really is" and one that trains students to recognize the expression of "the inherent superiority of the creative effort of the human spirit"—a methodological split that remains important in the debate over the contemporary academy. The first of these models includes approaches as diverse as formalisms like the New Criticism and historicisms as diverse as the Old and New Historicisms and cultural materialism while the second relates more to a discourse of moral improvement, which is also an important part of the Arnoldian legacy to literary criticism. I do not intend to provide an exhaustive discussion of the modern academic study of literature or of the job system or of the culture wars, but instead wish to suggest that claims for the distinctiveness and value of the intellectual labor of literature faculties need pay more careful attention to the discipline's historical and social context as they respond to the changing university than has been the case under the pressure of the job crisis and the culture wars.[16] In the pages that follow, I will sketch some of the contours of this history as a way to introduce a more specific discussion of the fraught status of historicism in early modern studies. I cite Arnold here not to suggest that nothing has changed, but to argue that current struggles over the definition, meaning, and function of criticism have a long history, a history that inevitably structures the profession and that needs to be addressed in current responses to the 'crisis of the humanities.'[17]

This crisis, *mutatis mutandis*, lies at the heart of the discipline's institutional history and dates at least as far back as Immanuel Kant's inaugural discussion of conflict between the various disciplines in his *The Conflict of the Faculties* (1798), which posits a distinction between higher and lower faculties based on their relation to the power of the state and their varying commitments to the development of knowledge. The higher faculties of law, medicine, and theology are, in Kant's view, intimately involved in the government of the state—they are concerned with the health of the body politic—and the state has a compelling interest in the content and conduct of their teaching.[18] The lower faculty (philosophy), on the other hand, lacks such direct connections to the state. In other words, it is or ought to be free from what Kant describes as the legitimate pressure that the state can bring to bear on the faculties of law, medicine, and theology. However, this freedom is only ever relative—the autonomy of the faculty of philosophy (a rubric under which both humanistic and scientific disciplines are gathered) is not absolute and depends on its institutional location.[19] Moreover, the philosophy faculty's autonomy comes with both the ability and the responsibility to "control" the higher faculties:

> A university must have a faculty of philosophy. Its function in relation to the other faculties is to control them and, in this way, be useful to them, since *truth* (the essential and first condition of learning in general) is the main thing, whereas the *utility* the higher faculties promise the government is of secondary importance. We can also grant the theology faculty's proud claim that

> the philosophy faculty is its handmaid . . . provided it is not driven away or silenced. For the very *modesty* [of its claim]—merely to be free, as it leaves others free, to discover the truth for the benefit of all the sciences and to set it before the higher faculties to use as they will—must commend it to the government as above suspicion and, indeed, indispensable.[20]

Kant's claim for the necessity of the philosophical faculty centers on that faculty's ability and obligation to serve the interests of the state by testing the edicts, laws, and prescriptions of the theological, legal, and medical faculties. The philosophical faculty is concerned with truth "the essential and first condition of learning in general" and that concern affords it the ability to control the higher faculties by verifying or falsifying their pronouncements. The direct utility of the higher faculties is secondary to the lower faculty's commitment to truth. However, that commitment to truth is useful only indirectly, only as it shapes or corrects disciplines with more direct public effect. Essentially, Kant claims that the lower faculty is necessary because as it advances knowledge (truth) it performs an invaluable service to the state by making it increasingly rational. In order for the lower faculty to do this it must be free, but this freedom is only meaningful in the context of the institution and of the state.

Kant's argument for the autonomy and necessity of the disciplines gathered together as "philosophy" thus depends on their necessarily indirect utility and despite changes in the definition of that utility, such claims remain at the heart of defenses of the humanities. Kant, of course, does not imagine any kind of simple, direct relationship between the lower faculty's work and its usefulness, but neither does he imagine that its work can proceed as though in isolation, nor is he imagining a scholarship determined by a utilitarian ideal, but instead argues that the pursuit of "truth" occurs in an institutional context and that that pursuit has effect by virtue of that context. The conflict of the faculties, a conflict that advances human society, can only occur in an institution where there are faculties and can only be socially useful in a mediated way. There is no way to circumvent this mediation—to imagine or act as though there is endangers the enabling relative autonomy of a discipline.[21] Kant's argument serves as a kind of blueprint for Humboldt's foundation of his university in Berlin—which collected various faculties into one institution—and in turn becomes the foundation of the modern

North American university with its divisions between departments, schools, and colleges. For Kant, conflict between the faculties is a necessary and inevitable part of the university's structure, but that conflict only has meaning in the context of a mediated relationship to the state of which the university constitutes one part.

University-based literary studies in the United States has been in a continual state of ferment at least since the advent of "theory" in the '60s and '70s.[22] One source of this ferment is a desire for "relevance" on the part of the discipline, a relevance that, as Guillory shows in the context of the canon debate, tends to elide the mediations that, at least in Kant's view, enable the lower faculty to effect change. Graff describes the modern Department of English as arising out of a conflict between philology and criticism in the context of the development of the North American research university in the late nineteenth and early twentieth centuries.[23] Graff argues that philology was able to assert itself as a research discipline—engaged in the production of "truth"—while criticism, at least initially, had more trouble making a place for itself in the new institution. This split is homologous to that described by Arnold in his "Function of Criticism at the Present Time"—distinguishing disciplines invested in the production of knowledge and those interested in enculturation—and remains important in current discussions about the field.[24] Philology's ascendancy waned under pressure from a criticism meant to provide access to literature "as it really is"—especially the New Criticism—and this institutional struggle in turn gives rise to the conflicts of the 1960s and '70s over the American reception of Continental literary and philosophical theory which purported to offer a new way to see literature.

In the course of these internal conflicts, the professional study of literature has come under external pressure from a wide variety of sources. Probably the most significant of these forces to the structure of the field are the exigencies of the job market, but the public debate over the usefulness of the teaching and scholarship literature faculty engage in has had profound effects on the profession. Recent claims for the continuing value of literary studies in a social order considerably different from that which grounded the foundation of academic literature departments have generally taken two paths. One of these claims, more pedagogically inflected, focuses on the practical use of the kinds of skills inculcated in students by taking a degree in English.[25] The other, more research oriented, defends its practice in the name of knowledge, often asserting a latent politics to its inquiry. Both of these defenses are related and are occasionally articulated as complementary, using the rhetoric of the intimate connection of research and teaching in the university. Both also refract structuring distinctions suggested by Kant's *Conflict of the Faculties* and by Arnold, distinctions between the immediate practical use of a discipline and the more mediated effects of its theoretical program.[26] The positions taken in defense of literary study have, I have been suggesting, a history and that history depends crucially on literary study's institutional location—a position that is and has been defined by intellectual and social conflict at least as far back as *The Conflict of the Faculties*.

Theoretical conflict is thus endemic in the field of literary study and the more recent turn to historicism can be seen as an epiphenomenon of a structural conflict between disparate elements of the field most straightforwardly represented by the researcher on one side and the pedagogue on the other.[27] Two suggestions or, perhaps, imperatives can be derived from the profession's history. First, the profession's autonomy is only ever relative but that does not imply that it is not real or vital and that autonomy needs vigorous defense. Second, that autonomy enables and obligates the disciplines grouped together in the lower faculty to comment on, correct, and, to some extent at least, control the higher faculties of (in the contemporary context) law and medicine and in doing so exert an effect on the field of power. If "history" is one of the dominant means by which literary studies imagines that it contributes to the truth that Kant sees as controlling the higher faculty, it is imperative that that history actually do the thing it claims to do. Thus, the next section turns to historicism in early modern studies and argues that historicism's history needs more careful analysis than has previously been the case. This analysis is particularly pressing as historicism seems to have become a dominant methodological principle. If historicist scholarship is to have an effect, however mediated, on the state, it is essential that practitioners have a clear sense of the implications of their practice. It will be my suggestion that at least some versions of early modern historicist scholarship precludes such effects by tending to be more antiquarian than historical.

II

This book's discussion of the early history of the professions engages with the broadly historical turn in early modern studies that has been the prevailing mode of scholarship since the 1980s. Whether labeled "New Historicism," "Cultural Materialism" or just "historicism," historicist work has taken center stage in early modern studies if not in literary studies more generally.[28] As John Brannigan writes in his 1998 book, *New Historicism and Cultural Materialism*:

> New historicism and cultural materialism have become a central part of the repertoire of literary studies, and new work using their approaches is supported by journals like *Representations, Textual Practice, Literature and History, English Literary History, American Literary History, Social Text*, and *News from Nowhere*, and by series of books like *The New Historicism* (California), *Cultural Politics* (Manchester), *Cambridge Studies in Renaissance Literature and Culture* (Cambridge), *New Cultural Studies* (Pennsylvania), and *Literature in History* (Princeton). New historicism and cultural materialism are regularly included on courses on literary or critical theory, and in guides to theory and critical practice, and are largely responsible for the turn toward the study of historical contexts in literary studies.[29]

What this list (which is not, naturally, exhaustive) suggests is the pervasiveness of scholarship presented under the aegis of history and its centrality in the profession's imagination of itself.[30] Historicism (of whatever variety—new, old, etc.) has moreover been associated with materialism in the current critical discourse in early modern studies. But this association has not been particularly well theorized in the professional discourse of early modern studies. At times the terms seem to function synonymously— with materialism being a version of historicism—or as designators of intellectual affiliation—cultural materialism being both more English and more Marxist than New Historicism which is more Foucauldian and American. The link between materialism and the various configurations of historicism has thus been variously accepted, disavowed, rejected, or celebrated but not, it seems, thoroughly theorized or conceptualized.[31] The New Historicism in particular is notoriously undertheorized and the recent move away from the "new" label still leaves the key term more or less undefined.[32] As alluded to above, the current centrality of historical scholarship in the humanities comes in the ongoing aftermath of the theory "revolution" and the so-called culture wars of the late 1980s and early 1990s.

Since at least the publication of Jean Howard's "The New Historicism in Renaissance Studies" in *English Literary Renaissance*, the return to history has been both hailed and criticized as a transformation of the field.[33] Criticism has come from both the right and the left, questioning the usefulness of historicist work in general for understanding literary texts, questioning the quality of the history produced by literary scholars, and questioning just how new the New Historicism is.[34] This book is indebted to the insights of the New Historicism, but has attempted to avoid some of its familiar pitfalls by recourse to Bourdieu's sociology. My approach is not a rejection or disavowal of theory, a move that seems latent in some recent historical scholarship that turns to an undertheorized archive in a labor of recovery rather than analysis.[35] In contrast to a postmodern critique of narrative history as tending to produce distorting or coercive teleologies, my work argues for the necessity of a historical project that depends on the creation of a narrative within which it is possible to investigate both specific events and broader developments.

History has nevertheless come to stand at the center of contemporary literary scholarship. "History" and "theory" have recently appeared to be the twin poles that structure our critical endeavor.[36] In some accounts, theory appears to have either exhausted itself or become so much a part of the discourse that its status as one pole of the scholarly world may be questionable.[37] This seems not to be the case with history. Nevertheless, the term remains contestable, loosely defined, and thus the right to define its content is a site of struggle in the profession. As with early modern administration, law, and theater, struggles over the right to define what counts as legitimate and illegitimate work and ways of doing work define the structure of the profession. "History" serves as one marker of that legitimacy in literary study and thus needs careful definition.[38]

In what follows, I will offer an account of some of the philosophical and theoretical questions surrounding the practice of historical scholarship, beginning with the problem of narrative in historiography and its relationship with historical knowledge. I then turn to an examination of a mode of historical thought that sees history as having come to an end—a position that alters historical scholarship in a number of ways, ways I argue are problematic—and responds to that end with either despair or hope. I will suggest that elements of this mode of thinking are latent in the New Historicism's approach to history and that that latency helps explain the increasing particularist, if not antiquarian, focus of historical scholarship in literary studies. Finally, I will argue, in agreement with critics of posthistory, that posthistory might best be understood as a hermeneutical crisis—not the end of history but the end of a certain kind of historical meaning—and that one among many productive responses to this interpretive crisis lies in what Pierre Bourdieu calls genetic or structural sociology, an approach that structures this book.[39] As Nietzsche notes in "The Uses and Disadvantages of History for Life," an essay important to posthistorical thought as well as postmodern philosophy, the problem is not with history as such, but with what one does with history. This problem is the subject of the following discussion.

To many theorists of history, the category itself is a problem. Is history simply another name for the past? Is history the name of a specific genre of discourse about events that occurred at some point in the past? Are the facts of the past even accessible to contemporary scholars in any kind of objective way? What kind of knowledge does historical scholarship produce? These questions are central to Hayden White's thought on historiography and his insights have immediate relevance to the historical turn in literary scholarship.[40] In the course of his ongoing project, White addresses the "problem of the relation between narrative discourse and historical representation."[41] This problem is, in many ways, the central problem of historicist scholarship in literature, which takes much of the evidence for its historical narratives from various modes of narrative discourse while at the same time producing a narrative discourse about the past—many different forms of narrative all invested in "history." In an essay called "The Question of Narrative in Contemporary Historical Theory," White asserts that the field of historical studies has traditionally viewed narrative as neither "a product of a theory nor as the basis for a method but rather as a form of discourse that may or may not be used for the representation of historical events" depending on the intention of the historian.[42] The distinction between fictional and historical narratives thus has to do with content, not form:

> The content of historical stories is real events, events that really happened, rather than imaginary events, events invented by the narrator. This implies that the form in which historical events present themselves is found rather than constructed. For the narrative historian, the historical method consists in investigating the documents in order to determine what is the true or most plausible story that can be told about the events of which they are evidence . . . The form of the discourse, the narrative, adds nothing to the content of the representations.[43]

Narrative, the form of traditional historiography as well as of fiction, is thus not an object of analysis. White's essay goes on to discuss several different approaches to the issue of narrative in historical theory and argues that differences over the role of narrative in describing historical events have to do with "how one construes the function of the faculty of the imagination."[44] White argues that the historiographical recourse to narrative expresses a desire to see the past as coherent, as meaningful, and that historians describe past events in narrative form to achieve that coherence—to engage in the production of a "specifically human truth."[45] White's discussion suggests the necessity of narrative form in representing what he calls the truth of the past, narrative is a mode of representation that allows the past to gain meaning—what this meaning is and where it comes from is an ideological question.[46]

White's work demonstrates the centrality of the question about narrative's ideological character to contemporary thought about historiography. Narrative and its relation to meaning has also been a thematic of much recent literary theory and a skeptical disposition toward the truth claims made by various narratives undergirds much poststructuralist philosophy. Philosophical and historical questions about the ideological effects (and content) of narrative are related to the recent turn to historical scholarship in literary studies. Ambivalence toward the version of early modern history represented by Tillyard's *Elizabethan World Picture*, a version that made sense of the period in terms of a totalizing model of social, intellectual, and political life, has given rise to a more fragmentary and partial kind of history, especially in literary studies. The New Historicism, as mentioned above, is one response to a totalizing history that attempts to avoid the ideological dangers of unifying accounts—metanarratives, to use Lyotard's term—while still holding on to the idea of history as a useful practice.[47]

Historicism, as distinguished from history, itself has a fraught and contradictory history. The term's status as one of the key designators for early modern scholarship makes its definition as important as that of history. Hayden White describes discussions of historicism by practicing historians that depict historicism as though

> it consists of a discernible and unjustifiable distortion of a properly "historical" way of representing reality. Thus, for example, there are those who speak of the particularizing interest of the historian as against the generalizing interests of the historicist ... while the historian studies the past for its own sake or, as the phrase has it, "for itself alone," the historicist wants to use his knowledge of the past to illuminate the problems of the present or, worse, to predict the path of history's future development.[48]

In the course of arguing that all historical writing is inescapably figural, White contends that the distinction between "history" and "historicism" is, in his terms, "virtually worthless" because "every 'historical' representation—however particularizing, narrativist, self-consciously perspectival, and fixated on its subject matter 'for its own sake'—contains most of the elements of what conventional theory calls 'historicism.' "[49] In other words, no matter how much effort is made to represent historical events without imposing the historian's ideas (of whatever sort) on those events, such impositions are inevitable and necessarily derive from a more or less conscious set of ideas deriving from a philosophy of history. White's dismissal of the distinction, though intellectually sound, obscures the ways that the two terms do imply distinct professional dispositions toward the writing of history.[50]

The status of historicism as an object of debate helps explain how prominent practitioners of the New Historicism have alternately distanced themselves from and embraced it as a term. Paul Hamilton's *Historicism* (part of Routledge's *New Critical Idiom* series of "introductory guides to today's critical terminology") defines historicism as a "critical movement insisting on the prime importance of historical context to the interpretation of texts of all kinds."[51] The interpretations that this insistence leads to are as variable as the interpreters. This is the most general and least loaded definition of historicism and, as such, is largely unexceptionable and the historicism of the New Historicism depends primarily on this sense of the term. Written primarily for an audience of literary critics and students, Hamilton's opening definition focuses on the recent literary critical meaning of historicism but also introduces the term's roots in the philosophy of history and in debates about historiography.[52] This philosophical legacy is often overlooked or selectively passed over in recent historicist literary criticism. For example, Stephen Greenblatt and Catherine Gallagher's recent and tellingly titled *Practicing New Historicism* prefers the relativistic historicism of Herder and the skepticism of Nietzsche to the universalizing and teleological historicism of a barely mentioned Hegel or Marx.[53] Johann Gottfried von Herder is cited approvingly (and repeatedly) in the introductory chapters while Hegel is mentioned in passing only once as a figure whose confidence in a unifying and progressive history is to be rejected in favor of an "existential skepticism" deriving from Erich Auerbach's work that lacks faith in a "meaningful higher order."[54] Herder's historicism seems to be more attractive because of his radical cultural relativism—his reluctance to apply modern schemes of judgment to a past that has to be evaluated more or less on its own terms—and because his work suggests that "the task of understanding then depends not on the extraction of an abstract set of principles, and still less on the application of a theoretical model, but rather on an encounter with the singular, the specific and the individual."[55] This emphasis on the singular lies at the heart of the New Historicism's use of the anecdote as a means of securing what the book's second chapter terms the "touch of the real" and also indicates hostility to generalizing explanatory models.[56] In addition, this focus on the singular can isolate event from event and thus may obscure potentially meaningful patterns. As Gallagher and Greenblatt's title announces, the book is more interested in the practice of the New Historicism even as it engages in its (disavowed) theory. History functions here as a practice that grounds the reading and interpreting of the literature of the past, a practice that has an ambivalent relationship with theory. This ambivalence seems to derive from both the postmodern suspicion of meta- or master narrative best represented by Lyotard's *Postmodern Condition* and the latent hostility of the practicing historian for theory.

Writing from a Marxist tradition without that hostility, Raymond Williams offers a general definition of history in his *Keywords* that suggestively points to the ambivalent ways that history and historicism function in cultural criticism. Of historicism he writes that it "has three senses": "(i) a relatively neutral definition of a method of study which relies on the facts of the past and traces precedents of current events; (ii) a deliberate emphasis on variable historical conditions and contexts, through which all specific events must be interpreted; (iii) a hostile sense, to attack all forms of interpretation or prediction by 'historical necessity' or the discovery of general 'laws of historical development.' "[57] The first of these agree with Hamilton's definition, but Williams goes on to suggest that the third sense, the attack on historicism, derives from what he calls a "related attack" on the idea of a future that uses the lessons of history. History in this figuration changes from a narrative of achievement or progress to one of "frustration and defeat" generating a feeling of hopelessness.[58] History thus becomes a narrative of loss, a tragic trajectory from potential freedom into actual constraint. It is this hopelessness that provides a great deal of the impetus toward the formation of the idea of the end of history as iterated in the twentieth century. The terms "history" and "historicism" evoke all these various senses in varying proportions and, rather than leaving them more or less unexamined, historical scholarship in literature would do well to explore them more fully than has generally been the case.[59]

One exploration of recent suspicions about the status and usefulness of the related ideas of history and historicism, Lutz Niethammer's *Posthistoire*, surveys the origins of the ideas linked together under the rubric of posthistory or "the end of history."[60] Niethammer refers in passing to Francis Fukuyama's more well-known recent work, but spends a great deal more time discussing German and French philosophers who have developed a theory of posthistory. The central premise, as Niethammer narrates it, derives from the work of the French philosopher Antoine Augustin Cournot (1801–77). Cournot held that philosophy was well on the way toward discovering the "laws" that govern society (and thereby history) and that this discovery would lead to the transcendence of history (its "end") and thus to a new world of freedom from the irrationality of historical change governed by chance. Cournot writes, "We are leaving the historical phase in which caprices of fate and acts of personal or moral vigour have had so much influence, to enter a new phase in which people weigh up the masses pen in hand, and are able to calculate the exact results of a clockwork mechanism."[61] Cournot depicts this departure from history as an achievement, a liberation of humanity from a historical condition he recognizes as chaotic and destructive. Cournot presents this liberated condition "as an overcoming of chaotic historicity."[62] History here is represented as the realm of caprice, of remarkable but individual acts, and as something to be abandoned.[63] Overcoming historical contingency and substituting a "clockwork mechanism" for it would lead to the development of a truly free civilization unburdened by the past and this civilization would somehow naturally produce peace and prosperity across the globe.

Another urtext of posthistory, Nietzsche's 1874 essay "On the Uses and Disadvantages of History for Life" was written roughly contemporaneously with Cournot's work. [64] Nietzsche does not envision an end to history in the same way as Cournot or, more immediately for him, Hegel does, and still less does Nietzsche desire an escape from a historical condition influenced by "personal or moral vigour," instead he argues that the study of history must subordinate itself to the needs of "life"—of culture. Writing in a German intellectual milieu dominated by a neo-Hegelianism that places history at the center of the human sciences, he writes: "We need history, certainly, but we need it for reasons different from those which the idler in the garden of knowledge needs it, even though he may look nobly down on our rough and charmless needs and requirements. We need it, that is to say, for the sake of life and action, not so as to turn comfortably away from life and action. . . . We want to serve history only to the extent that history serves life: for it is possible to value the study of history to such a degree that life becomes stunted and degenerate."[65] Reacting to the dominance of versions of historicism that downplay human agency in favor of historical determinism, Nietzsche argues for a history that is critical, that makes judgments about what elements of the past are to be kept and which are best swept away and replaced.[66] History can only be useful for "Life" when "it is dominated and directed by a higher force and does not itself dominate and direct."[67] That higher force could be called culture, agency, action—forces the essay depicts as properly human and under serious threat by versions of history that either monumentalize the past or uncritically memorialize it.[68]

Nietzsche is an important figure in posthistorical thought because of his deep skepticism about the usefulness of historical knowledge—though it is important to note that he does not dismiss history *tout court*, but only insofar as it limits freedom of action. Nietzsche does not argue that history can be transcended or ended, but more modestly argues that its study must not become an all-consuming end in itself, an end that determines all others. His skepticism responds to the danger presented by a Hegelian philosophy of history that describes the present as the completion of world-history. He writes that the idea that "one is a latecomer of the age is . . . paralyzing and depressing" but it is more destructive when "such a belief one day by a bold inversion raises this latecomer to godhood as the true meaning and goal of all previous events, when his miserable condition is equated with a completion of world history."[69] Posthistorical humanity can then lapse into a self-satisfied torpor having nothing left to accomplish or struggle for. Nietzsche rejects this version of Hegel's thought that envisions the end of world-historical process when humankind "achieves" the present which is then seen as the culmination of history. Instead, Nietzsche envisions an ongoing struggle to produce culture and meaning in the context of a constantly developing history.

Partly under the influence of a Nietzschean skepticism, Cournot's optimism about the end of history is transformed into despair in the writers Niethammer groups together under the Posthistoire label (whether on the left or the right) who see the discovery—or, more accurately, the belief in the discovery—of these laws as disastrous and productive of a one-dimensional social reality akin to that described by Herbert Marcuse. Nietzsche's skeptical influence is clear in this transformation, but Niethammer describes a mode of thought that sees the kind of struggle Nietzsche advocates as purposeless in the face of postwar social and political developments. Marcuse's "administered society" is a kind of nightmare version of the fully understood world that Cournot saw as utopian. Marcuse's *One Dimensional Man* opens with an ironic passage on contemporary society:

> A comfortable, smooth, reasonable, democratic unfreedom prevails in advanced industrial civilization, a token of technical progress. Indeed, what could be more rational than the suppression of individuality in the mechanization of socially necessary but painful performances; the concentration of individual enterprises in more effective, more productive corporations; the regulation of free competition among unequal economic subjects. . . . The rights and liberties which were such vital factors in the origins and earlier stages of industrial society yield to a higher stage of society: they are losing their traditional rationale and content.[70]

The rationalized society Cournot imagines as liberating instead leads to this comfortable unfreedom of technocratic management that leaves little or no room for traditional "rights and liberties." These writers argue that history no longer has meaning in the present context—that its explanatory power and relevance have faded in the face of new forms of social organization.[71] This rejection of history as an indication of future developments is based in a suspicion that historical discourse has a coercive effect on the present and future. This coercion can be seen as either a feature of the narrative nature of historical writing (see the discussion of White above) or of the effects of various philosophies of history on the kind of knowledge produced by historical research.[72] He argues that in most of the discussions of the end of history, "the history which is supposed to end with posthistory is a conceptual construction about the course of the world as a whole. Its core consists in the generalization of empirical knowledge about reality . . . in such a way that it does not conflict with, but rather gives support to, the setting of a comprehensive goal."[73] Such conceptual constructions about the world are meant to encompass analyses of the past, readings, and plans for the future. As Niethammer writes, "the problematic of posthistory is not the end of the world but the end of meaning."[74] This end of meaning—an historical as much as hermeneutical crisis—relates to a broader suspicion of the effects of a desire to understand and thus shape human activity in the aftermath of the events of the first several decades of the twentieth century.

With the "end" of this kind of history, what remains varies from the faceless uniformity of some versions of postmodernity to a liberatory moment of freedom from past constraint.[75] In ei-

6 / CONCLUSIONS

ther case, Niethammer argues that the idea of history as progressive, as moving, and as meaningful is no longer a significant factor in these thinkers' work. To take a prominent example, though one that Niethammer does not dwell on, Francis Fukuyama's much-discussed *The End of History and the Last Man* offers an account of the end of history in the Hegelian sense—an end to progressive history—in the achievement of liberal democracy in the West.[76] In Fukuyama's account of Hegel,

> [Hegel] did not believe that the historical process would continue indefinitely, but would come to an end with an achievement of free societies in the real world. There would, in other words, be an end of history. This did not mean that there would be an end to events rising out of the births, deaths, and social interactions of humankind, or that there would be a cap on factual knowledge about the world. Hegel, however had defined history as the progress of man to higher levels of rationality and freedom, and this process had a logical terminal point in the achievement of absolute self-consciousness. This self-consciousness, he believed, was embodied in his own philosophical system, just as human freedom was embodied in the modern liberal state that emerged in Europe after the French Revolution and in America after the American Revolution.[77]

Once the modern liberal state appears on the world stage, the historical process ceases and is replaced by events whose meaning is not progressive in Hegel's sense. In Fukuyama's work, historical knowledge will not help in solving the problems of the posthistorical world—solutions derive instead from the expansion and universal application of the norms of liberal democracy. Fukuyama, following Kojeve's version of Hegel, sees history as a tragedy from which humankind has been delivered by the advent of liberal states. Fukuyama's reading of the end of history is an optimistic one, seeing it as liberating. Fukuyama's optimism may simply have to do with his location in the conservative intelligentsia in the United States and with the fact that his book was written in the immediate aftermath of the first Gulf War while many of the less optimistic commentators come from European or left-leaning positions in the academy. The darker side of the end of the history, the pessimistic reading, could be said to see the end of history as tragedy—the process stops too early, leaving society unredeemed. Writing of the European version of posthistory, Niethammer suggests that "the hopelessness of the posthistorical perspective is bound up with the presumption, tragedy and decline of educated middle-class individualism in the political practice of the wartime years."[78] The hopelessness, in other words, derives from the failure of a model of individual action in the face of mass movements, warfare, and an advancing technocracy.

Niethammer goes on to argue that "the inflation of the various 'post' concepts might suggest that we are no longer able or willing to define the content of where we are and where we want to go; that we seek only to know where we came from."[79] This inflation of "post" concepts in the face of the "tragedy and decline of educated middle-class individualism" leads to a historiography that is purely backward looking, that does not care to project trajectories of change. In this view, historical scholarship neither can nor will make broad claims about social change over time; it is instead merely archival, dedicated to the recovery of knowledge about the past from which we come without reference to the future.[80] Niethammer does not argue that this analysis of history is useless or lacking in substance, but rather that it is insufficient. Perhaps, he concludes, a particular variety of history is finished, but only a variety, not history itself.

Rather than join the chorus of despair he describes, Niethammer suggests ways to at least begin responding to what he depicts as a crisis of historical meaning: "The quest for a critical alternative [to posthistory] would have to begin by asking what kind of service historians, or people with an education in history, can perform to support the subjectivity of individuals in their historical perceptions of themselves."[81] Outlining one alternative, he argues that "historical groundwork linked to clarification of one's own experience breaks open the apparent certainties of that experience" allowing individuals to orient themselves more effectively toward an active engagement with the world, an engagement that would replace the despairing retreat of posthistory. This project is not unlike the project described by Bourdieu in the epigraph to this chapter in that an alternative to the "end of meaning" perceived by the posthistorical school would be to support the development of a subjectivity in the context of history—to contribute to the development of, to cite Bourdieu, "something like a subject."

Niethammer's book leads to suggestive reflections on some of the concerns about metanarratives, *grands récits*, and teleological histories expressed by the recent turn toward materially specific historicist work in Shakespeare studies. The emphasis on particularism—narrowly focused studies of events, phenomena, or texts—reflects some of the anxieties Niethammer describes as characteristic of posthistorical thought. Specifically, the promise of history to explain events, to give reasons for the past, is seen as participating in a kind of determinism that "was increasingly felt to be a danger—of a history without alternatives, and without the possibility of establishing in historical research those degrees of freedom which threaten to disappear in the contemporary experience of all-powerful systemic connections."[82] Current preoccupations about anachronism and particularity participate in this reaction to the perceived coercion implicit in traditional narrative history. Materialist criticism (and literary history) of this narrowly construed variety can avoid the anachronistic imposition of a historical narrative composed from a later perspective and provides immensely important and exciting insights into particular practices, events, and discourses. However, this same avoidance of narrative can lead to less positive outcomes, including the failure to see or acknowledge connections between successive historical states of specific fields. An otherwise salutary focus on the moment can potentially obscure the way that moment relates to other moments.[83]

Douglas Bruster examines a less than satisfying response to this problem in his chapter on the "new materialism" in his *Shakespeare and the Question of Culture* when he describes a genre of criticism that sees materialism as an "attention to physical things—'matter,' that is, interpreted literally. In place of class struggle, hegemony, or ideology, the new materialism attends to objects in the world: clothing, crockery, sugar. It often does so with 'culture' (rather than 'society') as its organizing concept."[84] There exists, for example, a critical "school" that pays extraordinarily close attention to what we can recover of the items associated with playwriting—props, costumes, "stuffe" as some of the Revels records usefully call it—producing what sometimes bear a closer resemblance to lists than to arguments.[85] Such work attempts to recover the past—to bring it back somehow—and by doing so also seems to posit an absolute break from that past.[86] Like the anecdote in the new historicism, the matter (whatever it might be) here provides criticism with the "touch of the real"—a kind of token of authenticity that legitimizes it as "history" and as true. At the same time, however, it turns the past into an object like those which it describes. Discussing the new materialism, Bruster writes, "many critics have taken the word and practice of 'materialism' to depend strictly on concrete 'matter' as its ultimate ground. Scholars who 'read' mirrors and other physical objects . . . are doing materialism. Those who talk about seemingly abstract entities like 'capitalism' are not."[87] Bruster depicts this "new materialism" as a product of a deep suspicion of Marxist thought as insufficiently materialist because of its attention to such nontangibles as ideas. I would add to this characterization by suggesting that its avoidance of categories like capitalism also has much to do with a postmodern anxiety about the distorting, teleological effects of so-called master narratives on the "truth" of historical scholarship. Materialism does not, however, have to avoid ideas or the use of theoretical narratives and relinquishing the explanatory (or representational) power of narratives—whether Marxist or not—is too high a price to pay for the doubtful profits of the "new materialism."[88]

This turn to physical material represents less a new materialism than a new antiquarianism that falls into the pitfalls identified by Nietzsche under that rubric in his essay on the uses of history. He writes, "The antiquarian sense of a man, a community, a whole people, always possesses an extremely limited field of vision; most of what exists it does not perceive at all, and the little it does see it sees much too close up and isolated; it cannot relate what it sees to anything else and it therefore accords everything it sees equal importance and therefore to each individual thing too great importance."[89] The narrow focus of the antiquarian excludes much from vision and, more troublingly to Nietzsche, obscures the relational nature of historical phenomena in such a way as to make evaluation or judgment impossible.[90] Historical writing, as the writers discussed in this chapter note, ought first to be an act of judgment, of selection. Antiquarianisms of whatever variety choose recovery over judgment and thus agitate against any kind of critical or interpretive disposition toward the past—unselective recovery, as Nietzsche notes, makes all history the same, and all events are equally important, which amounts to making them equally unimportant.

6 / CONCLUSIONS

I have dwelt at some length on these questions about the status of history, historicism, and materialism in recent thought because, as noted above, that status remains an important issue for early modern studies. "History" has functioned as a dominant marker of intellectual affiliation and has arguably become the central research program in early modern studies in the past two or three decades. Bruster's suggestion that "culture" is coming to be more central as a term in early modern studies seems accurate, but "history" remains a crucial category in the field. Historical approaches that diminish narrative in favor of richly detailed and fascinating discussions of very specific events or items from history finally contribute little to our knowledge of how social or cultural change comes about and, I would argue, instead contribute to the obscuring of the ways that history structures those developments.

The shape of this book's argument demonstrates that constructing a history of early modern professional fields that does not do violence to the materiality of the phenomena described requires a mode of analysis that can synthesize the virtues of a kind of thick description with those of a broad view of historical time.[91] This synthesis is particularly important in studying developments that take place over most of a century. Responding to some of the problems implicit in such a project, Pierre Bourdieu argues that "what we need, in effect, is a form of structural history that is rarely practiced, which finds in each successive state of the structure under examination both the product of previous struggles to maintain or to transform this structure, and the principle, via the contradictions, the tensions, and the relations of force which constitute it, of subsequent transformations."[92] Bourdieu's sociology offers one way out of the dilemma posed by the crisis in historical thought Niethammer's book describes by encouraging the projection of trajectories for future developments in particular fields as well as in society more generally in the interest of changing the "relations of force" that constitute society. In addition, and not least importantly, this method demands a high degree of self-consciousness in the investigator and avoids the pitfalls of anachronism while allowing research to draw more general conclusions about trends and developments than more narrowly focused studies sometimes can.

III

> The philosophers have only *interpreted* the world, in various ways; the point, however, is to *change* it.
> —Karl Marx, *Theses on Feuerbach*

> The object of social science is a reality that encompasses all the individual and collective struggles aimed at conserving or transforming reality, in particular those that seek to impose the legitimate definition of reality, whose specifically symbolic efficacy can help conserve or subvert the established order, that is to say, reality.
> —Pierre Bourdieu, *The Logic of Practice*

I conclude with these epigraphs from Marx and Bourdieu in part to endorse them but also to suggest that our collective interpretations have at least the potential to contribute to the change they call for.[93] My intention is that this book will contribute to the double purpose of articulating a method and contributing to the history of the subject by showing how the study of related fields (as, in my case, law, writing, theater, and administration) affords me an opportunity to make larger claims about the shape and trajectory of an emergent professional field, a field I would suggest forms a major component of the field of power that structures contemporary society and one that structures individual agents' experience of that society. In other words, the kind of detailed sociological and historical study this book engages in may help early modern scholarship to describe and critique the shape of the totality of the social field over broad spans of time. Rather than turning away from such arguments, a tactic that seems to me likely to lead to a real and ever-increasing irrelevance—the kind of purely backward-looking scholarship that Niethammer and Nietzsche critique—early modern studies and literary studies more generally can contribute to the awareness of the wide range of determinations that have and continue to structure individual practice and society more generally. In this way, we can contribute to the construction of something that might resemble a subject. Abandoning, or, perhaps better, yielding up the control Kant argues is the province of the lower faculty ignores both the institutional history of the humanities in the university and forfeits one of the most historically powerful defenses of the importance of the humanities.

Where "posthistory" can be read as a kind of despairing response to the perceived ineffectuality of historical knowledge in contemporary society, I have argued that the kind of work this book represents can produce historical scholarship that avoids the pitfalls rightly recognized by critics of the New Historicism and of historicisms more generally. This work is part of an historical project that recognizes the necessity of being suspicious of *grands récits* with aspirations to total explanations, but that at the same time offers middling-sized narratives sensitive to both specific events and their broader contexts. It is both an archival project and a speculative one that intends to make broad claims about historical developments that are grounded in material evidence. And, it has faith in the usefulness of historical scholarship in understanding both where we come from and where we might be heading.

Notes

INTRODUCTION

1. See Pierre Bourdieu and Loïc Wacquandt, *Invitation to Reflexive Sociology* (Chicago: University of Chicago Press, 1992), 93–94, 107, and 109–10. Bourdieu discusses the historical genesis of the category of artist and cautions against the tendency to import a modern definition of "artist" into periods when that definition simply does not exist.

2. See Anthony Giddens, *The Consequences of Modernity* (Stanford, CA: Stanford University Press, 1990), 21–29. Giddens argues that modern societies disembed "social relations from local contexts of interaction" and restructure them "across indefinite spans of time-space" (21). This restructuring consists of a reembedding of social systems into an abstract space he calls modernity.

3. Christopher Marlowe's *The Jew of Malta*, William Shakespeare's *Merchant of Venice*, and Ben Jonson's *Volpone* all have central characters whose identities are defined in terms of their place in a series of marketplaces. I will avoid market language in what follows to avoid the kind of economism that "market" implies. Andrew Abbott's *System of Professions: An Essay on the Division of Expert Labor* (Chicago: University of Chicago Press, 1988) polemically discusses the professions in terms of a system, not of a market.

4. "Literature" does not acquire its modern definition until the late eighteenth century. In early modern England according to the *Oxford English Dictionary*, "literature" refers to "acquaintance with 'letters' or books; polite or humane learning; literary culture." The *OED* quotes Skelton (1581) and Bacon (1605) as using the word in this sense of familiarity with letters. Not until the 1820s does the term acquire its modern definition. For more detailed discussions of this point see Raymond Williams, *Marxism and Literature* (Oxford: Oxford University Press, 1977), 47; John Guillory, *Cultural Capital* (Chicago: University of Chicago Press, 1993) 122–23; and Timothy Reiss, *The Meaning of Literature* (Ithaca, NY: Cornell University Press, 1992), 229–30. This fact presents terminological difficulties in describing the activities of the writers discussed below. No useful collective term applies to the diverse writing of the period and it cannot be called "literature" in our contemporary sense of the term. The work discussed below—plays, pamphlets, and poetry—is the product of a loose group of writers whose competitions give rise to a field we recognize as

literary. These competitions are, in part, the subject of the final chapter on the Poet's War.

5. Stephen Greenblatt, *Renaissance Self-Fashioning* (Chicago: University of Chicago Press, 1980); Jean-Christophe Agnew, *Worlds Apart: The Theatre and the Market in Anglo-American Culture 1550–1750* (New York: Cambridge University Press, 1986); Richard Helgerson, *Self-Crowned Laureates* (Berkeley and Los Angeles: University of California Press, 1983); Catherine Belsey, *The Subject of Tragedy* (London: Methuen, 1988); Joel Fineman, *Shakespeare's Perjured Eye* (Berkeley and Los Angeles: University of California Press, 1986).

6. Greenblatt, *Renaissance Self-Fashioning*, 113.

7. Ibid., 162.

8. For example, he writes "Iago knows that an identity that has been fashioned as a story can be unfashioned, refashioned, and inscribed anew in a different narrative" (ibid., 238).

9. "They dismissed the usurpers as poetasters, versifiers, or riming parasites and elevated the great writers as *vates*, they translated 'poet' into 'maker,' equated it with 'priest,' 'prophet,' 'lawmaker,' . . . and adorned it with adjectives like 'right' and 'true'" (Helgerson, *Self-Crowned Laureates*, 3).

10. "Among poets, Spenser and Milton appear to possess their laureate identity as an inherent, positive attribute. Not so Jonson. His most obvious positive attribute is rather the constant, sweaty effort to mark a difference" (ibid., 183).

11. Agnew, *Worlds Apart*, 4.

12. Ibid., 114.

13. Ibid., 5.

14. This is much like Greenblatt's discussion of More and Tyndale.

15. Agnew, *Worlds Apart*, 113.

16. This is, admittedly, a reductive treatment of Agnew's important work but it does make the point that privileging one social phenomenon as the driving force of others does not do justice to the complexities of the dynamic structure of social space. Bourdieu calls this the "Marxist short-circuit" that explains all social phenomena in terms of economics. See Pierre Bourdieu, *The Field of Cultural Production* (New York: Columbia University Press, 1993), 181.

17. See Sally-Beth MacLean and Scott McMillin, *The Queen's Men and Their Plays* (Cambridge: Cambridge University Press, 1998); Roslyn Knutson, *Playing Companies and Commerce in Shakespeare's Time* (Cambridge: Cambridge University Press, 2001). The recent upsurge of interest in book history is likewise symptomatic of this shift of focus.

18. This is in part the subject of my concluding chapter. The Shakespeare Association of America seminar "Into the Archives and Back Again: Shakespeare and the End(s) of History" chaired by Shankar Raman in 2000 raised some of these questions in the context of a collective investigation of historicist scholarship in early modern studies. The International Shakespeare Association seminar on "Material Shakespeare" in 2000 raised similar questions. I am indebted to discussions in both seminars.

19. See Jill Lepore, "Historians Who Love Too Much: Reflections on Microhistory and Biography," *Journal of American History* (June 2001): 129–44, for a helpful discussion of this point.

20. Church courts were losing jurisdictions at the same time that common law and equity jurisdictions were expanding all over England. See W. J. Jones, *The Elizabethan Court of Chancery* (Oxford: Clarendon Press, 1967), especially chapter 1. For developments in government see G. R. Elton's *Tudor Revolution in Government* (Cambridge: Cambridge University Press, 1953), B. W. Beckingsale's biographies of Cecil and Walsingham, and Robert Tittler's biography of Sir Nicholas Bacon. For the theater business, see chapter 4 below and recent theater histories such as William Ingram's *The Business of Playing* (Ithaca, NY: Cornell University Press, 1992). For writing as grudgingly acceptable for gentlemen see Philip Finkelpearl, *John Marston of the Inner Temple* (Cambridge, MA: Harvard University Press, 1969), 126 and passim.

21. As noted above, I am using "literary" with caution here, since term carries very different meanings in the sixteenth and seventeenth centuries than it does today. Timothy Reiss argues that "we must distinguish the 'literary' from such earlier categories as those of the 'poetical' or the 'rhetorical.' The modern concept of literature was born simultaneously with a professional and semiprofessional criticism: Bouhours, Rymer, Rapin, Boileau, Dryden, Dacier, Dennis, Addison, etc." (Reiss, *Meaning of Literature*, 229). Marston, for example, saw himself as a satirist, a playwright, and, sometimes, a poet, but not as a producer of literature. Professional writing emerged before professional criticism, and, according to Reiss, professional criticism arose before "literature." The development of professional paradigms enabled these successive changes, but they had not yet occurred in early modern England.

22. This is a primary reason for Agnew's focus on the theater in *Worlds Apart*. He argues that the Elizabethan and Jacobean theater was a major site of experimentation and testing of ways of understanding social change. See also Bourdieu on classification struggles in *Distinction: A Social Critique of the Judgment of Taste* (Cambridge, MA: Harvard University Press, 1984), 99–168, 466–84.

23. Richard Helgerson, *The Elizabethan Prodigals* (Berkeley and Los Angeles: University of California Press, 1976), 23.

24. Abbott's *System of Professions* argues that professions interact as part of a complex "professional ecology" and that this interaction is an important factor in the constitution of individual professions. I will argue the occupations I discuss in this book develop into professions at the same time that they contribute to the constitution of a professional field—Abbott's system of professions.

25. His fate is equally prototypical. He is doomed by the very professional knowledge by which he hoped to gain freedom, power, and enlightenment. Faustus can be read as a harbinger of what the professional logics of modernity imply—in this, he is modern. See Theodor Adorno and Max Horkheimer, *Dialectic of Enlightenment* (New York: Continuum, 1994) for an extended discussion of Odysseus as the representative modern man. Adorno and Horkheimer could as easily have selected Faustus because he exhibits the same characteristics of commitment to abstraction and rationality and is graphically doomed by his own aspiring mind.

26. He also indulges in theatrical production.

27. This is one of the forces driving the increase in the number of active students at the Inns of Court throughout the period. The law was becoming an important means of social advancement.

28. See the discussion of the early modern redefinition of profession in chapter 1 below. The attitude represented here (however dimly) derives from a combination of Reformation practical theology, economic and social change, and status struggles among the various groups constituting the early modern English polity. See also Paul Marshall, *A Kind of Life Imposed on Man: Vocation and Social Order from Tyndale to Locke* (Toronto: University of Toronto Press, 1995), for a thorough discussion of the reformation theology of work.

29. This is not to say that early modern (or modern) professionals are actually not interested in status, merely that their interest in status can be misrecognized as a commitment to their work and that their rewards are compensation for the service their work provides. The early modern barrister's fees were often referred to as a gratuity—a free gift—despite there being a schedule stating what specific services cost. This too is fundamental to professional ideology.

30. And that power derives from diligence as an artisan in the craft of magic, from diligence in an occupation. If Faustus is a "studious artisan" he imagines that he will receive the "world of profit and delight" fantasized in his early speeches. See his comments about what he will do with his power later in this scene (1.1.78–96). I am using "Enlightenment" in Adorno and Horkheimer's sense of a commitment to instrumental reason intended to liberate that produces domination instead. See the opening remarks in *Dialectic of Enlightenment* where Adorno argues that this kind of rationality goes at least as far back as Francis Bacon.

31. Marlowe himself is a good example of the phenomenon the play responds to. A scholarship boy from Canterbury, Marlowe's education provided him with access to a "world of power and delight" won by rejecting divinity as a career path.

32. Jurgen Habermas's *Philosophical Discourse of Modernity* (Cambridge, MA: MIT Press, 1987) argues that adherence to the rational intellectual discourse of the Enlightenment still offers the best hope for the establishment of a just society. Giddens' *Consequences of Modernity* argues that modern social practices define and will continue to define global society for the foreseeable future. Rather than seeing recent changes (represented in part by the "theory" revolution in the humanities and social sciences) as the heralds of an oncoming postmodern cultural order, he argues that they are symptomatic of a kind of "radicalised modernity." Both thinkers hold that "modern" remains the best description of contemporary society.

33. Fredric Jameson, *Postmodernism, or, The Cultural Logic of Late Capitalism* (Durham, NC: Duke University Press, 1991) and *Late Marxism: Adorno and the Persistence of the Dialectic* (London: Verso, 1990).

34. Peter Sloterdijk, *Critique of Cynical Reason* (Minnesota: University of Minnesota Press, 1987). Sloterdijk argues that while "enlightenment" values are still widely held, their holders have developed a kind of unhappy cynical consciousness that derives from those very same ideals and that that cynical attitude is making the claims of enlightenment ring false.

35. Ibid., 5.

36. Sloterdijk posits a philosophy rooted in the body—in what he terms "kynicism" (after Diogenes' intentionally crudely physical rebuttals to Socratic philosophy)—that will, if not resolve, at least criticize and expose the contradictions of modern thinking while at the same time embodying an alternative. He writes: "Since philosophy can only hypocritically live out what it says, it takes cheek to say what is lived. In a culture in which hardened idealisms make lies into a form of living, the process of truth depends on whether people can be found who are aggressive and free ('shameless') enough to speak the truth" (ibid., 102). Kynicism has this "cheek" for Sloterdijk.

37. In this, Sloterdijk is quite close to the Frankfurt School thinkers he critiques. None of the major figures (Adorno, Horkheimer, Marcuse, or Habermas, for example) propose scrapping modernity in favor of some new order, but rather they advocate the critique and resolution of problems so that modernity can live up to its promises.

38. Bruno Latour, *We Have Never Been Modern* (Cambridge, MA: Harvard University Press, 1993).

39. I am aware of the problem of the relation of "the Middle Ages" to the early modern. I do not intend to suggest that something happened around 1485 to transform a late medieval social order into a modern one. This issue is discussed in the *King John* chapter below. Briefly, the later medieval period makes a transition into modernity in much the same way that the early modern becomes modern. No radical break need be imagined.

40. See *PMLA* 109, no. 5 (1994): 1025. The Forum section of this issue contains a discussion of the difficulties and usefulnesses of the term. See also Richard Halpern, *Shakespeare Among the Moderns* (Ithaca, NY: Cornell University Press, 1997) for a discussion of the refiguration of the "Renaissance" as "early modern." He writes that "recent critics have also been inclined to avoid the term 'Renaissance,' and I believe that this habit has something to do with a persistence of modernist sensibilities. . . . 'Renaissance' denotes a repetition of past (classical) glories while 'early modern' reconfigures the same period into an anticipation of the present" (9). "Postmodern" uses of "early modern" bespeak the persistence of what Halpern calls modernist historical allegory in contemporary critical practice. He differentiates it from postmodern pastiche, writing "modernism's historical allegory is not yet postmodern pastiche, for its allegorical mappings generally continue to be haunted by a sense of incompatibility and dissonance. Allegorical collapse still takes place against a backdrop of historical distance, it has not yet subsumed the latter into an amnesiac play of styles" (14). Allegory is thus productive, but not totally anachronistic. My own position is close to Halpern's, and I consider "early modern" useful in that it points to continuities between periods and affords space in which to discuss those continuities in a historically responsible way. I hope to avoid the teleological dangers that Halpern and Dubrow warn of while exploiting the potential of both modernist historical allegory and the emphasis on transition that the term "early modern" offers.

41. Dubrow, "forum," 1026.

42. In David Aers, ed., *Culture and History, 1350–1600: Essays on English Communities, Identities, and Writing* (Detroit, MI: Wayne State University Press, 1992).

43. We also have to avoid false teleologies that look at early modern developments in terms of later conditions. This is one of the dangers that Dubrow's commentary in *PMLA* addresses.

44. "Modernity," *OED*. It has been used in this sense since at least 1585, the date of the earliest citation in the *OED*.

45. See Giddens, *Consequences of Modernity*, 1.

46. "Modernity," *OED*. The earliest supporting quotations date to 1900 and have a pejorative sense that fades through the first half of the century.

47. Alan MacFarlane, *The Origins of English Individualism* (New York: Cambridge University Press, 1978). MacFarlane's periodizing is polemic and open to question but his work points to the fact that accounts that posit a break between the Middle Ages and the Renaissance necessarily ignore important evidence about social life.

48. Jean-Christophe Agnew's *Worlds Apart* and Richard Halpern's *Poetics of Primitive Accumulation* (Ithaca, NY: Cornell University Press, 1991) offer persuasive discussions of this point. See also Robert Matz, *Defending Literature* (Cambridge, MA: Cambridge University Press, 2001) for a discussion of the development of a "modern" sense of "literature" out of a classical and medieval tradition.

49. See A. L. Beier, "Engine of Manufacture," in *London 1500–1700: The Making of a Metropolis*, A. L. Beier and Roger Finlay eds., 141–67 (London: Longman, 1986) for a discussion of London as a manufacturing center in the seventeenth century.

50. Giddens, *Consequences of Modernity*, 16–17.

51. On this topic Giddens writes "the reflexivity of modern social life consists in the fact that social practices are constantly examined and reformed in the light of incoming information about those very practices, thus constitutively altering their character" (38). This sounds very much like some of Greenblatt's comments regarding the impact of self-fashioning on society (particularly in the *Othello* chapter in *Renaissance Self-Fashioning*) as well as Agnew's comments about the developing awareness of the transactional, fictive, nature of social interaction.

52. A shift Burckhardt's *Civilization of the Renaissance in Italy* (1860) discusses at length—also see Greenblatt's discussion in chapter 4 of *Renaissance Self-Fashioning*. Ernst Cassirer's *The Individual and the Cosmos in Renaissance Philosophy* (New York: Harper and Row, 1964) and his edited volume *The Renaissance Philosophy of Man* (Chicago: University of Chicago Press, 1948) both contain extended commentary on this shift.

53. The classic discussion being Karl Marx's *Capital*. A. L. Beier's work on London manufacturing in *London 1500–1700* and Christopher Brooks's work on apprenticeship (Christopher Brooks, "Apprenticeship, Social Mobility and the Middling Sort" in *The Middling Sort of People: Culture, Society and Politics in England 1550–1800*, eds., Jonathan Barry and Christopher Brooks, (New York: St. Martin's Press, 1994), 52–83 show how London society was developing in recognizably modern directions. Many other social historians have discussed the reshaping of English society in the wake of early modernization—see for example Keith Wrightson, Susan Amussen, and Alan MacFarlane.

54. Despite such exceptions as Chaucer in the fourteenth century. The highest ranks of the civil administration were typically occupied by clerics—the office of Lord Chancellor being perhaps the best example.

55. *Invitation to Reflexive Sociology* offers perhaps the most comprehensive and accessible introduction to Bourdieu's intellectual project. It outlines the use of his major theoretical terms, describes research projects, and addresses many of the common objections to his work.

56. As are most social phenomena, which is not necessarily to castigate them as deceitful, but to point out that social structures depend on a series of foundational impostures that society mistakenly recognizes as true or natural. See my discussion of the Bastard's choice in the second chapter for a more full development of this idea.

57. See Bourdieu, *Distinction* chapter 3 for an extended discussion on the utility (even the necessity) of systems of misrecognition.

58. The misrecognition of professional contingency explains, in part, the way that "profession" has become a singularly important stake in the struggles for distinction that pervade the occupational world. Ironically, these struggles for professional status often exchange one form of contingency for another, better misrecognized one.

59. John Guillory, "Bourdieu's Refusal," *Modern Language Quarterly* 58, no. 4 (1997): 367–98.

60. Ibid., 368.

61. Guillory's argument demonstrates that, rather than signalling economic determinism, Bourdieu's use of traditionally economic terminology like capital or profit is part of a polemic against the subordination of other social sciences to economics. Guillory writes that "Bourdieu regards sociology as a challenge to the very entitlement of economics to the language of exchange" (ibid., 377).

62. Pierre Bourdieu, *The Logic of Practice* (Stanford, CA: Stanford University Press, 1990), 21.

63. Bourdieu argues that sociology has to treat "individuals" as bearers of structured sets of dispositions ("agents") constructed by each biological individual's family background and history of encounters with society and this is why he consistently prefers "agent" to "individual" in his work.

64. "Relative autonomy" is a crucial notion in Bourdieu's sociology. To say that fields are relatively autonomous is to say that the field in question, the intellectual field for example, has a set of norms and practices that structure terms of success or failure that are specific to that field. But, at the same time, the logic of the field exhibits a homology with the logic of what Bourdieu calls the field of power. The intellectual field is autonomous, but still responds to external determinations.

65. Bourdieu, *Field,* 64.

66. Criteria such as these are also changeable—subject to being revised as a result of struggles over the definition of what does or does not count as "good" or worthwhile work. See chapter 5 below for an account of the 1599–1603 Poet's War as such a struggle.

67. See "The Field of Cultural Production, or, The Economic Field Reversed" *Poetics* 12 (1983): 311–56.

68. Bourdieu writes: "Social capital is the sum of the resources, actual or virtual, that accrue to an individual or a group by virtue of possessing a durable network of more or less institutionalized relationships of mutual acquaintance and recognition" (Bourdieu and Wacquandt, *Invitation*, 119). Bourdieu posits several different kinds of capital (cultural, economic, etc.) that contribute to an agent's total volume of social capital, and the composition of this total volume is as important as its size. For example, agents with the same total volume of social capital may have widely divergent chances in a given conflict depending on the proportions of economic and cultural capital in their total volume of social capital. See Pierre Bourdieu, "Forms of Capital," in *Handbook of Theory and Research for the Sociology of Education*, ed. John G. Richardson (New York: Greenwood Press, 1986) 241–58) for a more detailed discussion of the forms and function of the various kinds of capital. See also *Distinction* chapter 2 ("The Social Space and its Transformations") on the role of cultural capital in mechanisms of domination.

69. Bourdieu, *Distinction*, 122. Bourdieu makes a distinction between economic capital which can simply be wealth, not capital in the sense of economics, and "economic life," which is business—the stock market, industrial production, etc.

70. Bourdieu uses "disposition" to refer to the fact that particular agents are predisposed to act in certain ways in given situations. For example, if people from a specific social group tend to react in similar ways in similar situations, it is because they share a disposition that encourages such reactions.

71. Bourdieu and Wacquandt, *Invitation*, 121–22.

72. See *Distinction*, 32–41. "Everything takes place as if the 'popular aesthetic' were based on the affirmation of continuity between art and life, which implies the subordination of form to function, or, one might say, on a refusal of the refusal which is the starting point of the high aesthetic, i.e., the clear-cut separation of ordinary dispositions from the specifically aesthetic disposition" (32). Bourdieu argues that the "continuity between art and life" suggested by the dominated classes' refusal of formalism has everything to do with the necessities of life imposed by their dominated position in social space.

73. This point is taken up in more detail in chapter 2 with regard to the Bastard in Shakespeare's *King John*.

74. Habitus's responses to social capital enable the exercise of symbolic violence, the violence attendant on the coerced recognition of social stratification, either by granting an agent symbolic power or predisposing an agent to recognize its authority. Symbolic violence is violence that operates with the (often unwitting) complicity of its victims and this complicity is secured by the operations of habitus. See "On Symbolic Power" in Bourdieu, *Language and Symbolic Power* (Cambridge, MA: Harvard University Press, 1991). He writes "symbolic power . . . is a power that can be exercised only if it is recognized, that is, misrecognized as arbitrary. . . . What creates the power of words and slogans, a power capable of maintaining or subverting the social order, is the belief in the legitimacy of words and of those who utter them" (170). See also *Masculine Domination* (Stanford, CA: Stanford University Press, 2001) for a discussion of gender hierarchy as the basic example of symbolic violence.

75. Pierre Bourdieu, *In Other Words* (Stanford, CA: Stanford University Press, 1990), 63.

76. Bourdieu uses sports as a metaphor for the way that habitus structures social action. His example is that of the soccer player who, through a combination of practice and theoretical knowledge of the rules of the game, seems to know where a pass will fall or where to position him or herself on the field almost intuitively. Bourdieu argues that this kind of "feel for the game" characterizes social action, which has regularities without explicit rules and operates more through a kind of feel than through a conscious awareness of rules. For Bourdieu's differences with Rational Action Theory, see *Invitation to Reflexive Sociology*, passim.

77. *Distinction* demonstrates how individual habitus tend to be homologous across a class, sharing many characteristics indicative of a broad "norm," while remaining individual to particular agents. Each agent possesses a variation of a class habitus.

78. Bourdieu, *Logic*, 60. Individual variation is limited, of course, and a large part of Bourdieu's project is dedicated to exposing those limitations in the hope of changing or ameliorating them in the interest of expanding the space of freedom for agents in society.

79. See *Distinction*, chap. 1 "The Aristocracy of Culture" for a discussion of the ways in which the habitus structures an agent's encounter with culture (and with other fields) while at the same time that agent's habitus is changed by the encounter.

80. See "The Field of Cultural Production, or, The Economic World Reversed" in Bourdieu, *Field*, 29–73.

81. Bourdieu, *Field*, 163.

82. One set of these relations is temporal. Bourdieu writes of the time lag between developments in the field of power and those within the field of cultural production, a lag he calls *hysteresis*. Hysteresis can, for example, lead to respect for a particular artistic practice or to disdain of it. The final effect depends less on the state of individual fields than on the dynamic state of the relation between fields.

83. Bourdieu and Wacquandt, 105–6.

84. Toril Moi, "The Challenge of the Particular Case: Bourdieu's Sociology of Culture and Literary Criticism," *Modern Language Quarterly* 58, no. 4 (1997): 508.

85. Bourdieu and Wacquandt, *Invitation*, 234–35 (my italics). See also p. 233ff. on object-construction, analogical, or relational research practices, and the double-object.

86. Ibid., 90.

87. Ibid., 91.

88. Andrew Abbott's *System of Professions* provides important theoretical justification for this position. See chapter 1.

89. For London as "modern" see Beier and Finlay, *London 1500–1700*. See also *Material London, ca. 1600*, ed. Lena Cowen Orlin (Philadelphia: University of Pennsylvania, 2000).

90. See Abbott, *Systems of Professions*, for a detailed discussion of the interrelations of professions.

91. Michael Bérubé, *Public Access* (New York: Verso, 1994); Stanley Fish, *Doing What Comes Naturally* (Durham, NC: Duke University Press, 1989) and *Professional Correctness* (Oxford: Oxford University Press, 1995); Gerald Graff, *Professing Literature*, John Guillory, *Cultural Capital*, Cary Nelson, *Manifesto of a Tenured Radical* (New York: New York University Press, 1997), Bruce Robbins, *Secular Vocations* (London: Verso, 1993); and Andrew Ross, *No Respect* (New York: Routledge, 1989). There is an extensive literature on the cultural right as well including William Bennett's *To Reclaim a Legacy* (Washington, DC: National Endowment for the Humanities, 1984), Lynne Cheney's *Telling the Truth* (New York: Simon and Schuster, 1995), Dinesh D'Souza's *Illiberal Education* (New York: Free Press, 1991), and Roger Kimball's *Tenured Radicals* (New York: Harper and Row, 1990). All of this outpouring of work (an outpouring which continues) shares a focus on the content of literary education and only intermittently addresses institutional or professional histories in the various books' efforts to characterize the role and function of literary culture.

Chapter 1. "To sound the depths..."

1. See the brief discussion of this idea in the introduction above. Much of Bourdieu's work is devoted to creating just such a sociology—a sociology that is always historical even when dealing with the most contemporary of issues.

2. For a later example, see Thomas Dekker's *Gull's Horn Book* (1609), where he describes the theater as the poet's exchange.

3. This kind of slippage between terms appears in other texts from the period. See William Blandy, *The Castle of Commonwealth* (1581) (New York: Da Capo, 1972); Thomas Heywood, *An Apology for Actors* (1612) (New York: Garland, 1973); Nathan Field, *The Remonstrance of Nathan Field* (1616) (London: Chiswick Press, 1865); and *The Actors' Remonstrance* (1643) (London: Reeves and Turner, 1873). William Perkins's famous treatise on vocation uses vocation and calling almost interchangeably and so does much contemporary religious thought on the question of work (see Paul Marshall, *Kind of Life*, chapters 2–4).

4. I. M., *A Health to the Gentlemanly Profession of Serving Men* (London: Oxford, 1951), B2r.

5. Ibid., K1v–1.

6. And *not* in whose service they used those skills. I. M. acknowledges that the highest place for a servingman is in a noble household, but does not denigrate those who serve in lesser establishments. I. M.'s position may be compared to the discussion of "professionals" in Kazuo Ishiguro's *Remains of the Day* (New York: Vintage Press, 1988). Stevens, the butler in Ishiguro's novel, makes a similar point about the status of butlers.

7. Ingram, *Business of Playing*, 15.

8. See A. P. Carr-Saunders and P. A. Williams, *The Professions* (Oxford: Oxford University Press, 1933) for the classic development of this argument about professionalism.

9. Christopher Brooks, "Professions, Ideology and the Middling Sort," in Barry and Brooks, *The Middling Sort*, 118.

10. Other examples can be found in the names of the London livery companies—they are typically styled "noble" or "ancient" or "worshipful" in urban records.

11. This move is also characteristic of professions such as the law and, as Heywood's *Apology for Actors* argues, for playwrights and players. The avowal of public service is a hallmark of modern professions.

12. See the introduction to Michael Burrage and Rolf Torstendal, eds., *Professions in Theory and History* (London: Sage, 1990) for a discussion of historians' and sociologists' recognition of the importance of professions to modernity.

13. Giddens, *Consequences of Modernity*, 27.

14. Ibid., 1.

15. Ibid., 17–28.

16. For a discussion of the transformation of traditional elites in the fifteenth through seventeenth centuries, see Mervyn James's chapter on the concept of honor in English politics in his *Society, Politics, and Culture* (Cambridge: Cambridge University Press, 1986). G. R. Elton's *Tudor Revolution* argues that the Tudor monarchs oversaw a transformation of English government from being dominated by the household politics of the King and the great magnates to a more or less modern centrally administered state. Despite the title of Elton's book, this process was more of a transition than a revolution—proceeding slowly and haphazardly. Both historians argue that changes in traditional hierarchy empowered new groups to enter what Bourdieu calls the field of power.

17. See chapter 3.

18. Agnew tends to hypostatize the market into a unitary phenomenon, which causes him to pay less attention than he might otherwise to the ways in which "the market" might be better described as a series of interlocking markets—economic, symbolic, and professional to give a few examples.

19. Agnew, *Worlds Apart*, 4.

20. I am using "economy" in a broad sense to refer to sets of homologous practices only one of which is the strictly financial one studied by "economists." Early modern professions develop in response to a wide variety of influences, only one of which is the fraught and slow transition to a capitalist fiscal economy.

21. Some of these studies will be discussed below. The sociology of the professions only really begins in the 1920s with the publication of A. P. Carr-Saunders and P. A. Wilson's pioneering work on the professions.

22. Lawrence Stone, *The Crisis of the Aristocracy* (Oxford: Clarendon, 1965); Ian Archer, *The Pursuit of Stability* (Cambridge: Cambridge University Press, 1991); and Keith Wrightson, *English Society 1580–1680* (New Brunswick, NJ: Rutgers University Press, 1984).

23. The so-called estates system, of course, never provided a totally adequate model of—or authorizing structure for—premodern society, but it did nevertheless offer one among several stable and widely recognized means of recognizing one's place in society.

24. Examples include the livery companies that consolidated and reinforced their control of London's civic government and lawyers who claimed that their

knowledge of the law made them qualified to debate policy (see the succession debate in the Inns of Court). Both of these groups sought to secure their places in the social hierarchy but also to define the specific capital that would define their internal hierarchies.

25. Brooks, "Professions," 118. Brooks suggests that since professionals lived off their intellectual skills, not the labor of their hands, they occupied a rung in the ladder of rank similar to those who lived off of rents. This however does not account for professions like that of the servingman encomized by I. M. or those associated with the theater—who make claims for distinction as well and whose claims are based on a kind of learning.

26. Pierre Bourdieu writes of the way that acts of recognition are as much acts of creation in, for example, *Language and Symbolic Power*, especially in the chapter on political delegation. The recognition of a profession as a profession marks the success of its practitioners' efforts to transform it from an occupation.

27. Abbott, *System of Professions*; Magali Larson, *The Rise of Professionalism* (Berkeley and Los Angeles: University of California Press, 1977; Stanley Fish, *Doing What Comes Naturally*.

28. Important recent studies that deal with this question include Wilfred Prest ed., *The Professions in Early Modern England* (London: Croom Helm, 1987) and Barry and Brooks's *Middling Sort*.

29. See the various essays in Prest, *Professions*, for examples. All of these scholars demonstrate that to imagine "professionalism" as a nineteenth-century development ignores the long and, more importantly, continuous history of the idea in Western culture.

30. Wilfrid Prest, "Why the History of the Professions Is Not Written" in *Law, Economy, and Society: Essays in the History of English Law*, eds., G. R. Rubin and David Sugarman (Oxford: Professional Books, 1984); 306.

31. Burrage and Torstendal, *Professions in Theory and History*, 2.

32. Ibid., 2.

33. Ibid., 22. Note Friedson's adherence to the almost universal association of profession with industrialization and modern Anglo-American capitalism—historians have taken pains to question this association.

34. Ibid., 27.

35. Carr-Saunders and Wilson, *Professions*, and Talcott Parsons, *Essays in Sociological Theory* (New York: Free Press, 1954).

36. Examples of the "real world" problems they refer to are health, legal, and engineering problems. One of the old professions, religion, does not fit into this scheme (save in religion's connection to counseling), which reveals the inadequacy of their model.

37. Abbott, *System of Professions*, 4.

38. Larson, *Rise of Professionalism*, x.

39. Larson rightly emphasizes that this definition is as ideological as it is "true," and serves the interests of occupational groups maneuvering for power in the "professional market" she treats.

40. Larson, *Rise of Professionalism*, xiii.

41. Ibid., 4.

42. The well-developed market for cultural goods (for the product of professional writers) is totally ignored in Larson's account. She pays only glancing attention to the legal profession, which leads her to overlook, to use her terminology, the ways in which early modern lawyers strove to control their market. Lawyers, judges, and the Crown spent a great deal of time striving to define and control the "market" on which legal services were bought and sold. The recurrent attempts to reform fee schedules and the definition of the barrister's compensation as a "gratuity" rather than a fee are only two examples. The Inns of Court, as both an educational institution and a site of professional practice, structured both the learning and practice of the law in ways that Larson's model cannot explain. Larson's basic assumption that "modern" professions have a necessary link with nineteenth-century developments in market and industrial capitalism results in the exclusion of early modern professions from her narrative, professions that exhibit many of the traits she asserts only arose later and in conjunction with industrialization.

43. This slippage is similar to that found in Agnew's book. Larson does not adequately theorize how particular professional markets fit into the larger, and relatively unexamined, market that, in her model, contains them.

44. Larson, *Rise of Professionalism*, 16.

45. By extension, industrial capitalism spawns modern social structures more generally. Larson treats the Industrial Revolution as the "great transformation" whose effects pervade every aspect of society. Prest criticizes this idea of a complete break in "Why the History of the Professions Is Not Written."

46. See the discussion of the legal profession in chapter three.

47. Much of the earlier literature holds to the idea that the status of professionals owed more to the value of their services than to the efforts of the professionals to assert that value. Larson exposes this as fundamentally ideological.

48. Burrage and Torstendal, *Professions in Theory and History*, 19.

49. Law, administration, theater, and writing thus develop in a complex interaction with each other, other professions, and the economy in which they operate.

50. Talcott Parsons, *Men and their Work* (Glencoe, IL: Free Press, 1958) as well as his *The Sociological Eye* (Chicago: Aldine, 1971); Eliot Freidson, *The Profession of Medicine* (New York: Dodd and Mead, 1970); and T. J. Johnson, *Professions and Power* (London: MacMillan, 1972).

51. Abbott, *System of Professions*, 19.

52. Abbott's example is medicine, specifically the battle between physicians and other practitioners in the nineteenth century. The sixteenth- and seventeenth-century conflicts between legal practitioners (civilians vs. barristers, barristers vs. attorneys or solicitors) are analogous struggles over the jurisdiction which defines a profession.

53. Abbott, *System of Professions*, 19–20.

54. I will share in this focus in the chapters below, examining how changes in work change those doing that work. Institutional change responds to workplace change in early modern England as much as it does in twentieth-century America.

55. For a more detailed look at the history of "insanity" see Michel Foucault's *Madness and Civilization* (New York: Vintage, 1973). Abbott provides a narrowly focused discussion of the way "madness" was successfully medicalized in nineteenth-century America.

56. Abbott, *System of Professions*, 22.

57. Ibid., 22.

58. Ibid., 22.

59. Ibid., 33.

60. Vacancy models describe systems in which change only occurs when a position becomes vacant for whatever reason. Abbott's example is the episcopate where bishoprics only change when an occupant vacates his position, either taking up a new one, itself opened by a vacancy or by leaving the system altogether.

61. Abbott, 90. *System of Professions*, Vacancies occur when a profession vanishes or is suppressed and "bumps" are the product of one profession seizing the jurisdiction of another. Often, both occur at the same time. The history of public administration in early modern England can be seen in these terms. As the clerical role in government declined (and was actively suppressed in some cases) a new professional grouping formed to take over that part of the clergy's former jurisdiction. This new profession is the subject of chapter 2 below.

62. Profession language such as this recurs at several points in the *Apology*. Sidney is, of course, responding to Stephen Gosson's *Schoole of Abuse* (1579), which reviled plays and poetry as incitements to vice rather than spurs to virtue. This exchange was followed by a whole series of controversial writings that increasingly recognized writers and actors as being engaged in a profession (see Heywood's *Apology* [1612], Field's *Remonstrance* [1616], and the 1643 *Actors' Remonstrance* for examples). According to Abbott, public debate such as this is an integral part of the development of professions and is a primary source of the contacts with adjacent professions that define the system as a whole. The *Apology* also makes a claim for the dignity of the poet's calling by asserting that it is a vocation given by God—exploiting the resources of the religious dimensions of the term. This point will be taken up later in this chapter.

63. Sir Philip Sidney, *An Apology for Poetry* (1583), in *Critical Theory Since Plato*, ed., Hazard Adams, ed., (San Diego: Harcourt, 1971), 159.

64. Ben Jonson is, perhaps, the best example of a poet taking a moralist's role. His close ties to the Inns of Court put him in contact with lawyers' developing self-definitions and he began formulating an ideal of the poet's role, an ideal expressed in *Poetaster*.

65. Again, his treatment of medicine is a typical example. Developments in professional practice and jurisdiction are the result of conscious responses to situations objectively recognized by the professionals in question.

66. The recent history of professional literary study serves as an example of the way history determines choices more than reason. The profession has responded to demographic shifts, changes in the academy's public role, and increasing fiscal pressure in ways determined by its institutional history, not wholly by a rational assessment of its future. See Michael Berubé and Cary Nelson, eds., *Higher Education Under Fire: Politics, Economics, and the Crisis*

of the Humanities (New York: Routledge, 1995) and the final chapter of this book.

67. Bourdieu, *Distinction,* 110.

68. Symbolic power, symbolic violence, linguistic capital, and trajectory will all be important to my argument, but the central categories will be those of habitus and field.

69. Bourdieu discusses the notion of profession briefly but provocatively in his and Wacquandt's *Invitation to Reflexive Sociology* and my discussion here makes extensive use of his work, looking specifically at the question of profession/professionalization in early modern English culture.

70. Bourdieu and Wacquandt, *Invitation,* 242–43.

71. Burrage and Torstendal, *Professions in Theory and History,* 27. Friedson's call for a phenomenological approach to studies of profession has the salutary effect of questioning received definitions, but does not guard research against the residual effects of those definitions. If profession *is* a folk concept, then it is not an unambiguous object of research. Friedson's questions are good ones, but they do not go far enough in asking about the history that structures the perceptions that are to be examined "phenomenologically."

72. Recent historical scholarship has changed this to some extent but the effects of this historical work on professions is only slowly making its way into sociology (and literary criticism). Outside of a few seminal works that base their notions of profession on the common-sense definition Bourdieu is at pains to question, serious study of early modern writers as professionals is only a comparatively recent phenomenon. See James Forse, *Art Imitates Business* (Bowling Green, OH: Popular Press, 1993), Richard Helgerson, *Elizabethan Prodigals* and *Self-Crowned Laureates,* Ingram, *Business of Playing,* and Kathleen McLuskie, *Dekker and Heywood: Professional Dramatists* (New York: St. Martin's, 1994).

73. For example, there are a whole series of works on the theater that more or less uncritically use the term to describe actors and writers working on the public and private stages (many of which are immensely useful—see bibliography). Few such works question their use of the terms "profession" or "professional" in any kind of rigorous way.

74. Bourdieu and Wacquandt, *Invitation,* 243.

75. Ibid., 245.

76. See Abbott, *System of Professions,* 59ff. The academy is one of the important publics that professions make their jurisdictional claims before, and studies recognizing their claims are valuable tools in securing broader recognition.

77. Bourdieu, *Language and Symbolic Power,* 106.

78. In *Invitation to Reflexive Sociology* Bourdieu discusses the way that American studies of poverty create groups that take on an administrative life of their own even when the descriptions are manifestly inadequate to the diversity of those in poverty. See pages 240–41. See also "Did You Say popular?" in *Language and Symbolic Power.*

79. Bourdieu and Wacquandt, *Invitation,* 229–30.

80. See Archer, *Pursuit of Stability,* and Beier and Finlay, *London 1500–1700,* for discussions of London's response to the economic changes that occurred in the course of the sixteenth century.

81. Chapter 2 discusses the professionalization of administration in the period. Administration becomes a profession open to those who choose it and demonstrate ability over the course of the Tudor century under the pressure of social change that demanded that the government be staffed by men of ability, rather than by the clients of this or that noble or by churchmen.

82. "Profession," *Oxford English Dictionary* (second edition). The OED uses Chaucer's *Summoner's Tale* to provide examples for this definition as well as for profession as referring to a specific religious order.

83. See also I. M., *Health*, (1581), William Blandy, *The Castle of Commonwealth* (1581), as well as the various defences of playing and writing published in the early seventeenth century.

84. "Profession," *OED*.

85. "Vocation," *OED*. The supporting citation dates to 1426 and comes from Lydgate's *De Guileville's (G. de) Pilgrimage of the life of man* (translated in 1426).

86. Bourdieu, *Distinction*, 110.

87. "Vocation," *OED*.

88. There is a use of profession in the B Fragment of the *Romaunt of the Rose*, but this fragment is not thought to be Chaucerian. Nevertheless, the usage there is consistent with that in the *Tales* in that it refers to religious vows. See the Chaucer Concordance webpage at the University of Maine at Machias. http://www.umm.maine.edu/faculty/necastro/chaucer/concordance/index.asp.

89. When the friar reaches into Thomas's "bak," all he finds is a fart.

90. *Troublesome Raigne*'s Bastard is called to a profession, while Shakespeare's Bastard chooses one. See the *King John* chapter below for a more detailed discussion of these plays.

91. Marshall, *Kind of Life*, 10.

92. See chapter 3 below on the association of legal professionals and social unrest.

93. It is important to note that culture responds to changes in "objective" conditions through many layers of mediation, all of which exert their influence on a particular response. The redefinition of profession in early modern culture is not, therefore, a straightforward reflection of social changes but a refraction of a response to objective changes layers of mediation. In this case, the layers include the field of cultural production, the field of power, and the emerging professional field.

94. William Perkins, *A Treatise of the Vocations or Callings of Men, with the sorts and kindes of them and the right use thereof* (London, 1603) 931.

95. Easy because he refers to secular occupations in ways that resemble professions and foolhardy because he prefers vocation or calling to describe these occupations.

96. Perkins, *Treatise*, 904.

97. He explicitly excludes the writing of plays from the group of divinely sanctioned professions. This expresses more of his religious position than of the lack of professionalism in the ranks of playwrights. Perkins's exclusion of playwriting from the ranks of legitimate professions is part of broader cultural prejudices that would have encouraged the status-anxiety that forms part of the field's drive toward professionalization.

98. See the *OED* for additional definitions, most of which stress the received nature of vocation over the element of choice that Perkins focuses much of his attention on.

99. Perkins, *Treatise*, 909. It is worth noting that Perkins states that both men and women have callings that they are bound to follow by the law of God. He does not make any gender distinction in the basic fact that all people are called to labor in their vocation. Of course, he does not go so far as to say that all vocations are open to both genders, but it would not stretch his work far to suggest that his treatise at least implies that to be the case.

100. Ibid., 913.

101. In most cases. Some work is inherently illegitimate, like playing.

102. Perkins, *Treatise*, 906.

103. However, linking occupation to land as a reliable means of help does suggest a status claim for callings of whatever nature.

104. See Marshall, *Kind of Life*, 41–50 for a discussion of the link between the urban clergy and the theory (and theology) of calling/vocation/profession.

105. R. G. Lang, "Social Origins and Social Aspirations of Jacobean London Merchants," *Economic History Review* second series 27 (1974): 28–47. This is a topic taken up in greater detail below in the law chapter.

106. See Middleton's *Michaelmas Term* for an example of a merchant's son placed in university and then the Inns of Court in order to secure gentility for the family name. Law was, it seems, privileged over trade, but both served as reliable means of either ennobling or securing the family future.

107. See the law and administration chapters below for a more detailed discussion of this practice. Christopher Brooks makes this argument in his "Apprenticeship."

108. Ibid., 61.

109. This may have been partly due to the relative ease of reasserting that status if the apprentice succeeded in joining the livery of his company. As Brooks notes, many people who attached "gent" to their names belonged to the mercantile or professional populations.

110. Brooks, "Professions," 114.

11. In an earlier state of the field, practicing lawyers below the rank of serjeant were called apprentices. This demonstrates how close legal and craft methods of training were. See the law chapter below.

112. Brooks, "Professions," 115.

113. Lawyers were subject to a series of regulatory initiatives from both the City of London and from the Crown that were designed to control the production of lawyers and of legal business. That such measures were less than fully successful attests to the relative autonomy of the legal profession.

114. Brooks, "Professions," 134.

115. See chapter 2 on merit and birth, the Poetomachia chapter on theater, and chapter 3 on professional authority.

116. Brooks, "Professions," 118.

117. Some were more successful at this than others, law and administration being obvious examples. Playwriting, however, was not.

118. This is as true of professional writing as it is of law. Ben Jonson described himself as a poet-moralist, and as I demonstrate below, his example had a powerful effect on the development of the field.

Chapter 2. "I mean to learn"

1. James, *Society, Politics, and Culture*, 94.
2. Ibid., 136.
3. Elton, *Tudor Revolution*, 30.
4. Elton, 36.
5. This term is a conscious anachronism. England lacked a formal professional civil service until long after the period under investigation here ended, but, as Michael Pulman writes in his *The Elizabethan Privy Council in the Fifteen-Seventies* (Berkeley and Los Angeles: University of California Press, 1971): "Modern bureaucracy was still undreamed of, but its procedures in a basic simple form, were already in existence" (169). The bureaucracy was as systematic and its staff as professional as the situation allowed it to be.
6. Important recent collections of essays such as Christopher Coleman and David Starkey's *Revolution Reassessed* (Oxford: Oxford University Press, 1986), Alistair Fox and John Guy's *Reassessing the Henrician Age* (Oxford: Basil Blackwell, 1986), and Paul Fiedler and T. F. Mayer's *Political Thought and the Tudor Commonwealth* (London: Routledge, 1992) qualify certain of Elton's central propositions and suggest the reforms carried out under Thomas Cromwell's aegis in the 1520s and '30s were more returns to older administrative models or were developments in trends set in motion in the fifteenth century rather than genuine innovations that utterly reinvented government under the Tudors. Despite such challenges, Elton's work remains a significant formulation for the field, and if the Tudor "revolution" proceeded in a more fitful way than Elton suggests, it remains that administration underwent dramatic change in the period.
7. It is important to note that the impetus toward this professionalization was, at least in part, generated by humanist educational and social ideals that were held by many of the period's leading reformers from Cromwell to Cecil. These ideals were also, of course, important to the development of writing and law in the period.
8. See Alan G. R. Smith, *Servant of the Cecils: The Life of Sir Michael Hickes* (Totowa, NJ: Rowman and Littlefield, 1977). Beginning with an education at Cambridge and at Lincoln's Inn, Hickes' career trajectory took him from a mercer's family in London to being one of Burghley's principal secretaries, a holder of high office in central and local administration, an important financial consultant to individuals and the Crown, and lifelong confidant of Robert Cecil.
9. Cromwell, Bacon, and Cecil all rose from relative obscurity to the heights of power, often against the opposition of traditional elites, and it is important to note that these early administrators pursued the titles and honors of the traditional nobility, even though the original basis of their authority came from the pen rather than the sword.
10. Jones, *Elizabethan Court of Chancery*, 7.
11. His choice may be enabled by his blood, but blood is not the final determinant in that choice.
12. Sigurd Burckhardt, *Shakespearean Meanings* (Princeton, NJ: Princeton University Press, 1968); Virginia Vaughan, "Between Tetralogies: *King John* as

Transition," *Shakespeare Quarterly* 35 (1984): 407–20); Michael Manheim, *The Weak King Dilemma in the Shakespearean History Play* (Syracuse, NY: Syracuse University Press, 1973); Marsha Robinson, "The Historiographic Method of *King John*" in *King John: New Perspectives* ed. D. Curren-Aquino (Newark: University of Delaware Press, 1989), 29–40.

13. Vaughan, "Between Tetralogies," 409.

14. See Douglas Wixson, "'Calm Words Folded up in Smoke': Propaganda and Spectator Response in Shakspeare's *King John*," *Shakespeare Studies* 14 (1981): 111–27, which examines the play's dramaturgy in terms of contemporary political pamphleteering. See also John R. Elliott, "Shakespeare and the Double Image of King John," *Shakespeare Studies* 1 (1965): 64–84. Elliott discusses as politically motivated the conflict between two historical images of King John, as a proto-Protestant martyr king and as a weak, usurping, bad king.

15. See Jacqeline Trace, "Shakespeare's Bastard Faulconbridge: An Early Tudor Hero," *Shakespeare Studies* 13 (1980): 59–69, for a genealogy of the character in *King John* as well as in *The Troublesome Raigne*. She finds no direct historical analog to the Bastard, and looks instead at such figures as Henry VIII's bastards, Wolsey's son Thomas Winter, and other Henrician and Elizabethan bastard adventurers as possible models for the character. A real Bastard Falconbridge fought for Henry VI in the Wars of the Roses and was executed in 1471. Shakespeare and the anonymous author of *The Troublesome Raigne* likely found the name in Holinshed.

16. All citations of *King John* will be from the Arden edition. *The Troublesome Raigne* is quoted from G. Bullough, *Narrative and Dramatic Sources of Shakespeare*, vol. 4 (London: Routledge Kegan Paul, 1975). I am not particularly interested here in questions of chronology; it is more important for my argument that both were extant at roughly the same time, suggesting that the ideas presented in both were likewise contemporaneous.

17. See Phyllis Rackin, *Stages of History: Shakespeare's English Chronicles* (Ithaca, NY: Cornell University Press, 1990), chap. 4 for a discussion of the similarity of this succession dispute to that between John and Arthur.

18. As do the legalities of the claims. In the *Troublesome Raigne*, bastardy seems automatically to disqualify Philip from the inheritance while in *King John* the fact that Philip is born in wedlock and is the elder gives him the right to the land regardless of who his father actually was.

19. And he does not do even this: his claim evaporates when he is determined to be illegitimate. Volition is not an issue.

20. Wrightson's *English Society* demonstrates the complex and deeply ingrained awareness of rank and position in contemporary English society. He writes, "the most fundamental structural characteristic of English society was its high degree of stratification, its distinctive and pervasive system of social inequality" (17). The very bulk of contemporary writing on order and degree attests to a conscious awareness of the importance of attempting to maintain these distinctions. Philip is no exception.

21. Voices call Philip "regius filius" carrying him away with the "glorie" of his birth, voices that only fall silent when another, more pragmatic, voice reminds him of what he is and whence he comes.

22. Bourdieu, *Logic*, 81–82.

23. The Bastard in Shakespeare's play shows a more explicit awareness of this "game" in the "I mean to learn" speech and his learning project is designed to replace that awareness with the practical sense of the game that *Troublesome Raigne* represents here through Philip's reverie outside of normal dramatic time.

24. He is called to the nobility in the sense of a divine and preordained vocation. In this kind of vocation, choice is nonexistent.

25. Where the Bastard says "my Liege," Robert says "my gracious Liege." Robert's speech is markedly more deferential and conventionally polite. Interestingly, Shakespeare's Bastard never reminds himself of his "place" or to whom he is speaking.

26. In an article important to my thinking, David Scott Kastan writes that the Bastard "chooses his bastardy.... He denies himself access to a lineal history that would grant and guarantee name and position in favor of a freedom in which he can create both" (" 'To Set a Form Upon That Indigest': Shakespeare's Fictions of History," *Comparative Drama*. I would suggest that the freedom to create "name and history" that Kastan alludes to is far smaller than he argues it is: the Bastard chooses a fairly conventional pattern for his new identity as a nobleman (that of the royal servant) and, as I hope to demonstrate, works to assimilate himself ever more fully to that pattern as the play progresses.

27. John himself acknowledges the Bastard's right to the land saying: "My mother's son did get your father's heir; / Your father's heir must have your father's land" (1.1.128–29).

28. Countenance here includes the sense of face, the physical semblance. Eleanor asks if the Bastard wants to be like his brother, not just in terms of blood, but in a physical sense as well.

29. Note that in *Troublesome Raigne* Elinor discounts the physical resemblance's relevance to the question of Philip's bastardy, saying "Know you not, *Omne simile non est idem!*" (l. 197), going on to suggest that their mother thought of Richard as she lay with her husband and that this thought caused the resemblance.

30. It is important to note that *he* settles the squabble himself without reference to the King's judgment. The Bastard takes full charge of his affairs, as is fitting for one elevated to his status. John himself points to the Bastard's right to do this in his final lines to Robert: "Go, Faulconbridge: now hast thou thy desire; / A landless knight makes thee a landed squire" (1.1.176–77). The authority is clearly the Bastard's and this is the first of many scenes where he summarily takes matters into his own hands.

31. Wallace T. MacCaffery argues that "the Queen's service" was seen as a "career" for "the young man of good birth, poor estate, and average talents" (qualifications roughly matching those of Shakespeare's Bastard) with the possibility of "the solid respectability and substantial rewards of an official career" ("Place and Patronage in Elizabethan Politics," in *Elizabethan Government and Society*, ed. S. T. Bindoff et al. [London: University of London Press, 1961] 101). John Guy, Penry Williams, and the various biographers of the Cecil family attest to the role of talent in the selection of administrators.

32. B.W. Beckingsale, *Burghley: Tudor Statesman 1520–1598* (London: MacMillan, 1967) 134.

33. The Bastard's emphasis on chance here shows that his success is by no means sure—his ascent is made possible by the chance of his begetting, but is only secured by his ability.

34. And this is not the case in *Troublesome Raigne*. The Bastard is acknowledged as Plantagenet and offered the chance to "wait upon me and on thine Unckle heere, / Who shall give honour to thy noble mind" (ll. 297–98). John knights him immediately—without waiting for a response—and the Bastard Fauconbridge is transformed.

35. "Habitus" is defined by Pierre Bourdieu as "a disposition that generates meaningful practices and meaning-giving perceptions; it is a general transposable disposition which carries out a systematic, universal application—beyond the limits of what has been directly learnt—of the necessity inherent in the learning conditions" (*Distinction*, 170). It is a structure of dispositions which structures an agent's responses to events.

36. Wrightson, *English Society*, 25.

37. The Cecil family's fortunes might serve as a good example of this (infrequent) movement up the ladder of rank– from being minor courtiers and country landholders under Henry VII, the family grew in stature to become one of the most important and influential ones in Elizabeth's England.

38. Rather than its presence. His rhetorical failures before the walls of Angiers in act 2, scene 1 can be seen as more evidence of incomplete mastery of "royal" rhetoric.

39. Michael Mannheim, "The Four Voices of the Bastard," in Curren-Aquino, *King John: New Perspectives*, 127.

40. Ibid., 128. Mannheim's assertion that Old Faulconbridge was too dull to have been the Bastard's father, a "fact" that Mannheim claims the Bastard's language demonstrates, ignores the fact that Faulconbridge was knighted on the field, presumably for valor, and that Richard I clearly valued him.

41. The Arden edition footnotes lines 169–75 (the Bastard's last speech before his "soliloquy" at line 182ff.): " 'The proverbial sayings which follow are characteristic of the Bastard's rusticity of breeding' (Wright, comparing *Cor.* I.i.211)," underscoring the fact that despite his royal blood, he was raised with the manners of the country.

42. "Joan" was apparently a common name for a "female rustic" (OED cited in Arden ed.).

43. Pierre Bourdieu discusses the ideal of performative language in *Language and Symbolic Power*. See especially "Price Formation and the Anticipation of Profits."

44. See *Language and Symbolic Power*. Habitus is a multivalent word in Bourdieu's work, for now I am commenting only on the strictly linguistic aspect of the concept.

45. Ibid., 51.

46. Or perhaps three. The Bastard occupies a continuum of habitus that range from that of his brother to that of the King and the other nobles. Schematically: Robert—the Bastard—the King. The second term, of course, splits in the course of the play—the Bastard of the early part of the action metamorphoses into a dramatically different one by the end—but this schema is basically accurate.

47. He engages in the same kind of wordplay that "noble" characters do in this and other Shakespearean plays. The difference lies in the vocabulary, the stock of linguistic capital, he has at his disposal. Structurally, the Bastard's speech approximates that of "madcap" noble figures such as, for example, *Romeo and Juliet'* s Mercutio or *Much Ado About Nothing'* s Don Benedick. This relation is, I think, what Mannheim discusses in his article cited above.

48. Robert Beale, "A Treatise of the Office of a Councellor and Principall Secretarie to her Majestie" ca. 1592, in Conyers Read, *Mr. Secretary Walsingham and the Policy of Queen Elizabeth* (Oxford: Clarendon Press, 1925), 427. The manuscript is in the British Library (BL MS Add Manuscript 48149, Yelverton MS. 161 part 1 [ff 3b–9b]). I have consulted this MS to compare it the Read's transcription.

49. Ibid., 440.

50. Elsewhere in the treatise Beale gives long list of the information and references the secretary must have available. It ranges from lists of all the gentle families in the shires, to a list of judges, to notes on resources and their role in foreign trade. See ibid., 428ff. The British Library preserves many of Beale's papers in the Yelverton MS. One manuscript (BL Add. Ms. 48150) is a formulary containing examples of various different documents a secretary would have to draw up. Folio page 15 has examples of "sauve conduicts, commissions for horses, carriages" and is followed by a blank leaf and then examples of "Actes of Appearances before the Councell, discharges of bonds." It appears to have been a working notebook of the kind the treatise describes.

51. Ibid., 442–43.

52. Sir George Puttenham's treatise on poetry makes a similar shift from specific commentary on composition to a lengthy discourse on comportment. In the eyes of "theorists" at least, he practice of a profession could not be separated from the behavior of those occupying it.

53. Sir Thomas Smith, *De Republica Anglorum,* ed. Mary Dewar (Cambridge: Cambridge University Press, 1982), 80.

54. This does not necessarily have anything to do with *actual* representation—only the forms are at issue here.

55. In which he is of course participating as "Question."

56. Both our modern sense of observation as taking notice of or studying something and what the Arden editor calls the "secondary sense" of obsequiousness are at work here. The Bastard, in order to be fully integrated into his new rank, must observe the conventions of observation. Only then will he not be a "bastard to the time." In contrast to other scholars who see the Bastard as either remaining a "bastard to the time" and those who view his becoming a "son to the time," to use Ronald Stroud's phrase, as a kind of sellout, a corruption of his critical virtue, I view his "conversion" as part and parcel of his ascent up the ladder of rank and not as an example of cynicism or deception. He does not lose the honesty most critics see him as possessing in acts 1, 2, and 3 in the course of acts 4 and 5, his honesty is of a different nature, one in keeping with the position to which he has assimilated himself. This transfigured honesty is troubling, not because it is a lie, but precisely because it is not—the Bastard is not being deceptive because he has forgotten the perspective that would show his practice to be deceit. As part of his professional ascent, the Bastard's sense of the world is transformed.

57. Linguistic habitus could be said to be a constitutive component of the class habitus that encompasses not only linguistic practice but what Bourdieu calls bodily hexis and the whole constellation of more or less conditioned responses that produce an agent's actions. See Bourdieu, *Language*, 83: "what expresses itself through the linguistic habitus is the whole class habitus of which it is one dimension."

58. Linguistic habitus also contains the whole history of a speaker's relation to various linguistic markets. The fact that the Bastard comes from the country remains apparent in his speech no matter how fully he takes on the voice of his new rank. He approaches asymptotically near to the habitus of the King, for example, but never actually gets there and that slight gap sounds in his utterances.

59. He does not take full advantage of this performativity until much later in the play—at this point it is merely a source of amusement—by the end he exercises surprising amounts of power through his speech.

60. It appears that Shakespeare is less troubled in this play by the deceit implicit in such linguistic role-playing—even when the new role appears to replace the old almost completely. Later, in *1 and 2 Henry IV* and *Henry V* the capacity for this kind of linguistic transformation is more troubling (and less total). Hal's ability to speak with any tinker in his own language is the mirror image of the Bastard's adoption of noble linguistic practices, but the attitude of the playwright toward that ability seems more ambiguous.

61. Hotspur's speech in *1 Henry IV* is characterized by its more or less univocal quality—he cannot recognize or exploit shifts in rhetoric. Indeed, he claims not to "profess" talking (5.2.90).

62. Bourdieu, *Language*, 77. See the rest of this chapter ("Price Formation and the Anticipation of Profits") especially pages 66–72 for further discussion of the interactions of linguistic habitus and linguistic market.

63. These being Philip's oath to Constance and Arthur, the demands of honor, and Arthur's claims to the English throne, all of which are bypassed in the making of the contract.

64. See the exchange between Lewis, Blanche, Philip and John at 2.1.495ff. The marriage is proposed, the massive dowry offered, the love language begins to be used, the dowry is confirmed (and expanded), and then the marriage is confirmed. The role of land and money in all this is made clear by this sequence of events—the dowry precedes the "love" expressed by Lewis and Blanche.

65. Note that Constance mentions only the land here, not the thirty thousand marks of English money King John adds to the five provinces (2.1.530). She overlooks the explicitly financial component of the marriage.

66. I do not wish to treat this, as some critics have, as a speech betraying only the Bastard's essential cynicism and disillusionment. It *is* that of course, but I think it also demonstrates his ever-deepening awareness of how far his learning project must take him if it is to succeed. And in this, it is more troubling than a straightforwardly cynical speech—especially as his aware of the "bias of the world" evaporates as the play proceeds.

67. See the different attitudes toward honor expressed by Hotspur, Hal, and Falstaff in that play.

68. Bourdieu, *Logic*, 17.

69. Mannheim, "Four Voices."

70. All through the play, Hal has described Hotspur as a kind of storehouse whose contents he will later appropriate to his own use. For example, in the "Percy is but my factor" exchange with Henry IV, Hal describes Hotspur as an agent collecting honor for Hal's benefit. In the final scenes of the play, Hal withdraws the honor stored up by Hotspur and, as Hotspur dies, takes over even his speech.

71. For the facts of the Cecil family's rise, see Beckingsale's *Burghley: Tudor Statesman*, to which this discussion is much indebted. Burghley himself entered the royal service as a page, acting as a personal servant of the monarch, and rose from there to the highest offices in England.

72. Both Burghley and his son Robert Cecil were instrumental in shaping policy including (and this is a parallel to *King John*) the succession.

73. According to the treatise, the secretary must be able to act on all matters foreign and domestic, he must be informed on all legal, economic, political, and social issues and must be prepared to act appropriately on all of these issues. There is no sense that officers operated in distinct departments with specific responsibilities. The Elizabethan "man of business" had to be willing and able to do everything.

74. See John's reaction to the Bastard's taunting of Austria in act 3 cited above for another response to the Bastard's efforts to occupy a high social position.

75. "May" carries overtones both of a beneficent wish for the prince's happy coronation and the sense that the Bastard is somehow granting him permission.

76. Note the contrast between this scene and the final scene of *Troublesome Raigne*. The Bastard Philip of *Troublesome Raigne* says "Then Kings & Princes, let these broils have end, / And at more leasure talke upon the League. / Meanewhile to *Worster* let us beare the King, / And there interre his bodie, as beseemes. / But first, in sight of *Lewes*, Heire of *Fraunce*, / Lords take the crowne and set it on his head, / That by succession is our lawfull King" (ll. 1178–84). He then shifts into a choric mode for the final patriotic speech of the play, losing his already tenuous individuation as he speaks the epilogue. This Bastard defers to the lords in a way Shakespeare's does not, and this speech carries far less of the assured and commanding tone conveyed by the end of Shakespeare's play.

77. See the succession of the Cecil family in the service of the Tudors. Burghley served Henry VIII, Edward VI, Mary (briefly), and Elizabeth I—rising in importance and trust with each successive monarch, a trust he passed on to his son Robert.

78. Note also that *knights* pledge service to their lords; in pledging thus, he consolidates a position that might have remained ambiguous. The Bastard exercises his control over his future (and that of the kingdom insofar as he is authorized by John to "have the ordering of this present time") from a posture of submission (on his knees), exemplifying his mastery of the symbolic practices of the aristocratic habitus.

79. It is laden with "sweet, sweet, sweet poison for the age's tooth," "poison" which does indeed "strew the footsteps of [his] rising." It is also not deceptive. This is a sincere offer, even as it strategically ensures the continuance of his role in the court.

80. Philip begins his royal service as a soldier and remains such throughout the play. *Troublesome Raigne* does not give him the same kind of specifically administrative duties that Shakespeare's Bastard has by the end of his play.

81. Shakespeare's Bastard's power in the government is as legitimate as his birth is not, and his power's legitimacy has less to do with his birth than his ability and choice of "profession."

82. "Near or far off, well won is well shot, / And I am I, howe'er I was begot" (1.1.174–75), as cited above. Regardless of his "base" birth, he is still who he is and that becomes "Sir Richard Plantagenet," the trusted adviser and half-brother to the King. Merit takes the place of birth but only, of course, to a limited extent.

83. Smith, *Servant*, 144.

84. Note the Bastard's reference to the courtier's manual's dialogue of Question and Answer. The "dialogue of compliment" educated many courtiers—see Castiglione's *Book of the Courtier*.

85. Beale, "Treatise," 428.

86. St. Germain's *Doctor and Student* being only one of the more famous of such works. See the next chapter for a more developed discussion of this text.

87. Beale, "Treatise," 424.

88. Ibid., 423–24.

89. See Mervyn James's discussion of the politics of honor in *Society, Politics, and Culture*. One of the Essex rebellion's greatest grievances was the Queen's refusal to accept the "right" of the great nobles to a role in the national government represented by a seat on the Privy Council. The Privy Council jealously guarded the privilege of advising the Queen. Michael Pulman writes that there existed a convention that the Queen would only discuss matters of public import with her council (Pulman, *Elizabethan Privy Council*, 53). This will be discussed further below.

90. See Beckingsale, *Thomas Cromwell, Tudor Minister* (Totowa, NJ: Rowman and Littlefield, 1978) for a discussion of his work in the Court of Wards; Burghley and Bacon built on his reforms in the court and enhanced its revenues as a consequence. As discussed above, Mervyn James argues that under Cromwell the local elites in the Marches were slowly replaced by men who owed their position more to the central government than to local eminence, focusing authority on the Crown. This was true under Elizabeth as well, perhaps the best example being the institution of the Lords Lieutenant who were appointed centrally and exercised considerable power in the shires.

91. Beale, *Treatise*, 431. Beale goes on to provide just such a means of training—but it is not an academic program, it is a practical program that stresses the importance of assimilating the habits of a secretary.

92. See Richard Halpern's *Poetics of Primitive Accumulation* (Ithaca, NY: Cornell University Press, 1991) for a discussion of the central importance of imitation in Renaissance pedagogical theory.

93. Beale, "Treatise," 426.

94. The Privy Council had its own clerks, usually four in number, to manage the bulk of this paperwork, but individual secretaries had their own staffs as well. Michael Hickes's colleague in Burghley's secretariat was responsible for this task under Burghley's secretaryship. Other figures had similar personal staffs that operated alongside the Privy Council's official staff. This fact suggests that control of information played a major role in the exercise of power, a suggestion Beale's commentary reinforces.

95. In a way, Beale is arguing that the secretary needs to be a kind of living description of England. Beale's list of the things necessary for the secretary bears a close resemblance to the chapter headings in Harrison's *Description of England* (1587) and Smith's *De Republica Anglorum*.

96. Beale, "Treatise," 428. This list goes on to list several more items, extending the range of knowledge expected of a secretary to foreign trade and other matters beyond England's borders.

97. British Library Additional Manuscripts 48018–48167 (the Yelverton Papers). These papers include formularies recording usual ways of composing particular kinds of documents, indexes of the justices of the peace for the counties, and similarly practical documents related to the office. The attention to language in this material also demonstrates the need for secretaries to be aware of and facile with the intricacies of government discourse.

98. Baptist Hickes went on to amass an immense fortune and died as a viscount (he was raised to the peerage in 1628) partly through his brother's help early in his career.

99. Leslie Stephen and Sidney Lee, eds., *Dictionary of National Biography* (London: Oxford University Press, 1921–22) 810.

100. Many of these "gentlemen" were only gentle by virtue of education. Hickes was a grocer's son. To look at a dramatist example, Marlowe was trained in Cambridge for an ecclesiastical career and had gentle status because of his Master of Arts degree. See Helgerson, *Elizabethan Prodigals,* for more details.

101. Robert Tittler, *Nicholas Bacon: The Making of a Tudor Statesman* (Athens: Ohio University Press, 1976), 19. My discussion of Bacon's life and career owes much to this work.

102. Bacon was always a dedicated Protestant and spent the years of Mary's reign out of service rather than change his public position on religion. His work ethic and the interests expressed by his work in the Court of Wards (where he strove to reform the generally bad treatment accorded minor wards by their guardians), his work on the Denton-Bacon-Cary report on the state of the Inns of Court, and his work in Chancery derive from the humanist ideals and Reformist religion inculcated by his education.

103. Tittler, *Nicholas Bacon,* 22.

104. Ibid., 25. G. R. Elton's *Reform and Renewal* (Cambridge: Cambridge University Press, 1972) argues that Cromwell was an active recruiter of talented men with ideas compatible with his into various positions in the government. Bacon would hardly have escaped his notice.

105. Tittler, *Nicholas Bacon,* 26. The solicitor examined matters to be heard in Augmentations, as well as prosecuting and setting forth suits, actions, and process.

106. Ibid., 71.
107. B. W. Beckingsale, *Burghley: Tudor Statesman 1520–1598* (London: MacMillan, 1967), 25.
108. Ibid., 51.
109. Ibid., 51.
110. It is an interesting irony that Cromwell was created Earl of Essex immediately before his attainder and execution. He represented the apotheosis of the kind of upstart whose ascendancy Robert Devereux, Earl of Essex, agitated against at the turn of the sixteenth century.
111. Elton, *Reform and Renewal*, 13.
112. Ibid., 23.
113. Ibid., 29.
114. Ibid., 25.
115. See Beale discussion above. Beale's attention to comportment resembles that of the Bastard.
116. Shakespeare makes some use of the Protestant hagiography of John as an early resister to Rome's power, this being one of the more explicit references. However, the play does not go to the lengths John Bale's *King Johan* (or *The Troublesome Raigne*) does to establish John's proto-Protestant credentials.
117. Nicholas Bacon, Thomas Smith, Thomas More, and others are good examples of this kind of individual.
118. See Elton's *Reform and Renewal*, James' *Society, Politics, and Culture*, and Penry Williams's *The Tudor Regime* (Oxford: Oxford University Press, 1979) for discussions of the role of humanist ideas in the public intellectual life of the period.
119. Elton, *Reform and Renewal*, 1.
120. Ibid., chap. 1. A glance through the *Dictionary of National Biography* will serve to show that Tudor administrators tended to have scholarly ambitions. These men combined a will to public service with a scholarly disposition, and it seems likely that the kind of scholarship they engaged in helped to reinforce that will to service.
121. The profit here was not, of course, merely personal. The Queen's government profited mightily by having educated and capable servants. It is important to note that not all such men were able to find positions in the government, and a number of those turned to other developing fields such as writing or law. This is part of Richard Helgerson's argument in his *Elizabethan Prodigals*.
122. Bourdieu and Wacquandt, *Invitation*, 98.
123. The clerks of the Privy Council in the 1570s (Edmund Tremayne [from 1571], Robert Beale [from 1572], Thomas Wilkes [from 1576], and Henry Cheke [from 1576]) were all "men of ability, experienced, particularly in foreign affairs, long before they were attached to the council in an official capacity, and in social standing at least on a par with the secretaries themselves" (Pulman, *Elizabethan Privy Council*, 157). All four were learned men as well as being capable administrators.
124. Bourdieu and Wacquandt, , *Invitation*, 101.
125. Pulman, *Elizabethan Privy Council*, 169.
126. In 1568, the Council numbered fifteen, and five of the members were of the old nobility (the Duke of Norfolk, the Earl of Arundel, the Earl of Lincoln,

the Earl of Pembroke, and Lord Howard of Effingham). Three of the five were appointed for their ability as much as their pedigree. See Pulman, *Elizabethan Privy Council*, 3.

127. Ibid., 53.

128. James, *Society, Politics, and Culture*, 433.

129. The contrast between the careers of Michael and Baptist Hickes illustrates the consequences (and costs) of this kind of choice. Michael Hickes entered Burghley's service and worked in the Queen's government in one way or another for most of his life while his brother inherited the family business and, with Michael's help, became immensely wealthy in trade and died a viscount. Both brothers were educated similarly but chose different paths.

Chapter 3. "This! . . ."

1. A writ of demur—otherwise known as a demurrer—moved the court to delay action because of a disputed point of law. A procedendo was a writ from a higher court ordering a lower to proceed to judgement. A sursurrara (certiorari) called proceedings in a lower court into a higher (as from a local jurisdiction into a Westminster court). The capiendo was a writ of arrest—for debt, trespass, or other offense. English law operated by means of such writs and much of an attorney's training involved mastering the various forms and purposes of writs.

2. Citations to Middleton's *Phoenix* and *Michaelmas Term* are to the forthcoming Oxford Middleton edition. *The Phoenix* is edited by Lawrence Danson and Ivo Kamps. *Michaelmas Term* is edited by Theodore Leinwand. Massinger's *A New Way to Pay Old Debts* is cited from the New Mermaids edition. *The Honest Lawyer* does not exist in a modern edition and I cite the play from the photographic facsimile in the Tudor Facsimile Texts series. Legal materials are generally cited from modern editions where they exist.

3. See my " 'From Wronger and Wronged Have I Fee': *Thomas Middleton and Early Modern Legal Culture*" in *Thomas Middleton and Early Modern Textual Culture: A Companion to the Collected Works*, ed. Gary Taylor (Oxford: Oxford University Press, forthcoming) for a discussion of Middleton's lifelong entanglements with the law. They begin in his youth and continue for the rest of his life. Parts of this chapter appear there as well.

4. See Luke Wilson's *Theatres of Intention: Drama and the Law in Early Modern England* (Stanford, CA: Stanford University Press, 2000) for a discussion of the ways that legal conceptions of intention influence early modern dramaturgy.

5. Jonson's *Poetaster* (1601) closes with Horace (Jonson) administering a purgative to the bad poets Crispinus (Marston) and Demetrius (Dekker) that forces them to vomit up the fustian vocabulary that has contaminated their minds and work. Jonson's purge itself revises his classical source—Lucian's *Lexiphanes*. Here, Quieto's bloodletting purges Tangle of both the vocabulary and the material—ink—which has poisoned him. See chapter 5.

6. See for example, the draper Quomodo's hopes for his son Sim in *Michaelmas Term*—by sending Sim to the Inns of Court, Quomodo hopes to secure a place for his family in the gentry.

7. Wilfred Prest, *The Inns of Court in Elizabethan England* (London: Longman, 1972), 21–22.

8. This is not an exhaustive list, and it excludes some of the civil jurisdictions and other smaller courts. Courts were, however, thick on the ground in early modern London.

9. Parliament tried, for example, cases of treason and handled the impeachment of public officials.

10. "Pettifogger" is a term first recorded in the *OED* in 1576 and refers to "a legal practitioner of inferior status, who gets up or conducts petty cases; esp. in an opprobrious sense, one who employs mean, sharp, cavilling practices; a 'rascally attorney.' " It is never applied to barristers—those lawyers trained at the four Inns of Court and entitled to appear before the superior courts—and only refers to attorneys. Berger, Bradford and Sondergard list 13 attorneys and pettifoggers, 120 judges and justices, and 65 other lawyers in their *Index of Characters in Early Modern English Drama* (Cambridge: Cambridge University Press, 1998). By comparison, about 60 "poets" appear in the *Index*. Clerks, bailiffs, constables, scriveners, bailiffs, solicitors, and other legal functionaries raise this total considerably.

11. The title character of the play is a disguised prince traveling among his soon-to-be subjects. Phoenix's father, the Duke of Ferrara, is dying and sends his son, he thinks, on a grand tour to finish Phoenix's education. However, Phoenix decides to travel through his city in disguise. Like the Duke in *Measure for Measure*, Phoenix observes various kinds of corruption in a series of vignettes illustrating different offenses he will have to respond to upon taking power. Legal corruption is only one kind in a large catalog.

12. Printing houses produced large numbers of law-related texts; scriveners producing deeds, bonds, indentures, and some writs abounded; and copies of proclamations, statutes, and ordinances circulated like playbills announcing the law to its audiences. Legal books far outnumbered printed plays throughout the period. For example, in 1580, the year of Middleton's birth, the *Short Title Catalog* records fourteen legal texts and Greg records no plays. In 1627, the year of his death, thirty law books were printed and Greg cites only four plays. I count conservatively, only including texts that are unambiguously linked to the law by title. This number could well be higher.

13. Moreover, the statutes produced by Parliament circulated in manuscript and later came to be printed. Statutes *were* law, and their force depended crucially on their written transmission.

14. See E. F. J. Tucker's *Intruder Into Eden: Representations of the Common Lawyer in English Literature, 1350–1750* (Columbia, SC: Camden House, 1984) for a discussion of the image of the common lawyer.

15. As will be discussed below, the "legal profession" existed under that name from as early as the beginning of the fifteenth century, but it functioned much more like a craft guild than a modern profession.

16. Controls were imposed on the numbers of attorneys who could practice in a given court (with little success), fee charts were repeatedly published, and educational standards were made explicit by royal proclamation and by statute. Few of these measures were effective and lawyers were far more successful in controlling themselves than external authorities were. See Prest, *Inns*, chaps. four and five.

17. See Brooks, *Pettyfoggers and Vipers of the Commonwealth: The Lower Branch of the Legal Profession in Early Modern England* (Cambridge: Cambridge University Press, 1986), 193–95; Wilfred Prest, *Rise of the Barristers*, (Oxford: Oxford University Press, 1986), chap. 4, and his essay "The English Bar, 1550–1700," in Prest, ed., *Lawyers in Early Modern Europe and America* (New York: Holmes and Meier, 1981), 73–80.

18. Tucker's study of representations of common lawyers argues that upswings in legal satire have more to do with social and economic upheavals than real disaffection with the legal system and its participants (*Intruder into Eden*, 11–12 and passim) and therefore legal satire often bears little resemblance to actual contemporary practice.

19. Ibid., 36.

20. Ibid., 38.

21. L. C. Knights, *Drama and Society in the Age of Jonson* (London: Chatto and Windus, 1951); Brian Gibbons, *Jacobean City Comedy: A Study of Satiric Plays by Jonson, Marston, and Middleton* (Cambridge, MA: Harvard University Press, 1968); Susan Wells, "Jacobean City Comedy and the Ideology of the City," *ELH* 48 (1981): 37–60; and Theodore Leinwand, *The City Staged* (Madison: University of Wisconsin Press, 1986).

22. To prevent terminological confusion, a confusion encouraged by the historical literature, I will call the medieval legal "profession" a guild, because it acts like one even though it had none of the public and formal attributes of a guild. This "guild" evolves into a profession over the course of the sixteenth and seventeenth centuries.

23. Brooks, *Pettyfoggers*, 96.

24. In particular, the conciliar courts, whose jurisdictions expanded under the Tudors and Stuarts, were crucially important to the exercise of royal authority.

25. Brooks argues that "one of the reasons why this period was so litigious was simply that a desirable service was for a while quite within the financial reach of a large number of customers" (*Pettyfoggers*, 101).

26. W. J. Jones's *Elizabethan Court of Chancery* clearly describes the function and jurisdictions of the various courts. Christopher Brooks's *Pettyfoggers and Vipers of the Commonwealth* and Wilfrid Prest's *Rise of the Barristers* examine the practice of common lawyers (barristers and attorneys or solicitors), while Brian Levack's *Civil Lawyers in England, 1603–1642* (Oxford: Oxford University Press, 1973) describes the education and work of the civilians. Wilfrid Prest's *Inns of Court in Elizabethan England* offers a detailed description of legal training at the Inns of Court.

27. This process went on in tandem with the progressive centralization of political authority in London under the Tudors. Provincial jurisdictions were not only courts of law but also administrative centers. Provincial courts' legal authority waned as they lost their status as semiautonomous sites of government. The great provincial councils were increasingly subordinated to the central government.

28. Chancery was fairly efficient in the period—*Jarndyce v Jarndyce* being yet to come. Some the reforms made in the sixteenth and seventeenth centuries had ossified into delays by the nineteenth when Dickens imagines this eternal Chancery suit in *Bleak House*.

29. Prest's *Inns of Court*, Brooks's *Pettyfoggers and Vipers*, and Brian Levack's *Civil Lawyers in England* all describe the growth of the legal profession as well as changes in legal training. Regularization and improved training also served the interest of lawyers by giving them something of a defense against charges of incompetence, venality, and corruption.

30. J. H. Baker, *Readings and Moots at the Inns of Court in the Fifteenth Century*, vol. 2. (London: Selden Society, 1990), xvi.

31. I use "faculty" for lack of a better term for those who taught lawyers. However, only civilians teaching in the universities fit the definition, since common law teachers were practicing lawyers first, and educators second, if at all. This is an important professional distinction, one that shapes the nature of common law training from its beginnings.

32. Baker, *Readings*, xviii. Writs in particular were practical procedural documents that lawyers needed to know how to produce on demand. They derive from precedent, the record of practice, not from a code. Later lawyers attempted to order writs into a more adequately theorized form (see the edited *Natura Brevium* volumes of the seventeenth century) but the acquisition of the knowledge of how and when to use them remains rooted in practice.

33. Baker, *Readings*, xxvi.

34. This is in contrast to the universities whose civil law curriculum concentrated on theoretical texts to the exclusion of practical issues. Newly graduated civilians had to spend several years in Doctor's Commons (which was, interestingly, structured very much like the Inns of Court) learning procedure before they could practice in any of the civil jurisdictions. See Levack's *Civil Lawyers* for a detailed discussion.

35. This practical mode of training, one which persisted through the rationalizing of legal education, resembles the Bastard's learning in *King John* and is not far off from contemporary training in fields such as business. The academic qualification of the MBA is granted by both classroom training and "experience," and the experience is that of immersion in what is sometimes termed the culture of business. Note the readiness of some business schools to grant credit hours for "real world" experience—early modern legal training did much the same thing.

36. Bourdieu, *Logic*, 54.

37. Ibid.

38. Later manuals in logic for budding lawyers emphasize the need for the student to conceptualize problems in terms of legal categories. For example, a limited number of actions and remedies were available to a plaintiff and if his (or her) complaint could not be made to fit under one of the existing rubrics, the plaintiff could not bring suit. One of the lawyer's functions was to find ways to fit real-world conflicts into the categories of legal contention. Recommendations a physical comportment is a frequent component of such tracts—see the discussion of Beale's advice for secretaries above.

39. This aspect of legal education has not disappeared. Learning how to socialize like a lawyer is an integral part of the informal training aspiring lawyers undergo even today. As Bourdieu notes, social connections and "networking" are vital components of a professional's social capital. See *Distinction* especially pages 283–87.

40. Pierre Bourdieu, "The Force of Law: Towards a Sociology of the Juridical Field," *Hastings Law Journal* 38 (1986–87): 820.

41. Middleton's *Phoenix* satirizes this tendency of lawyers by showing Tangle translating events into legal terms—the "law-bout" in the play translates a fencing match into a legal battle.

42. See Maxine MacKay, 15, no. 4 *"The Merchant of Venice*: A Reflection of the Early Conflict Between Courts of Law and Courts of Equity," *Shakespeare Quarterly* (1964): 371–75 for a discussion of the way the play exploits the relationship between common law and equity jurisdictions in the service of the plot.

43. Bourdieu, "Force," 820. Responding to the putative impartiality of the law, the American Repertory Theatre's 1998 production of the play staged this scene with Portia in a full face mask—utterly concealing her identity—and her lines were delivered through the theater's sound system in an exaggeratedly affectless tone. This staging relentlessly underscored the lack of neutrality in Portia's practice by overemphasizing the show of impartiality.

44. Legal training responded to the growth in business by at least attempting to regularize (by textualizing) legal education, an effort that coincided with public claims for the depth and sophistication of contemporary lawyers' legal learning.

45. Bourdieu, *Logic*, 55–56. See these pages for a discussion of habitus as a principle of innovation, but innovation limited by the logic of a field and by history. Lawyers faced changing circumstances but responded to them in ways structured by the history of the profession.

46. The central place of Littleton's treatise on land tenure in the printed discourse of the common law points to the centrality of property law to legal education and practice. Common law is identified closely with property law and with the maintenance of stable property relations.

47. These changes will be discussed in more detail below.

48. "The medieval legal profession had been in effect a guild, whose journeyman members practiced their trade within the narrow confines of the ancient common-law courts, under the oversight of a body of masters, the judges and serjeants-at-law. The dominance of the 'order of the coif' depended on a congruence of rank, seniority, academic learning, courtroom skills, and earning power" (Prest, *Rise*, 74). No lawyer could rise to a position of eminence without attention to both the academic side of his career and the more clearly social aspects of it. Rank and seniority depend as much on social interaction as it does to training.

49. The internal hierarchy of the Inns was more complicated, and when litigation expanded in the later sixteenth century some of the Inns' internal ranks became public ones. For example, call to the bar originated as a purely internal mark of a certain degree of learning on the part of students not yet admitted to practice.

50. Prest, *Inns*, 54.

51. The traditional course of learning exercises came under increasing strain in the later sixteenth century, as their inadequacy to the changing times became clearer to practicing lawyers. Coke's massive commentaries on Littleton respond, despite their complexity and bulk, to a perceived need for clarifi-

cation and expansion of this classic text on property law. The guild structure of the old profession was forced to adapt to radically altered conditions in ways that brought it closer to a modern one by adopting new text-based training methods, by formalizing qualifications for practice, and by paying more attention to the ethics of practitioners.

52. David J. Seipp, "The Structure of English Common Law in the Seventeenth Century," in *Legal History in the Making*, ed. W. M. Gordon and T. D. Fergus (London: Hambledon, 1991), 61.

53. If theoretical approaches were made necessary by changes in the legal system, they were made possible by the advancing technology of print, which made the texts of the law more easily accessible and, thus, synthesizable.

54. The *content* lagged behind, but the habits of mind inculcated by the kinds of practices the exercises demanded remained relevant and essential. Later attempts to revive the exercises (which had lapsed entirely during the Civil War) focused on their role in the intellectual formation of aspiring lawyers. See Prest, *Inns*, chap. 6.

55. In *Learning the Law: Teaching and the Transmission of English Law 1150–1900* ed. Jonathan Bush and Alan Wijffels (London: Hambledon, 1999). The attention to the usefulness of legal texts in the sixteenth and early seventeenth centuries suggests that this market was already in existence, if smaller than its late seventeenth century descendant.

56. Baker, *Readings*, 207–8.

57. Walter Cecil Richardson's *History of the Inns of Court* (Baton Rouge, LA: Claitor's, 1975) provides a useful survey of these texts.

58. This is only one example of a concern with training. Even as early as the 1530s, Henry VIII commissioned a report on the status of learning at the Inns of Court. The Denton-Cary-Bacon report (so named for its compilers) provides important early evidence of the nature and quality of legal education in the early part of the century. The report was first printed in *Fortescutus Illustratus* (1663). No period manuscript survives.

59. The various manuscripts of the *Brevia Placitata* that date as far back as the middle of the thirteenth century list precedents, writs, and forms of pleading without indexes or much in the way of organization. Nevertheless, they "aimed at giving instruction to the young advocate" (G. J. Turner and T. F. Plucknett, *Brevia Placitata* [London: Selden Society, 1951] xvi). Later versions of similar tracts acquire indexes, tables of contents, and other finding aids.

60. Baker, *An Introduction to English Legal History*, 3rd ed. (London: Butterworths, 1990), 216–17.

61. Christopher St. German, *Doctor and Student*, (ed. T. F. T. Plucknett and J. L. Barton (London: Selden Society, 1974), 95.

62. Or what ought to have been the structuring principles. St. German's work is filled with similar definitions that explain specific issues while offering insights into general principles. St. German alternates between a descriptive and prescriptive mode throughout *Doctor and Student* often within the same sentence.

63. William Fulbecke, *A Direction, or Preparative, to the Study of Law* (Aldershot: Wildwood House, 1987).

64. The content of legal education would have been readily accessible to a student in printed reports, abridgments, yearbooks, and, of course, through the oral exercises that remained the core of legal training in the Inns.

65. Abraham Fraunce's successful *Lawiers Logike* (1588) was one of many legal textbooks produced under the systematizing influence of Ramist logic.

66. Brooks, *Pettyfoggers*, 174.

67. See for example the 1662 *Brevia Judicialia* (Wing B5192) printed from the papers of Richard Brownloe, prothonotary of the Common Pleas. Its title page asserts that it will be "ufeful not only for all Clerks and Attornies, but alfo for the moft Learned in the Law, as fhewing the whole Series of Legal Proceedings in the faid Court, in all Actions, as well Real, as Perfonal." It, like other similar volumes, lists and gives examples of the writs through which the law functioned. Brownlow (1553–1638) was a Bencher of the Inner Temple and was prothonotary from 1591 until his death. The *Brevia Judicialia* acquires a detailed and highly practical index in the printed version. Anthony Fitzherbert (1470–1538) produced a *Natura Brevium*, another compilation of writs, which was printed in a massively unfriendly black-letter version in 1533. By 1662, the *New Natura Brevium*, based on the old book, organizes the contents and provides both the examples of writs and also comments on them. The 1662 volume is aimed explicitly at students of the law: "there are divers Maxims and Fundamentals in the knowledge of the Common Laws of the Land, which a man ought for to believe very neceffary for thofe who will underftand the fame Law . . . for that purpofe was there compofed by a Learned man a Book called *Natura Brevium*, which Book doth declare and fet forth the Diverfities of Natures of many Original Writs, with their Procefs; which Book helped much to the understanding not onely of the Regifter, but alfo of the Law of the Land" (A2r–v). The table of contents was compiled by William Rastall in 1539, likely in response to the difficulty of using an unindexed collection. This text and its "table" was in use for over a century, constantly revised and updated, and this kind of editorial practice mirrors that of the successive publishers of Littleton's *Tenures*.

68. The structure of a handbook like the *Boke of Presidents* is mirrored by later texts like the *Attorney's Academy*. Part of this has to do with the list-making influence of Ramist logic, but a large part has to do with the imitation of models. Coke's commentary on Littleton, rather than being a systematic treatment of the content of Littleton, proceeds as a line-by-line glossing of the older texts with the result that Coke's massive work's organization depends on Littleton.

69. See Brooks, *Pettyfoggers*, 48ff. Cases in late stages are cases that are past the point where they might settle out of court; the number of suits filed was, naturally, much larger.

70. Baker, *Introduction*, 185. These "old branches" were the serjeants-at-law and the attorneys working in Common Pleas. Before the sixteenth century, Common Pleas saw the bulk of important litigation and its officers, judges, and practitioners were therefore the elite corps of the legal profession. This was to change under the Tudors.

71. The Inns had a simple internal hierarchy with the benchers at the top; below them were the outer and inner barristers who were students at different

stages in their training. Both ranks of barrister were prohibited from pleading in the central courts and were not part of the "professional" membership of the Inns.

72. Baker, *Introduction,* 185. As members of a new profession, barristers would have been in search of ways to distinguish themselves from other practitioners. This need underlies some of the conflicts between attorneys and barristers in the later sixteenth century.

73. See Prest, *Inns,* 47 for a more detailed discussion of the Inns' internal hierarchy.

74. Ibid., 174. Also see Prest *Rise of the Barristers* for a detailed discussion of the rise, influence, and history of the barristers in early modern England.

75. Baker, *Introduction,* 179.

76. Ibid., 182.

77. Prest, *Inns,* 43.

78. And of struggles for social distinction.

79. This included producing the paperwork that initiated lawsuits and the gathering and presentation of evidence for many of the pretrial motions in "fairly simple common law cases" (Brooks, *Pettyfoggers,* 191).

80. Ibid., 18–19.

81. Ibid., 191.

82. See Baker's description of the medieval legal system in his *Introduction.* He shows that litigants were required to conduct their business in local courts. The superior courts of the common law were only to be used in cases where local justice failed (or was relinquished to the central courts) requiring the King's justice to settle an issue and even then required royal consent. There was no automatic recourse to the higher courts in the Middle Ages. In other words, before the Renaissance the central courts' role in national justice was fairly limited.

83. Christopher Brooks, "The Common Lawyers in England, 1558–1642" in Prest, *Lawyers,* 46–47.

84. Of Court or of Chancery. The Chancery Inns tended to concentrate on writs and procedure in their learning exercises and thus by the end of the sixteenth century were havens for attorneys (but not for barristers). The Inns of Chancery became increasingly marginal and lacked the social cachet the Inns of Court maintained as "nurseries of the gentry."

85. See James's *Society, Politics, and Culture* for a discussion of the erosion of provincial conciliar power (and legal jurisdictions) as the Tudors gathered power to themselves in London.

86. Brooks, "Common," 52.

87. Bourdieu and Wacquandt, *Invitation,* 101.

88. Even London had its own courts that heard causes originating in the city. In the fourteenth and fifteenth centuries, the superior courts tended to hear London cases only in the event of a city court's failure or abdication of authority.

89. Brooks, "Common," 42.

90. Prest, *Rise* 287.

91. Tucker, *Intruder into Eden,* 11.

92. Ibid., 12.

93. Jonson's *Staple of News* satirizes lawyers in these terms as do many other city comedies.

94. Thirty-six percent of the men in his sample were the sons of citizens of London, another twenty-one percent were sons of provincial tradesmen, sixteen percent were the sons of yeomen or husbandmen, and twenty-seven percent were the sons of "knights or gentlemen" (Lang, "Social Origins," 31).

95. See Archer's *Pursuit of Stability.*

96. I am very much in debt to Ian Archer's account of London governance for what follows.

97. Examples would include food riots, whose intent was generally the enforcement of city or Crown regulations, and attacks on foreigners. Typically, these riots expressed dissatisfaction with the way in which authority was exerted, not with authority itself. See Archer, *Pursuit of Stability*, 3–9.

98. Ibid., 5. The targets include, ironically enough, lawyers and especially law students. Many apprentice riots were directed at students in the Inns of Court who were, by virtue of their student status, both peers of and superiors to the apprentices.

99. The elite was primarily composed of successful merchants, and the resident gentry had little role in city government. Archer asserts that "although London harbored many gentleman residents, their role in City government was heavily circumscribed. They lacked any representation on the common council" (ibid., 50). There was no competition for power between gentlemen and citizens.

100. Keith Wrightson writes of the period's preoccupation with the maintenance of rank, order, and degree in *English Society;* "The most fundamental structural characteristic of English society was its high degree of stratification, its distinctive and pervasive system of social inequality" (17). Contemporary writers often mention the importance and necessity of maintaining status distinctions.

101. Nor was it in fiction. See Thomas Deloney's *The Gentle Craft* (1598) for its story of Simon Eyre's rise from obscurity to the office of Lord Mayor. See also Thomas Dekker's dramatization of Deloney's novel, *The Shoemaker's Holiday.* Unlike the rapacious and destructive social climbers depicted in other fictions, Deloney's Eyre rises from humble beginnings to high office without destructive consequences for his neighbors.

102. Archer, *Pursuit of Stability,* 51. This may have had the double effect of making assimilation attractive and increasing anxiety about status. See the discussion of the Bastard Faulconbridge's trajectory in chapter 2.

103. See the "law-bout" in Middleton's *Phoenix* that links legal rhetoric with physical violence in surprising ways. Tangle, the poseur attorney, and his mentor the justice Falso engage in a fencing bout that confuses the rapiers and daggers they wield with the legal terms they throw at each other. Both do physical damage. As Falso says at the close: "I perceive by this trial if a man have a sound fall in law, he shall feel it in his bones all his life after" (9.274–75).

104. Middleton's drama is particularly consumed with legal matters. See my " 'From Wronger and Wronged Have I Fee' " for a more detailed discussion of how Middleton's legal interests find their way into his writing.

105. See the above discussion of the operations of the juridical sense.

106. MacKay, "Reflection," 372.

107. MacKay refers to the case of *Throckmorton v. Finch* (1598 [3 Inst. 124]), which resulted in Chancery being denied its former right to review "judgments at law" (372) despite there being "apparent matter in equity" (3 Inst. 124).

108. The injustice of Shylock's fate in the eyes of the audience is irrelevant to the ways that characters on stage recognize it as just. The slipperiness of the question of justice in Shakespeare's play only reinforces the notion that the law's relations to ethical questions about ends are murky at best. Jonson's legal system is even murkier on the same issue.

109. Citations of Jonson are to Herford and Simpson.

110. See Joel Altman, *Tudor Play of Mind: Rhetorical Inquiry and the Development of Elizabethan Drama* (Berkeley and Los Angeles: University of California Press, 1978) for a detailed discussion of the importance of arguing both sides of a position to Tudor education.

111. Each of the punished characters receives a punishment symbolically appropriate to his nature. There is no attempt at legally inflected sentencing.

112. This is not unlike Mosca's trajectory in *Volpone*. Mosca employs Volpone's will as his instrument of ascent, despite Volpone not being dead before its implementation.

113. Cockstone asks, surprised, as Rearage moves to avoid Quomodo, "How then, afraid of a woolen draper?" (1.1.72). Rearage replies in justification, "He warn'd me his house, and I hate he should see me abroad" (1.1.73). Cockstone's surprise suggests that avoiding a draper is abnormal behavior for men of their status.

114. Ironically enough, while Quomodo is busy about Easy's lands, Easy is busy about Quomodo's wife, which leads to Quomodo's downfall. The proverb he quotes accurately portrays citizen-gentry relations in the play.

115. "Your revenge is more glorious: / To be a cuckold is but for one life, / When land remains to you, your heir, or wife" (1.1.108–10).

116. He makes reference to this throughout the play. In conversation with his daughter and wife he says: "Thou know'st, beside, we undo gentlemen daily" (2.3.55).

117. Contemporary cony-catching pamphlets discuss tactics like those Quomodo employs to put Easy in his debt. Thomas Dekker, among others, discusses the use of bonds to extract cash from gullible people new to the city. See *Lanthorn and Candlelight* (1608) and *The Guls Hornebook* (1609) for examples. *Measure for Measure* refers to such a swindle as well in a part of the play arguably contributed by Middleton.

118. In 3.4, Quomodo exults, "Now shall I be divulged a landed man / Throughout the Livery; one points, another whispers, / A third frets inwardly, let him fret and hang! / Especially his envy I shall have" (3.4.5–8). His goal is clearly enhanced status among his peers. His envy is bad for good order and demonstrates the conventional wisdom about the dangers of envy.

119. Note the conflation of thrifty and covetous in Quomodo's speech. This linkage responds to anxieties about the results of mercantile thrift (and economic success) for the established order.

120. By convention, students and graduates of the universities or the Inns were accorded gentle status, but that status did not pass down to their descendants.

121. There is a suggestion that Sim's education will protect him from the wiles of men like his father. His legal knowledge ought, Quomodo hopes, to inoculate him against the kind of trickery that got him his land in the first place.

122. "Our works" here refers to those of the law, the works appropriate to a judge, and, more importantly to a play called *Michaelmas Term*, works appropriate to term time. The judge appears not only to punish the malefactors and restore order, but also to purge the law of the errors introduced by Quomodo's misuse of it.

123. Unclear is the final status of Easy's relationship to Mrs. Quomodo given that Quomodo is not dead, but the play suggests that the marriage will stand.

124. *A New Way to Pay Old Debts* is far more strident about this than Middleton's play is. Quomodo is merely stripped of his ill-gotten gains and his mercantile business, not driven mad and carried off to Bedlam like Sir Giles Overreach.

125. Griffin's practice resembles exactly what Mosca praises in Voltore's legal career. See above.

126. Note that Griffin himself speaks in these terms, though not to condemn. He says "I loue peace, though I cannot liue by't. I respect my conscience aboue my purse—when't has no money in it" (C3ʳ).

127. Sager wins—despite the efforts of the corrupt Griffin—in an offstage hearing. The play keeps what Middleton's *Phoenix* calls "sober Law" offstage to preserve it from the workaday corruptions typified by Griffin's work.

128. Sager holds property of Bromley for a lease of one life—when Sager dies, the land reverts to Bromley. Bromley's losing cause argues that that life is already done and therefore the land ought to be returned to his possession. This was not an uncommon kind of lawsuit between tenant and landlord.

129. The final judgments are, significantly, not made by a judge, but by an Abbot. The play abandons the common law system completely in favor of a religious judge who sets matters right.

130. Tucker, *Intruder into Eden*, 59.

131. Character names in Massinger's play are more obviously allegorical than in *Michaelmas Term*: Welborne, the prodigal of good blood; the Alworth family, honored by all; Overreach, the "cruel extortioner" and social climber; Marrall, the unscrupulous attorney; and a host of lesser characters are all typed by their names. The auditor can hear the natural order in the names of characters, and those names predict their fates at the end of the action.

132. This concern with status and reputation is quite similar to Quomodo's in *Michaelmas Term*. Where Quomodo seeks to force his peers in the Livery of his company to show him respect and honor, Overreach seeks to force his gentle neighbors to show him respect and honor. The play suggests that neither deserve this on their own merits.

133. This was not, of course, usually the case. The lower branch of the legal profession—attorneys and solicitors—*was* seen as a craft, however, its members trained by apprenticeship, and this guild language would not have seemed inappropriate to an early modern audience, nor would the demonizing of attorneys as charlatans and tricksters have been unfamiliar. See Brooks, *Pettyfoggers*, for details on attorneys' training and public perceptions of their professional activities.

134. It is important to note that while this kind of legal activity is condemned in the play, the law itself is not. Lady Alworth's servant Order speaks of this distinction, talking of Overreach: "He frights men out of their estates, / And breaks through all law-nets, made to curb ill men, / As they were cobwebs" (2.2.114–18). The "law-nets" are good, Overreach's actions are bad. Deceit and exploitation are not inherent to the law, only to its abusers.

135. Overreach is one of Harrison's "gentlemen made good cheap," and the play registers anxiety over the numbers of such persons.

136. Or how virtuous she is. Note that Overreach's London origins are a primary reason for Lovell's disdain of him. "London-blue," glossed as "servants' livery," forever bars him from access to the heights he so desires to reach.

137. That the common lawyers were divided on the question of the rule of law and royal authority only reinforces the profession's status as a field. Lawyers converted political questions into legal ones, expressing the depth to which their legal habitus structured their perceptions.

138. See the bleeding scene in Middleton's *Phoenix* discussed above where this transformation is literalized.

139. J. H. Baker, "The English Legal Profession, 1450–1550," in *The Legal Profession and the Common Law: Historical Essays* (London: Hambledon, 1986) 76.

140. Baker, "English" 77.

141. Baker, "Counsellors and Barristers," in *Legal Profession,* 109.

142. What statutory regulation did exist seems more to legitimate existent practices than initiate new ones. See Prest, *Inns,* chaps. 3 and 4.

Chapter 4. "The Art of Revels..."

1. See Jeffrey Masten's *Textual Intercourse* (Cambridge: Cambridge University Press, 1997) and Robert Weimann's *Author's Pen and Actor's Voice* (Cambridge: Cambridge University Press, 2000) among others.

2. See chapter 5 below on the Poetomachia and an extensive scholarship.

3. With the important exceptions of the work of William Ingram, John Orrell, Bruce Smith, and Susan Cerasano.

4. Most famously, Inigo Jones's fights with Jonson turn on the relative importance of stage and script. Less well known are the repeated references to the artificers of civic pageantry who are often recognized above the writers of the various shows.

5. Sir George Buc, *The Third Universitie of England* (London, 1615): sig Oooo3v. Copy in British Library.

6. Nor does the treatise described in the section on poets and musicians. Buc's *Third Universitie* is appended to Stowe's *Survey* in the editions of 1615 and 1632. Buc discusses every conceivable educational institution in London—from the churches to the Inns of Court and Chancery to schools of music, dancing, and fencing and includes the Revels in his list of things taught in London.

7. This institutionalization—the imagination of a curriculum—marks the regularization and rationalization of specifically Revels-related skills. This kind of rationalization in an educational context is a mark of a profession. Buc

may be imagining this—motivated by his own position as Master—but the fact that such a thing is imaginable is important to the development of a profession (or group of them).

8. Detailed records are readily available from the reign of Edward VI on, and many of the individuals associated with the Revels Office remain in the payment records for decades. Transcriptions of records for Lord Mayor's Shows and Midsummer Shows are available from the beginning of the sixteenth century.

9. The combination of this practical and theoretical orientation toward the work of the office is professional. See the discussion of shifts in legal practice as it moves from a guild to a profession in chapter 3.

10. Greene's play stands in many ways at the beginning of the self-conscious professionalization of playwriting while Beaumont's follows the Poetomachia's restructuring of the terms of the debate and what I would argue is Jonson's refashioning of at least parts of the profession in his image.

11. Much of the historical research for this chapter has been supported by a grant from the College of Liberal Arts at the University of South Carolina. My comments on Greene's play derive from work on Willing Suspension Productions' 1997 production of *James IV* at Boston University (Director: Kirk Melnikoff; Assistant Directors: Ed Gieskes and Mike Walker). Likewise, my comments on *Knight of the Burning Pestle* come out of work on Willing Suspension Productions' 1999 performances of Beaumont's play (Directed by Ed Gieskes and Sarah Lyons).

12. G. E. Bentley, *The Profession of Dramatist in Shakespeare's Time* (Princeton, NJ: Princeton University Press, 1971), James S. Shapiro, *Rival Playwrights* (New York: Columbia University Press, 1991), and Lynne Magnusson, *Shakespeare and Social Dialogue* (Cambridge: Cambridge University Press, 1999).

13. Ingram, *Business of Playing*.

14. W. R. Streitberger, *Court Revels* (Toronto: University of Toronto Press, 1994) and David M. Bergeron, *English Civic Pageantry* (Columbia: University of South Carolina Press, 1971). There are notable exceptions to this, Orgel and Strong's work on the masque and Inigo Jones being chief among them, but in general scholars have not focused much attention on craftspeople since the major transcription projects of the first third of the twentieth century (Stephen Orgel, *The Jonsonian Masque* [Cambridge, MA: Harvard University Press, 1965] and Stephen Orgel and Roy Strong, *The Theatre of the Stuart Court* [Berkeley and Los Angeles: University of California Press, 1973]). The ongoing Malone Society *Collections* series offers vitally important access to records as well.

15. Abbott, *System of Professions*.

16. This is analogous to the way that John Bulwer's *Chirologia* (1644) describes in very detailed ways how gesture conveys meaning. Regrettably, we do not have a similar period work on props, but the plays provide evidence of a kind of language of the prop.

17. See John Orrell's *The Human Stage: English Theatre Design 1567–1640* (Cambridge: Cambridge University Press), 162–63. Street's specialized tools and skills were used by the Works office in making some stage pillars.

18. One example is Richard Munday—Anthony Munday's son—who was employed as a painter on a series of Lord Mayor's Shows in the early seventeenth century only some of which were written by his father. Richard's employment extends past his father's death. James Peele and his son George offer devices and scripts for several Lord Mayor's Shows over the period as well. In the Revels records, one John Ogle and his son (John Ogle "iunior") are paid as "propertymakers" in many of Cawarden and Blagrave's accounts. This is also true of several other father/son teams among the artisans working for the Revels Office. See MSC 3 for Munday and Feuillerat, *Elizabeth*, for details.

19. See the discussion of property-making below.

20. MSC 3 contains a variety of citations to people like Munday, Dekker, John Grinkin, Middleton and others being paid large sums (£190 and upwards) for the pageants. The scale of these payments suggests that they were coordinating the whole of the production for the year. See discussion below.

21. Malone Society *Collections* 3, 5, 6, and 10 (hereafter referred to as MSC 3, etc). There are some useful records in MSC 13 as well as the first volume of the collections. However, 3, 5, 6, and 10 are the most relevant to my work here. Feuillerat's transcriptions of the Revels material appear in two volumes: *Documents Relating to the Office of the Revels in the Time of Elizabeth* (Louvain, 1908) and *Revels at Court in the Time of Edward VI and Queen Mary* (Louvain, 1914).

22. As many commentators have noted, after the mid-1560s, plays came to dominate the Revels season and the labor-intensive and expensive production of masques declined until the Jacobean resurgence. The craftsmen associated with the office thus lost a major and more or less reliable source of income at around the same time the public theaters are being built.

23. After 1587, the records become far less detailed and tend to report the payments to the officers rather than to the craftsmen. For example, the 1587–88 record in Feuillerat reads "for 2 yeres: The *Master* of Thoffice for his attendance aswell for choise, makinge, and reforminge of plaies and Commedies as otherwise in Christmas & Shrovetide by the space of ccxxxj. daies and xxx. nightes . . . lx li iiij s" (Feuillerat, *Elizabeth*, 395—from BL MS Lansdowne 59, no. 26). The records collected in the MSC volume of Revels records from 1603 on are less useful for my purposes as they tend not to include detailed accounts of payments to individual craftsmen.

24. William Ingram has discussed the Revels Office's practice of lending costumes out in his *Business of Playing*. The Revels "stuffe," as it is often called, was a substantial inventory of props, costumes, lighting apparatus, set pieces, and other theatrical items—products of artisans in the employ of the Office. The "stuffe" circulated in London, as Ingram demonstrates, and it stands to reason that the makers of that "stuffe" did too.

25. John Astington, *English Court Theatre, 1558–1642* (Cambridge: Cambridge University Press, 1999), 11. Much of the critical literature on the Master of Revels has dealt with his function as a licenser and sometime censor of playtexts. See Richard Burt, *The Administration of Aesthetics* (Minneapolis: University of Minnesota Press, 1994) and Richard Dutton, *Mastering the Revels* (Iowa City: University of Iowa Press, 1991).

26. Astington argues that the Revels Office was only closely involved in the "business" of theater until the advent and growth of the professional acting

companies (*English Court Theatre*, 11). This fact is of crucial importance—the Revels Office ceases being a production company at the same moment that the professional theaters begin being producers.

27. Ibid., 19. Cawarden thus served under Henry VIII, Edward VI, Mary, and the beginning of Elizabeth's reign. His ability to continue as Master under four monarchs with very different religious and political dispositions speaks to a recognition of the skill Astington describes. It is also indicative of a developing professional civil service; see chapter 2.

28. The structure Astington describes here resembles that which develops in the production of London's Lord Mayor's Shows in the early seventeenth century. The pageants were produced by a kind of production company under the lead of experienced producers. See discussion below.

29. W. R. Streitberger mentions that the Revels of 1549–50, for which Clatterbooke headed a group of twenty-one tailors, were "on Reformation subjects" (*Court Revels, 1485–1559* [Toronto: University of Toronto Press, 1994] 185–86). It seems that the skill of the craftsmen (and their Master) allowed them to remain in place despite the various changes in religion that took place over the next several years. There were functionaries in the Crown's administration (most famously Lord Burghley) whose ability to survive changes in monarch, policy, and religion resembles this—skill being the primary criterion.

30. The Bosums vanish sometime between 1559 and 1567. The records from those years are abstracts that attest to the scale of the Office's expenses (some £4,900 over those years) but do not name individual payees. The Lyzard family takes over the painting duties when William Lyzard becomes the Sergeant Painter to the Queen—he and his sons appear in the Revels accounts from 1567–85 (after which the records become far less detailed). See Astington, *English Court Theatre*, for a detailed discussion of the painting involved in Revels productions. Also see Feuillerat for the lists of names.

31. Orrell, *Human Stage*, and *The Theatres of Inigo Jones and John Webb* (Cambridge: Cambridge University Press, 1985).

32. A John Carrowe is recorded in the Carpenters' Company records in 1547—"resd of Wyllam frances for p[re]senting of John Carrowe for vij yere bynding at or ladyday in lent" (*Records* IV.9) but this seems not to be the same Carrowe. In addition, the Revels Carrowe is consistently referred to as a carver or joiner, not a carpenter. It is conceivable that the Carrowe in the Carpenters' records is a relative, but, this is only conjecture. I have not been able to locate other records related to Carrowe.

33. The *OED* cites Feuillerat's 1559 record as the first instance of the term's use: "wages of taylours, karvars, propertie makers" and in 1582: "Property makers being Paynters the firste at ii s the day." Feuillerat first records the term somewhat earlier, in 1552. The *OED* also refers to Shirley's 1633 *Triumph of Peace* (a masque, not coincidentally) as having a "Property-Mans Wife" rush onto the stage. "Property" in the theatrical sense has a somewhat longer pedigree, dating at least as far back as 1425 and the *Castle of Perseverance*.

34. The carver Robert Trunckewell and his men Robert and James are paid for their services and attendance during the 1555 and 1556 Christmas seasons and seem to have worked as a group on a variety of tasks. Trunckewell is paid on several occasions for making furniture for the office as well. Details like

these point to the range of skills required of Revels workers. Trunckewell's first appearance in the records transcribed by Feuillerat is in 1551 and his last is in 1559.

35. The Nicholas Ross mentioned here may be a relative, but it is difficult to be certain. What seems clear is that the designation "junior" points to a son—the accounts use it repeatedly of various people associated with the Revels Office. John Ogle and his son appear in the accounts under tailors for the bulk of the period, and there are other suggestive repetitions of family names throughout the records. See below on the Christmas family and civic pageantry—Garrett Christmas and his sons built the pageants for the vast majority of Jacobean Lord Mayor's Shows in collaboration with a variety of playwrights.

36. Feuillerat, *Elizabeth*, 156.

37. Feuillerat transcribes several long lists of costumes, properties, and "stuff" as part of the records for the periodic "airings" during which the stock was repaired, cared for, and inventoried. The extravagance of the costumes and other items points, as many writers have noted, to a spectacular theater of display.

38. BL MS Harleian 146. f. 15 recto in Feuillerat, *Elizabeth*, 119.

39. The name for the form, interestingly, derives from a property associated with it. This fact is obscured by the usual modern spelling—sixteenth-century records consistently use "maske" to describe these kinds of entertainments.

40. Cited from the New Cambridge Shakespeare edition edited by M. M. Mahood.

41. David M. Bergeron, *Practicing Renaissance Scholarship* (Pittsburgh, PA: Duquesne University Press, 2000). See chap. 10: "Pageants, Masques, and Scholarly Ideology."

42. Players are paid by the Drapers as early as 1485 and they continue to be paid for entertaining at mayoral inaugurations all through the early sixteenth century. They only disappear with the advent of the Guildhall banquets. Payments were made to various companies—the King's Men, the Prince's Men, Sly's company, the earl of Essex's and others. Dramatic entertainments were clearly an important part of the Drapers' public life from the late fifteenth century onward. Interestingly, Anthony Munday, who wrote a great many of the speeches for civic pageants, repeatedly identifies himself as "Citizen and Draper of London" on title pages. He appears in the Drapers' books in 1585 when he is made free by his father's copy: 23 June, Drapers' Freedom List, 1567–1656, 278.53: 21 Iunij Mondaie Anthonie filius / Mondaie Cxpofers patrimon'/ } a Poet by Criplegate" (MSC 3:165). He is described as a poet in the Drapers' Freedom List. Munday was apprenticed to a stationer but freed as a draper.

43. Writing of late medieval lay drama, Lawrence Clopper argues that "cycles of drama are to be associated with the secular or lay guild government, perhaps as an expression of civic control, civic pride, and civic concern for the religious education of the townspeople" (*Drama, Play, and Game: English Festive Culture in the Medieval and Early Modern Period* [Chicago: University of Chicago Press, 2001]). Clopper shows that vernacular drama has strong associations with civic oligarchies, associations that continue through the early modern period.

44. When George the grocer calls for "something notably in honor of the commons of the city" in the induction to Beaumont's *Knight of the Burning Pestle* (1607), he is calling for something recognizable both to himself and to the actors and writers from whom he demands it. The pageant-like additions to the play participate in an old and immediately comprehensible tradition.

45. Substantial gaps in the records exist due to several of the companies having lost their records in fires and other disasters. MSC 5 supplements MSC 3 by including more records from the Clothworkers' Company. However, the surviving records are full for the whole span from the early decades of the sixteenth century to the effective cessation of the civic pageants on the eve of the Civil War. They become more detailed in the seventeenth century attesting to the growth in importance of a ritual that was an innovation in the mid-sixteenth century.

46. This likely has to do with both the increasing availability of skilled craftsmen and a kind of emulative rivalry between the Crown and City.

47. MSC 3:41–44. Chambers suggests that this John Holt is the Holt who was Yeoman of the Revels, Feuillerat discounts this idea for two reasons. His first reason, that John Holt was a fairly common name seems reasonable, while his second, that the actor Holt mentioned here couldn't possibly have been the Holt of the Revels Office because the Yeoman Holt was illiterate makes considerably less sense. The identification is tempting, but in the absence of evidence, it seems best to assume that these were different men.

48. The descriptions are of fairly elaborate set pieces—Arion sits on a "Dolphyn in the sea playeng on the harpe Topas so, before a table of princes and eu'y of theis to haue his posie" (44)—from which the speakers are to deliver their orations. Most of the Shows follow a similar pattern in which allegorical figures voice their hopes for the good government of the incoming Lord Mayor from a stable set of positions along the processional route.

49. A foist is a stand or other structure from which fireworks were fired.

50. John Lyon was Lord Mayor in 1554. The barge was for members of the company and was part of the procession. The practice of seating the Bachelors of the Company on a barge in the river falls into disuse, but the tradition of elaborate water shows ("othr pleasure on the water") remain important throughout the history of the Shows.

51. Shakespeare appears not to have written pageants, but members of the King's Men participated in the shows. In 1611, John Lowen "one of his Ma.ties players and brother of this Companie [the Goldsmiths] was required by Mr Wardeins to perforrne the part of Lepston in the shew" (81).

52. Another Richard Munday—a tailor—is a repeated payee in the Revels records from about 1572 on. I cannot ascertain what, if any, relation there is between the tailor and the playwright aside from both being associated with the cloth trades.

53. Similarly elaborate stage pieces appear routinely in the Revels accounts demonstrating a dynamic of influence between the Court and the City.

54. MSC 3:85.

55. Middleton also wrote the pageant in 1613 for the installation of Sir Thomas Middleton, grocer, as Lord Mayor. It appears as though Munday was involved that year as well since he was paid £40 by the Grocers for "the devyse of the Pageant and other shewes . . . and for the ordering overseeing and writing

of the whole Devyse" (MSC 3:87). Munday and Dekker receive payment in 1617 for their "paines" in drawing up proposals "offered to the Comytees" (3:93). Munday got £5 and Dekker received £4. The practice of submitting what are here called "proiects" for the shows is increasingly well documented in the records over the course of the seventeenth century.

56. Christmas becomes the dominant artificer in civic pageantry from 1618 to 1639. See David Bergeron, "The Christmas Family: Artificers in English Civic Pageantry," *ELH* 35, no. 3 (1968): 354–64. His role will be discussed more fully below.

57. Ibid., 356.

58. Christmas worked with Middleton, Munday, Dekker, and Heywood.

59. In the Shows, the visual spectacle is more important than the speeches—not least because the pageants were visible over greater distances than they were audible—and design thus had to be what Orrell calls "iconic" in order for the message to be clear.

60. Bergeron, "Christmas," 364. Bergeron's essay downplays the "cleavage" between artificer and author in civic pageantry as opposed to masque, but I would suggest that there is more common ground here than the article allows. The cleavage may have been more profound in the court masque, but the separation here does point to a kind of specialization in tasks that is characteristic of modern professions.

61. MSC 3:115.

62. MSC 3 reprints a manuscript description of the Show on pages 117–19. Notice too that Christmas and Dekker are to provide land and water carriage "as is accustomed"—another signal of customary practice and related expectations.

63. See note 55 above. The various committees mentioned also have clear, if not articulated, expectations of what they want to see and how much it should cost: "Anthonie Mundaie, Thomas Middleton, and Richard Grimston, poettes, all shewed to the table their severall plottes for devices for the shewes . . . itt is wholie referred to the Consideracon of the Comittees formerlie Appointed for business of the like nature and they are to make Choice of whome they shall best approve of" (MSC 3:99). There are a number of records where the company decides the bid is too high and offer a lesser payment.

64. MSC 3:99.

65. Writing, in fact, is nowhere mentioned in the contractual material regarding this show. The speeches are part of the furniture of the pageant. This is no accident given the importance of visual spectacle to the Shows.

66. Henslowe's attention to properties and costumes in his *Diary* points to this kind of practice as well.

67. *Londini Artium & Scientiarum Scaturigo; OR, Londons Fountaine of Arts and Sciences* sig. A4r. This was the Show for the installation of Nicholas Raynton of the Haberdashers as Lord Mayor in 1632.

68. The repetitive nature of the Show underscores the cyclic nature of civic life—much as the cycle plays marked the religious year, the Lord Mayor's Show marks the bounds of London's civic year.

69. Ben Jonson, *The Devil Is an Ass* (Herford and Simpson, volume 6) 1.1.83–89.

70. Quoted from the Riverside Shakespeare.

71. Sidney famously pokes fun at such things in his reference to the sign on stage indicating that the scene has moved to Thebes. See also the players in Marston's *Histriomastix* who are equally foolish but whose folly is structured by a sense of the parameters of the drama. This is a common feature of such moments. Brome's *The Antipodes*, a relatively late play, contains a rehearsal scene and other theatrical elements that refer to specific elements of the theaters. Imagination and audience expectation structure each other explicitly in Brome's play and implicitly elsewhere.

72. See Bruce Smith's *The Acoustic World of Early Modern England* (Chicago: University of Chicago Press, 1999).

73. Detailed records reappear in the Works accounts in the seventeenth century as masque production becomes more important, and similar patterns of repeated employment appear in those records.

74. Henslowe's diary is particularly frustrating in this regard. He records inventories of what the Revels Office termed "stuff"—costumes and properties—but very rarely mentions particular names. However, he does tend to return to the same artisans repeatedly for the same kinds of services—the "little tayler" (later identified as one Radford) appears repeatedly in the accounts. Also, a Mrs. Goosen/Gossen/Gosson is often paid for head tyres. And, of course, he hired Street for the building of the Fortune to the specifications of Street's recently built Globe.

75. Orrell, *Human Stage*, 49. Orrell's immensely useful book, along with his book on Jones and Webb, provides a clear and provocative discussion of the theoretical underpinnings of the early modern theaters in memories of antiquity, in Serlian architecture, and in other well-articulated theories of design.

76. An extensive literature on "reconstructions" of early modern theaters has described these requirements and various ways the buildings might have satisfied them. What is most important for my argument is the fact that were these three factors the only important ones, innyard theaters would have been sufficient. Sisson's discussion of the Boar's Head theater in *The Boar's Head Theatre* (London: Routledge Kegan Paul, 1972) makes this clear. Purpose-built theaters are, to reiterate the obvious truism, something else entirely.

77. The existence of a theory is, of course, important and it is likewise important that there were at least some discussions of the proper way to design a theater, but I will be more interested in discussing the effects of the theory than the theory itself. John Orrell's work provides an exemplary discussion of these matters.

78. Banquet halls were designed to be demountable—Henry VIII's banqueting hall at the Field of the Cloth of Gold was movable and the great Banqueting Hall at Whitehall was, for most of its life, based on a temporary building constructed of timbers and canvas. This, as Orrell writes, is an important legacy for the London theater builders.

79. William Ingram, "The Early Career of James Burbage," *The Elizabethan Theatre X* (Ontario: PD Meany, 1983), 36. Ingram notes that a Daniel Burbage, minstrel, appears in the St. Stephens records though there is nothing firmly linking him to James Burbage. A John Perkin also appears in the register and Ingram asserts that this is the only John Perkin he can find in any period parish register—one John Perkin signed (with James Burbage) a petition imploring Le-

icester to take them into service in 1572. And, a Richard Perkin, son of John, lived in Clerkenwell, adjacent to St. Stephens.

80. Susan Cerasano has described Street's career in her unpublished dissertation (University of Michigan, 1981), from which I derive much of the information I am working with in this chapter.

81. The Rose, Henslowe's 1587 theater, was built by John Griggs and the Hope (1613–14) was built by Gilbert Katherens. John Brayne's pre-Theatre venture, the Red Bull, was built by William Sylvester and Francis Langley employed someone to build the Swan. Street, though an important figure in the theater-building enterprise, hardly had a monopoly. Like the livery companies choosing production syndicates, theater entrepreneurs could choose a builder.

82. Smith, *Acoustic World,* 209.

83. Writing of the Works Office's renting of specialized tools from Street, Orrell asserts that "the transaction is of small consequence in itself, but it does illustrate the dependence of the Whitehall administration of the supply of technical prowess and specialized skills available in the city of London and its surroundings" (*Human Stage,* 160). The Revels establishment depended on these skills in the same way the theater companies did.

84. He was elected warden, one of the highest offices in the guild in the 1590s.

85. Street was involved in more theater projects than any other theater builder for whom any records exist.

86. Even the Office of Works turned to Street for help with theatrical problems.

87. Herford and Simpson, volume 3.

88. The criticism of the rapid aging of characters complains of the use of beards to mark that aging and beard maker is the trade of Belch, one of the buffoon players in Marston's *Histriomastix.* See chapter 5. Two of Marston's tradesman players abandon already theatrically inflected occupations for playing.

89. This move is as strategic as his attacks on his rivals in *Poetaster*—Jonson, despite his comments here, is as opportunistic and eclectic about his tools as any of the writers discussed in this book.

90. Peter Womack, "Imagining Communities: Theatres and the English Nation in the Sixteenth Century" in *Culture and History 1350–1600: Essays on English Communities, Identities and Writing,* ed. David Aers (Detroit, MI: Wayne State University Press, 1992): 91.

91. One of the underlying thematics of the play is, of course, the issue of semblance—Henry says he will "be like a king" in 1.2, for example. The Chorus's stress on the work of representation calls attention to the artifice of the theater that refracts the artifice of Henry's kingship, itself a kind of theatrical product.

92. Bourdieu's focus in this book is on the French field in the nineteenth century (which explains his focus on the novel) but the idea that generic upheavals depend on this kind of conjunction of changes makes sense of the transformation of the early modern literary field in the period following about 1570.

93. His "imitations" of Marlowe are evidence of his search for ways to unite his learning to more popular elements by imitating Marlowe's successful combinations.

94. Slipper and his brother Nano's position, both inside the play and outside it, resembles that occupied by Rafe in Beaumont's later *Knight of the Burning Pestle* and that liminal position enables the characters to comment (if not explicitly) on the ways the plays they occupy operate.

95. See chapter 5 below for a discussion of the term "literature" in the period. See also Reiss's *Meaning of Literature*.

96. My own "demonstration" depends in part on a production of the play produced by Willing Suspension Productions at Boston University in 1997. Kirk Melnikoff directed and Mike Walker and I served as assistant directors. Our direct engagement with Greene's dramatic practice clarified many of the oddities of the play and pointed toward some of my conclusions here. The conflict the play dramatizes is a long-lasting one that provides one of the structuring oppositions of the literary field.

97. Kenneth Muir, "Robert Greene as Dramatist" in *Essays in Elizabethan Drama* ed. R. Hosley (Columbia: University of Missouri, 1962), 50. The reception of Greene's work tends to be divided between those who study the prose and those who study the drama. Very few monographs treat the drama and most view Greene as a failed precursor of Shakespeare and a bad imitator of Marlowe—maybe overstated but not, I think too much.

98. The two poles imagined here come to be associated with the comic realism of Heywood, for example, on the one hand, and what McLuskie terms "the elite style of satiric iconoclasm" (*Dekker and Heywood*, 15). McLuskie argues that Heywood linked himself with a "theater of exciting physical action, a theater which was a spectacle and an entertainment, a magical vision of unexperienced riches before it was a theater of ideas" (*Dekker and Heywood*, 15). What is interesting here, and, I will suggest, later, with Beaumont's *Knight of the Burning Pestle*, is the way that Greene juxtaposes these poles rather than necessarily choosing one over the other in any kind of clear fashion.

99. James has, he thinks, had Dorothea, his queen, murdered so he can pursue the "Scottish Ida" who, being virtuous, wants nothing to do with him. Dorothea's father, the King of England, vows revenge and attacks Scotland, winning battles and killing thousands as he makes his way to meet James. When they meet, James makes lame offers of ransom or reparation and matters seem headed for disaster when the disguised Dorothea reveals herself and almost instantaneously resolves the situation. She forgives James for his adulterous plot and attempt to murder her ("Tush, but a little fault") and causes her father to vow continued friendship with James, and all parties go in to dinner. If this synopsis sounds contradictory, it is because the narrative *is* contradictory, largely due to the way Greene orchestrates Oberon's intervention in Bohan's play.

100. All quotations from Greene's play are from Norman Sanders's edition in the Revels series (London: Methuen, 1970).

101. In one of the most affecting moments in the play, Bohan begs Oberon to save Slipper from execution for colluding with Ateukin—forgetting for the moment that what he's watching is only a "demonstration"—Oberon obliges out of "love."

102. See the discussion of the generic significance of the term "jig" below. Bohan always refers to his "demonstration" with this term that locates the

play, or, better, Bohan's part of it, in a particular theatrical tradition distinct, I will argue, from Oberon's interventions in the play. Bohan's words also call attention to the built nature of his tomb-retreat.

103. In our staging, Bohan and Oberon were seated just off the stage proper (in front of the curtain) throughout the play, visibly reacting to and, at times, intervening in the action. Oberon's antics danced before, after, and during the play, and served as the actors in the dumb shows. Modern editions of the play print the several dumb shows as appendices ("additional choruses"). In the several readings we gave the play, it became clear that the choruses reflect moments where Oberon's aesthetic gains ground on Bohan's and that there were logical places in the text to insert them. On stage, as the play progressed and Oberon's influence became more and more important, the action of the choruses spill over more and more into the starker play world of Bohan's narrative. The spillover suggests the contest between the principles represented by Oberon and Bohan—which we came to see in terms of a professional conflict.

104. Kirk Melnikoff, Directors' Notes, Program for Willing Suspension Productions *James IV*, 1997.

105. It is not my intention to posit some kind of teleological movement here—out of the meeting of these two traditions comes the theater of the later 1590s—but to describe tensions in the field, problems writers and companies appear to have faces, and to suggest that the failure to resolve these problems and tensions helps define the field by defining the terms of discussion. It is not, in other words, solutions that describe the theatrical field, but the enacted discussion of failures in a wide range of plays.

106. A. R. Braunmuller, "The Serious Comedy of Greene's *James IV*" *English Literary Renaissance* 3 (1973): 338. Braunmuller also notes the resemblance of the framing situation to the inductions of later plays by Jonson (*Bartholomew Fair* and *Every Man Out*).

107. Alexander Leggatt, "Bohan and Oberon: The Internal Debate of Greene's *James IV*," in *The Elizabethan Theatre XI*, ed. Lynne Magnusson and Ted McGee (Ontario: P. D. Meany, 1985), 98–99.

108. J. Clinton Crumley, "Anachronism and Historical Romance in Renaissance Drama: *James IV*," *Explorations in Renaissance Culture* 24 (1998): 88.

109. The same applies to the critical discussion of Jonson's *Poetaster*, a play often discussed more in terms of its philosophical or biographical interest than in terms of its place in a changing theatrical field.

110. Greene appears to be calling attention to the visual aspect of the play even at the level of the terms used to describe how it is to be received. The stress on vision, on looking at the show, remains constant throughout the play and both Oberon and Bohan call attention to the particular things they are looking at ("jig" vs. "pomp," for example). This despite the fact that James's story could be told with almost no set and little in the way of props. The technically demanding part of Greene's play lies in the dumb shows.

111. Placement of the choruses is a major difficulty in the play—the Quarto of 1598 prints several of them following the first act, but it seems clear that they belong elsewhere in the play. It is not obvious, however, where they do belong. Sanders's edition prints them as "additional choruses" in an appendix to the play.

112. Using the *OED*, Sanders glosses "jig" as "a performance normally of a lively or comical nature usually applied to a piece given in the intervals or at the end of a play" and suggests that here it refers to the play as a whole. The more usual sense of the word has to do with a dance at the end of a play. Why Bohan would call his "ruthful" play a jig is difficult to say, but the term allies the work with a particular kind of theater.

113. Sanders conjectures that the chorus may have appeared after 1.2 where Ateukin employs his craft, but to no harmful ends—thus not justifying Bohan's loathing of the world.

114. See Orrell, *Human Stage*. Note too that unlike the Semiramis show, this one comes with signs that are read by the performers. Oberon seems to be responding to Bohan's earlier inability to understand what the dumb shows mean without commentary. Bohan's orientation is consistently toward words and away from spectacle and Oberon revises the dumb shows in light of this.

115. Greene remains dubious about the play's capacity to convey a message to the end—Bohan's final speech tells the audience that they've witnessed a kind of morality play, but his remarks bear almost no resemblance to the action actually presented.

116. Citations of the play are from Michael Hattaway's New Mermaids edition (New York; W.W. Norton, 1998).

117. The play assumes that these are real distinctions—that there are populations with distinct tastes that are incompatible. The citizen norm and the gentleman norm are understood, at least by the Prologue Boy, as impossible to reconcile—see all the apologies to the gentle members of the audience. One part of what the play is engaged in is the creation of such norms—an initially unsuccessful effort to produce a shift in the taste of the audience which was always comprised of a mixture of social groups.

118. Laurie Osborne, "Female Audiences and Female Authority in *The Knight of the Burning Pestle*" Exemplaria 3, no. 2 (Fall 1991): 491–517; Glenn Steinberg, " 'You Know the Plot/We Both Agreed On?': Plot, Self-Consciousness, and The London Merchant in Beaumont's *The Knight of the Burning Pestle*," *Medieval and Renaissance Drama in England* 5 (1991): 211–24.

119. See the above discussion of generic transformations. While *James IV* seems more engaged with the production end of the process of generic change, *Knight* engages with audiences and fails partially because it does not, at least initially, find an audience properly constituted to appreciate it.

120. The apparent distaste for *Knight* in its early appearances interestingly parallels the contemporary distaste for *James IV*—early modern audiences appear to have rejected the play because of its unfriendliness in much the same way critics have rejected Greene's play for its supposed formlessness. In both cases, responses appear to have been mediated by generic expectations.

121. Keysar, a London goldsmith, was a theater entrepreneur who financed a children's company at Blackfriars for some years shortly before the King's Men took over the theater. From all accounts, his interest in plays was pecuniary, seeing theater as a good investment opportunity. In 1609, to take one example, Keysar sued Middleton over a debt, a debt Middleton claims to have repaid with a manuscript for a lost play (see Bruce Hillebrand, "Thomas Middleton's *The Viper's Brood*," *Modern Language Notes* 42 [1927]: 35–38). Keysar appears to have wanted the cash. William Ingram's article "Robert Keysar, Theatrical

Speculator" offers a useful account of Keysar's life and career, (*Shakespeare Quarterly* 37, no. 4 [Winter 1986]: 476–85.

122. The avenging child image here appears related to the armed prologue motif that Jonson uses in *Poetaster*. Plays need some kind of protector.

123. *Knight* can be read as a kind of premature sign of a generic upheaval—it represents a new category of product in search of a consumer in print as much as on the stage. This kind of archly metadramatic play becomes, in less extreme forms, more common later in the seventeenth century (Massinger, Brome, Jonson, etc.).

124. Jonson's armed Prologue in *Poestaster* speaks to this desire in other writers, as does the elaborate contractual prologue of *Bartholomew Fair*.

125. Zachary Lesser, "Walter Burre's *Knight of the Burning Pestle*," *English Literary Renaissance* 29 (1999): 23.

126. Ibid., 32.

127. Slipper and Nano's insertion into *James IV* also inserts characters from the frame into the main action of the play with similarly plot-deforming results.

128. Merrythought's song, of course, is disruptive, but not in the same way as Rafe's presence and the constant directorial commentary shouted in by the citizens. The Prologue Boy at several occasions strives to quiet the Citizens lest they spoil the play.

129. *Mucedorus* in particular links their taste to the mixed forms of the 1570s and 80s—"gallimaufrey."

130. See Kathleen McLuskie's discussion of the banning of theatrical performances in the Merchant Taylor's Hall by the livery of that company in 1573. Performances were banned not out of an overarching hostility to theater as such, but because the purpose of the plays had shifted in ways the livery did not like. Company records show the livery comparing the virtues (and costs) of rival proposals to mount the annual Show. The decisions were both informed and deliberate. See MSC 3 for details of such discussions.

131. In production, the blurring of lines between categories is apparent—particularly at moments where the Rafe-centered romance narrative comes into contact with the parts of *The London Merchant* that survive the Citizens' revisions—all which underscores the difficulty of maintaining such distinctions in a theater that itself necessarily (and institutionally) combines widely divergent stage traditions.

132. George's criticism of the "girds" the boy's companies have been having at citizens is more evidence of his knowledge of theatrical types.

133. George appears to be a fan of Heywood's plays. In the induction, Nell says that he's seen Heywood's *Edward IV* and the lost *Bold Beauchamps*.

134. Thomas Heywood, *The Four Prentices of London*, in *The Dramatic Works of Thomas Heywood* 6 vols. 1874s repr. New York; (Russell and Russell, 1964), 2:165. This edition has no line numbers. I have changed the long s to a standard s.

135. The final lines (delivered by Prologue 1) refers judgment to the audience: "Our Author submits his Labours to you, as the Authors of all the content he hath within this Circumference" (Heywood, *Four Prentices* 2.166]. Note that even this statement makes reference to the fabric of the building within which the show takes place. See McLuskie, *Dekker and Heywood*, for more on the play's interrogation of its discourse.

136. The innovative play here is the whole of the production—*The Knight of the Burning Pestle*—not any individual element of the play. When the Boy implies that the *London Merchant* is novel, largely because it is not "stale" like a Red Bull play, serves primarily as an assertion of distinction, an assertion that need not have any actual content.

137. Here again the insistence that George and Nell's interventions may ruin the play suggest that the actors have a sense of what they are doing that is distinct from the kind of show the Citizens seems to want. This generic distinction implies a social hierarchy that the Boy is at times forced to point out—asking the gentlemen for pardon, asserting that the Citizens will have to explain the play's botching to the gentle audience, etc. Interestingly, George's suggested reading, *The Four Prentices*, consistently addresses its auditors as gentlemen as well suggesting that the social division the Boy attempts to play to is more discursive than actual.

138. And, after all, what Nell really wants is for Rafe to "talk with" Pompiona. Speeches are not so bad. Nell's occasional failures to distinguish stage events from real ones notwithstanding, she demonstrates both knowledge of and taste for specific kinds of performances. In addition, George's "well, lets ha't as you can then" can read as sarcastic or pitying, rather than as a kind of defeated settling for what the Boy puts on offer, which is one of the more usual readings for that line. George knows that spectacle is possible elsewhere but makes allowances for this company's shortcomings.

139. George's call for "something notably to the honor of the city" in the induction is, in some ways, a call for the kind of pageantry that Nell describes here, which, as it turns out, does honor the city as Rafe rejects the Lady Pompiona for his true love, black-thumbed Susan, the cobbler's girl. It is also, as the Boy notes and makes fun of, a call for a play like those Heywood is producing at about the same time.

140. Thomas Heywood, *Londons Ius Honorarium* (London, 1631), A3v–B1r.

141. See Hattaway's note to this speech in his New Mermaids edition.

142. Rafe's fifty-line death speech, delivered with an arrow through his head, reiterates his entire trajectory through the play, from his becoming a grocer errant to his military adventures at Mile End to his participation in apprentice Shrovetide riots. It embodies the combination of romance and historical drama (and associated props—the arrow) that Rafe interjects into the *London Merchant*. The speech also parodies elements from *Richard III*, *The Spanish Tragedy*, and some echoes of *Eastward Ho!* See Hattaway's note to this speech as well.

143. Bergeron's call for closer attention to civic drama in his *Practicing Renaissance Scholarship* is a response to this exclusion of some modes and techniques from scholarly consideration.

144. Buc, *Third Universitie*, Oooo3v.

Chapter 5. "Honesty and Vulgar Praise"

1. "Value" here refers to aesthetic value along with commercial value and other kinds of judgments—all of which combine in the evaluation of the work of art.

2. This autonomy is always only relative—external forces do act within fields, but are mediated through the laws of the field. See Bourdieu's argument about the emergence of "art for art's sake" in "Field of Cultural Production," 29–73

3. See Pierre Bourdieu, "Intellectual Field and Creative Project," *Social Science Information* 8, no. 2 (1969), for a discussion of the development of a relatively autonomous intellectual field. He argues that in the course of the Renaissance "the intellectual field becomes an increasingly complex system, increasingly independent of external influences . . . a field of relations governed by a specific logic: competition for cultural legitimacy" (90). It is this struggle that I will be discussing below.

4. Edwin Havilland Miller in his *Professional Writer in Elizabethan England: A Study of Nondramatic Literature* (Cambridge, MA: Harvard University Press, 1959) describes this Grub Street in terms of a constant and difficult struggle by writers for financial support for their work whether from printers or from wealthy patrons.

5. "Poetomachia" refers to a group of plays written between about 1598 and 1602 (the dates are subject to debate as are the numbers of plays involved) that engage in a combination of personal satire and poetic competition. See below for a more developed definition.

6. The Parnassus plays make specific reference to Jonson ("the wittiest fellow of a bricklayer" in England), Shakespeare, and to the Chamberlain's Men as representatives of what the Parnassians struggle futilely against.

7. See Miller, *Professional*; Helgerson, *Elizabethan Prodigals* and *Self-Crowned Laureates*; Bentley, *Profession of Dramatist*; Ingram, *Business of Playing*; Forse, *Art Imitates Business*. On print more generally, see Eisenstein's work on the printing press and related social and technological changes and Neil Rhodes and Jonathan Sawday, eds., *The Renaissance Computer* (New York: Routledge, 2000)

8. See David Cressy's *Literacy and Social Order* (Cambridge: Cambridge University Press, 1980) for data on literacy rates in Tudor England.

9. See Pierre Bourdieu, *Rules of Art* (Stanford, CA: Stanford University Press, 1996), 252ff. on generic upheavals.

10. The plays offer a kind of gloss of Cuddie's complaint in Spenser's "October" eclogue from the *Shepheardes Calender* that "Mecaenas is yclad in claye." For the Parnassians, Mecaenas is replaced by the inadequate substitutes of the players and the printers. Greene's repentance pamphlets, discussed below, speak to this sentiment as well.

11. The modern literature on the Poetomachia dates from the late nineteenth century and works like F. G. Fleay's *Chronicle of the English Drama* (London, 1891), J. H. Penniman's *War of the Theatres* (Boston, 1897), and R. A. Small's *Ben Jonson and the Poetasters* (1899; repr. New York: AMS Press, 1966) establish the outlines of the war (its participants, the plays involved, and the dates). Early twentieth-century work continues the project of deciphering what real writers characters in the plays refer to and make efforts to understand the conflict in terms of rivalries between companies (see Robert Sharpe, *The Real War of the Theatres* (1935; repr. New York: Kraus Reprint Association, 1966). Later work, like James Bednarz's *Shakespeare and the Poet's War* (New York: Columbia University Press, 2001), explores particular plays as they relate to bi-

ography, individual careers, or changes in public taste. See also Alan Sinfield "*Poetaster*, the Author, and the Perils of Cultural Production" in *Material London, ca. 1600*, ed. Lena Cowen Orlin (Philadelphia: University of Pennsylvania Press, 2000).

12. For example, a late poet's war among Brome, Davenant, Shirley, Suckling, and Massinger makes use of terms current in the 1599–1601 Poetomachia. See Matthew Steggle, *Wars of the Theatres: The Poetics of Personation in the Age of Jonson* (Victoria: University of Victoria Press, 1998). See also Peter Beal, "Massinger at Bay: Unpublished Verses in a War of the Theatres" *Yearbook of English Studies* 10 (1980): 190–203.

13. Pierre Bourdieu, *Field*, 78.

14. These are not rigidly defined groups, of course, but writers at the time recognized the fundamental divide between the generally nongentle professionals working in London's commercial markets and university-educated or gentle writers working in a patronage economy.

15. The Parnassus plays document this shift in the lamentations of the patronless writers and their unwillingness to work in the new, more explicitly commercial, market. See below.

16. See Reiss, *Meaning of Literature*, for a thorough treatment of the development of "literature" as a category. He locates its full development in the eighteenth century, but I would argue Jonson and his contemporaries laid a great deal of the groundwork.

17. See Jeffrey Masten's *Textual Intercourse* for a useful reconsideration of the development of authorship as practice and concept in the period.

18. See also the raucous debate about theater and its social role and the status of those who write and act in plays. Where a Ben Jonson would argue for the edifying potential of a play, a Stephen Gosson would rail at the immorality and depravity of both plays and playwrights. Antitheatrical writings play a significant role in the kinds of defenses writers produce. See Thomas Heywood's *Apology for Actors* (1612).

19. See lines 140–60 of the *First Return*.

20. The treatment of the awarding of clerical livings in the plays demonstrates the corruption of a system that once, in the world of the play at least, provided places for learned men. See especially the *Second Return*.

21. Satire, interestingly, is the genre Marston begins writing before turning to drama and the Parnassians' place of retreat refers to a lost satirical play written by Jonson and Nashe in 1597—just before the composition of the Parnassus plays. Jonson and Nashe found themselves in trouble with the Privy Council and audience members may have expected a similar fate for Ingenioso, Furor Poeticus, and Phantasma, particularly after the Bishops' Ban in 1599.

22. Notice that only at the nadir of their fortunes do Parnassian characters turn to playing or entertaining of any kind. The Parnassians' reduction to fiddling is portrayed as an act of desperation, the play makes In the play, such employment is a last resort to be avoided at all costs.

23. Miller, *Professional* 18. See also the discussion of Greene's *James IV* in the preceding chapter. Greene stages this conflict in that play.

24. Helgerson, *Elizabethan, Prodigals* 13.

25. Robert Greene, *Greene's Groatsworth of Witte, Bought With a Million of Repentance* (1592), Ed. G. B. Harrison (New York: Barnes and Noble, 1966), 43.

26. Ibid., 45.

27. Ibid., 46.

28. This is an issue to which I shall return. The conflict is not merely moral, but social as well, the rise of player-authors (and other professionals) threatened the places of gentlemen-authors in an already crowded market. See Marotti on the idea that a homology existed between genre and rank. Drama was, or ought to have been, beneath educated men.

29. Greene's repentance pamphlets famously complain about the fickleness of the public and the theater companies. The stridency of Greene's (and by extension the Parnassians') complaints has a great deal to do with the fact that the players and the printers are fast becoming the only game in town. Greene is deeply ambivalent about print and theater.

30. Thomas Dekker, *The Guls Horn-Booke*, in *Nondramatic Works of Thomas Dekker*, ed. A. B. Grosart (New York: Russell and Russell, 1963), 2:246–47. Kathleen McLuskie uses this passage as the epigraph for her important article "The Poet's Royal Exchange: Patronage and Commerce in Early Modern Drama" *Yearbook of English Studies* 21 (1991): 53–62.

31. Field refers to areas of practice and their symbolic patterns that are understood to be relatively autonomous. The literary field is a subfield of the more general intellectual field that can be equated with the field of cultural production. Pierre Bourdieu, "Intellectual, 90.

32. Ibid., 91.

33. Ibid., 90. Shakespeare, for example, attached what some critics have called fawning dedications to his poetic works (i.e., works in the conventional "domain of literature") but the published dramas have no such apparatus until the 1623 Folio. He seems not to have been particularly interested in controlling or influencing the reception of the printed texts of his plays suggesting that, for him at least, the theater provided its own source of legitimacy. Shakespeare's interest in publishing would have been in preventing others from profiting from the plays when they were published (Forse and Bentley remark on this aspect of play publishing). This is not, of course, to say that the drama was necessarily recognized as "literature" in the period but to suggest that it was developing internal distinctions and thus was relatively less dependent on external authorities than other forms of cultural production. Jonson, of course, is another story entirely.

34. Bourdieu, "Intellectual," 90.

35. And not Art or Poetry or Literature or Society in any more general sense. This is not, of course, to say that drama did not affect other areas of society but that the competition for success within the theater was seen and experienced as such.

36. Bourdieu, *Rules*, 224.

37. Ironically, the only social difference between Jonson the bricklayer's son and Marlowe the cobbler's son is a Cambridge degree. Socially, Marlowe is as much a "new man" as Jonson. That the Parnassus writers champion Marlowe

points to both the complex and contradictory nature of their thinking and their (reluctant) awareness that the battle is already lost.

38. Interestingly for my later argument, these very qualities are those that Jonson claims as positive signs of his distinction. In Jonson's self-presentation, his worth as a writer depends on the care he takes with his work.

39. In *Distinction*, Bourdieu argues that this contrast serves as a basic marker of social distinction. Works characterized by ease and grace are, by this logic, recognized as being of higher status while work that displays the signs of its making is, by the same logic, lesser. The same logic applies to the producers. Early modern conduct manuals recognize this in their emphasis on sprezzatura, freshness, and surprise.

40. "Plays, together with the commercial trade in books, afforded an opportunity for the unlearned to appear learned, removing the controls on the trade in learning which a closed patronage system would have imposed" (McLuskie, "Poet's Royal Exchange," 56). This is precisely what the Parnassian characters are complaining about.

41. This is, of course, only a representation and not necessarily an accurate reflection of the facts. Successful poets without the marks of gentility did exist and succeed, but prevailing definitions of the "poet" expected that he be gentle.

42. Greene's *Groatsworth of Witte* was published in 1592 and the first Parnassus play has been dated to 1598, and the *Second Return* to about 1600. By this point the great "university wit" writers are either dead or retired from writing, and the field belongs to the Jonsons and Shakespeares they once scorned.

43. This move is both a mystification—these writerly struggles are, at least in part, involved in status conflicts—and an effort to develop alternative principles of distinction. Marston's own ambiguous status as a gentleman, a member of the Inner Temple, and poet and playwright drives some of his efforts to secure distinction much as Jonson's own bricklaying background does his. Struggles over principles of authorship refract a series of social determinations at the same time as they remain struggles over "poesy."

44. I will not make any claims that these writers were engaged in any kind of conscious group forming, but rather that the struggles for ascendancy in the late Elizabethan literary field resulted in the formation of a stable and recognizable social type: the writer.

45. Thomas Dekker, *Thomas Dekker*, ed. E. D. Pendry (Cambridge, MA: Harvard University Press, 1968), 27.

46. Ibid., 28.

47. Dedications *did* typically address readers as "learned" or "gentle." This kind of flattery was part of the conventional rhetoric of the dedication. See Franklin Williams, "Commendatory Verses: The Rise of the Art of Puffing," *Studies in Bibliography* 19 (1966): 1–14.

48. Dekker, *Thomas Dekker*, 28.

49. Ibid., 28.

50. See Bourdieu, "Field of Cultural Production" for a discussion of the way popular rejection functions as a signal of artistic success in a later state of the field.

51. See Williams, "Commendatory Verses," 1–14, for a discussion of dedicatory practices. These kinds of disclaimers become conventional feature of ded-

ications in the period. See also J. W. Saunders's "The Stigma of Print: A Note on the Social Bases of Tudor Poetry," *Essays in Criticism* 1 (1951): 139–64. Whether print really was a stigma is, of course, open to question, but the practice of disavowing print function rhetorically in struggles for distinction. See Steven May, "Tudor Aristocrats and the 'Stigma of Print,' " *Renaissance Papers* (1980): 11–18.

52. Jonson and Dekker appear on the playwriting scene ca. 1597–98 while Marston's first play seems to have been produced in 1599. Henslowe records a payment of two pounds to a "Mr Maxton the new poete" in September of 1599 and Chambers holds that this is a reference to Marston (*Elizabethan Stage* 3:428). It is unclear what this play was, but Marston is unlikely to have begun his career as a playwright much before 1599.

53. David Riggs, *Ben Jonson: A Life* (Cambridge, MA: Harvard University Press, 1989), 79. Riggs argues that Jonson saw Marston as an "enemy twin" (80)—a doppelganger—and thus psychologizes a professional conflict.

54. The insistence on the identity of the author in many early pamphlet titles—Greene, Nashe, etc.—points to a need for writers to claim their place in an emergent hierarchy within the sphere of writing. Greene's digs at Shakespeare can be read both as a kind of social or educational snobbery and as an effort to establish rankings within the field of cultural production. The lack of authorial attribution for many dramatic texts may be sign of a different kind of hierarchical principle at work in the professional theater—principles organized in terms of companies, not writers. This does, however, change, as Masten's book shows.

55. Note that these are specifically writerly categories, as opposed to the fundamentally status-centered categories at play in the Parnassus plays.

56. *Imitation and Praise in the Poems of Ben Jonson* (New Haven, CT: Yale University Press, 1981), 6. This is not the "aping"—mere copying—that the poetasters are guilty of. See the discussion of the trial scene in *Poetaster* below.

57. "Poetaster" is a Jonsonian coinage, first cited in the OED in his 1599 play *Cynthia's Revels*. It refers to "a petty or paltry poet; a writer of poor or trashy verse; a rimester." Jonson consistently uses the term to refer what he depicts, from his position in the field, as writers who pander to their audiences.

58. Jonson happens to be the person making these claims, but the claims themselves have much to do with positions in the field. In many accounts, Jonson figures as a kind of heroic figure championing a model of early modern authorship, what I would like to argue is that though this may be the case, his position taking depends on the field as much as it does on Jonson's individual agency.

59. This shift away from persons is something Jonson refers to disingenuously throughout his plays and poems. In this play, it is particularly disingenuous because Demetrius and Crispinus are transparent caricatures of Dekker and Marston respectively.

60. This characterization is typical of the early literature on the Poet's War, and is based, at least in part, on Jonson's late "Ode: To Himself." See also Kathleen McLuskie, *Dekker and Heywood*, for a discussion of the opposition between a popular and an elite stage.

61. See Chambers *Elizabethan Stage* vol. 2. All three men appear as playwrights for the first time in Henslowe's records, and his theaters have been associated with a more "popular" mode of playwriting.

62. No solid information about *Histriomastix*'s place of performance exists. Conjecture has ranged from it being Marston's first play for the Children of Paul's to it being performed by Derby's men at the Curtain to it being composed for revels at the Inns of Court. This fact alone makes the usual lines of opposition—between the child companies and the adult players—untenable. Dekker's *Satiromastix* was written for the Lord Chamberlain's Men and was also performed by the Children of Paul's.

63. See Bentley, *Professional,* for a useful discussion of the distinction between an "attached playwright" like Shakespeare and unattached ones like Jonson, Marston, and Dekker.

64. William Shakespeare, *Hamlet,* ed. H. Jenkins (New York: Routledge, 1990), 2.2.340–42; 350–54. Rosencrantz's comments are another source of the idea that the Poet's War is really a war between theaters, not writers.

65. What complaints there are about players in the various plays have more to do with skill or lack thereof than with their being adults or children—Jonson's episode with Histrio and the pyrgi in *Poetaster* criticizes both kinds of actor. Marston's players in *Histriomastix* are castigated for being bad, not for being professionals.

66. It is ironic that Rosencrantz's representation of the Poetomachia has been accepted as an accurate picture when he proves himself to be at best an inattentive listener and observer.

67. Hamlet's comment also bears witness to the links between child and adult players, links that make rigid distinctions between child and adult companies difficult to maintain. See Joseph Loewenstein, "Plays Agonistic and Competitive: The Textual Approach to Elsinore" *Renaissance Drama* 19 (1988): 63–96. Loewenstein discusses the eyases passage as evidence of current events in the London theater world.

68. See Jonas Barish on Jonson's commitment to what Jonson terms the "plain style" in his *Ben Jonson and the Language of Prose Comedy* (Cambridge, MA: Harvard University Press, 1960). The complexity of Jonson's diction does not belie this commitment—what he attacks in Marston and Dekker is what he depicts as a willful obscurity of vocabulary. As with other moves in the Poetomachia, this too is strategic and aims at separating Jonson from his rivals.

69. The play has been dated variously (from a few years earlier to a few later), placed in various performance contexts (from the Inns of Court to the Children of Paul's), and described as a revision of an earlier play. Marston's authorship has been generally accepted, however. See Finkelpearl, *John Marston* 119–24 for a discussion of various theories about the play's first performances. Recently, Roslyn Knutson has argued that *Histriomastix* is not by Marston and that it has little to do with the Poet's War *(Playing Companies).* James Bednarz accepts Marston's authorship of the play in his *Shakespeare and the Poet's War.* The jury appears still to be out on the play's authorship and I accept the traditional ascription. It does seem that Jonson responds to the play and its depiction of Chrisoganus and the actors make it relevant to the Poet's War and to my argument.

70. John Marston, *Plays of John Marston,* ed. H. Harvey Wood (Edinburgh: Oliver and Boyd, 1934), 3:281. All citations of *Histriomastix* are to this edition which is unlineated.

71. Players could make a considerably better income than laborers or artisans. Some successful actors made large fortunes—Alleyn endowed a college with money earned as an actor and Sharer—larger than those Belch, Incle, and Gut could ever hope for from their trades. Incle's comment on Plenty's effect on trade make the economic dimension of their ambitions clear.

72. Finkelpearl, *John Marston,* chap. 7.

73. Lynda Boose has argued that the Bishop's Ban on print satire drove writers to the theater as they sought a venue for their work. See "The 1599 Bishops' Ban, Elizabethan Pornography, and the Sexualization of the Jacobean Stage," in *Enclosure Acts: Sexuality, Property, and Culture in Early Modern England,* ed. Richard Burt and John Michael Archer (Ithaca, NY: Cornell University Press, 1994): 185–200.

74. That this scene owes its structure to Shakespeare's *Midsummer Night's Dream* seems obvious, but the criticism is not of "rude mechanicals" but professional players (however short their career).

75. The *Conversations with Drummond* record that Jonson said "he had many quarrels with Marston, beat him, and took his pistol from him, wrote his *Poëtaster* on him; the beginning of them were that Marston represented him in the stage" (282–84). The edition quoted is Ben Jonson's *Complete Poems,* ed. George Parfitt, (London: Penguin, 1988).

76. Marston, *Plays,* 258. All of these insults make the identification with Jonson clearer: Jonson was a "translating-scholler" and he did write satires and epigrams.

77. James Bednarz, "Representing Jonson: *Histriomastix* and the Origins of the Poet's War," *Huntington Library Quarterly* 54 (1991): 1–30.

78. Ibid., "Representing" 23.

79. The discourse of professionalism operates in largely the same way. As Abbott and Larson argue, discussions of and claims for the value of an occupational groups ideas serves those groups' efforts to claim professional status and thus (in Abbott's terms) control over an area of work. This is in many ways precisely what is at stake in the Poet's War.

80. Demetrius and Crispinus are ridiculed for their ludicrous vocabulary and the base content of their work, not their theoretical positions that are left unstated in the play.

81. This is not to say that Bednarz is wrong about Chrisoganus. The philosophical element of the Poet's War is important and he makes a persuasive case for this interpretation, but the War remains at root a professional conflict. Even assuming that *Histriomastix* responds to *Every Man In/Every Man Out,* the debate is still over *quality* not *philosophy.* Theory and philosophy serve more as weapons in a conflict between professional dramatists for preeminence than issues in their own right. Alan Sinfield's article on *Poetaster* suggests that Jonson's embrace of Augustan Rome's intellectual world was itself a response to the situation of the writer in the early seventeenth century.

82. See also the opening poems of his *Epigrams* which make a similar claim about his honest labors. See Halpern's discussion of Spenser's industry in *Poet-*

ics of Primitive Accumulation. See also Robert Matz on the importance of figuring poetry as work in his *Defending Literature in Early Modern England* (Cambridge: Cambridge University Press, 2000).

83. This hierarchy is described in more detail below.

84. Jonson lines himself up with the worthy few in contrast to his competitors, the "common spawne of ignorance, / Our frie of writers." Importantly, he also asserts that theater can be art fit for noble consumption. Here as elsewhere in his work, Jonson claims a status traditionally denied to theater and, at the same time, this claim intervenes in the market for performed and printed drama by asserting the superior value of his work as opposed to that of his envious and vulgar detractors.

85. Another collection laden with personal attacks, if not under real names.

86. Or a short term intervention in a trivial writers' tiff.

87. See for example Timothy Murray, *Theatrical Legitimation* (Oxford: Oxford University Press, 1987), for a discussion of Jonson's monumentalizing efforts in the Folio publication.

88. Dekker, like Marston, appears not to have held to this animosity, if animosity it was, for long. He and Jonson collaborated on the *King's Entertainment* in 1604.

89. See passages on poets, critics, and how to behave at the theater in *The Gull's Horn Book*.

90. It is Jonson's play that contains a literary court presided over not by Apollo but by Caesar Augustus and Dekker loses in that court.

91. It is all but impossible to see how Dekker's Tucca and Horace fit into the already chaotic main plot of his play and Marston's players (and Chrisoganus too, for that matter) are out of place in the morality structure that characterizes the bulk of *Histriomastix*. Dekker in particular seems to have opportunistically dressed up (to appropriate Jonson's insult) his play with an attack on Jonson at a moment when this "stage-quarrel" was current and drawing large audiences.

92. Tucca has, in a radical act of misreading, taken an epigram in progress to be a treasonous libel and, supported by Demetrius and Crispinus, accuses Horace of this crime. The charges are laughingly dismissed and the tables turned on Horace's accusers.

93. This is not to say that Jonson actually achieved these goals, but to say that he articulated them *as goals*.

94. Marston's praise of Jonson's skill in the dedication to *The Malcontent* (1604) may be a kind of peace offering, but one that tellingly uses the same vocabulary Jonson uses to describe worthy poets.

95. His failure with *Sejanus* aside. Though the fact that it was performed publicly speaks to the King's Men's willingness to trust his skill.

96. See Bourdieu and Wacquandt on habitus in *Invitation*.

97. In later poetic conflicts, rivals claim to be the legitimate heirs of Jonson's comic legacy—his language becomes a marker of distinction in subsequent battles over literary status. See Brean S. Hammond's " 'An Allusion to Horace,' Jonson's Ghost and the Second Poet's War" in *Reading Rochester*, ed. Edward Burns, (New York: St. Martin's, 1995), 166–86. Hammond argues that Jonson's image and language play an important role in a conflict between Rochester and Dryden.

Chapter 6. Conclusion

1. Bourdieu, *Logic* 37.
2. Ibid., 41. See also chap. 6, "The Work of Time."
3. Ibid., 50.
4. Ibid., 50.
5. Psychoanalysis, being one of the most powerful and pervasive of these accounts, has this as its therapeutic purpose. Analysis is intended to produce change by the process of analysis.
6. Bourdieu, *Logic*, 21. Bourdieu writes "like a subject," rather "of a subject," because he remains, as I do, suspicious of the term's investment in positing a position absolutely free of determinations. Bourdieu denies the possibility of a wholly transparent and self-authoring subject because human individuals are always involved in history and that involvement necessarily has structuring effects on one's sense of self.
7. See Larson and other "power theorists" discussed in chapter 1.
8. See Abbott, *System of Professions*, on jurisdictions.
9. My usage of "legitimation crisis" derives from Jurgen Habermas, *Legitimation Crisis* (Boston: Beacon Press, 1975). That there was an early modern version has been a commonplace of historical scholarship since Burckhardt. Interpretation of the content, meaning, and pace of the crisis have changed, but there remains a consensus that some kind of change did occur.
10. For example, my argument about the Poet's War strives to locate the specific struggle of Jonson, Marston, and Dekker in early seventeenth-century culture in ways that account for the emergence of a relatively autonomous literary field.
11. Even in so banal a fashion as the curricular division between "English" and "Creative Writing" in literature departments.
12. See Terry Eagleton, *Literary Theory* (2nd ed. Minneapolis: University of Minnesota Press, 1996) and Gerald Graff, *Professing Literature*, for discussions of the conflicts that structure the development of literary study.
13. I am using Bourdieu's phrasing here to describe the way that the Arnoldian distinction between creative and critical endeavors and his investment in the critical become guiding principles for the field.
14. This desire also articulates the goal of one variety of historical scholarship—to see the past as "it really was." See Graff, *Professing Literature*, and Chris Baldick, *The Social Mission of English Literature* (Oxford: Oxford University Press, 1983) for discussions of the historical justifications of the profession. Baldick demonstrates that Arnold held that criticism was necessary and antecedent to poetry—providing it with material, in effect. This position has the double effect of making criticism valuable in its own right and, at least to some extent, prior to the literature it criticizes. Baldick is particularly useful in describing the Arnoldian legacy in English criticism up to the founding of *Scrutiny* in 1932. He makes clear the way that Arnold and his successors saw "English" as a discipline with a social purpose beyond the cultivation of letters.
15. *Culture and Anarchy* is Arnold's most developed discussion of the role and importance of literature and its social function, but "The Function of Criticism" offers an early defense of criticism.

16. There is an extensive literature on "the profession" and its ongoing crisis. Much of this work focuses pretty narrowly on present concerns and seems to at times forgetful of the current crisis' social and historical antecedents. The work of Cary Nelson and Michael Bérubé avoids this problem while edited volumes such as Jeffrey Williams, ed., *The Institution of Literature* (Albany: State University of New York Press, 2002), Peter C. Herman, ed., *Day Late, Dollar Short: The Next Generation and the New Academy* (Albany: State University of New York Press, 2000), David Shumway and Craig Dionne, eds., *Disciplining English* (Albany: State University of New York Press, 2002), and James Sosnoski, *Token Professionals and Master Critics: A Critique of Orthodoxy in Literary Studies* (Albany: State University of New York Press, 1994) tend be more narrowly (and understandably) present-focused. Bill Readings' *The University in Ruins* (Cambridge, MA: Harvard University Press, 1996) is one of the more useful and interesting of these considerations of the status of the university in late modernity—too many of which are overpowered by lament or jeremiad. Readings' book also offers the important reminder that Lyotard's *Postmodern Condition* originates as a "report on knowledge" to Canadian authorities on higher education—placing it firmly in the context of debate about the nature, future, and function of the academy.

17. John Guillory's *Cultural Capital* (Chicago: University of Chicago Press, 1995) describes a crisis in the value of the cultural capital produced by literary education and relates it to the emergence of a professional-managerial class.

18. This connection to the state accounts for their designation as "higher."

19. This is an important aspect of the argument and one that is often lost in contemporary discussions about the relation of literary studies to its various publics.

20. Immanuel Kant, *The Conflict of the Faculties* (Mary J. Gregor, trans. Lincoln: University of Nebraska Press, 1992), 45.

21. See Guillory, *Cultural Capital*, on the canon debate. This does not preclude political or social engagements in one's work—it almost demands them—but serves as a reminder that the two cannot be collapsed into each other. Scholarship and activism are, after all, distinct no matter how related they may be.

22. If not before, see Gerald Graff's *Professing English* for a wide-ranging historical discussion of the conflicts that have surrounded English at least since its institutionalization in the university curriculum in the later nineteenth century.

23. Johns Hopkins serves as the best example of this development in Graff's book. It was founded in 1876 explicitly on the German model. Daniel Coit Gilman's inaugural remarks stated that the new institution's goal was to be "the encouragement of research . . . and the advancement of individual scholars, who by their excellence will advance the sciences they pursue, and the society where they dwell" (cited from JHU's Web presence). Teaching was intended to be part of the mission, but it was a teaching intimately related to the research agenda of the professor and of the university.

24. The traditional distinction between a teaching school and a research school is one effect of this split. The teaching institution—best exemplified by the liberal arts college—derives from the older enculturation model of educa-

tion while the research institution derives from its opposite. Graff offers an illuminating analysis of the nineteenth-century role of the liberal arts school as distinguished from the nascent university. More recently, the distinction in intellectual mission between these two general types of institution has begun to fade in the face of the ever-increasing professionalism of literary studies which encourages both types of institution to value the same cultural capital—the research Ph.D. See various articles in the MLA annual *Profession* on this shift.

25. This claim has a long history—see Baldick, *Social Mission*, on the Leavis's belief that literary knowledge would serve as a defense against the powers of advertising—and is an important part of the authority of composition and rhetoric as much as it is of English.

26. A third justification—one that appeals to the self-evident value of art on its own terms—remains powerful as well despite its occasional disavowal by practicing scholars. This justification also has an Arnoldian pedigree—the task of criticism being to preserve and transmit touchstones of the culture. The recent return of aesthetics in literary studies seems indicative of both this disavowal (since it is a turn) and the durability of the *ars gratia artis* rationale.

27. This is, naturally, a more or less fictional distinction since the two roles are almost always united in each member of the profession, but such fictions have effects.

28. Despite the fact that the New Historicism and cultural materialism have well-documented differences, I link them here because both are part of a broad movement of scholarship toward history. The lower case "h" in "historicism" is, of course, deliberate and reflects what appears to be a turn away from labels which for various reasons have become either passé or overly laden with negative connotations.

29. John Brannigan, *New Historicism and Cultural Materialism* (New York: St. Martin's Press, 1998) 126. Brannigan calls this a "turn"—echoing the "linguistic turn"—which suggests that this move is something rather than a return to history with a different emphasis.

30. This is most true of early modern studies, but the New Historicism has colonized other fields as well. See Jon Klancher, "English Romanticism and Cultural Production," *The New Historicism*, ed. H. Aram Veeser (New York: Routledge, 1989), 77–88, for a discussion of the influence of the New Historicism on Romanticists.

31. With notable exceptions including David Kastan's recent *Shakespeare After Theory* (New York: Routledge, 2002) and Douglas Bruster's *Shakespeare and the Question of Culture* (New York: Palgrave, 2003).

32. The definition of "historicism" is a question that will be taken up below. The usage of the term in early modern studies seems oddly forgetful of its deep connections to the philosophy of history and its function as a term of abuse used by historians to criticize work that they deem not properly historical. See Karl Popper's *Poverty of Historicism* (London: Routledge Kegan Paul, 1957) for one of the more influential deployments of this term. See also Raymond Williams's "history" entry in his *Keywords* (Oxford: Oxford University Press, 1976). This is, as Douglas Bruster points out, just as true of materialism.

33. Jean Howard, "The New Historicism in Renaissance Studies," *English Literary Renaissance*, 16, no. 1 (1986): 13–43.

34. H. Aram Veeser's edited collection *The New Historicism* includes essays by Jon Klancher, Vincent Pecora, and others that question the New Historicism's theoretical and historical underpinnings. David Scott Kastan's *Shakespeare After Theory* represents the New Historicism as neither particularly new nor particularly historical. This charge, interestingly enough, was already being made when the New Historicism really was new. The persistence of this criticism suggests both its accuracy and its professional usefulness as a marker of distinction separating its author from those he or she critiques.

35. See my discussion of Niethammer's argument on this issue below.

36. This is, of course, an unstable and not fully tenable opposition and begs the question of what either term actually means. The untenability of the opposition is demonstrated, ironically enough, by a history journal called *History and Theory*.

37. I am suspicious of such claims, but it remains that "history" appears in a great many book titles, series names, and articles in the field while "theory" appears to be less prevalent. Certainly, fewer job ads include theory as part of the position title than was the case in the 1980s and early 1990s.

38. My effort here is, of course, not innocent of involvement with this struggle for authority.

39. See the discussion of Lutz Niethammer's conclusions in his *Posthistoire: Has History Come to An End?* (London: Verso, 1992) below.

40. Beginning with *Metahistory* (Baltimore, MD: Johns Hopkins University Press, 1974) and continuing to his recent *Figural Realism* (Baltimore, MD: Johns Hopkins University Press, 1998), White has considered the relationship between historiography and that which it purports to describe.

41. Hayden White, *The Content of the Form: Narrative Discourse and Historical Representation* (Baltimore, MD: Johns Hopkins University Press, 1987), ix.

42. White, *Content* 27.

43. Ibid.

44. Ibid., 57. He describes five strains in the discussion of narrative in historical theory: one influenced by Anglo-American analytical philosophy, one deriving from the social science–inflected work of the *Annales* school, one related to semiologically influenced literary theorists and philosophers, one coming from the thought of hermeneutically oriented philosophers, and one, less theoretical, that comes from the practical dispositions of working historians.

45. White, *Content*, 57. That truth has to do with the effort to make meaning out of a series of occurrences that can just as easily be described as a meaningless collection of unrelated events. See his discussion of medieval annals and chronicles in the first essay in this collection. Annals, in his discussion, list events without positing relations between them or causation, while chronicles do.

46. In White's view, the production of this meaning depends in every instance on a philosophy of history—a historicism—that is present whether avowedly or not.

47. Jean-François Lyotard's *Postmodern Condition* (Minneapolis: University of Minnesota Press, 1984) posits the postmodern as a condition suspicious of any metanarrative's authority, instead imagining a congeries of micronarra-

tives that do not pretend to total explanations. Ironically, the antitotalizing impulse represented by the rejection of Tillyard in early modern studies has had the result of replacing one totalizing narrative with another—a subversion-containment model that derives from Foucault. Greenblatt's famed paraphrase of Kafka's comment on hope ("there is subversion, no end of subversion, only not for us") points to this substitution.

48. Hayden White, *Tropics of Discourse* (Baltimore, MD: Johns Hopkins University Press, 1978), 101.

49. White, *Tropics,* 101–2.

50. Moreover, competitions over what counts as properly historical writing define the boundaries of the field regardless of the specific content of the competing definitions. White is, of course, more interested in the product of historical scholarship than in intentions, but intentions do have important effects on production.

51. Paul Hamilton, *Historicism* (New York,: Routledge, 1996), 2.

52. This makes his book an exceptionally useful text for thinking about the role of history in literary study.

53. See Catherine Gallagher and Stephen Greenblatt, *Practicing New Historicism* (Chicago: University of Chicago Press, 2000). In a moment that Douglas Bruster also notes, Gallagher and Greenblatt express an at least somewhat disingenuous amazement at the new historicism's position as a recognized method in early modern studies. In the course of their remarks on their surprise, they articulate the usual assertion that New Historicism lacks a theory and that it "resists systematization." See Bruster, *Shakespeare,* 208ff., where he discusses the many publications associated with both scholars that avow the label they here express surprise over. Taking their title seriously means that Gallagher and Greenblatt actively refuse to offer a theory, instead offering a series of exemplary practices. Whether or not this is possible or desirable or even true is another question.

54. Gallagher and Greenblatt, *Practicing,* 35. This skepticism is clearly related to the kind of skepticism characteristic of posthistorical thought in which the meaning of history is evacuated at the same time as the sense of progress in history is abandoned.

55. Ibid., 6.

56. This is paradoxical, of course, due to the enormous influence of Foucauldian theory on the early practice of the New Historicism.

57. Williams, *Keywords,* 147.

58. Ibid.

59. This is particularly true since the mode of historicism implicit in the New Historicism seems more akin to posthistory than to history proper.

60. Niethammer's book is an intellectual history that explores the genesis of this position and attempts to account for it in the social and historical context of twentieth century Europe's experience with war and dictatorship, among others.

61. Cournot cited in Niethammer, *Posthistoire,* 17. No English translation of the 1861 work (*Traité de l'enchaînement des idées fondamentales dans les sciences et dans l'histoire*) from which this quotation is drawn exists. In contrast, Cournot's work on economics remains important to contemporary

economists while this work remains obscure to the English-speaking academy.

62. Niethammer, *Posthistoire*, 17.

63. Cournot's picture of history as concerned with the singular resonates with the New Historicism's focus on isolated striking events.

64. This essay is curiously underdiscussed in much recent early modern scholarship that takes up the question of history. Recent neoconservative thought echoes much of Cournot's vision of history especially with regard to the spread of liberal democracy.

65. Friedrich Nietzsche, "On the Uses and Disadvantages of History for Life" in *Untimely Meditations*, trans. R. J. Hollingdale (Cambridge: Cambridge University Press, 1997), 59. Nietzsche's position in many ways is the reverse of "end of history" thinking—what he criticizes here is the full domination of history and what he argues is the concomitant end of "Life" in the face of that domination.

66. The things to be swept away and replaced are those related to the human propensity to weakness and violence. See Nietzsche, "Uses," 76 on confronting "our inherited and hereditary nature" with knowledge so as to "implant in ourselves a new habit" that will cause the negative aspects of that inherited nature to wither away.

67. Ibid., 67.

68. See discussion of Bruster on the "new materialism" below.

69. Nietzsche, "Uses," 104.

70. Herbert Marcuse, *One Dimensional Man* (Boston: Beacon Press, 1964), 1.

71. Daniel Bell's work on post-industrial society and the "end of ideology" is related to this suspicion of history in a putatively new era. The end of ideology appears to be necessary for the end of history.

72. One example would, of course, be particular versions of Marxist historiography that, as Lyotard would argue, impose an economic master narrative on historical events and, by extension, on the future they are meant to prefigure.

73. Niethammer, *Posthistoire*, 138.

74. Ibid., 3. Notice the resemblance to what Gallagher and Greenblatt represent as Auerbach's skepticism about a "meaningful higher order." This doubt about higher order meaning is symptomatic of both posthistory and the new historicism.

75. Niethammer cites Marcuse's *One Dimensional Man*, and I would add the analysis of postmodernism in Fredric Jameson's *Postmodernism, Or, The Cultural Logic of Late Capitalism* as examples of warnings about this faceless postmodernism. Lyotard and Hutcheon would be exemplary of the other side of the argument.

76. Francis Fukuyama, *The End of History and the Last Man* (New York: Free Press, 1992). Fukuyama is most concerned with questions of world politics in the aftermath of the end of the Cold War, but his argument that historical progress ends with the spread of liberal democracy is homologous to the posthistorical thought Niethammer describes—with the major difference that Fukuyama sees the end of history as a consummation devoutly to be wished.

77. Ibid., 64.

78. Niethammer, *Posthistoire*, 85.

79. Ibid., 10.

80. My "merely" is deliberate here and echoes Niethammer's assessment of the idea of posthistory—to abandon historical scholarship as at least instructive about social change seems like more an act of despair than anything else.

81. Niethammer, *Posthistoire*, 149.

82. Ibid., 19. These thinkers see society as increasingly dominated by a technocratic, historyless order, and part of what they refuse by embracing the posthistory concept is the extension of that model to the past—partly because it might legitimate the current order and partly because historical research might mirror the lack of freedom this quotation refers to. Interestingly, the totalizing impulse of which the New Historicism is often accused seems to participate in the creation of a "history without alternatives"—a history it is rhetorically aligned against.

83. I want to stress that my position here is complementary to the one I am describing—it seems to me that a distrust of a coercive or distorting historical narrative is a positive thing, but that that distrust does not necessarily mean that *all* narratives are coercive or distorting. The creation of historical narratives is inevitable, the question is thus not about whether we create them, but what kinds we want to create. And, not least, how reflexively we create them. For some suggestive reflections on this problem see Kastan, *Shakespeare After Theory*.

84. Bruster, *Shakespeare*, 192.

85. By this I do not mean to refer to the invaluable work in the Malone Society *Collections* and other transcriptions of early modern theater records that are the sources of my argument in the theater chapter above.

86. The shift from society to culture refracts this break—"society" has historical and political associations that culture can transform into objects of contemplation.

87. Bruster, *Shakespeare*, 203. He goes on to suggest that this version of materialism could benefit from attention to the extensive history of materialist thinking in early modern England that comments extensively on the relations between things and thoughts, objects and knowledge.

88. Raymond Williams offers a typically provocative and helpful account of "materialism" in his *Keywords*. Williams points out that a narrow—matter-focused—definition of materialism is only one definition and not one that does justice to the complexity and richness of the term's intellectual legacy.

89. Nietzsche, "Uses," 74.

90. There is also more than a little of what Nietzsche calls the damaging side of "monumental history" in which the past is valued simply because it is past, not because of any judgment of lasting value or usefulness, or, more importantly for me, relevance to the present. See ibid., 67–72.

91. Bruster calls for "thin description" to supplement the thick description of the New Historicism and other "materialisms" and this thin description has affinities to the kind of work I describe in this book. I am in agreement with much of what he says about the need for breadth as well as depth in early modern scholarship and believe that a Bourdieuian approach can offer both.

92. Bourdieu and Wacquandt, *Invitation*, 91.

93. Though of course not in any simple way. As argued above, the notion that "radical" interpretation can have immediate social effects short-circuits the more mediated process by which change occurs.

Bibliography

Abbott, Andrew. *The System of Professions: An Essay on the Division of Expert Labor*. Chicago: University of Chicago Press, 1988.

Adams, Hazard. *Critical Theory Since Plato*. San Diego: Harcourt Brace Jovanovich, 1971.

Adorno, Theodor, and Max Horkheimer. *Dialectic of Enlightenment*. New York: Continuum, 1994.

Aers, David, ed. *Culture and History 1350–1600: Essays on English Communities, Identities, and Writing*. Detroit, MI: Wayne State University Press, 1992.

Agnew, Jean-Christophe. *Worlds Apart: The Theatre and the Market in Anglo-American Culture 1550–1750*. New York: Cambridge University Press, 1986.

Altman, Joel. *The Tudor Play of Mind: Rhetorical Inquiry and the Development of Elizabethan Drama*. Berkeley and Los Angeles: University of California Press, 1978.

Amussen, Susan. *An Ordered Society: Gender and Class in Early Modern England*. Oxford: Blackwell, 1988.

Anonymous. *The Actor's Remonstrance or Complaint*. London, 1643. London: Reeves and Turner, 1873.

———. *Mucedorus*. London, 1598.

———. *A Newe Boke of Presidentes in Maner of a Register*. London, 1543.

———. *The Old Natura Brevium*. London, 1518. STC 18388.

———. *The Troublesome Raigne of King John*. Edited by G. Bullough. In *Narrative and Dramatic Sources of Shakespeare*, vol. 4. London: Routledge Kegan Paul, 1975.

Archer, Ian. *The Pursuit of Stability: Social Relations in Elizabethan London*. Cambridge: Cambridge University Press, 1991.

Arnold, Matthew. *Culture and Anarchy*. Cambridge: Cambridge University Press, 1993.

Astington, John, ed. *The Development of Shakespeare's Theatre*. New York: AMS Press, 1992.

———. *English Court Theatre, 1558–1642*. Cambridge: Cambridge University Press, 1999.

Baker, J. H. *The English Legal Profession and the Common Law.* London: Hambledon, 1986.

———. *An Introduction to English Legal History.* 3rd ed. London: Butterworths, 1990.

———. *Readings and Moots at the Inns of Court.* Vol. 2. London: Selden Society, 1990.

———. *The Third University of England.* London: Selden Society, 1990.

Baldick, Chris. *The Social Mission of English Literature.* Oxford: Oxford University Press, 1983.

Barish, Jonas. *Ben Jonson and the Language of Prose Comedy.* Cambridge, MA: Harvard University Press, 1960.

Barry, Jonathan and Christopher Brooks, eds. *The Middling Sort of People: Culture, Society and Politics in England 1550–1800.* New York: St. Martin's, 1994.

Barton, Anne. *Ben Jonson, Dramatist.* Cambridge: Cambridge University Press, 1984.

Baudrillard, Jean. *The Transparency of Evil.* London: Verso, 1993.

Beal, Peter. "Massinger at Bay: Unpublished Verses in a War of the Theatres" *Yearbook of English Studies* 10 (1980): 190–203.

Beale, Robert. "A Treatise of the Office of a Councellor and Principall Secretarie to her Majestie." ca. 1592. In *Mr. Secretary Walsingham and the Policy of Queen Elizabeth,* edited by Conyers Ready, vol. 1. Oxford: Clarendon Press, 1925. Transcribes BL MS Add. 48149:161 (Yelverton MSS) fol 3b–9b.

Beaumont, Francis. *The Knight of the Burning Pestle.* New York: Norton, 1986.

Beckingsale, B. W. *Burghley: Tudor Statesman 1520–1598.* London: MacMillan, 1967.

———. *Cromwell: Tudor Minister.* Totowa, NJ: Rowman and Littlefield, 1978.

Bednarz, James. "Marston's Subversion of Shakespeare and Jonson: *Histriomastix* and the War of the Theatres." *Medieval and Renaissance Drama in England* 6(1993): 103–28.

———. "Representing Jonson: *Histriomastix* and the Origins of the Poet's War." *Huntington Library Quarterly* 54 (1991): 1–30.

———. *Shakespeare and Poet's War.* New York: Columbia University Press, 2001.

Beier, A. L., and Roger Finlay, eds. *London 1500–1700: The Making of a Metropolis.* London: Longman, 1986.

Bell, Daniel. *The End of Ideology.* New York: Free Press, 1965.

Belsey, Catherine. *The Subject of Tragedy.* London: Methuen, 1988.

Bennett, William. *To Reclaim a Legacy.* Washington, DC: National Endowment for the Humanities, 1984.

Bentley, G. E. *The Profession of Dramatist in Shakespeare's Time.* Princeton, NJ: Princeton University Press, 1971.

Berger, Thomas L. *Index of Characters in Early Modern English Drama.* Cambridge: Cambridge University Press, 1998.

Bergeron, David M. *English Civic Pageantry.* Columbia: University of South Carolina Press, 1971.

———. "Patronage of Dramatists: The Case of Thomas Heywood." *English Literary Renaissance* 18 (1988): 294–304.

———. *Practicing Renaissance Scholarship.* Pittsburgh, PA: Duquesne University Press, 2000.

Bérubé, Michael. *The Employment of English.* New York: New York University Press, 1998.

———. *Public Access.* London: Verso, 1994.

Bérubé, Michael, and Cary Nelson, eds. *Higher Education Under Fire: Politics, Economics, and the Crisis of the Humanities.* New York: Routledge, 1995.

Bindoff, S. T., Joel Hurstfield, and C. H. Williams, eds. *Elizabethan Government and Society.* London: University of London Press, 1961.

Blandy, William. *The Castle of Commonwealth.* London, 1581. New York: Da Capo, 1972.

Bourdieu, Pierre. *Algeria 1960.* Cambridge: Cambridge University Press, 1979.

———. *Distinction: A Social Critique of the Judgment of Taste.* Translated by Richard Nice. Cambridge, MA: Harvard University Press, 1984.

———. *The Field of Cultural Production.* New York: Columbia University Press, 1993.

———. "The Field of Cultural Production, Or, The Economic Field Reversed." *Poetics* 12 (1983): 311–56.

———. "The Force of Law: Towards a Sociology of the Juridical Field." *Hastings Law Journal* 38 (1986–87): 805–53.

———. "The Forms of Capital." In *Handbook of Theory and Research for the Sociology of Education,* edited by John G. Richardson, 241–58. New York: Greenwood, 1986.

———. "Intellectual Field and Creative Project." *Social Science Information* 8, no. 2 (1969): 89–120.

———. *Language and Symbolic Power.* Translated by Gino Raymond and Matthew Adamson. Cambridge, MA: Harvard University Press, 1991.

———. *The Logic of Practice.* Stanford, CA: Stanford University Press, 1990.

———. *Masculine Domination.* Stanford, CA: Stanford University Press, 2001.

———. *The Rules of Art: Genesis and Structure of the Literary Field.* Stanford, CA: Stanford University Press, 1996.

Bowdieu, Pierre, and Loïc Wacquandt. *Invitation to Reflexive Sociology.* Chicago: University of Chicago Press, 1992.

Brannigan, John. *New Historicism and Cultural Materialism.* New York: St. Martin's, 1998.

Braunmuller, A. R. "*King John* and Historiography." *ELH* 55, no. 2 (1988): 309–22.

———. "The Serious Comedy of Greene's *James IV*" *English Literary Renaissance* 3 (1973): 335–50.

Brennan, Michael. *Literary Patronage in the English Renaissance.* London: Routledge, 1988.
Bretzius, Stephen. *Shakespeare in Theory: The Postmodern Academy and the Early Modern Theatre.* Ann Arbor: University of Michigan Press, 1997.
Brome, Richard. *The Antipodes.* Lincoln: University of Nebraska Press, 1966.
Brooks, Christopher. *Pettifoggers and Vipers of the Commonwealth: The Lower Branch of the Legal Profession in Early Modern England.* Cambridge: Cambridge University Press, 1986.
Brownlow, Richard. *Brevia Judicialia.* London, 1662.
Buc, Sir George. *The Third Universitie of England.* London, 1615.
Bulwer, John. *Chirologia, or, The Natural Language of the Hand.* London, 1644.
Burckhardt, Jacob. *The Civilization of the Renaissance in Italy.* New York: Modern Library, 1954.
Burckhardt, Sigurd. *Shakespearean Meanings.* Princeton, NJ: Princeton University Press, 1968.
Burns, Edward, ed. *Reading Rochester.* New York: St. Martin's, 1995.
Burrage, Michael, and Rolf Torstendal. *Professions in Theory and History.* London: Sage, 1990.
Burt, Richard, *The Administration of Aesthetics.* Minneapolis: University of Minnesota Press, 1994.
Burt, Richard and John Michael Archer. *Enclosure Acts: Sexuality, Property, and Culture in Early Modern England.* Ithaca, NY: Cornell University Press, 1994.
Bush, Jonathan, and Alain Wijffels, eds. *Learning the Law: Teaching and the Transmission of the Law in England, 1150–1900.* Rio Grande, OH: Hambledon Press, 1999.
Calhoun, Bruce et al., eds. *Bourdieu: Critical Perspectives.* Chicago: University of Chicago Press, 1993.
Carr-Saunders, A. P., and P. A. Wilson. *The Professions.* Oxford: Oxford University Press, 1933.
Cassirer, Ernst. *The Individual and the Cosmos in Renaissance Philosophy.* New York: Harper and Row, 1964
———, ed. *The Renaissance Philosophy of Man.* Chicago: University of Chicago Press, 1948.
Chambers, E. K. *The Elizabethan Stage.* 4 vols. Oxford: Clarendon, 1951.
———. *The Medieval Stage.* 2 vols. Oxford: Clarendon, 1903.
———. *Notes on the History of the Revels Office under the Tudors.* New York: B. Franklin, 1967.
Cheney, Lynne. *Telling the Truth.* New York: Simon and Schuster, 1995.
Christian, Mildred G. "A Sidelight on the Family History of Thomas Middleton" *Studies in Philology* 44 (1947): 490–96.
Clopper, Lawrence. *Drama, Play, and Game: English Festive Culture in the Medieval and Early Modern Period.* Chicago: University of Chicago Press, 2001.

Coleman, Christopher, and David Starkey, eds. *Revolution Reassessed.* Oxford: Oxford University Press, 1986.

Cressy, David. *Literacy and Social Order.* Cambridge: Cambridge University Press, 1980.

Crumley, J. Clinton. "Anachronism and Historical Romance in Renaissance Drama: *James IV.*" *Explorations in Renaissance Culture* 24 (1998): 75–90.

Curren-Aquino, Deborah T., ed. *King John: New Perspectives.* Newark: University of Delaware Press, 1989.

Dekker, Thomas. *Dramatic Works.* Vol. 1. Edited by Fredson Bowers. Cambridge: Cambridge University Press, 1962.

———. *Londons Tempe.* London, 1629.

———. *Nondramatic Works.* Edited by A. B. Grosart. New York: Russell and Russell, 1963.

———. *Thomas Dekker.* Edited by E. D. Pendry. Cambridge, MA: Harvard University Press, 1968.

D'Souza, Dinesh. *Illiberal Education.* New York: Free Press, 1991.

Dubrow, Heather et al. "Forum." *PMLA* 109, no. 5 (1994): 1025–30.

Duby, Georges. *The Three Orders.* Chicago: University of Chicago Press, 1980.

Dutton, Richard. *Mastering the Revels.* Iowa City: University of Iowa Press, 1991.

Eagleton, Terry. *Ideology: An Introduction.* London: Verso, 1991.

———. *Literary Theory.* Minneapolis: University of Minnesota Press, 1996.

Eccles, Mark. "Middleton's Birth and Education." *Review of English Studies* 7 (1931): 431–41

———. "'Thomas Middleton A Poett.'" *Studies in Philology* 54 (1957): 516–36.

Eisenstein, Elizabeth. *The Printing Press as an Agent of Change.* 2 vols. Cambridge: Cambridge University Press, 1979.

Elliott, John M. "Shakespeare and the Double Image of King John." *Shakespeare Studies* 1 (1965): 64–84.

Elton, G. R. *Reform and Renewal: Thomas Cromwell and the Common Weal.* Cambridge: Cambridge University Press, 1973.

———. *The Tudor Revolution in Government.* Cambridge: Cambridge University Press, 1953.

Evans, Robert. *Ben Jonson and the Poetics of Patronage.* Lewisburg, PA: Bucknell University Press, 1989.

Feuillerat, Albert. *Documents Relating to the Office of the Revels in the Time of Elizabeth.* Louvain, 1908.

———. *Revels at Court in the Time of Edward VI and Queen Mary.* Louvain, 1914.

Field, Nathan. *The Remonstrance of Nathan Field, one of Shakespeare's Company of Actors.* London: Chiswick Press, 1865.

Fiedler, Paul and T. F. Mayer eds. *Political Thought and the Tudor Commonwealth.* London: Routledge, 1992.

Fineman, Joel. *Shakespeare's Perjured Eye*. Berkeley and Los Angeles: University of California Press, 1986.
Finkelpearl, Philip. *John Marston of the Inner Temple*. Cambridge, MA: Harvard University Press, 1969.
Fish, Stanley. *Doing What Comes Naturally*. Oxford: Oxford University Press, 1989.
———. *Professional Correctness: Literary Studies and Political Change*. Oxford: Oxford University Press, 1995.
Fitzherbert, Sir Anthony. *New Natura Brevium*. London, 1652.
Fleay, F. G. *Chronicle of the English Drama*. London, 1891.
Forse, James. *Art Imitates Business*. Bowling Green, OH: Popular Press, 1993.
Fortescue, John. *De Laudibus Legum Angliae*. Cambridge: Cambridge University Press, 1942.
Foucault, Michel. *Madness and Civilization*. New York: Vintage, 1973.
Fox, Alistair, and John Guy, eds. *Reassessing the Henrician Age*. Oxford: Basil Blackwell, 1986.
Fraunce, Abraham. *Lawiers Logike*. London, 1588.
Freidson, Elliot. *The Profession of Medicine*. New York: Dodd and Mead, 1970.
Fukuyama, Francis. *The End of History and the Last Man*. New York: Free Press, 1992.
Fulbecke, William. *A Direction, or Preparative, to the Study of the Law*. Aldershot: Wildwood House, 1987.
Gallagher, Catherine, and Stephen Greenblatt. *Practicing New Historicism*. Chicago: University of Chicago Press, 2000.
Gebert, Clara. *Elizabethan Dedications and Prefaces*. Philadelphia: University of Pennsylvania Press, 1933.
Gibbons, Brian. *Jacobean City Comedy: A Study of Satiric Plays by Jonson, Marston, and Middleton*. Cambridge, MA: Harvard University Press, 1968
Giddens, Anthony. *The Consequences of Modernity*. Stanford, CA: Stanford University Press, 1990.
Gosson, Stephen. *The Schoole of Abuse*. London, 1579.
Graff, Gerald. *Professing Literature*. Chicago: University of Chicago Press, 1987.
Greenblatt, Stephen. *Renaissance Self-Fashioning*. Chicago: University of Chicago Press, 1980.
Greene, Robert. *Greene's Groatsworth of Witte, Bought With a Million of Repentance*. 1592. Edited by G. B. Harrison. New York: Barnes and Noble, 1966.
———. *James IV*. London: Methuen, 1970.
Greg, W. W. *Bibliography of the English Printed Drama to the Restoration*. 4 vols. London: Bibliographic Society, 1939–59.
Grennan, Eamon. "Shakespeare's Satirical History: A Reading of *King John*." *Shakespeare Studies* 11 (1978): 21–37.
Guillory, John. "Bourdieu's Refusal." *Modern Language Quarterly* 58, no. 4(1997): 367–398.

———. *Cultural Capital.* Chicago: University of Chicago Press, 1993.
Gunn, S. J. *Early Tudor Government, 1485–1558.* New York: St. Martin's, 1995.
Gurr, Andrew. *Playgoing in Shakespeare's London.* Cambridge: Cambridge University Press, 1987.
Guy, John, ed. *The Reign of Elizabeth I: Court and Culture in the Last Decade.* Cambridge: Cambridge University Press, 1995.
———. *Tudor England.* Oxford: Oxford University Press, 1988.
Habermas, Jurgen. *Legitimation Crisis.* Boston: Beacon Press, 1975.
———. *The Philosophical Discourse of Modernity.* Cambridge, MA: MIT Press, 1987.
Haigh, Christopher, ed. *The Reign of Elizabeth I.* Athens: University of Georgia Press, 1985.
Halpern, Richard. *The Poetics of Primitive Accumulation.* Ithaca, NY: Cornell University Press, 1991.
———. *Shakespeare Among the Moderns.* Ithaca, NY: Cornell University Press, 1997.
Hamilton, Paul. *Historicism.* New York: Routledge, 1996.
Harrison, William. *Description of England.* London, 1587.
Helgerson, Richard. *The Elizabethan Prodigals.* Berkeley and Los Angeles: University of California Press, 1976.
———. *Self-Crowned Laureates.* Berkeley and Los Angeles: University of California Press, 1983.
Henslowe, Philip. *Diary.* Cambridge: Cambridge University Press, 2002.
Herman, Peter, ed. *Day Late, Dollar Short.* Albany: State University of New York Press, 2000.
Heywood, Thomas. *An Apology for Actors.* 1612. New York: Garland, 1973.
———. *The Dramatic Works of Thomas Heywood.* 1874. 6 vols. Russell and Russell: New York, 1964.
———. *Londini Artium & Scientiarum Scaturigo; OR, Londons Fountaine of Arts and Sciences.* London, 1632.
———. *Londons Ius Honorarium.* London, 1631.
Hillebrand, Howard. "Thomas Middleton's *The Viper's Brood.*" *Modern Language Notes* 42 (1927): 35–38.
Hosley, R., ed. *Essays in Elizabethan Drama.* Columbia: University of Missouri Press, 1962.
Howard, Jean. "The New Historicism in Renaissance Studies." *English Literary Renaissance* 16, no. 1 (1986): 13–43.
Howard, Jean, and Marion F. O'Connor. *Shakespeare Reproduced.* London: Routledge, 1987.
Hurstfield, Joel, ed. *The Tudors.* New York: St. Martin's, 1973.
I. M. *A Health to the Gentlemanly Profession of Servingmen.* 1581. London: Oxford, 1931.
Ingram, William. *The Business of Playing.* Ithaca, NY: Cornell University Press, 1992.

———. "The Early Career of James Burbage." *The Elizabethan Theatre X.* Ontario: PD Meany, 1983.

———. "Robert Keysar, Playhouse Speculator." *Shakespeare Quarterly* 37, no. 4 (Winter1986): 476–85.

Ishiguro, Kazuo. *The Remains of the Day.* New York: Knopf, 1989.

James, Mervyn. *Society, Politics, and Culture.* Cambridge: Cambridge University Press, 1986.

Jameson, Fredric. *Late Marxism, Adorno, or the Persistence of the Dialectic.* London: Verso, 1990.

———. *Postmodernism, or, The Cultural Logic of Late Capitalism.* Durham, NC: Duke University Press, 1991.

Johnson, Paul. *The Birth of the Modern.* New York: HarperCollins, 1991.

Johnson, T. J. *Professions and Power.* London: MacMillan, 1972.

Jones, W. J. *The Elizabethan Court of Chancery.* Oxford: Clarendon Press, 1967.

Jonson, Ben. *Ben Jonson.* Vol. 4. Edited by C.H. Herford and Percy Simpson. Oxford: Oxford University Press, 1932.

———. *Complete Poems.* Edited by George Parfitt. London: Penguin Books, 1988.

———. *Poetaster.* Edited by Thomas Cain. New York: Manchester University Press, 1995.

Kant, Immanuel. *The Conflict of The Faculties.* Lincoln: University of Nebraska Press, 1979.

Kastan, David Scott. *Shakespeare After Theory.* New York: Routledge, 1999.

———. " 'To Set a Form Upon That Indigest': Shakespeare's Fictions of History." *Comparative Drama* 17, no. 1 (1983): 1–16.

Kimball, Roger. *Tenured Radicals.* New York: Harper and Row, 1990.

Klancher, Jon. "English Romanticism and Cultural Production." In *The New Historicism*, edited by H. Aram Veeser, 77–88. New York: Routledge, 1989.

Knights, L. C. *Drama and Society in the Age of Jonson.* New York: G. W. Stewart, 1951.

Knutson, Rosyln. *Playing Companies and Commerce in Shakespeare's Time.* Cambridge: Cambridge University Press, 2001.

Lang, R. G. "Social Origins and Social Aspirations of Jacobean London Merchants." *Economic History Review* second series 27 (1974): 28–47.

Larson, Magali. *The Rise of Professionalism.* Berkeley and Los Angeles: University of California Press, 1977.

Latour, Bruno. *We Have Never Been Modern.* Cambridge, MA: Harvard University Press, 1993.

Leggatt, Alexander. "Bohan and Oberon: The Internal Debate of Greene's *James IV.*" In *The Elizabethan Theatre XI*, ed. Lynne Magnusson and Ted McGee. Ontario: P. D. Meany, 1985.

Leinwand, Theodore. *The City Staged.* Madison: University of Wisconsin Press, 1986.

Leishman, J. B., ed. *The Three Parnassus Plays.* London: Ivor, Nicholson, and Watson, 1949.

Lepore, Jill. "Historians Who Love Too Much: Reflections on Microhistory and Biography." *Journal of American History* 88, no. 1 (June 2001): 129–44.

Lesser, Zachary. "Walter Burre's *Knight of the Burning Pestle*." *English Literary Renaissance* 29 (1999): 22–43.

Levack, Brian P. *The Civil Lawyers in England, 1603–1642*. Oxford: Oxford University Press, 1973.

Littleton, Sir Thomas. *Lytylton Tenures Newly and Most Truly Correctyd & Amendyd*. London, 1528.

Loewenstein, Joseph. "For a History of Literary Property: John Wolfe's Reformation." *English Literary Renaissance* 18 (1986): 389–412.

———. "Plays Agonistic and Competitive: The Textual Approach to Elsinore" *Renaissance Drama* 19 (1988): 63–96

———. "The Script in the Marketplace." *Representations* 12 (1985): 101–14.

MacFarlane, Alan. *The Origins of English Individualism*. New York: Cambridge University Press, 1978.

MacKay, Maxine. "*The Merchant of Venice*: A Reflection of the Early Conflict Between Courts of Law and Courts of Equity." *Shakespeare Quarterly* 15, no. 4 (1964): 371–75.

MacLean, Sally-Beth and Scott McMillin, *The Queen's Men and Their Plays*. Cambridge: Cambridge University Press, 1998

Magnusson, Lynne. *Shakespeare and Social Dialogue*. Cambridge: Cambridge University Press, 1999.

Malone Society. *Collections*. 5 vols. London: Malone Society, 1954–

Manheim, Michael. *The Weak King Dilemma in the Shakespearean History Play*. Syracuse, NY: Syracuse University Press, 1973.

Marcuse, Herbert. *One Dimensional Man*. Boston: Beacon Press, 1964.

Marlowe, Christopher. *Complete Plays*. New York: Penguin, 1969.

Marotti, Arthur. *John Donne, Coterie Poet*. Madison: University of Wisconsin Press, 1986.

———. "Patronage, Poetry and Print." *Yearbook of English Studies* 21 (1991): 1–26.

Marshall, Paul. *A Kind of Life Imposed on Man: Vocation and Social Order from Tyndale to Locke*. Toronto: University of Toronto Press, 1995.

Marston, John. *The Malcontent*. London: A. & C. Black, 1991.

———. *The Plays of John Marston*. 4 vols. Edited by H. Harvey Wood. Edinburgh: Oliver and Boyd, 1934.

Marx, Karl. *Capital*. 3 vols. New York: International Publishers, 1967.

———. *The German Ideology*. New York: International Publishers, 1970.

Massinger, Philip. *A New Way to Pay Old Debts*. T. W. Craik ed. London: Ernest Benn, 1964.

Masten, Jeffrey. *Textual Intercourse*. Cambridge: Cambridge University Press, 1997

Matz, Robert. *Defending Literature*. Cambridge: Cambridge University Press, 2001

May, Steven. "Tudor Aristocrats and the 'Stigma of Print'" *Renaissance Papers* (1980): 11–18.

McLuskie, Kathleen. *Dekker and Heywood: Professional Dramatists.* New York: St. Martin's, 1994.

———. "The Poet's Royal Exchange: Patronage and Commerce in Early Modern Drama." *Yearbook of English Studies* 21 (1991): 53–62.

Moi, Toril. "The Challenge of the Particular Case: Bourdieu's Sociology of Culture and Literary Criticism" *Modern Language Quarterly* 58, no. 4 (1997): 497–508.

Miller, E. H. *The Professional Writer in Elizabethan England.* Cambridge, MA: Harvard University Press, 1959.

Middleton, Thomas. *A Chaste Maid in Cheapside.* London: Methuen, 1969.

———. *A Mad World, My Masters.* Lincoln: University of Nebraska Press, 1965.

———. *Michaelmas Term.* Edited by Richard Levin. Lincoln: University of Nebraska Press, 1966.

Middleton, Thomas and William Rowley. *A Fair Quarrel.* Lincoln: University of Nebraska Press, 1976.

Murray, Timothy. *Theatrical Legitimation.* New York: Oxford University Press, 1987.

Neale, J. E. *Essays in Elizabethan History.* New York: St. Martin's, 1958.

Nelson, Cary. *Manifesto of a Tenured Radical.* New York: New York University Press, 1997.

Niethammer, Lutz. *Posthistoire: Has History Come to an End?* London: Verso, 1992.

Nietzsche, Friedrich. *Untimely Meditations.* Translated by R. J. Hollingdale. Cambridge: Cambridge University Press, 1997.

Orgel, Stephen. *The Jonsonian Masque.* Cambridge, MA: Harvard University Press, 1965.

Orgel, Stephen, and Roy Strong. *The Theatre of the Stuart Court.* Berkeley and Los Angeles: University of California Press, 1973.

Orlin, Lena Cowen, ed *Material London, ca. 1600.* Philadelphia: University of Pennsylvania Press, 2000.

Orrell, John. *The Human Stage: English Theatre Design 1567–1640.* Cambridge: Cambridge University Press, 1988.

———. *The Theatres of Inigo Jones and John Webb.* Cambridge: Cambridge University Press, 1985.

Osborne, Laurie. "Female Audiences and Female Authority in *The Knight of the Burning Pestle.*" *Exemplaria* 3, no. 2 (Fall 1991) 491–517.

Parsons, Talcott. *Essays in Sociological Theory.* New York: Free Press, 1954.

———. *Men and Their Work.* Glencoe, IL: Free Press, 1958.

———. *The Sociological Eye.* Chicago: Aldine, 1971.

Payne, Deborah. "Patronage and the Dramatic Market under Charles I and II." *Yearbook of English Studies* 21 (1991): 137–52.

Penniman, J. H. *The War of the Theatres.* Boston, 1897.

Perkins, William. *A Treatise of the Vocations or Callings of Men, with the sorts and kindes of them and the right use thereof.* London, 1603. STC 19647.

Peterson, Richard. *Imitation and Praise in the Poems of Ben Jonson.* New Haven, CT: Yale University Press, 1981.

Phialas, P. G. "Middleton's Early Contact with the Law." *Studies in Philology* 52 (1955): 186–95.

Pollard, Alfred William and G. R. Redgrave. *A Short Title Catalog of Books Printed in England, Scotland, and Ireland and of English Books Printed Abroad, 1475–1640.* 3 vols. London: Bibliographic Society, 1976–91.

Popper, Karl. *The Poverty of Historicism.* London: Routledge Kegan Paul, 1957.

Powell, Thomas. *The Attorneys Academy.* London, 1623.

Prest, Wilfred. *The Inns of Court, 1590–1640.* Totowa, NJ: Rowman and Littlefield, 1972.

———. ed., *Lawyers in Early Modern Europe and America.* New York: Holmes and Meier, 1981.

———. *The Professions in Early Modern England.* London: Croom Helm, 1987.

———. *The Rise of the Barristers.* Oxford: Oxford University Press, 1986.

———. "Why the History of the Professions Is Not Written." In *Law, Economy, and Society: Essays in the History of English Law,* edited by G.R. Rubin and David Sugarman, Oxford: Professional Books, 1984.

Pulman, Michael. *The Elizabethan Privy Council in the Fifteen-Seventies.* Berkeley and Los Angeles: University of California Press, 1971.

Puttenham, George. *Arte of English Poesie.* London, 1589.

Rackin, Phyllis. *Stages of History: Shakespeare's English Chronicles.* Ithaca, NY: Cornell University Press, 1990.

Rand, Richard, ed. *Logomachia: The Conflict of the Faculties.* Lincoln: University of Nebraska Press, 1992.

Read, Conyers. *Lord Burghley and Queen Elizabeth.* New York: Knopf, 1960.

———. *Mr. Secretary Cecil and Queen Elizabeth.* New York: Knopf, 1955.

Reiss, Timothy. *The Meaning of Literature.* Ithaca, NY: Cornell University Press, 1992.

Richardson, Walter Cecil. *History of the Inns of Court.* Baton Rouge, LA: Claitor's, 1975.

Riggs, David. *Ben Jonson.* Cambridge, MA: Harvard University Press, 1989.

Robbins, Derek. *The Work of Pierre Bourdieu.* Boulder, CO: Westview Press, 1991.

Saint German, Christopher. *Doctor and Student.* London: Selden Society, 1974.

Saunders, J. W. "The Stigma of Print: A Note on the Social Bases of Tudor Poetry." *Essays in Criticism* 1 (1951): 139–64.

S. S. *The Honest Lawyer.* New York: AMS Press, 1970.

Rhodes, Neil, and Jonathan Sawday, eds. *The Renaissance Computer.* New York: Routledge, 2000.

Robbins, Bruce. *Secular Vocations.* London: Verso, 1993.

Ross, Andrew. *No Respect.* New York: Routledge, 1989.

Seipp, David J. "The Structure of the English Common Law in the Seventeenth Century." In *Legal History in the Making,* edited by W. M. Gordon and T. D. Fergus, 61–84. London: Hambledon, 1991.

Shakespeare, William. *Hamlet.* H. Jenkins ed. New York: Routledge, 1990.

———. *Merchant of Venice.* Edited by M. M. Mahood, Cambridge: Cambridge University Press, 1987.

———. *King John.* Edited by E. A. J. Honigmann. London: Methuen, 1954.

———. *The Riverside Shakespeare.* Boston: Houghton Mifflin, 1997.

Shapiro, James S. *Rival Playwrights.* New York: Columbia University Press, 1991.

Sharpe, Robert. *The Real War of the Theatres.* 1935. New York: Kraus Reprint Association, 1966.

Shumway, David, and Craig Dionne, eds. *Disciplining English.* Albany: State University of New York Press, 2002.

Sisson, C. J. *The Boar's Head Theatre.* London: Routledge Kegan Paul, 1972.

Sloterdijk, Peter. *Critique of Cynical Reason.* Minnesota: University of Minnesota Press, 1987.

Small, R. A. *Ben Jonson and the Poetasters.* 1899. New York: AMS Press, 1966.

Smith, Alan G. R. *Servant of the Cecils: The Life of Sir Michael Hickes.* Totowa, NJ: Rowman and Littlefield, 1977.

Smith, Bruce. *The Acoustic World of Early Modern England.* Chicago: University of Chicago Press, 1999.

Smith, Sir Thomas. *De Republica Anglorum.* Edited by Mary Dewar. Cambridge: Cambridge University Press, 1982.

Sosnoski, James. *Token Professionals and Master Critics: A Critique of Orthodoxy in Literary Studies.* Albany: State University of New York Press, 1994.

Spenser, Edmund. *Edmund Spenser's Poetry.* New York: W. W. Norton, 1993.

Steggle, Matthew. *Wars of the Theatres: The Poetics of Personation in the Age of Jonson.* Victoria: University of Victoria Press, 1998.

Steinberg, Glenn. " 'You Know the Plot/We Both Agreed On?': Plot, Self-Consciousness,and The London Merchant in Beaumont's *The Knight of the Burning Pestle."* *Medieval and Renaissance Drama in England* 5 (1991): 211–24.

Stephen, Leslie, and Sidney Lee, eds. *Dictionary of National Biography.* London: Oxford University Press, 1921–22.

Stone, Lawrence. *The Crisis of the Aristocracy.* Oxford: Clarendon, 1965.

Stow, John. *A Survey of London.* London, n.d.

Streitberger, W. R. *Court Revels.* Toronto: University of Toronto Press, 1994.

Stroud, Ronald. "The Bastard to the Time in *King John." Comparative Drama* 6, no. 2 (1972): 154–65.

Thomson, Patricia. "The Literature of Patronage, 1580–1630." *Essays in Criticism* 2 (1952): 267–84.

Thomson, Peter. *Shakespeare's Professional Career.* Cambridge: Cambridge University Press, 1992.
Tittler, Robert. *Nicholas Bacon: The Making of a Tudor Statesman.* Athens: Ohio University Press, 1976.
Trace, Jacqueline. "Shakespeare's Bastard Falconbridge: An Early Tudor Hero." *Shakespeare Studies* 13 (1980): 59–69.
Tucker, E. F. J. *Intruder into Eden: Representations of the Common Lawyer in English Literature, 1350–1750.* Columbia, SC: Camden House, 1984.
Turner, G. J., ed. *Brevia Placitata.* London: Quaritch, 1951.
Vaughan, Virginia Mason. "Between Tetralogies: *King John* as Transition." *Shakespeare Quarterly* 35 (1984): 407–420.
Veeser, H. Aram, ed. *The New Historicism.* New York: Routledge, 1989.
Voloshinov, V. N. *Marxism and the Philosophy of Language.* Cambridge: Massachusetts Institute of Technology Press, 1973.
Waith, Eugene M. "*King John* and the Drama of History." *Shakespeare Quarterly* 29, no. 2 (1978): 192–211.
Waterhouse, Edward. *Fortescutus Illustratus.* London, 1663.
Weimann, Robert. *Author's Pen and Actor's Voice.* Cambridge: Cambridge University Press, 2000.
Wells, Susan. "Jacobean City Comedy and the Ideology of the City." *ELH* 48 (1981): 37–60.
White, Hayden. *The Content of the Form: Narrative Discourse and Historical Representation.* Baltimore, MD: Johns Hopkins University Press, 1987.
———. *Figural Realism.* Baltimore, MD: Johns Hopkins University Press, 1998.
———. *Metahistory.* Baltimore, MD: Johns Hopkins University Press, 1974.
Wilkes, G. A., ed. *The Complete Plays of Ben Jonson.* 4 vols. Oxford: Clarendon, 1981.
Williams, Franklin B. "Commendatory Verses: The Rise of the Art of Puffing." *Studies in Bibliography* 19 (1966): 1–14.
Williams, Jeffrey.ed. *The Institution of Literature.* Albany: State University of New York Press, 2002.
Williams, Penry. *The Later Tudors.* Oxford: Oxford University Press, 1995.
———. *The Tudor Regime.* Oxford: Oxford University Press, 1979.
Williams, Raymond. *Keywords.* Oxford: Oxford University Press, 1976.
———. *Marxism and Literature.* Oxford: Oxford University Press, 1977.
Wilson, Luke. *Theatres of Intention: Drama and the Law in Early Modern England.* Stanford, CA: Stanford University Press, 2000.
Wing, Donald. *Short-Title Catalogue of Books Printed in England, Scotland, Ireland, Wales, and British America, and of English Books Printed In Other Countries, 1641–1700.* 4 vols. New York: Modern Language Association, 1982–98.
Wixson, Douglas C. " 'Calm Words Folded Up In Smoke': Propaganda and Spectator Response in Shakespeare's *King John.*" *Shakespeare Studies* 14 (1981): 111–27.

Worshipful Company of Carpenters. *Records of the Worshipful Company of Carpenters.* 7 vols. Oxford: Oxford University Press, 1913–

Wright, Louis B. *Middle-Class Culture in Elizabethan England.* Chapel Hill: University of North Carolina Press, 1935.

———. "William Perkins: Elizabethan Apostle of Practical Divinity." *Huntingdon Library Quarterly* 3, no. 2 (1940).

Wrightson, Keith. *English Society 1580–1680.* New Brunswick, NJ: Rutgers University Press, 1982.

Žižek, Slavoj. *The Sublime Object of Ideology.* London: Verso, 1989.

———. *Tarrying with the Negative.* Durham, NC: Duke University Press, 1993.

Index

Abbott, Andrew: ecology of professions, 51, 52–53; on emergence of psychiatry, 51–52; on professional ecologies, 279 n. 24; on vacancy models, 290 n. 56; system model of professions, 50
Acting companies, 229
Administration: professionalization of, 70; royal, 101
Administrators: education of, 103–4
Adorno, Theodor, and Max Horkheimer: *Dialectic of Enlightenment* and modernity, 279 n. 25
Aers, David, 22
Agency, 26, 28, 29
Agnew, Jean-Christophe, 16
Alleyn, Edward, 187
Altman, Joel, 313 n. 110
Anon., *Honest Lawyer*, 151–54
Anon., *Troublesome Raigne of John* 71, 72; and essentialist notions of identity, 76, 98–99; on order and degree, 75; on social status, 74–75; and recognition scene, 74
Antiquarianism, 272
Apprenticeship: as training model, 65
Archer, Ian, 131
Arnold, Matthew, 254, 337–38 n. 15
Astington, John, 169, 317 n. 25
Attorneys, 135
Attourney's Academy (1623), 132–33, 129
Auerbach, Erich, 264
Autonomy: artistic, 13

Bacon, Sir Nicholas, 105–6
Baldick, Chris, 337 n. 14
Barish, Jonas, 334 n. 68
Barristers, 134
Bastardy, 72–73; in law, 79
Beal, Peter, 330 n. 12
Beale, Robert, 96, 111, 298 n. 48; "Treatise of the Office of a Councellor and Principall Secretarie to Her Majestie," 85; as handbook, 101; on administration, 102–3; on councillor's language, 85; on secretary's comportment, 86; on Sir Thomas Smith, 101; papers (Yelverton MSS) and practical nature, 298 n. 50
Beaumont, Francis: *Knight of the Burning Pestle*: "privy mark of irony" and audience, 204, 141, 165, 202–12, 213; and aesthetic conflict, 202; and civic drama, 207–8, 209; and generic experimentation, 211; and parody, 210; dramatic tastes in, 205–7; early reception, 204–5; mixed styles of, 205
Beckingsale, B. W., 104
Bednarz, James, 233, 329–30 n. 11; on Poet's War, 234
Bell, Daniel, 342 n. 70
Bentley, G. E., 316 n. 12
Bergeron, David, 174, 178, 316 n. 14
Berube, Michael, 337 n. 16
Blandy, William, 286 n. 3
Boose, Lynda, 335 n. 73

Bourdieu, Pierre, 13, 24, 25, 26, 27, 28, 32, 111, 218, 249–50, 329 nn. 2 and 3, 332 n. 39, 337 n. 6; agent defined, 283 n. 63; and genetic sociology, 32; and patronage, 223; as not economic determinist, 283 n. 61; disposition defined, 284 n. 70; *Distinction*, 29; on "Marxist short-circuit," 278 n. 16; on acts of recognition, 288 n. 26; on aesthetics and class, 284 n. 72; on categories of perception as products of struggle, 38; on category of artist, 277 n. 1; on field, 332 n. 50; on field, 54, 62; on field of power, 58; on forms of capital, 284 n. 68; on genre, 191–92; on habitus, 284 n. 74; on habitus as feel for the game, 285 n. 76; on history, 261, 273; on hysteresis, 285 n. 82; on linguistic habitus, 84; on literary field, 215; on performative language, 297 n. 43; on relative autonomy, 283 n. 64; on symbolic violence, 284 n. 74; on vocation, 59; sense of the game and status, 76; on profession, 55

Brannigan, John, 339 n. 29
Braunmuller, A. R., 197, 325 n. 106
Brayne, John, 323 n. 81
Brome, Richard, 322 n. 71
Brooks, Christopher, 122; on professions and middling sort, 64–65
Bruster, Douglas, 271–72, 339 n. 31
Buc, Sir George, 163, 328 n. 144
Bulwer, John *Chirologia* (6144), 316 n. 16
Burbage, Daniel, 322–23 n. 79
Burbage, James, 322–23 n. 79
Burbage, Robert, 186
Bureacracy: Tudor, 294 n. 5
Bureaucrats: Tudor, 109–11; education of, 109
Burkhardt, Sigurd, 294–25 n. 12
Burre, Walter, 203
Burt, Richard, 317 n. 25

Calling, 20
Capital: social, 27

Carow, John: propertymaker, 171
Castiglione, Baldessar: *Book of the Courtier*, 301 n. 84
Cawarden, Sir Thomas, 169
Cecil family, 96
Cecil, William Lord Burghley, 96, 106
Cerasano, Susan, 323 n. 80
Chancery, Court of, 306 n. 28
Chaucer, Geoffrey: profession as religious term, 60–61
Children of Paul's, 229, 231
Children of the Queen's Revels, 229
Christmas, Garrett, 178, 179, 181, 319 n. 35, 321 n. 56
City comedy, 115; lawyers in, 120
Civic pageantry, 173; playwrights and, 174; production syndicates, 178
Class, 28
Clatterbook, Thomas tailor, 169
Clopper, David, 319 n. 43
Consecration, 219
Cournot, Antoine Augustin, 265–66, 341–42 n. 61
Cressy, David, 329 n. 8
"crisis of the humanities," 37, 253, 255
Cromwell, Thomas, 106–8; and reform, 70, 101; and Shakespeare's Bastard, 108; as administrator, 69
Crumley, J. Clinton, 197, 325 n. 108
Cultural Materialism, 259–60, 339 n. 28
Curren-Aquino, D., 294–95 n. 12

Dedications, 332 n. 47
Dekker, Thomas, 176, 177, 179, 217, 222, 225–27, 227–28, 244, 246–48, 312 n. 101, 313 n. 117, 331 n. 30; and Thomas Middleton: *Newes from Gravesend*, 117; and *Gull's Hornbook*, 286 n. 2; and *Satiromastix*, 237–40; and *Satiromastix* and performances, 334 n. 62
Deloney, Thomas, 312 n. 101
Dionne, Craig, 338 n. 16
Drapers Company, 319 n. 42
Dubrow, Heather, 22
Dutton, Richard, 317 n. 25

Eagleton, Terry, 337 n. 12
Early modern drama: and social change, 16; as period designation, 21, 281 n. 40; and field of power, 58
Education: and social capital, 110
Elizabeth I, 96
Elliott, John R., 295 n. 14
Elton, G. R., 106, 107, 294 n. 3; on Tudor changes in government, 287 n. 16; *Tudor Revolution in Government,* 70; and critiques of, 294 n. 6
Equity: in law, 131
Erosion: of traditional elites and professionalization of royal service, 112–13

Feuillerat, Albert, 168
Field, 13, 24, 27, 33, 112, 331 n. 31; and competition, 26; legal, 125, 137; professional, 14; and social space, 29–30, 32
Finkelpearl, Philip, 232, 334 n. 69
Fleay, F. G., 329–30 n. 11
Foucault, Michel: on insanity, 290 n. 55
Fukuyama, Francis, 265, 269–70, 342 n. 76
Fulbecke, William, 131

Gallagher, Catherine, and Stephen Greenblatt: *Practicing New Historicism,* 265, 341 n. 53
Giddens, Anthony, 19, 20, 62; *Consequences of Modernity,* 23; and expert systems and modernity, 42; on modernity, 277 n. 2
Globe Theatre, 186
Graff, Gerald, 257, 337 n. 14, 338 n. 22
Greenblatt, Stephen: *Renaissance Self-Fashioning,* 15
Greene, Robert, 192, 221; and professional theater, 192; *James IV,* 165, 183, 192–202, 213; and aesthetic conflict, 202; and dramaturgy, 197; and field of cultural production, 196, 201; and form, 201; and problem of representation, 200; and visual spectacle, 198–99; as theatrical contest, 193, 194, 197; didacticism vs aestheticism, 194
Grinkin, John, 177
Guillory, John, 257, 338 nn. 17 and 21; and *Bourdieu's Refusal,* 26

Habermas, Jurgen, 20, 337 n. 9
Habitus, 28, 297 n. 35; class, 29; and legal ("juridical sense"), 125, 160, 315 n. 137; and legal changes in, 126
Halpern, Richard, 301 n. 92, 335–36 n. 82
Hamilton, Paul, 263
Hammond, Brean S., 336 n. 97
Hegel, Georg W. F., 269
Helgerson, Richard, 221; *Self-Crowned Laureates,* 15
Hemynge, Mr., 177
Henry VII, 68–69
Henslowe, Philip, 187; on Marston, 333 n. 52
Herder, Johan Gottfried von, 264
Herman, Peter, 338 n. 16
Heywood, Thomas, 176, 134, 135, 140, 327 n. 133, 330 n. 18; and *Four Prentices of London,* 208
Hickes, Michael, 103, 104, 111, 294 n. 8; and administrative career, 104
Hillebrand, Bruce, 326–27 n. 121
Historical knowledge and narrative, 262; as problem, 261
Historicism, 36, 251, 253, 254, 258, 263–65, 273, 275, 339 n. 32
History, 36, 260, 270; of the subject, 251; structural, 273
Holt, John Yeoman of the Revels, 169, 320 n. 47
Howard, Jean, 260, 339 n. 33
Humanitie, 274

I. M., on society as marketplace, 39
Identity: conceptions of, 72; personal, 24
Imitation, 228

Ingram, William, 317 n. 24, 326–27 n. 121
Inns of Court: structure, 308 n. 49
Institutions: as forming identities, 24

James, Mervyn, 294 n. 1; *Society: Politics and Culture* on transformation of traditional elites, 287 n. 16
Jameson, Fredric, 20, 342 n. 75
Jig, 326 n. 112
Johns Hopkins University, 338 n. 23
Jones, Inigo, 315 n. 4
Jones, W. J., 294 n. 10
Jonson, Ben, 176, 217, 224–25, 227–28, 229, 246–48, 304 n. 4, 323 n. 89, 331–32 n. 37; and 1616 Folio, 237, 238; as moralist, 290 n. 64; *Devil is an Ass*, 182; *Epigrams*, 245; *Every Man In His Humor*, 188–89; *Poetaster*, 235–38; *Poetaster*, trial scene, 243; *Volpone*, 144–47

Kant, Immanuel, 258, 338 n. 20; and *Conflict of the Faculties*, 255–57
Kastan, David Scott, 339 n. 31, 340 n. 34; on Bastard's choice, 296 n. 26
Katherens, Gilbert, 323 n. 81
Keysar, Robert, 203, 326–27 n. 121
Klancher, Jon, 339 n. 30
Knutson, Roslyn, 334 n. 69

Lang, R. G.: on merchant aspirations, 140
Langley, Francis, 323 n. 81
Larson, Magali, 48; professions as tied to industrial capitalism, 48
Latour, Bruno, 21
Law: admission to practice, 124, 135; and ambivalence toward, 150; and dramatic form, 143; and early modern drama, 115; and fraud, 149; and social status, 149; and violence, 312 n. 103; as corrupt, 156; as destructive, 154; as means of social advancement, 116; as profession, 35; as trickery, 155; as value-neutral, 151; civil, 307 n. 34; linked to social conflict, 142, 152, 157, 159; professionalization of, 133–34
Lawyers: as autonomous, 160; early modern, 28; influence on early modern culture, 66; linked to social change, 139; perceptions of, 138–39; stage, 143; stage as linked to social conflict, 158
Legal education, 123–24, 127–28, 308 n. 51
Legal institutions in London, 117; medieval, 121
Legal learning, 118
Legal practice: changes in, 119, 123; restrictions on, 305 n. 16
Legal printing, 118, 128–29, 305 n. 2; as aid to practice, 310 n. 67
Legal profession: and social aspirations, 158; and Tudor centralization, 306 n. 27; as corrupt, 153–54; as guild, 127; authority based in training, 160; structure of, 136, 314 n. 133
Legg, John, 177
Leggatt, Alexander, 197, 325 n. 107
Lepore, Jill: on microhistory, 278 n. 19
Lesser, Zachary, 204–5, 327 n. 125
Levack, Brian, 307 n. 34
Linguistic habitus, 299 nn. 57 and 58; change as troubling 299 n. 60
Literary education: controversy over, 285 n. 91
Literary field, 241, 243, 245, 247; and nineteenth-century France, 27
Literature, 219, 248; as category: history, 277 n. 3
Litigation: expansion of, 122, 133
Littleton's Tenures (1481), 118, 130
Loewenstein, Joseph, 334 n. 67
London: civic elite, 312 n. 99; civic order, 141
Lord Mayor's Show, 167, 174; 1561, expenses of; 175; and in 1609, 176; and in 1629, 179; and theater, 181–82; and planning, 180
Lyotard, Jean-François, 20–21, 338 n. 16, 340 n. 47; *The Postmodern Condition*, 265

MacCaffery, Wallace, 296 n. 31
MacFarlane, Alan, 23
MacKay, Maxine, 308 n. 42
Magnusson, Lynne, 316 n. 12
Malone Society, 168
Manheim, Michael, 295 n. 12; on Bastard's (*King John*) language, 83
Marcuse, Herbert, 267–68
Market of symbolic goods, 289 n. 42
Marlowe, Christopher, 192, 224–25, 331 n. 37; and *Doctor Faustus*, 19–20; *Doctor Faustus* and enlightenment, 280 n. 30
Marshall, Paul: on doctrine of vocation, 61
Marston, John, 217, 224–25, 227–28, 229, 244, 246–48, 322 n. 71, 323 n. 88; and verse satire, 232; and *Histriomastix*, 231–34; *Histriomastix* and performances, 334 n. 62; career, 28
Marx, Karl, 274
Massinger, Philip: *New Way to Pay Old Debts*, 154–59
Masten, Jeffrey, 330 n. 17
Materialism, 271
Matz, Robert, 335–36 n. 82
May, Steven, 332–33 n. 51
McLuskie, Kathleen, 324 n. 89, 327 n. 30, 331 n. 30
Melnikoff, Kirk, 196
Merchants: perceptions of, 140; and representations of 140–41; and social aspirations of, 157, 304 n. 5
Metadrama, 188; and theater crafts, 212
Middleton, Sir Thomas (Lord Mayor 1613), 320–21 n. 55
Middleton, Thomas, 176, 320–21 n. 55; and *Michaelmas Term*, 147–51; and *Phoenix*, 114; and *Triumphs of Honor and Industry*, 178
Miller, E. H., 221, 329 n. 4
Misrecognition, 25, 29; professional, 283 n. 58
Modern, 23; as best description of contemporary society, 280 n. 32; definitions, 22

Modernity 20, 21, 22, 23, 250; as abstraction, 24–25; as reflexive, 282 n. 51; transition to, 42–43
Moi, Toril, 31
Mucedorus, 327 n. 129
Muir, Kenneth, 193–94, 324 n. 97
Mulcaster, Richard, 176, 317 n. 18
Munday, Anthony, 176, 177; and Drapers' Company, 319 n. 42
Murray, Timothy, 336 n. 87

Nelson, Cary, 337 n. 16
New Boke of Presidents (1543), 128
New Historicism, 17, 252, 259–60, 262, 339 n. 29
Niethammer, Lutz, 265, 270, 341 n. 60
Nietzsche, Friedrich, 261, 272, 342 n. 65; and "The Use and Disadvantages of History for Life," 266–67

Objectivisim, 249
Office of Works, 170
Ogle, John, 319 n. 35
Orgel, Stephen, 316 n. 14
Orrell, John, 170, 316 n. 17
Osborne, Laurie, 326 n. 118

Painters, 170
Parnassus Plays, 216, 219, 221, 224–25
Patronage, 223, 243; failure of, 219–20
Peele, George, 176
Peele, James, 176; and George, 317 n. 18
Penniman, J. H., 329–30 n. 11
Percy Earls of Northumberland, 68
Perkin, Daniel, 322–23 n. 79
Perkin, John, 322–23 n. 79
Perkins, William, 20; and the *Treatise on the Vocations and Callings of Men*, 62–64
Peterson, Richard, 228
Philology, 257
Plagiarism, 228
Playwriting: as collaborative, 162; as profession, 36, 184; history, 163, 166

Poet's War (Poetomachia), 36, 216, 224, 225, 227–28, 229, 230, 246–48; and profession, 240; defined, 328 n. 5
Popper, Karl, 339 n. 32
Posthistory, 261, 265, 268, 270, 275
Practical mastery, 94
Prest, Wilfred, 116
Privy Council, 112; and structure, 302 n. 94, 303 n. 12
Profession, 18, 31–32, 99, 273; and division of tasks, 41; and social distinction, 44; as category critique of, 46; as folk concept, 291 n. 71; as similar to calling and vocation, 40; as status marker, 38; change in social meaning, 41; early modern definitions, 59; of servingman, 41; sixteenth-century ideas of, 40
Professional ideology: critique of, 49
Professional literary study, 257, 258; recent history, 290 n. 66
Professional study of literature, 37
Professional: as category critique of, 46; as status marker, 38
Professionalism, 45, 228, 242, 243, 335 n. 79; and humanism, 294 n. 7
Professionals: dramatic representation of, 34; place in society, 42
Professions, 14, 24, 250, 252; and agency, 25; and modernization, 43; and social differentiation, 66; as "public-spirited," 47; as fields, 56–57; early modern, 45, 58; sociology of, 43; struggle for title, 67
Propertymaker, 171, 318 n. 33
Psychoanalysis, 337 n. 5
Pulman, Michael, 294 n. 5; on Tudor bureaucracy, 111–12
Puttenham, George, 219, 298 n. 52

Rackin, Phyllis, 295 n. 17
Rational-Actor Theory, 249
Read, Conyers, 104
Readings, Bill, 338 n. 16
Red Bull Theatre, 323 n. 81
Reiss, Timothy, 330 n. 16
Renaissance: as period name, 22

Revels Office, 163–64, 223; and professional drama, 184–85; production values of, 172; structure, 169; workers, 168–70
Rhodes, Neil, 329 n. 7
Riggs, David, 227–28
Robinson, Marsha, 294–95 n. 12
Rose Theatre, 186
Ross, John, 172
Ross, John Jr., 172
Ross, Nicholas, 319 n. 35

Saunders, J. W., 333 n. 51
Sawday, Jonathan, 329 n. 7
Self-fashioning, 15
Shakespeare, William, 230; and *Midsummer Night's Dream*, 162, 183; *1 Henry IV*, 95; Hal and Hotspur, 95; Hotspur and language of honor as nostalgic, 95–96; *Hamlet*, 230; *Henry V*, 189–90; *King John*, 70–71, 72: and profession, 34; and service, 99; and social status, 77; and symbolic violence, 91; and voluntarist notions of identity, 80; as transitional play, 71; and Bastard and acquisition of new habitus, 88–89; and Bastard and administration, 81; and Bastard and continuum of habitus, 297 n. 46; and Bastard and honor, 81, 94; and Bastard and language, 82, 83, 89, 97; and Bastard and linguistic habitus, 82; and Bastard and mastery of noble practice, 300 n. 78; and Bastard and misrecognition, 94; and Bastard and professionalization, 98; and Bastard as administrative professional, 96–97; and Bastard as articulating analysis of linguistic habitus, 85; and Bastard as cynical, 299 n. 66; and Bastard hypostatization of rank, 84; and Bastard on "dialogue of compliment," 87; and Bastard's choice to give up land, 80; and Bastard's status change, 80, 298 n. 56; and Bastard's wordplay, 298 n. 47; and commodity speech, 91–93; on

land claim, 78; *Measure for Measure*, 313 n. 117; *Merchant of Venice*, 125–26, 144, Venice, 173
Shapiro, James S., 316 n. 12
Sharpe, Robert, 329–30 n. 11
Shumway, David, 338 n. 16
Sidney, Sir Philip, 219, 322 n. 71
Sinfield, Alan, 330 n. 11
Sloterdijk, Peter: *Critique of Cynical Reason*, 21
Small, R. A., 329–30 n. 11
Smith, A. G. R., 104, 294 n. 8
Smith, Bruce, 187
Smith, Sir Thomas: *De Republica Anglorum*, 85, 100; *Discourse of the Common Weal of England*, 100
Social conflict, 142
Social construction, 28
Social mobility, 142
Social space, 28, 36
Sociology, 26
Solicitors, 135
Sosnoski, James, 338 n. 16
Spenser, Edmund, 329 n. 10
St. Germain, Christopher: *Doctor and Student* (1528–31), 131
Steggle, Matthew, 330 n. 12
Steinberg, Glenn, 326 n. 118
Street, Peter, 165, 186–89; and Carpenters' Company, 187
Streitberger, W. R, 316 n. 14
Strong, Roy, 316 n. 14
Structure: and agency, 28
Subjectivism, 249
Subjectivity, 22
Swan Theatre, 323 n. 81
Sylvester, William, 323 n. 81

Tailors, 169

Teleology, 271
Theater craftspeople, 165, 167, 212; as professionals, 164
Theater: and professionalism, 315–16 n. 7; as profession, 35; craft traditions and language, 182–83; professional, 165
Theaters: building and festive architecture, 185; history, 184; technical capacities of, 190–91
Theory, 260
Trace, Jacqueline, 295 n. 15
Training, professional, 34
Trunckewell, Robert, 318 n. 34
Tucker, E. F. J., 305 n. 14; on legal satire, 120

Vaughan, Virginia, 294 n. 12
Veeser, H. Aram, 340 n. 34

Webster, John, 176
Weimann, Robert, 191
White, Hayden, 261–62, 340 nn. 40–46, 341 nn. 48 and 49
Williams, Franklin, 332 n. 47
Williams, Jeffrey, 337 n. 16
Williams, Raymond, 342 n. 88
Willing Suspension Productions, 324 n. 96
Wilson, Luke, 304 n. 3
Wixson, Douglas, 295 n. 14
Womack, Peter, 323 n. 90
Wrightson, Keith, 295 n. 18; on social order, 82–83
Writers: ranking, 241–43
Writing: and status, 232, 236; as profession, 18; professional, 21, 216, 218, 224, 246–48; professional and drama, 221; and Jonson as professional, 240–45